EARLY COGNITIVE DEVELOPMENT

EARLY COGNITIVE DEVELOPMENT

EDITED BY JOHN OATES

A HALSTED PRESS BOOK

JOHN WILEY & SONS
New York

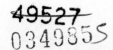

Selection and editorial material
copyright © The Open University 1979

Published in the USA
by Halsted Press, a Division
of John Wiley & Sons Inc.
New York

Library of Congress Cataloging in Publication Data

Main entry under title:

Early cognitive development.

   "A Halsted Press book."
   Includes index.
   1. Cognition in children — Addresses, essays,
   lectures. 2. Infant psychology — Addresses, essays,
   lectures. 3. Child psychology — Addresses, essays,
   lectures. I. Oates, John, 1946-
   BF723.C5E2   155.4'22   78-17694
   ISBN 0-47026431-4

Printed and bound in Great Britain by
Butler & Tanner Ltd, Frome and London

CONTENTS

EARLY COGNITIVE DEVELOPMENT

LARGE COOPERATIVE DEVELOPMENT

INTRODUCTION

The first five years of life have a perennial interest for those concerned with the understanding of human development, as the rapidity and scope of the changes that occur during this period are greater than in any other part of the life-span. In these few years, a dependent infant is transformed into a self-assured and autonomous five-year old, in command of language and able to take part in formal education. Developmental research has always tended to turn to early childhood to explore the causes and origins of behaviour, and it has long been thought that this is the most important stage of development for the formation of personality and intellect. The new-born child holds a particular fascination for those interested in the interplay of genetic and environmental forces, as the complex impact of environmental stimulation is at this point only just beginning to play its part. A further major influence in focusing interest on the pre-school years has been the contemporary concern of social policy with the alleviation of the effects of poor environments on mental development, and on achievement in school and later life. The pre-verbal child, also, is a challenging subject for the experimentally-inclined, who has to devise novel methods of investigation to explore the child's developing mental process.

In the last twenty years, all the factors mentioned here have worked together to produce a massive upsurge in the amount of research conducted with this age-range. Of all the areas of psychology, this is the one which has sustained a real knowledge explosion, which shows no signs of abating. Several major breakthroughs in experimental technique have generated a revolution in our views of the infant's capabilities which have barely begun to be assimilated into our current approaches to child-rearing. Stimulated by this research, a continuing critical analysis of theories of child development has led to the development of new, more sophisticated models of the developmental process. There is much to be gained, for the parent and the professional, in at least sampling the new insights that we now have into early development.

This reader sets out to provide an overview of the major developments in this area in the form of reports of original research that are central to the issues covered, and review papers written by people involved in research in the field.

The first topic is that of the role of culture in the course of cognitive

11

development. The main questions that this section addresses are the extent to which adult modes of thought are transmitted socially by parents and others with whom the developing child interacts and whether there are any features that are universally given by our biological heritage. The section raises a number of questions that are dealt with in more detail in later sections.

The second section contains descriptions of two of the areas of experimental research that have produced a real breakthrough in knowledge of the infant's abilities; these are visual and auditory perception. By progressive refinements of techniques first developed by Robert Fantz, it is now known that infants have consistent 'visual preferences' for certain sorts of patterns, and the judicious use of these can tell us a great deal about what, and how clearly, babies can see. Research into the perception of speech, and speech-like sounds has produced intriguing evidence that the infant may possess specialised systems for dealing with speech from birth, and that an 'innate sense of rhythm' may be every baby's endowment. The implications of this for language development are only just beginning to be explored.

Some thirty years ago, Jean Piaget made the somewhat surprising suggestion that the idea of 'objects' as permanent, bounded features of the world is not one that infants initially have, and that progress towards the 'object concept' is complex, and takes well over a year to reach completion. The third section is a representative selection of the large amount of experimental research that has been carried out on Piaget's hypothesis. It is arranged in chronological order, to give a sense of the research progression.

Another controversial area, and the subject of much research, has been the issue of whether infants are able to learn in the manner of the classic behaviourist paradigm, that is, through classical conditioning. At least in part because of the difficulty of working with infants, who have very few 'usable' responses, it proved initially very difficult to show evidence of this sort of conditioning. However, as experimenters began to discover forms of response to work with it became clear, as the research in the fourth section shows, that this form of learning can be operative from a very early age.

The fifth section deals with what many psychologists believe to be the most important form of learning in the pre-verbal period. Indeed, the authors of the two papers in this section suggest that the learning that is a result of the child's interaction with a parent (or caretaker) may be a *necessary* prerequisite of language and other aspects of cognitive development. Just as Margaret Mead, in the very first reading, sees the learning of sex-specific behaviour as arising from subtle variations in adult-child interaction, so the Newsons and Schaffer see adults as subtly helping children to make sense of their joint behaviour. Also, by involving objects and events in the interaction, the adult 'marks' these phenomena as meaningful. Thus, social interaction is seen as the arena for the basic learning of concepts; as the Newsons term it, symbolic functioning.

A very different form of interaction between adults and children is when assessments are made of children's developmental status, whether for research or diagnostic purposes. Many of the reports and discussions in earlier sections of this volume refer to the use of tests with pre-school children, and this sixth section looks at the forms of tests that are used with the age-group, and at the interpretation of some of the resulting data. It has been known for some time that the results of tests carried out with very young children do not correlate at all highly with scores at later ages. Marjorie Honzik, in her paper, discusses this fact and the possible reasons for it. Robert McCall takes up this issue, and suggests that the sort of model which supposes that test results can be statistically analysed in this way is simplistic, and shows a direction that more elaborate models might take.

In the final section, which is concerned primarily with models of the development process, Jerome Kagan continues McCall's line of discussion, elaborating further on many of the points raised. Tom Bower, in his paper on continuities, discusses particularly the idea of the reiteration of many cognitive achievements, at progressively higher levels of co-ordination, such that these abilities, such as conservation, appear to wax and wane in the course of development. Continuity in development is the main focus of the final paper, by Judy Dunn, which argues that we should not think of the infant as simply receptive of environmental influences, but that we should tend to a transactional model, in which the child plays a part, as well as the parents (or caretakers).

SECTION ONE: CULTURAL CONTEXT

Introduction

This first section sets a background against which to interpret the various research reports and discussions later in this volume. Culture is an all-pervading context for cognitive development, and we ignore its potential effects at our peril. There is much we can learn by appreciating the different ways in which childhood experience is interpreted in cultures across the world. The initial reading is a series of eloquent passages by Margaret Mead, one of the most eminent and committed anthropologists, who has come to view childhood as a central component in culture. Writing in the context of the development of sex role differentiation, she stresses and illustrates here the astonishing variety in child-rearing practices, and introduces several themes that are treated later in this volume.

The three papers that follow each give a more detailed picture of early development in particular cultural settings: Mary Salter Ainsworth writes of infancy in Uganda, T. Berry Brazelton and his colleagues of life with the Zinacantecans of Mexico, and Jerome Kagan describes infancy in Guatemala. The paper by John and Elizabeth Newson then brings us back to our own culture, taking an historical look at how views of child-rearing have changed over the last 200 years or so.

The final paper, by Neil Warren, rounds off the section by giving a provocative contemporary view of the significance of the variations and common features across cultures in cognitive development.

1 MALE AND FEMALE

Margaret Mead

Source: *Male and Female* (Pelican Books, 1962), pp. 63-4, 75-9, 178-9.
Reprinted by permission of Victor Gollancz Ltd.

Back of the word 'man' stand in my mind a phalanx of images, men with white skins and brown skins and yellow skins and black skins; men with crew-cuts and shaved heads and great psyche knots; men in evening-dress in contemporary society and men wearing nothing but gleaming pearl-shell crescent ornaments on their chests; men with muscles that bulge and ripple and men with arms as slender as a girl's; men whose fingers are too clumsy to hold a tool smaller than an adze and men who sit threading tiny beads on a string; men whose manhood is offended by the smell of a baby and men who cradle an infant gently in a steady arm; men whose hands are always ready to fling upwards and backwards as if to throw a spear and men whose hands press easily palm to palm in a gesture of apology and entreaty; men of six feet six and men of five feet one. And beside them stand women, again with many-coloured skins; some with bald pates and some with long flowing hair; women with breasts that hang very low or can sometimes even be trained to a form which can be thrown over their shoulders and women with small high breasts like the figures on the Medici tombs in Florence; women who swish their grass skirts as they walk and women who handle these same grass skirts as if they were sheets of iron protecting their virtue; women whose arms look empty without a child in them and women who hold their children at arm's length as if they were clawing little wild cats; women who are readier to fight than their husbands and women who scatter like leaves before the sound of a brawl; women whose hands are never still and women who sit after a heavy day's work with hands flaccid in their laps. And in front and beside and behind them, in their arms, on their backs, clinging with hands tight around their necks, sitting on their shoulders, slung in slings and net bags and baskets, hanging on the tipi wall tightly laced in cradle-boards — there are the children. Children who may be dressed as tiny replicas of the adults, tripping over a long skirt as they learn to walk, and children who may go stark naked until ten or eleven; children who relax into passivity as their carriers pound rice or play rough running-games and children who brace themselves tightly as the punted canoe jams and mother and child fall into the water; children for whom there is no word, who are first referred to as 'mice' or 'beetles' and then as 'small men', children who have been wanted, children

17

whose very words are treated as prophecy; children who are subhuman until they have teeth and children who are monsters if their teeth come in irregularly; children who have no toys and who cling sullenly to the legs of adults and children who are as gay and frolicsome as laughter itself.

Children's experiences in a world in which the adults already have a way of life become in turn the stuff out of which they, as adults, are able either to conform to and use, or to rebel against and change, their ways of life. In following the steps by which the infant learns his civilization, we are tracing a process of transmission, not one of creation; but the path is none the less revealing.

Of the child's first experiences within the womb, and the way in which different cultures pattern these experiences, we still know very little. The Arapesh say the baby sleeps until ready for birth and then dives out. The Iatmul believe an unborn child can hurry or delay, as it wishes. 'Why do you rail at me?' said Tchamwole to her husband. 'This baby will be born when it likes. It is a human being, and it chooses its own time of birth. It is not like a pig or a dog to be born when others say it should.' 'The birth is hard,' said the Tchambuli, 'because the mother has not gathered enough firewood.' It is probable that in different societies, by the attribution of more or less autonomy of movement to the baby, by enjoining upon the mother active or placid behaviour, the process of learning may begin within the womb, and that this may be interpreted differently for the two sexes. It is possible that there may be deep biochemical affinities between mother and female child, and contrasts between mother and male child, of which we now know nothing. So, at birth itself, whether the mother kneels squatting holding on to two poles or to a piece of rattan hung from the ceiling — whether she is segregated among females or held around the waist by her husband, sits in the middle of a group of gaming visitors or is strapped on a modern delivery table — the child receives a sharp initial contact with the world as it is pulled, hauled, dropped, pitched, from its perfectly modulated even environment into the outer world, a world where temperature, pressure, and nourishment are all different, and where it must breathe to live. Here there may be cultural intervention, such as to save the boy-baby and strangle the girl, but we know nothing as to whether birth itself means something different to the boy-baby and to the girl. There seems to be a differential sensitivity in the skin of males and females; and a sensitive skin is one of the clues that may make a male classify himself as a female, a hard skin may tend to get a girl dubbed masculine, in her own eyes and those of others. Skin-shock is one of the major shocks of birth, and where there is a final difference, there may be an initial one. In our own society, our images of the carefully guarded rituals of the delivery-room, in which the mind conjures up an even temperature maintained by a thermostat, the most medically perfect oils and unguents, and the softest of appropriate materials in which to wrap the baby, overlay the realization of what a shock birth is. The shock is easy enough to realize when the baby is born on an unsheltered hillside, where the mother and attending women crouch shivering over a tiny fire until finally the baby falls with a soft little thud on a cold, dew-coated leaf — to be left there, perhaps five minutes, while the mother herself cuts and ties the cord, packs up the placenta, and wipes out the baby's eyes and nose. Only then can the squirming, exposed little creature be gathered up and laid against the mother's breast. Whether or not this initial experience differs for the two sexes in any basic way, their later realization of their sex can reinvolve the experience they know has occurred. A longing for a world where pressure is even on the body and breathing is effortless, an experience that mystics of all times have sought, can be very differently woven into the phantasies of two parents expecting a child. To the expectant mother it means an increased sense of her sheltering relation to the child within her womb, to the expectant father such memories may come as a threat or as a temptation. For him, identification with the unborn child is at least partially unacceptable, for it turns his wife into his mother. For both expectant father and mother, such phantasies may arouse memories of the time before a younger child was born to his or her own mother, and then father and mother will defend themselves differently against these memories. What actual traces remain of the specificities of the birth-shock in the nervous system we do not know, but a careful examination of the ways in which new-born babies are handled — cradled gently against the breast, held up by the heels and slapped, wrapped so close that no light comes to them until they are many weeks old, stood out on the mother's iron-stiff arm to fend, like tiny frogs, for themselves — shows that these early ways of treating them are strictly congruent with later handling and later phantasies. However little the baby learns from its own birth, the mother who bears it, the midwife who assists, the father who stands by or walks the floor outside or goes off to consult a magician, all bear the marks of the birth experience and can again communicate it to the growing child. It will make a difference ultimately in our theories of human learning whether males and females are found actually to remember, differentially, their first shocking experience of temperature and breathing, or whether they learned about it from the imagery and poetry of the adult world. But in either case, whether the boy learns something different from his mother's voice because he has remembered, at some very deep level, a lesser shock upon his skin, or because he realizes that he can experience birth only once, while the girl pre-lives at that moment the day her own baby will be thrust out into the world – in either case, the birth experience becomes part of the symbolic equipment of women, who are formed to bear children, and of men, who will never bear them.

From the moment of birth – probably always from before birth also – contrasting types of behaviour can be distinguished in a mother's attitude towards her child. The infant may be treated as a whole little creature – little animal, little soul, little human being, as the case may be, but whole, and to a degree capable of setting its own will and needs over against those of its mother. Such behaviour may be called *symmetrical*, the mother behaves as if the child were essentially similar to herself, and as if she were responding to behaviour of the same type as her own. Or she may treat the child as one who is different from herself, who receives while she gives, with the emphasis upon difference between the mother's behaviour and that of the child as she cherishes and shelters and above all feeds a weak, dependent creature. This patterning of the relationship may be called *complementary*, as each of the pair is seen as playing a different role, and the two roles are conceived as complementing each other. A third theme occurs when the behaviour of the mother and the child is seen as involving an interchange when the child takes in what the mother gives it, and later, in elimination, makes a return. The emphasis is not on the symmetrical or the complementary character of the roles, which include a feeling about the two personalities – as of the same kind or, in terms of the particular relationship, with different appropriate behaviours – but rather on an exchange of commodities between mother and child. Such behaviour can be called *reciprocal*. In reciprocal phrasings of relationship, love, trust, tears, may become commodities, just as much as physical objects, but the interchange of physical objects remains the prototype. All these themes are present in every cultural phrasing of the mother-child relationship. To the extent that the child's whole individuality is emphasized, there is symmetry; to the extent that its weakness and helplessness are emphasized, there is complementary behaviour; and to the extent that the mother gives not only her breast, but milk, there is the beginning of reciprocity. But cultures differ greatly as to which they emphasize most.

So we may contrast mothers in different societies with these different emphases. The Arapesh treat a baby as a soft, vulnerable, precious little object, to be protected, fed, cherished. Not only the mother, but the father also, must play this over-all protective role. After birth the father abstains from work and sleeps beside the mother, and he must abstain from intercourse while the child is young, even with his other wife. When the mother walks about she carries the child slung beneath her breast in a bark-cloth sling, or in a soft net bag in which the child still curls as he curled in the womb. Whenever it is willing to eat, even if it does not show any signs of hunger, it is fed, gently, interestedly. The receptiveness of the mouth is emphasized in both boys and girls. Through the long, protected infancy, during which children are carried, slung in bags from their mother's foreheads or high on their father's shoulders, up and down the steep mountain trails, and are never asked to perform tasks that are difficult or exacting, their whole interest remains focused on the mouth. Not even the almost ever present breast provides enough stimulation for a mouth that has been so heavily stressed, and small children sit playing endless gentle games with their lips, bubbling them, teasing them, puckering them lightly between their fingers. Meanwhile the grasping action of the mouth has never been developed. A readily offered breast does not have to be vigorously seized upon or bitten. The method of carrying places no emphasis on teaching the hands to grasp — which when it occurs can reinforce the grasping possibilities of the mouth. The Arapesh child, male and female, continues to take in, receptively, passively, what is offered it and to fly into tempers if food is ever refused — as it sometimes may be from necessity, for the people are very short of food.

Both boys and girls have learned about life from using their mouths. When they use their eyes, their eyes reflect the same passive expectancy. Eyes light up and mouths shout with excitement when some lovely colour is presented to them, but hands do not reach aggressively, eyes do not probe and seek with active curiosity. The Arapesh are a people among whom communication between infants and others has been very heavily specialized to one part of the body, the mouth, and to one aspect of that part, passive receptivity.

We speak in our current folk-language of the beast in man, of the thin veneer of civilization, and either statement simply means that we do not trust mankind to be continuously human.

For our humanity rests upon a series of learned behaviours, woven together into patterns that are infinitely fragile and never directly inherited. The ant we discover imbedded in a block of Baltic amber, which the geologist dates 20,000,000 years ago, may be trusted to reproduce its typical ant behaviour wherever it can survive. It is trustworthy for two reasons: first, because its complex behaviour, by which its society will be divided into minute castes that carry out predetermined tasks, is built into the very structure of its body, and second, because even if it should learn something new, it cannot teach it to the other ants. The repetitious pattern in which countless generations of a single species repeat a pattern more complicated than the dreams of a technocratic Utopian is protected by these two circumstances: behaviour imbedded in physical structure and an inability to communicate new learnings. But man does not even carry the simplest forms of his behaviour in such a way that a human child without other human beings to teach it can be relied upon to reproduce spontaneously a single cultural item. Long before his small fist is strong enough really to deliver a blow, the angry gestures of the human child bear the stamp not of his long mammalian past, but of the club-using or spear-throwing habits of his parents. The woman left alone to bear her child calls not upon some reliable instinctive pattern that will guide her through the complexities of cutting the umbilical cord and cleansing the new infant from the traces of birth, but fumbles helplessly among bits of folk-lore and old wives' tales that she has overheard. She may act from the memory of what she has seen animals do, but in her own living nature she finds no reliable cues.

2 SENSORIMOTOR DEVELOPMENT OF GANDA INFANTS

Mary D. Salter Ainsworth

Source: *Infancy in Uganda: Infant Care and the Growth of Love* (Baltimore: Johns Hopkins Press, 1967), pp. 319-30.

Most of the babies in the sample [of Ganda infants] were clearly accelerated in their rate of sensorimotor development. The rate of their physical growth, as checked by measurements of height and weight upon visits to the clinic, was not accelerated. On the contrary, most of the babies were average in height and weight when compared with Western norms. But they sat and crawled and stood and walked much earlier than the average baby in Western societies. Although the focus of my interest was upon the development of interpersonal relations, the striking acceleration of these Ganda babies in sensorimotor development merits consideration.

Although I lacked training in infant testing, I had intended to teach myself from a test manual and to administer an infant intelligence test at regular intervals to each baby in order to have some kind of base line of developmental rate against which I could check my findings in regard to social development. Test equipment was ordered, but delays in shipping prevented it from arriving in time to be used. In order to obtain the base line which I sought, I made note of each baby's locomotor attainments and of his language development, both in terms of first words and language comprehension. I soon realized that the infants in my sample were very accelerated in regard to these aspects of development, and much regretted the lack of test equipment.

I was delighted when Dr Marcelle Geber arrived in Kampala just before the end of my project. She was not only expert in infant testing but also wished to test a sample of Ganda infants. It was agreed that I should introduce her to the families in my sample on the occasion of my last visit and seek to gain their cooperation in her work. Then, a week or so after I had left Kampala, she was to visit each home, accompanied by Mrs Kibuka, to administer the Gesell Developmental Schedules.[1] In about half the cases this plan worked out. In a few instances we had been unable to arrange a joint visit to introduce Dr Geber; in other instances families who had agreed to cooperate refused to do so when Dr Geber came at the appointed time.[2] Consequently test results are available for only thirteen children.[3]

When I began my project it was not generally known that African infants are accelerated in sensorimotor development, especially throughout the first year of life. Dr Geber's findings, not only with the Ganda but also with infants in other African societies, were the first to draw widespread attention to this significant phenomenon. Since there is some controversy about the factors responsible for this acceleration in development, and since I believe that my observations have some light to throw on the issue, I wish to present what I found, despite the fact that my observations of sensorimotor development are imprecise.

Working retrospectively I have ascertained the age level of each of the items of behavior which appear both in my records of home visits and in the Griffiths Infant Intelligence Scales[4] — the infant test with which I am now currently working — and estimated an Intelligence Quotient on the basis of the discrepancy between the age of the child when observed and the age level at which the behavioral item appears in the test norms. In all but one case there was fairly close agreement between this estimated IQ[†] and DQ[†] found by Dr Geber. This agreement lends support to the validity of the conclusions that can be drawn from my relatively imprecise observations.[5]

Locomotor Development

In the case of all infants, I inquired from the mother about the age of the infant when the locomotor milestones were achieved — sitting alone, crawling, standing alone, and walking. Although only the mother's retrospective report is available for milestones achieved before our observations began, my notes of the baby's behavior during visits provide a check on the achievement of later milestones and also provide details that could not be obtained in interview.

Sitting

Sitting alone is a very important milestone for the Ganda infant. I suspect that its importance traditionally was that the naming ceremony could not take place until the infant was able to sit. None of the mothers in our sample made any reference to the naming ceremony, which among Christians has been replaced by christening. Nevertheless, it was generally acknowledged that a baby ought to be able to sit alone by the time he was three months old. My informants of ancient customs told me that a baby was given training in sitting as he approached three months of age. A hole of suitable size was dug in the ground. Barkcloth was wrapped around the

---

[†]   Words or phrases accompanied by this symbol are explained in the Glossary.

baby to give support to his trunk, and he was placed in the hole in a sitting position for about fifteen minutes a day, until he was able to sit unsupported. Sixteen babies in this sample (see Table 2.1) were given 'training' of this sort. In only one case was a hole actually dug. More usually a basin of suitable size was used, and in some instances the only support was given by the cloths (no longer barkcloth) that were wrapped around him.

Can a baby be trained to sit? Or does he just naturally sit when maturation has proceeded to the point that he is able to? Widespread opinion in Western countries favors the maturational view, and even though the work of Piaget[6] and others leads to the inescapable conclusion that experience plays an important role in the development of intelligence and in the sensorimotor development that is the forerunner of intellectual development, there are grounds for skepticism that training of this sort imposed on an infant could substantially facilitate development. This sample can provide no support for the belief that training helps a baby to sit earlier than he might otherwise have done. But before considering the evidence, it is first necessary to consider a definition of what is meant by a baby's sitting 'alone'.

In several instances we observed the infant shortly after he was able to sit 'alone'. In these instances the mother placed him in a very special position to help him keep his balance. The soles of his feet were placed together in front of him, and he was tipped slightly forward so that his hands rested on the ground beyond his feet. His hands kept him from falling forward, and the spread of his legs counteracted a tendency to topple sideways. But the babies positioned thus nevertheless looked pretty wobbly and some expressed insecurity by crying. There are no norms in the infant tests for this item. The closest that one can approximate it is 'sits with slight support', which Griffiths places at the end of the sixth month. Being able to sit unsupported for a short time she places in the eighth month, and being able to sit on the floor more or less indefinitely she places at the end of the ninth month. With the few Ganda babies we observed who were seen first to sit when positioned and then at the next visit to sit indefinitely unsupported, there appeared to be a gap of two to four weeks between the two achievements. In cases where we have only the mother's report to guide us it seems safest to assume that she refers to the baby's being able to sit alone when positioned.

Combining mothers' reports with our own observations, babies who were 'trained' to sit achieved sitting 'alone' at a mean age of 4.6 months whereas babies who were not so trained achieved sitting at a mean age of 3.9 months. These figures must be taken as very approximate, however.

Table 2.1: Locomotor Achievements and Developmental Quotient

	Training in sitting	Sits with slight support	Sits alone, sustained	Crawls	Creeps	Stands held	Stands alone	Walks	Trots	DQ[b]
Griffiths' norms		6 mos.	9 mos.	9 mos.	11 mos.	10 mos.	13 mos.	14 mos.	16 mos.	
NAME										
Secure-attached										
1. Paulo	yes	6[a]		6[a]	6½		9½	11	13	114
2. Sembajwe	yes	3[a]		6[a]				8½[a]		70
3. Juko	yes	4[a]		5[a]	7	7				
4. Senvuma	yes							11		108
5. Petero	yes	8		6[a]		8	11½			102
6. Mutebe	yes	5[a]		6[a]	7½	7				120
7. Nakiku	no	4½[a]		6[a]	7½	6½	11½	10	11	
8. Alima	yes	3		6	4½					
9. Aida	no		4½	6	7½					
10. William	no		5	5½	7½	6½		9		122
11. Senkumba	yes	3	4½	4½	8½		6½[a]	9		
12. Kyimba			5½[a]	5[a]			6½[a]			
13. Samwendi	no	4	4½			4				
14. Maryamu	no	4[a]		9	9½		11½	11½	13	107
15. Lusiya	yes	5[a]		6[a]			7[a]	8½		102
16. Nabatanzi	no	3[a]		5½[a]	7		8½	9½	10½	102

Table 2.1: *cont.*

NAME Griffiths' norms	Training in sitting	Sits with slight support 6 mos.	Sits alone, sustained 9 mos.	Crawls 9 mos.	Creeps 11 mos.	Stands held 10 mos.	Stands alone 13 mos.	Walks 14 mos.	Trots 16 mos.	DQ[b]
Insecure-attached										
17. Muhamidi	no	4½[a]	5	4½[a]	7½	7	7½			130
18. Magalita	no	3[a]		6[a]			8[a]	12		104
19. Sulaimani	no	3[a]		6	6½	7½				
20. Nakalema	yes	4[a]	5½	8	9					
21. Kasozi	yes	4[a]		6[a]			10[a]	11½		109
22. Waswa (1)	yes	4[a]		6[a]			15	17		
23. Nakato (1)	yes	4[a]		5[a]			13	14		
Non-attached										
24. Nora	no	3[a]		7½	9	9	9½	10½		
25. Kulistina	yes	6½		7		9	10½			
26. Waswa (2)	yes	5½	6½	7		5½				105
27. Nakato (2)	yes	5½	6½	7		5½				120
28. Namitala	yes	3								

a   Based on the mother's retrospective report.
b   Gesell Developmental Quotient, courtesy of Dr Marcelle Geber.

Mothers' retrospective reports are notoriously unreliable, and this might be suspected to be the case especially in a non-literate community where calendars are less important and written records are not kept in baby books. For those babies who were already able to sit when we began to visit and for whom we had to rely on mothers' reports, the mean age of sitting alone was 4.0 months. For those babies whom we actually observed at, or close to, the achievement of sitting, the mean age was 4.8 months. I consider these figures essentially equivalent, for we could pinpoint the precise age at the time of observation whereas the mother was reporting in 'months old'; moreover, in some instances our observation did not take place until the baby already could sit without support for extended periods. All things considered, the mothers' reports match our own observations quite well, and a discrepancy of 0.8 months must be considered negligible. By the same token the discrepancy between those who were trained and not trained must be considered negligible. Our figures give no grounds for arguing that training slows the development of sitting. Indeed, it may well be that some babies were not trained because they sat spontaneously at the expected age and others were trained because they were considered to be slow. Nevertheless, and regardless of all the difficulties discussed above, it is clear that this sample of Ganda babies was accelerated in sitting in comparison with the London babies on whom Griffiths standardized her test.

Crawling and Creeping

We followed the standard usage in distinguishing between crawling and creeping. The term 'crawling' was used when the infant, placed in a prone position on the floor, moved body and limbs in such a way as to make some progress, even though he was still flat to the floor. Griffiths' norms place this behavioral item at the end of the ninth month. The term 'creeping' was used for locomotion on the hands and knees or on all fours – a 'bear walk'. This item is placed by Griffiths at the eleventh month. In interview I was not careful to make a distinction between these two modes of locomotion, although I did so when recording observations. Therefore, I assume that when the mother reported the age at which locomotion was first achieved she meant 'crawling' – the earlier form.

The findings suggest that the Ganda child achieves locomotion first at about six or six and a half months of age and is able to creep effectively about a month later. The mean age of 'crawling' from the mothers' reports was 5.6 months; that from our own observations 6.6 months. The mean age of 'creeping' from our own actual observations was 7.5 – but this could not refer to the very onset of creeping. All we knew was that the child was able to creep on the occasion of one visit and that we had not seen him do so on an earlier visit. On the basis of our own observations crawling occurred about two and a half months earlier than the Griffiths' norms and creeping about three and a half months earlier.

Standing

Standing alone is not quite as momentous a milestone as sitting or crawling or walking, and the age at which it is achieved is sometimes not remembered. But limiting ourselves to those babies in which standing alone could be pinpointed by our own observations, the mean age of achieving this milestone was eleven months — two months in advance of the Griffiths' norms. Moreover, the intermediate stages in development of standing were observed to be well in advance of the Griffiths' norms. Standing firmly when held supported was observed to occur at about seven months (Griffiths' eleven months); being able to pull oneself to a standing position while holding onto furniture was observed at about seven or eight months (Griffiths' eleven months).

Walking

Walking is an important landmark in present-day Ganda society because it is, more often than not, the signal that a child is old enough to be weaned. Fourteen of the sample were able to walk, and with one exception (Sembajwe) we were on hand to witness the event. The mean age of achievement of walking was eleven months, Sembajwe excluded. We used as our criterion for walking the ability to take a few steps before falling. Griffiths places this item at fourteen months. For those whom we observed long enough to ascertain when they could 'trot about well', we found this to occur at about twelve months whereas Griffiths places it at sixteen months. The intermediate steps toward walking were observed infrequently. Only four babies, ranging in age from seven and a half to eleven months were observed to 'cruise', that is, to side step while holding onto something — an item which Griffiths places at twelve months. We did not inquire about this — and indeed the sparse furniture in the typical house would make it difficult for a baby to cruise while holding onto furniture. We saw only one child walk when led with both hands held — Juko. He was seven and a half months old; Griffiths places the time at twelve months. My impression was that, despite the significance attached to walking, few of these mothers walked the child about while holding his hands whereas this is fairly common among the 'Western' mothers I have known.

Language Development

Unless one deliberately sets out to observe an infant's vocalization, one tends to ignore it because it is so undifferentiated. And even when one deliberately attempts to note and record it, this is a difficult task — difficult because the untrained person cannot reproduce in writing the sounds (phonemes) the baby makes. An exhaustive examination of my field notes made me realize that it was not until the baby was capable of the repetition of four or more syllables — and I most frequently recorded 'da-da-da-da' and 'ma-ma-ma-ma' — that I made notes of vocalization, except crying of course. When vocalization got to the point of approximating a word, I, as an alien, found it difficult to detect — except in the case of *mama*, which is the same in Luganda and English. I had to rely, therefore, on the mother's reports of the child's acquisition of words — although having been told, I could sometimes verify the report through my own observations. Similarly, we had to rely on the mothers' reports of what the child was able to comprehend — although, again, there was some opportunity for direct observation. In regard to locomotor development my inquiries about achievements were repeated frequently and observations were easily made. In regard to language development, my specific inquiries tended to be made toward the end of the project; consequently I missed some of the milestones, and direct observations were more difficult. Thus, my records of language development are much more incomplete than those pertaining to locomotor development.

But, since I found locomotor development to be so accelerated, it is a fair question to ask whether the acceleration was limited to locomotor achievements or was more general. It is only because of this question that I turn to my scanty notes on language development.

I recorded four-syllable vocalization in the case of nine infants, but there is no reason to suppose that my record caught anything approximating a first achievement. The mean age at which I observed this type of vocalization was thirty-eight weeks; Griffiths places this item at the beginning of the ninth month. My notes suggest that the mean age at which it was reported that the child 'knew his own name' was about eight and a half months; Griffiths places this at fourteen months. We inquired about all children who had begun to say words the number of words they could use appropriately. Of those who could use three or more words appropriately the mean age was ten and a half months. Griffiths places this item at the end of the twelfth month. She lists only one item pertaining to early language comprehension; thus she places appropriate response to simple requests, such as 'give me the cup', at twelve months. Although the nature of our inquiries did not give us a longitudinal picture of the development of comprehension, a number of children were responding appropriately to simple commands — 'come', 'stop', 'go away', 'hush', 'give it to me', and the like — by the time they were nine or ten months old.

Geber's Findings

In all, Geber examined 252 infants and young children in or near Kampala. Her findings[7] not only substantiate but greatly elaborate our own. She found precocious psychomotor development to be common and particularly marked in the first year of life. She found momentary sitting to be achieved at four months and sustained sitting at five months. Standing without support was achieved at seven months and the first steps alone at nine months. Although locomotor development was most accelerated, all aspects of development were precocious — prehension and manipulation, adaptivity, language, and personal-social behavior. All of the babies under six months of age had Developmental Quotients of better than 100, and the same was true of 95 per cent of the babies between six and nine months of age. The superiority of the African group to the European norms was less marked in the second year of life, but even then, 75 per cent of the DQs exceeded 100. From then on the rate of development slowed down even more, until after the age of three years the DQs tended to be below the European norms.

Although Geber found that even the newborn baby was in a more advanced state of development than newborn European children,[8] she placed most emphasis upon methods of infant care as the factor responsible for the accelerated development of African babies. She particularly emphasized the close infant-mother relationship throughout the first year of life, the breast feeding on demand, the intimate physical contact, and the mother's constant availability. She also suggested that the way that the baby is carried on his mother's back may strengthen his ability to hold his head steady by forcing him to compensate for her various movements, and that the 'sitting position' on her back may help him to sit alone earlier.

Furthermore, I was very much impressed with the way that the Ganda baby is held sitting face outward on his mother's lap as she pauses to visit with family or guests; this brings him, from the beginning, into the midst of the social group and gives him much stimulation. I also noted that from an early age he is often held standing. As soon as the baby can sit alone, he spends some time on the floor rather than being held or confined, and when he can crawl he is given complete freedom to move about. I have no doubt that this absence of confinement interacts with social stimulation to account for his very precocious locomotor development, and I agree with Geber in attaching importance to postural adjustments to being held and carried during the earliest months.

Geber suggests that the decline in rate of development is attributable to abrupt and traumatic weaning and the great diminution of mother-child interaction that follows, often culminating in mother-child separation. The findings on weaning . . . suggest that it is a misunderstanding to characterize Ganda weaning as abrupt, but there is no doubt that the advent of a new baby in the family very substantially reduces the amount of time that a mother has free for the toddler who has been weaned. Although William's mother managed not only to interact with him often but also to spread her attention over all the members of her large family, I felt that she was exceptional. The general impression I received was that the Ganda mother's all-absorbing preoccupation with the infant made it impossible for her to give adequate stimulation to her other young children. Additional factors contributing to too low a level of stimulation in childhood beyond the first year or so of life are the dearth of toys and other playthings, the absence of organized activities for the young child, and the traditional training in polite, submissive behavior.

Geber reported two additional sets of findings that lend further support to the view that the course of sensorimotor development of the Ganda child is much influenced by child-care practices. One group of children attended a nursery school; these children showed much less of a decline in DQ in the third and fourth years of life than the children without nursery school experience. Geber points out that their mode of life and the socio-economic level of their families were essentially the same as those of the group as a whole. Secondly, she reports[9] that a group of infants from highly acculturated Ganda homes failed to show precocity of development during the first year of life. They were slower than babies in village families and approximated the European norms. They tended to be kept in their cribs much of the time and were held and carried much less than the village children. They were also fed on schedule, and breast feeding was on the whole less satisfactory. But when they could walk they had a much richer experience than did the village children — more toys, more attention, and the stimulation of parents with a relatively high degree of education, and in due course nursery school. These children did not enter into the decline in rate of development characteristic of the village children after the first year of life but rather proceeded to develop regularly at an average or somewhat above average rate.

When Geber's findings first became known in this country, some psychologists in my acquaintance received them with critical disbelief. The belief that intelligence is predetermined by genetic endowment and develops through a process of maturational unfolding is so ingrained in our society that it is difficult for many to assimilate evidence that experiential factors could either facilitate or retard its course. Geber's methods were criticized.[10] The old argument was revived that tests of infant sensorimotor development do not examine the same abilities that are measured by intelligence tests at later ages, and, moreover, they have been found to have limited predictive value. Another argument implied that Africans must be viewed as a species other than Western man; chimpanzees are accelerated in early development in comparison to humans, but this early precocity is associated with a much lower limit for potential development. The relevance of this issue to the controversial question of the intellectual potential of Negroes versus whites is all too painfully evident.

If the issue of the role of experience in the development of intelligence rested solely upon Geber's reports and upon my own observations reported here, I would have to acknowledge that confirmation from other studies was required. But there is in fact a great deal of evidence from a variety of sources other than these which makes continued belief in predetermined intelligence uninfluenced by experience untenable. J. McV. Hunt[11] has summarized and discussed this evidence . . .

Assuming, therefore, that the major issue — that intellectual development is influenced by individual experience — is resolved, the question then can be examined: What kinds of experience, at what periods of development, can facilitate intellectual growth? Obviously much careful and intensive research is needed before this important question can be answered. In the meantime Geber's and my studies of the Ganda suggest that during the first year of life development is facilitated by the kind of infant care the Ganda give — with much physical contact, much interaction between the infant and his mother, much social stimulation, prompt gratification of creature-comfort needs, lack of confinement, and freedom to explore the world. Just which of these features are the crucial ones in facilitating development cannot, of course, be ascertained, for they are confounded in these studies. Furthermore, Geber's findings suggest that traditional Ganda methods of child rearing in the second year of life and beyond provide less adequate stimulation to development than the Western methods characteristic of the more acculturated members of the society.

Notes

1.   The Gesell Development Schedules are included in *Developmental Diagnosis* by A. Gesell and Catherine S. Armatruda (2nd ed; New York: Harper, 1947). Dr Geber used a revision of these schedules which had been standardized on French infants.

2.   Mrs Kibuka subsequently wrote to report the reasons for the refusal. Dr Geber was working in cooperation with Dr R.F.A. Dean, director of research in infant nutrition supported by the National Research Council of Great Britain. Dr Dean's unit wished to make anthropometric measurements on the same occasion that the Gesell Tests were to be given. Being unaware of this plan, Mrs Kikuba and I had not prepared the families for the prospects of two male visitors in addition to Dr Geber, nor for the fact that they wished to photograph each baby when naked and to measure his physical dimensions with calipers. Some of the first babies visited cried with fear when faced with male strangers and the strange procedures, and the mothers found it incomprehensible and somehow improper that their babies were stripped naked for the photographs. Word spread through the villages, and some of the families refused to cooperate when the team came to visit them at the appointed time.

3.   I am much indebted to Dr Geber for providing me with her findings and with permission to use them here. For some cases only the Development Quotient was recorded. For other cases she sent a full report of details of the test behavior and findings for the four separate scales of the Developmental Schedules. These reports have been summarized and appear at the end of each of the summaries of case history.

4.   Ruth Griffiths, *The Abilities of Babies* (London: University of London Press, 1954).

5.   The discrepancy occurred in the case of Sembajwe. His DQ of 70, which falls in the borderline-defective range, does not match the picture of healthy development which I report, and was, I believe, misleadingly low because he was so uncooperative in the testing.

6.   Jean Piaget, *The Origins of Intelligence in Children* (New York: International Universities Press, 1952). Further, for an excellent exposition of the role of experience in the development of intelligence see J. McV. Hunt, *Intelligence and Experience* (New York: Ronald Press, 1961).

7.   Marcelle Geber, 'Développement psychomoteur de l'enfant africain', *Courrier*, 1956, 6, pp. 17-29. Marcelle Geber and R.F.A. Dean, 'Gesell tests on African children', *Pediatrics*, 1956, 6, pp. 1055-65. Marcelle Geber, 'Problèmes posés par le développement du jeune enfant africain en fonction de son milieu social', *Le Travail Humain*, 1960, 23, pp. 97-111.

8.   Marcelle Geber and R.F.A. Dean, 'The state of development of newborn African children', *Lancet*, 1957, 1, pp. 1216-19.

9.   Marcelle Geber, 'L'enfant africain occidentalisé et de niveau social supérieur en Uganda', *Courrier*, 1958, 8, pp. 517-23.

10.   The criticisms were as follows: Her sample was relatively small and not selected in a way to ensure that it was representative; she does not provide adequate data in regard to measures of scatter and significance of statistical differences; she counts the same children twice or more by combining retest data with cross-sectional data. These criticisms are quite justified, and certainly my own data reported here are from an even smaller sample — some are based on retrospective report and are equally open to criticism.

11.   J. McV. Hunt, *Intelligence and Experience*.

3 INFANT DEVELOPMENT IN THE ZINACANTECO INDIANS OF SOUTHERN MEXICO

T.B. Brazelton, J.S. Robery and G.A. Collier

Source: *Pediatrics*, 1969, vol. 44, no. 2, pp. 274-93. Copyright American Academy of Pediatrics 1969.

. . . Of particular interest was Geber's report of the motor precocity of Ugandan infants evident from birth as compared with a control group of European infants (12, 13). Ainsworth documented the early development of these infants and their interaction with their culture (14). These cross-cultural studies suggested a method for observing in a natural experiment a variation in human behavioral genotype[†] and the influence of child-rearing practices on its eventual development.

This paper reports the findings of our study of infants and their development in an isolated group of Malayan Indians in southeastern Mexico. Neurological-behavioral examinations and unstructured observations of neonates at birth and in the first week of life revealed striking differences between these infants and a control group from our own culture. Developmental testing of Indian infants under 1 year of age showed minimal differences when compared to United States norms in the sequence and timing of developmental steps. The effects of their distinctive child-rearing practices on these infants were demonstrated in the development of personality characteristics and imitative learning of expected roles which enabled the child to fit into his environment and to perpetuate the culture of these isolated people.

Zinacantan: The Setting for the Study

The Zinacantecos of highland Chiapas, in southeastern Mexico, are a culturally distinct tribe of Indians who live in scattered mountain villages in relative isolation. For over 10 years, they have been the subject of intensive anthropological study by the Harvard Chiapas Project, led by Professor Evon Z. Vogt (15). Project members, including Dr George Collier, have gathered extensive background information on the society and have developed a fine rapport with its leaders which enabled us to observe deliveries, examine newborns, and test small infants, despite the pervasive suspicion with which outsiders are viewed (16-19).

Unlike many aboriginal hunting and gathering groups in the United States whose cultures were destroyed by the encroachment of civilization, the Zinacantecos have remained successful agriculturalists who have been able to defend themselves from assimilation by dominant Mexican civilization in spite of 400 years of close contact with it. Indeed, their cultural integrity and Indian identity are strong, and nonconformity leads individuals to unhappy roles outside of the society (18).

The total population of about 8,500 is surrounded by other Indian tribes with whom, however, there is little intermarriage. The Zinacantecos live in scattered mountain villages of up to 1,200 people in which the local descent group is the dominant structural unit (29). The typical living unit is headed by an elder male and made up of his children and his married sons and their offspring who live in his house or in adjacent dwellings. Men of such a unit co-operate in farming and share with each other the expenses of rituals, sickness, and all the life crises, while the women of the group prepare its food and clothing. Ordinarily, then, the immediate family group is much larger than our own, and the infant in a single household has many to mother him.

A typical house has one room about 20 feet square with a dirt floor, windowless walls of mud or split boards, and a high-peaked thatched roof with a smoke hole. Family members sleep on planks or mats around the periphery of this room where cooking is done over the quiet, perpetually burning fire in the center.

Theirs is not an idle life: men and grown boys are usually at work in the fields, while older girls and women are busy with household tasks and care of the young. A child is expected to assume adult tasks by the sixth or seventh year and is given increasingly difficult chores from infancy (19).

Zinacanteco artistic expressions are subtle and muted: their joy in speech, drinking and complex ritual is a more important creative outlet than are their handicrafts which, though extensive, tend to be prescribed, functional, and uniform. Unaware of the magnificent achievements of their Mayan ancestors, they are concerned only with survival and the present. They make sparse reference to past history in their folklore and worry little about future unforeseeable events. Individual self-expression is not a goal, and conformity is highly valued and respected.

As in most of the underdeveloped world, illness is widespread and untreated; sanitation is non-existent, and the incidence of gastrointestinal disorders and parasitism is high. Pneumonia, tuberculosis, and infectious diseases of childhood are endemic. Though precise figures do not exist, we estimate that 35 per cent of the children die before the age of 4 years, half of these in infancy (15). Although modern medicine is available at free clinics in a nearby Spanish town, they do not use these facilities for acute illness, relying on them for less severe chronic ailments, e.g. skin diseases or minor wounds. The Zinacantecos rely on local shamans or curers to treat most illness, which they believe has its origin in loss of the soul which comes about through supernatural causes. Children with pneumonia and meningitis must recover without medical intervention and many die.

Although we lack precise data on their nutrition, the Zinacanteco diet seems adequate — eggs and meat frequently supplement the staple bean and corn tortilla diet. The important question of malnutrition and its deleterious effect on development raised by Cravioto's work (20) and by others (21) cannot be ruled out as a variable affecting the children we saw. We did not see kwashiorkor or recognize other forms of clinical malnutrition in this group. The adults and children did not appear to be grossly anemic, but no hematologic tests have ever been done.

Zinacanteco cultural practices involving infant and child care are remarkably uniform. As in other primitive cultures with extended families, knowledge is passed on by the immediate presence of experienced older family members at the time of birth and thereafter.

No special rites or practices are carried out while a woman is pregnant, and no pharmacologic agents are given before or during delivery. The midwife, always present during childbirth, does not employ any particular obstetrical techniques but supports and encourages the mother in labor (16). Immediately after birth, elaborate rituals are performed with the newborn lying naked near the fire. Prayers and incantations by the midwife exhort the gods to bestow upon the child all the manly or womanly attributes necessary for success in the Zinacanteco world. The infant is then clothed. A long heavy skirt extending beyond the feet, which is worn throughout the first year by both sexes, is held in place by a wide belt or cinch wrapped firmly around the abdomen. Then the newborn is wrapped in additional layers of blankets in order to protect him from 'losing parts of his soul'. This wrapping, in effect, swaddles the baby and acts as a constant suppressant to motor activity (22, 23), as well as defending him from outside evil. Infants' faces are covered except during feedings, especially during the first 3 months, in order to ward off illness and the effects of 'the evil eye'.

During the first month after delivery, the mother is confined with the infant held wrapped in her arms or laid supine beside her as she rests. Thereafter, the child is carried in a rebozo[1] on the mother's or another woman's back when not feeding. Siblings often care for infants, carrying them on their backs in imitation of the mother, though rarely playing with them (16). Indeed, during the first year, they are never propped up to look around, talked to or stimulated by eye-to-eye contact with family members, nor are they put on the floor to explore on their own.

Striking in this culture is the frequent nursing of the infant which is facilitated by the dress of adult women – a woven shirt, slit deeply under the arms to provide easy access to the breast.

In general, social and visual stimulation are minimal throughout the first year, while kinesthetic and tactile forms of interaction are maximal.

Study

The authors carried out the study during the summers of 1966 and 1967. In both summers, the pediatricians participated for one month each; the anthropologist author and an Indian guide located subjects and interpreted language and cultural practices.

In an attempt to minimize the possible effect of chronic disease and malnutrition, subjects were chosen who appeared clinically healthy and who had no history of previous illness. Mothers were evaluated clinically as well; they appeared to be well nourished and were not anemic or toxic during pregnancy. Confirmation by laboratory studies was not possible.

The study consisted of three parts, the first focusing on characteristics of the newborn at birth and in the first week of life, the second on mother-child interaction in the first 9 months, and the third on developmental milestones during the first year of life.

Part I: Evaluation of Neonates

In this aspect of the study, we attempted to evaluate the inborn characteristics of the newborn as soon after delivery as possible and on two more visits during the first week. We observed two deliveries and were allowed to examine a total of five neonates in this first week of life. The observations of the newborns fell into three categories:

In an unstructured observation period of 30 minutes, the infant was with his mother. At this time, we recorded spontaneous activity and the neonate's responses to stimuli which occurred naturally – environmental sounds, light changes, handling by the caretakers, and internal stimuli from within the baby. Of particular interest to us was the infant's use of motor activity and states of consciousness, e.g. how the infant moved from state to state, the build-up of tension before he nursed, and his mode of falling asleep afterward. [Description of states omitted.]

We recorded the quality of his responses – his ability to attend to or modulate his response to a stimulus in these unstructured periods. Nursing and mothering practices were described in detail as we observed them.

A pediatric examination was made on each visit, with special attention to the infant's maturity, state of nutrition, and hydration. Since our equipment was necessarily limited to a stethoscope and tape measure because of the parents' fear of intrusion on the integrity of the infant's soul, a large part of this assessment depended on observation and palpation. No blood sampling was possible without endangering our chances of continuing our study.

A neurological-behavioral evaluation[2] was recorded on each infant twice in the first week. This assessment is described in a previous paper (10) and is based on that outlined by André-Thomas *et al.* (25), Prechtl and Beintema (26) and behavioral tests of Graham *et al.* (29). Presentation of stimuli and the elicitation of reflexes were flexible and we attempted to produce optimal responses. Our categories included:

Motor activity. Both spontaneous and elicited responses were recorded here; they included quantity, tempo, freedom, and fluidity of movement, tremulousness, startle activity, preferred movement, and positions at rest. A general assessment of the infant's buildup of activity, tempo, use of states, general tone, irritability, vigor, maturity, and organization of reflex activity was made. Passive movements were scored according to André-Thomas *et al.* (25).

Sensory responses. Stimuli were presented at appropriate times and reactions recorded: tactile — such as stroking around the mouth, on the belly and extremities; kinesthetic — handling, rocking and cuddling, and changing the subject's position; auditory — reaction to voice, rattle and bell; visual — reaction to observer's or mother's face, fixation and pursuit of red ball (30); sucking — mother's breast or observer's finger; temperature changes — observed when infant was undressed or uncovered for a period; restraint or swaddling — as was achieved by the tight cinch around the abdomen and the swaddling effect of the rebozo.

We scored the infants at the end of this 30-minute period of observation on a 5-point scale. A general assessment of the infant's state, behavior, motor activity and tempo, tonus,[†] maturity, irritability and consolability, vigor, adaptation to repeated sensory stimuli, and general behavioral organization was recorded at the end of this period of observation.

Part II: Mother-Child Interaction

Four-hour observation periods of mother-child interaction were made with infants of different ages during the first 9 months of life. We attempted to use Rheingold's schema (31) for sampling interaction at prescribed intervals; but we found that we had to modify it to suit our purposes. In this culture, interaction between mother and child was infrequent, and each event was extremely significant. Timed sampling[†] missed many of these events. Therefore, all events occurring in this dyad were recorded in detail and timed accurately; and, we focused on whether mother or infant initiated the interplay, for what purpose, and its outcome. Rhein-gold's categories for mothering activities and infant behavior were followed according to her criteria. The number and quality of each was recorded.

Part III: Developmental Milestones

In this aspect of the study, we used the Knobloch-Pasamanick adaptation (32) of the Gesell scales the first summer and the Bayley scales (33) the second summer. Motor development and social interaction were scored also. Testing of infants over 9 months of age proved impossible because of the marked degree of stranger anxiety which appeared before 12 months and interfered with observations. Each infant was tested once, and a second time 1 month later.

Results

Part I: Evaluation of Neonates

Of the five Zinacanteco newborns examined in the first week, two were examined at birth. The delivery was easy in each instance. The young mother was given no medication during labor. Toward the end of the second stage, she knelt before her own mother while her husband pulled on a cinch around her waist, exerting downward pressure on her fundus. The midwife instructed her with each labor pain, received the infant on delivery, and tied the cord. In one case, she manually extracted the placenta when it did not come easily. Then the young baby was kept undressed for a 30-minute period in front of the fire with no protection against the cold other than a blanket on his back while chants were sung and rituals performed on his behalf. This provided us with a rare oppor-tunity to observe and record his behavior immediately after delivery.

Both infants were typical of the other newborn Zinacantecos we examined later in the neonatal week. They were small, weighing about 5 lb and measuring 18 in. in length and 12½ in. in head circumference. Apgar† scores for both were 9, 9, 9 at 1, 5, and 15 minutes (34). In appearance and behavior they were mature, with no apparent anemia or dysmaturity. Although they were the size of premature infants in our country, they had none of the jerky movements or snapback of the limbs characteristic of a premature infant. Their limb movements were free and smooth, and they lay quietly on the blanket looking around the room with alert faces for the entire hour after delivery. In addition to quiet motor activity, they demonstrated a striking sensory alertness. Repeatedly in the first week, all five infants would become quiet and

Table 3.1: Observations of Neonates (Average Ratings of Performances Scaled from 1 to 5 – Low to High)

Age of examination	Birth		1 Day	2 Days	3 Days	4 Days	5 Days	7 Days (in cinch)	7 Days (out of cinch)
Zinacanteco infants (US controls in brackets)	2	(3)	3 (3)	2 (3)	2 (3)	1 (3)	1 (3)	2	2 (3)
Spontaneous movement									
Output	2	(2)	2.5 (1)	2 (2)	2 (2)	2 (3)	1 (4)	1	3 (4)
Tempo	2	(2)	2 (1)	2 (2)	2 (2)	2 (4)	2 (4)	2	2 (4)
Limb excursion	2	(3)	2 (2)	2 (2)	3 (3)	2 (4)	2 (4)	1	2 (4)
Hand to mouth: frequency	2	(4)	3 (3)	2 (3)	3 (4)	2 (4)	1 (4)	1	2 (4)
duration	1.5	(3)	3 (3)	1.5 (3)	2 (4)	2 (4)	1 (4.5)	1	2 (4.5)
Spontaneous startles	1	(4)	2 (4)	2 (4)	1 (3)	2 (3)	1 (3)	1	1 (2.5)
Tremulousness	1	(4)	1 (4)	1.5 (2)	1 (3)	1 (3)	1 (3)	1	1 (3)
Fluidity of movement	4	(2)	4 (2)	3 (2)	3.5 (2)	4 (3)	3 (3)	4	4 (3)
Freedom of movement	3	(4)	3.5 (2)	3.5 (3)	3.5 (3)	3 (4)	2 (4)	2	3 (4.5)
Elicited responses									
TNR	2	(2)	2.5 (3)	1.5 (3)	2 (3)	2 (3)	2 (3)	2	3 (4)
Pull to sit: head lag	2	(2)	2.5 (2)	2 (2)	2 (2.5)	3 (3)	2 (4)	3	2 (4)
head control	3	(3)	3 (2)	2 (2)	3 (3)	2 (3)	2 (4)	4	3 (4)
Prone placement: crawl	2	(3)	3 (2)	2 (2.5)	3 (3)	2 (3.5)	2 (3.5)	1	2 (4)
head raising and turning	2	(3)	3 (2)	2 (3)	3 (4)	2 (3.5)	2 (4)	1	2 (5)

Table 3.1: *cont.*

Age of examination	Birth	1 Day	2 Days	3 Days	4 Days	5 Days	7 Days (in cinch)	7 Days (out of cinch)
Zinacanteco infants (US controls in brackets)	2 (3)	3 (3)	2 (3)	2 (3)	1 (3)	1 (3)	2	2 (3)
Elicited responses (cont.)								
Moro:								
extension to flexion	3 (3.3)	3.5 (3)	2 (3)	3 (4)	2 (4)	2 (5)	1	3 (4)
Ankle clonus	1 (3)	2 (4)	1 (3.5)	1 (4)	2 (4)	3 (3)	1	1 (3)
Pinprick (intensity and spread)	1.5 (4)	3 (3)	2 (3)	3 (4)	2 (3)	3 (2)	1	3 (2)
Grasp (hands)	4 (4)	4 (3)	3 (3)	3.5 (3)	4 (4)	3 (4)	2	3 (3)
Placing	3 (4)	3.5 (3)	3 (3)	3 (2)	3 (3)	3 (3)	1	3 (4)
Stepping	3 (4)	3.5 (2)	3 (3)	3 (2)	3 (3)	3 (4)	4	3 (3)
Rooting	3.5 (3)	4 (2)	3 (3)	3.5 (4)	4 (4)	2 (2)	4	4 (3)
Sucking	4.5 (3)	5 (2)	4 (2)	4 (4)	5 (3.3)	4 (2)	5	4 (4)
Passive movement								
Range	4 (3)	4 (2)	4 (3)	4 (3)	4 (2.5)	4 (3)	2	4 (3)
Resistance	1 (3)	2 (2)	1 (2)	1 (3)	2 (4)	1 (4)	4	2 (4)
Recoil	1 (3)	1 (3)	1 (2)	1 (4)	1 (4)	2 (4)	1	2 (3)
Muscular consistency	2.5 (3)	2.5 (2)	2 (2.5)	2 (4)	2 (3)	2 (3)	2	3 (4)
Sensory responses								
Eyes:								
blink	3 (3)	2 (3)	3 (3)	3 (3)	3 (4)	3 (3)	3	3 (3)
adaptation	4 (3)	3 (4)	4 (4)	3 (3)	4 (3)	3 (4)	3	4 (3)
visual pursuit	4 (3)	4 (2)	3 (2)	3 (1)	3.5 (3)	3 (3)	4	4 (3)

Table 3.1: *cont.*

Age of examination	Birth	1 Day	2 Days	3 Days	4 Days	5 Days	7 Days (in cinch)	7 Days (out of cinch)	7 Days (US)
Zinacanteco infants (US controls in brackets)	2 (3)	3 (3)	2 (3)	2 (3)	1 (3)	1 (3)	2	2	(3)
Sensory responses (cont									
amp. persistence vestibular (head and eyes)	4 (3)	3 (2)	3 (2)	3 (2)	3.5 (2)	2 (2)	5	5	(3)
Auditory:	3 (3)	3 (3)	3 (3)	3 (3)	3 (3)	3 (3)	2	3	(3)
adaptation	4 (3)	3 (2)	3.5 (2)	3 (2)	3 (2)	2 (3)	3	4	(3.5)
General assessment									
Modulation of states	4 (3)	4 (2)	4 (2)	4 (1)	4 (2)	4 (3)	3	4	(3)
Organization (spread of responses, habituation, quality of performance)	4 (3)	4 (2)	3 (2)	4 (2)	4 (3)	3 (4)	3	4	(4)
Adaptation to repeated stimuli	4 (3)	4 (3)	4 (3)	3 (4)	4 (3)	4 (4)	3	4	(4)
Consolability	5 (3)	4 (2.5)	3 (2.5)	3 (3)	4 (3)	4 (5)	4	4	(5)
Maturity	4 (3)	4 (2)	3 (2.5)	3 (3)	4 (4)	4 (4)	3	3	(5)
Rapidity of build-up	2 (3)	3 (4)	2 (5)	2 (5)	3 (4)	1 (4)	1	3	(3)
Tempo at height	2 (4)	2 (4)	2 (4)	2 (3)	3 (4)	1 (3)	2	3	(3)
Irritability	1 (3)	2 (4)	2 (4)	2 (4)	1 (3)	1 (3)	1	2	(3)
Vigor	2.5 (3)	2.5 (3)	2 (3)	2 (4)	3 (4)	2 (4)	2	3	(5)
General tonus	2 (4)	3 (2)	3 (2)	2 (3)	3 (3)	2 (4)	3	2	(4)

alert, and then slowly turn toward a voice. When lighting was adequate in the dark huts, they alertly looked at the red ball visual stimulus and followed it back and forth as it was moved; on one occasion, a baby followed for 60 seconds without interruption. Vertical excursions of 30° from neutral were easy to elicit. We noted frequent head movement to augment such pursuit, and only rarely would startles or jerky motor activity interrupt this attentive state.

In order to evaluate the distinctive characteristics of these Zinacanteco infants, we compared their performance with that of three Caucasian infants to whom we administered, on each day of their first week of life, the same neurological-behavioral protocol used for their Zinacanteco counterparts. These controls had experienced normal spontaneous delivery from unmedicated and unanesthetized mothers after 40 weeks of normal gestation without any complications of pregnancy. Their Apgar scores were 8, 9, 9 or over; and, pediatrically and neurologically, they were normal in the first week after birth.

Table 3.1 shows tested performance differences for the two groups of infants. Each infant was rated on a scale from 1 to 5 (from low to high) on the test items listed by general category of response. The figures given for each item are the averages of the ratings for the infants of each group seen on the corresponding day after birth, and the data for the controls are listed in parentheses.

Although the small size of our samples does not allow statistical treatment of the data, certain differences speak for themselves. We shall summarize the most important ones.

Spontaneous Movement. While the output, tempo, and freedom and excursion of limb movements was initially low for both groups of infants, it increased gradually from day to day for the United States controls but not for the Zinacantecos. Both the frequency and duration of hand to mouth activity were initially lower in the Zinacantecos than in the controls and, by the fifth to seventh day, were much reduced in the Zinacantecos while increasing in the controls. Spontaneous startles and tremulousness were much lower at all times in the Zinacantecos, while their fluidity and freedom of movement were rated consistently high. In general, the Zinacantecos were distinguished by high freedom and fluidity but low output of spontaneous movement.

Elicited Responses. In tonic neck responses,[†] in head lag and head control on being pulled to sit, their crawling and head control when placed in a prone position, and the completeness of Moro reflexes,[†] Zinacanteco infants were similar to the controls during the first 2 or 3 days; but, thereafter, the controls scored increasingly higher in these responses. With ankle clonus[†] and in the intensity of spread of pinprick response, the Zinacantecos were consistently lower throughout the first week. In placing, stepping, and grasp, they differed little from the controls. In sucking and rooting, their performance was consistently excellent. Cinching[†] apparently restrained many of these responses by day 7. In general, the Zinacanteco infants maintained throughout the first week the muted level of these responses seen at birth, while their United States counterparts increased in the intensity of their responses.

Passive Movement. In range of passive movement, the Zinacantecos scored slightly but consistently higher than the controls; but, in resistance, recoil, and muscular consistency, their responses were noticeably more muted.

General Assessment. In modulation of states, the Zinacanteco infants scored consistently higher than their United States counterparts. Their moderately high organization of responses, adaptation to repeated stimuli, consolability, and maturity exceeded those of the controls in the first days, but the controls equalled or surpassed the Zinacantecos in their degree of these reponses by the end of the first week. In rapidity of build-up, tempo at height, irritability, and vigor, the Zinacantecos scored consistently lower than the controls throughout the first week, while both groups had roughly the same level of general tonus. In general, the Zinacanteco infants' scores did not change appreciably during the first week, while the controls increased in their level of organization, of adaptation, consolability, and maturity.

In summary, Zinacanteco infant motor activity from birth was freer, more fluid, non-tremulous, and only moderate in vigor, and without the 'over-shooting' or over-reaction which tends to interfere with prolonged or repeated responses to sensory stimuli as seen in North American infants. Spontaneous startles were rare, and responses to the elicited Moro were somewhat subdued in the Zinacantecos; the general disorganization of states and lack of coordination that we are accustomed to see on day 1 and 2 in North American infants (10) was not evident in these neonates. State behavior was also dissimilar to that of United States babies; the Zinacantecos maintained quiet, alert states for long periods, with slow, smooth transitions from one state to another. We recorded none of the deep sleep, intense crying, or intense sucking observed in the American controls. The apparent control of state and motor behavior in Indian infants seems to be of a higher order, permitting repeated and prolonged responses to auditory, visual, and kinesthetic stimuli in the first week of life.

Part II: Mother-Child Interaction

Twelve Zinacanteco infants ranging in age from 1 to 9 months were the subjects of our 4-hour observations of mother-child interaction. Parents though bewildered by the purpose of our 4-hour visits to their homes, quickly resumed their normal activities while other family members and occasional visitors chatted with them and with our guide.

Rheingold's categories of mothering and infant activities (31) were the basis for our observations. Rather than following her time sampling procedures, however, we recorded the frequency and duration of interaction continuously throughout each observation.

For each subject of the 4-hour observations, the number and duration of each mothering and infant activity is listed in Table 3.2. Although we have no controls for these observations, certain differences from mother-child patterns in our own culture are striking and obvious.

For example, mothers rarely attempted to elicit social responses from their infants by looking at their faces or talking to them. Even during feedings when the mother would preen the baby, her glances were perfunctory and without expectation of response.

The infants were rarely placed on the floor or bed, except when kept supine and swaddled beside the mother during the month of her postpartum confinement. Older infants were held in her lap, her arms, or on her back in the restraining rebozo.

Breast feedings were notably frequent, as high as nine times in a 4-hour period. In four families, siblings were breast fed as many as 10 times. The primary purpose of feeding appeared to be to quiet the child's restlessness when he would not be lulled in the rebozo on the mother's back by her rhythmic grinding of the corn.

Mothering activities tended to be perfunctory, with little scrutiny of the infant, and with only minimal assessment of his needs. Rather than eliciting responses from their children, Zinacanteco mothers tended to restrain the slightest disturbance or restlessness by frequent breast feeding.

The most striking feature of infant activity was the paucity of vocalizations. Indeed, during three observations, no vocalizations were heard. Cries were brief and were quickly terminated by the mothers' quieting activities.

These infants rarely mouthed their hands and never sucked their fingers. The youngest infants spent most of their time covered and asleep with the confined mother. Older infants were never offered pacifiers and only rarely toys, were never placed on the floor to crawl or stand at the

Table 3.2: Ratings from 4-Hour Observations of Mother-Child Interaction

Subject number	1	2	3	4	5	6	7	8	9	10	11	12
Age (mos.)	7	1	1	3	3	4	6	7	8	8	9	9
Mothering activities												
Total number of caretakers	1	1	1	1	4	2	1	1	1	1	2	5
Number of glances at infant's face	3	4	3	2	3	3	1	1	1	1	4	0
Number of times of talking to infant	10	0	0	4	1	5	0	1	4	3	2	0
Number of diaperings	4	4	1	2	1	1	1	1	3	1	4	0
Total minutes hold child in rebozo	0	0	0	50	94	0	180	30	0	0	58	111
Total minutes holding in arms or lap	25	40	110	185	143	142	60	210	176	240	182	227
Total minutes leaves child on bed	215	200	130	5	3	98	0	0	64	0	0	0
Number of breast feedings	3	6	3	7	9	4	2	5	3	6	7	9
Total length of feeding (minutes)	24	38	14	37	63	30	15	35	15.5	48	30	35
Number of times siblings were breastfed	3	3	—	—	—	—	—	—	—	9	2	10
Age of siblings (years)	1.5	3	—	—	—	—	—	—	—	3	2	3
Total minutes of sibling feeding	10	15	—	—	—	—	—	—	—	20	5	29
Infant anxieties												
Total minutes of sleep	205	55	100	33	30	93	180	30	60	15	58	111
Total minutes awake	35	185	140	207	210	147	60	210	180	225	182	129
Total number of vocalizations	0	0	0	1	3	0	0	1	3	2	5	5
Number of times cries briefly	7	5	8	3	2	0	3	3	1	1	3	3
Number of times mouths hands	0	0	1	3	3	0	3	5	3	3	5	5
Number of times plays with toys	0	0	0	1	1	0	0	0	7	3	2	1

furniture, and were mostly in their mother's arms or lap, or on her back in a rebozo. In her rebozo, they might reach for her braid, beads, or for passing objects as she moved, and they might sit up or bounce as though in a bouncing chair. Although they were quieter and less demanding than our infants, their activity and motor development came to the surface in spite of the limitations of the rebozo.

Part III: Developmental Milestones

Ninety-three healthy, normal infants, ranging in age from birth to 9 months were tested for gross and fine motor performance (Figure 3.1), mental age as judged by social behavior, language development, and adaptive behavior in response to test objects (Figure 3.2). Each infant

Figure 3.1: Estimates of Motor Age Plotted against Chronological Age Knobloch-Pasamanick scale (●), Bayley scale (○). The diagonal line indicates the statistical norm of United States infants

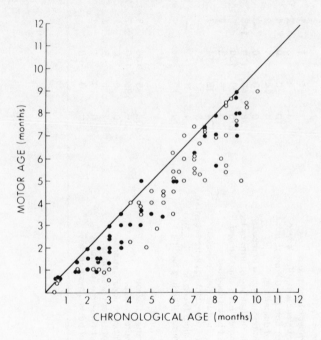

was tested once and, where possible, was re-tested by a second observer one month later using the Knobloch-Pasamanick adaptation of the Gesell scales in 1966 and the Bayley scales in 1967.

Test items were administered with the infant in his mother's lap in the hut or, occasionally, outside on a mat. The examiner sat nearby and presented blocks, toys, and other test items on a small square board platform held on his knees. Curious onlookers inevitably gathered around us in this setting and added their comments as we tested. This excitement produced enough stranger anxiety in infants older than 9 months to prevent their being tested. Both the Knobloch-Pasamanick and the Bayley scales required the use of test objects with which the Zinacanteco infants were totally unfamiliar, such as cubes, rattles, balls, spoons, and cups, and the children had to be taught how to use these objects before their performance could be scored. Novelty was met with impassive faces in tested children and parents alike. Repeatedly, infants watched us carefully as we demonstrated the use of test objects, imitated each movement we had made to score a success on the test, and then dropped the object without any of the exploration or experimental play we would have seen in United States babies.

Because Zinacanteco mothers never place their infants in a prone position, doing so, as required for certain items of motor development testing, uniformly elicited distress which masked the motor performance being tested. Finally, several items rating the quality of vocalization could not be scored because of the paucity of social babbling and imitation of language in the Zinacanteco infants.

In spite of these problems, the ratings using both the Knobloch-Pasamanick and the Bayley scales gave comparable results, though the administration of the latter and its scoring were somewhat easier and more precise. Both scales permitted performance on items to be grouped, resulting in an estimate of mental age and motor age for each child which could be compared with his chronological age. Although data were collected from three culturally similar Zinacanteco hamlets, there was no statistical difference in performance between these hamlets, and the results were pooled. These results are summarized in Figures 3.1 and 3.2 and in Table 3.3.

In Table 3.3, differences in performance of the Zinacantecos from United States norms are summarized. For each Zinacanteco infant, the estimated mental and motor ages in months were subtracted from his chronological age in months, yielding differences whose averages across subjects would be zero if the subjects did not differ from United States norms or would be significantly greater than zero if they lagged behind these norms. The table gives the mean and standard deviation in months of these differences from United States norms of the Zinacantecos' mental and motor age, derived from the Knobloch-Pasamanick scale the first summer and Robey's administration of the Bayley scale and Brazelton's administration of the Bayley scale in the second summer.

It can be seen from Table 3.3, that the differences from United States norms are significantly positive, and that though varying in size between scales and test administrators, the Zinacanteco infants lagged about one month, with no increasing decrement with increasing age (Figures 3.1 and 3.2).

The difference from United States norms in motor age is consistently higher than that of mental age.[3] Furthermore there was a Pearson product

Figure 3.2: Estimates of Mental Age Plotted against Chronological Age Knobloch-Pasamanick scale (●), Bayley scale (○). The diagonal line indicates the statistical norm of United States infants

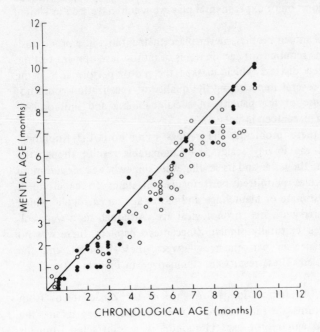

Table 3.3: Differences from United States Norms of Mental and Motor
Ages Observed in Zinacanteco Infants

Scale used	Difference in mental age from United States norms		Difference in motor age from United States norms		
	Mean	Standard deviation	Mean	Standard deviation	Number of subjects
Knobloch-Pasamanick Scale (administered by Robey and Brazelton)	.61	.60	.88	.61	40
Bayley Scale (administered by Robey)	1.24	.76	1.51	.91	36
Bayley Scale (administered by Brazelton)	.74	.59	.78	.75	17

moment correlation (r) between the differences from United States norms
in motor age and mental age of .66 for the Knobloch-Pasamanick ratings
and .42 for the Bayley ratings (both significant to the $p < .01$ level),
indicating a tendency for high lag in motor age to accompany high lag in
mental age.

Finally, the lack of agreement in Table 3.3 regarding the differences
from United States norms of Zinacanteco performance warrants some
comment. We attribute the considerable spread of the distribution of these
differences to the peculiar circumstances and difficulties inherent in the
testing situation, especially to those reactions to the novelty of the test
setting and procedures which modified the infant's test response. However,
the differences between Robey's and Brazelton's administration of the
Bayley scale reflected a definite observer effect.

In summary, in their first year's motor and mental development,
Zinacanteco infants seemed to lag consistently 1 month behind United
States norms. Nevertheless, this lag did not increase with age, reflecting
the Zinacanteco's apparent passage through essentially the same sequence
of development at approximately the same rate as is characteristic of
North American infants.

Discussion

Any attempt to understand infant development in another culture must
take into account the culturally distinctive practices of mothering and
socialization which constitute the infant's environment, as well as the

particular behavioral characteristics which the infant presents to this environment. In the Zinacanteco infants, we have discerned what we think to be inborn behavioral characteristics which may contribute to the mothering practices which have been observed. These are behaviorally valid for mother and child and become culturally adaptive as well.

Although intra-uterine malnutrition and infection are known to interfere with the full expression of individual genotype, we are relatively confident that, in Zinacantan, where diet and protein intake are adequate, these factors did not contribute significantly to the distinctive behavior of the newborns we examined.

These infants were uniform in their quiet, monitored motor activity, which permitted long, uninterrupted periods of alert response to auditory and visual cues, in contrast to United States infants and the African neonates described by Geber. The Zinacanteco infants exhibited a high order of control in the modulation of their states of alertness and in the suppression of motor behavior which might interfere with prolonged alertness.

Zincanteco mothering practices, while culturally uniform, seemed well fitted to these characteristics of their infants. By swaddling the infant, through the close physical contact maintained with the child during all the early months, and by nursing at the earliest signs of restlessness or vocalization, these mothers seemed to establish and maintain a kind of physical and kinesthetic communication with their babies which reinforced the suppression of extraneous motor activity and enhanced the fluid and moderate characteristics of the infants' state behavior.

This nexus of complementary mother and child behavior contrasted sharply with patterns that have been seen elsewhere. In the United States, for instance, great emphasis is placed on practising motor skills, on mastering a simple behavior such as crawling before acquiring a more complex one such as walking, and on teaching by the mother as a stimulus to progress. In Uganda, Ainsworth (14) describes the tremendous value placed on the infant's motor achievement. Despite the lack of such emphasis, however, the Zinacanteco infants underwent normal motor development and normal mental maturation during the first year, following a sequence and timing of progress parallel to that seen in our own culture, though lagging slightly behind it.

Zinacanteco mother and child interaction appeared to foster quiet alertness conducive to imitation and conformity. Striking was the quiet way in which older infants imitated our handling of unfamiliar test objects without the exploration and experimental play one might expect in the United States. In older children as well, imitation seems to be the chief mode of learning. Fantasy play, games of imagination, and innovation are rarely seen in Zinacanteco children. By age 4, they imitate in play the appropriate adult tasks. By ages 6 and 7, they take an active, responsible role in the household and are never confronted with the choice of roles our children must face.

In many other primitive societies, such as those described by Whiting (35) and Mead and Wolfenstein (36), this early role delineation seems to exist. Apparently missing in this method of learning is the exploration of the facets surrounding the simple imitated task which United States children are stimulated to pursue. Does this make the Zinacantecos less able in later life to master complex cognitive tasks requiring curiosity and aggressive exploration? Indeed, is there such a model in infancy which is necessary for later complex models? These are some of the questions which might be clarified on a return visit with psychologists equipped to study finer points of personality and cognitive development in older children.

Viewing Zinacantan in historical perspective, one is led to wonder if its cultural emphasis on uniformity, conformity, and imitation in role behavior do not, in themselves, constitute the selective pressure favoring the distinctive, apparently inborn neonatal behaviors observed there. During 400 years of contact with a dominant civilization, Zincantecos have avoided changes toward Spanish values which would have meant dissolution and loss of their culture. Self-conscious distinctiveness is maintained through the emphasis on conformity to a few culturally prescribed roles, causing non-conforming individualists to leave the society and effectively preventing outsiders from entering into it. Thus, in Zinacantan, where the population is small and where intermarriage, even with other Indian groups is rare, population shifts and interbreeding do not foster the wide range of genetic variability characteristic of most contemporary societies. Our intuition is that the neonatal behavior of Zinacanteco infants enhances the culturally valued imitative learning and role conformity and is the outcome of the interplay of these selective and isolating factors.

In retrospect, we would like to make a plea for infant scales which are more directly applicable to cross-cultural research. Inter-scorer agreement using infants in our culture does not mean that this agreement can be carried to another culture. Despite strict attention to the rules outlined by Knobloch-Pasamanick and well defined by Bayley, we had difficulty in translating their tests to this 'primitive' group. The paucity of cross-cultural literature in the behavioral field, such as Whiting's field guide (37), left us with much to learn in this area, and we relied heavily on the experience of our anthropological co-workers to anticipate many of the problems we encountered. It is likely, as Lévi-Strauss indicates (38), that 'primitive' peoples are not less complex than we, but are complicated in different ways. Behavioral tests must be constructed so as to deal with these subtle variations.

Finally, the importance of understanding the interrelation of cultural factors and genetic determinants in the early child-rearing practices of underdeveloped peoples cannot be overstated. We must be aware of their assets and their problems, for these are vital, constant, and important influences on the future of their countries.

Summary

Twelve neonatal observations, 93 tests of later infant development using Bayley and Knobloch-Pasamanick scales and 12 4-hour observations of child-rearing practices were recorded in the Zinacanteco Indians of southeastern Mexico. The quieting child-rearing practices of these isolated Mayan descendants seem well adapted to the quiet, alert infants they bear. The belly cinch, the rebozo, covered faces, and frequent breast feedings produce imitative, non-exploratory infants who develop in a slightly delayed (about 1 month) but parallel fashion to infants in the United States in motor, mental, and social parameters. The parallel progress, despite a very different kind of child-rearing stimulation, is evidence of a 'time table' in the development of milestones in infancy. This different, but nurturing environment produces strong, adequate, imitative children who may show subtle differences from North American children in cognitive tasks but who seem well adapted to their society's emphasis on conformity. The role of the infant who is presented to the environment in shaping this environment's response to him is discussed.

References

1.   Brody, S., *Patterns of Mothering*. New York: International University Press, 1956.
2.   Erikson, E., *Childhood and Society*. New York: Norton and Company, 1950.
3.   Escalona, S.K. and Heider, G.M., *Prediction and Outcome*. New York: Basic Books, 1959.
4.   Chess, S., 'Individuality in children, its importance to the pediatrician', *J. Pediat.*, 69: 676, 1966.
5.   Escalona, S.K., 'The use of infant tests for predictive purposes', *Bull. Menninger Clin.*, 14: 117, 1950.
6.   Fries, M., 'Psychosomatic relationships between mother and infant', *Psychosom. Med.*, 6: 159, 1944.
7.   Korner, A.F. and Gronstein, R., 'Individual differences at birth: Implication for mother-infant relationship and later development', *J. Child Psych.*, 6: 676, 1967.

8.   Ginsburg, B.E., 'The interaction of genetic and experiential factors in early life'. Presented at Joseph P. Kennedy Foundation Symposium, Chicago, 29 April, 1968.

9.   Freedman, D.G., in Washburn, S.L. and Jay, P.C. (eds.), *Perspectives in Human Evolution*. Chicago: Holt, Rinehart and Winston, Inc., 1968.

10. Brazelton, T.B. and Robey, J.S., 'Observations of neonatal behavior: The effect of perinatal variables, in particular that of maternal medication', *J. Amer. Acad. Child Psychiat.*, 4: 613, 1965.

11. Brazelton, T.B., 'Observations of the neonate', *J. Amer. Acad. Child Psychiat.*, 1: 38, 1962.

12. Geber, M. and Dean, R.A.F., 'The state of development of newborn African children', *Lancet*, 1: 216, 1957.

13. Geber, M. and Dean, R.A.F., 'Gesell tests on African children', *Pediatrics*, 20: 1055, 1957.

14. Ainsworth, M.D.S., *Infancy in Uganda*. Baltimore: Johns Hopkins Press, 1967.

15. Vogt, E., *Los Zinacantecos*. Mexico, D.F. Instituto Nacional Indigenista Publications, 1966.

16. Anscheutz, M., *A study of midwives in Zinacantan*. Thesis, Harvard University, Cambridge, Massachusetts, 1966.

17. Blanco, M.G. and Chodorow, N.J., *Children's work and obedience in Zinacantan*. Unpublished study, Harvard University, Cambridge, Massachusetts, 1964.

18. Colby, B.N. and Van den Bergh, P., 'Ethnic relations in southeastern Mexico', *Amer. Anthropologist*, 63: 4, 1961.

19. Collier, G.A., *The life cycle in Zinacantan*. Thesis, Harvard University, Cambridge, Massachusetts, 1962.

20. Cravioto, J., Delicardie, E.R. and Birch, H.G., 'Nutrition, growth and neuro-integrative development: an experimental and ecologic study', *Pediatrics* (Suppl.), 38: 319, 1966.

21. Stoch, M.G. and Smythe, P.M., 'The effect of undernutrition during infancy on subsequent brain growth and intellectual development', *S. Afr. Med. J.*, 41: 1027, 1967.

22. Lipton, E.L., Steinschneider, A. and Richmond, J.B., 'Swaddling, a child care practice: Historical, cultural and experimental observations', *Pediatrics* (Suppl.), 35: 521, 1965.

23. Bloch, A., 'The Kurdistani cradle story', *Clin. Pediat.*, 5: 641, 1966.

24. Brown, J., 'States in newborn infants', *Merrill-Palmer Quart.*, 10: 313, 1964.

25. André-Thomas, C.Y., Chesni, Y. and Saint-Anne Dargassies, S., *Neurological Examination of the Infant*. London: National Spastics Society Publications, 1960.

26. Prechtl, H. and Beintema, O., *The Neurological Examination of the Full Term Newborn Infant*. London: William Heinemann Medical Books, 1964.

27. Wolff, P.H., *The Causes, Controls and Organization of Behavior*. New York: International University Press, 1966.

28. Wolff, P.H., 'Observations on newborn infants', *Psychosom. Med.*, 21: 110, 1959.

29. Graham, R.K., Matarazzo, R.C. and Caldwell, B.M., 'Behavioral differences between normal and traumatized newborns', *Psychol. Monogr.*, 70: 427, 1956.

30. Brazelton, T.B., Robey, J.S. and Scholl, M.L., 'Visual behavior in the neonate', *Pediatrics*, 37: 284, 1966.

31. Rheingold, H.L., 'The measurement of maternal care', *Child Develop.*, 31: 565, 1960.

32. Knobloch, H., Pasamanick, B. and Sherard, E.S., Jr., 'A developmental screening

inventory for infants', *Pediatrics* (Suppl.), 38: 1095, 1966.

33.   Bayley, N., *Bayley Scales of Mental and Motor Development*, as used by the Collaborative Perinatal Research Project of the National Institute of Neurological Diseases and Blindness, Bethesda, Maryland, 1961.

34.   Apgar, V., 'A proposal for a new method of evaluation of the newborn infant', *Curr. Res. Anesth. Analg.*, 32: 260, 1953.

35.   Whiting, B. (ed.), *Six Culture Studies of Child Rearing.* New York: John Wiley and Sons, Inc., 1963.

36.   Mead, M. and Wolfenstein, M., *Childhood in Contemporary Cultures.* Chicago: Chicago University Press, 1955.

37.   Whiting, J.W.M. (ed.), *A Field Guide for a Study of Socialization.* New York: John Wiley and Sons, Inc., 1966.

38.   Lèvi-Strauss, C., *The Savage Mind.* Chicago: Chicago University Press, 1966.

Notes

1.   A rebozo is a shawl which is large enough to hold and enclose the infant; it is knotted over the mother's breast or back.

2.   Protocol will be in the reprints, and a manual describing its use is available on request from T.B.B.

3.   This difference is very significant for the Knobloch-Pasamanick data ($p < .01$), on the edge of significance for Robey's data ($.05 < p < .10$), and not significant but of the right order for Brazelton's Bayley data, as indicated by t tests performed on the values of mental and motor age differences across subject. Two extremely large values of motor age difference in Robey's data, 4.2 and 4.3, were Winsorized back to the next largest value, 3.2, in the computations so that they would not unduly influence the results. If left unaltered, they would only have decreased the p value.

4 THE IMPORTANCE OF SIMPLY GROWING OLDER

Jerome Kagan

Source: *New Society*, 14 June 1973, pp. 610-12. This article is condensed from a paper delivered to the American Association for the Advancement of Science conference in December 1972.

Most psychologists believe habits die hard, and that experience etches an indelible mark on the mind that is not easily erased. Psychological growth during the early years is thought to be under the strong influence of external events. The psychological structures established then are thought to last at least into early adolescence. This hypothesis owes part of its popularity to Freud.

I was certain that this was true, and set out to find the form of those initial structures, and the earliest time one might foresee a child's future. But, during a search that has lasted 15 years, I observed some children living in an isolated Indian village on Lake Atitlan, in the highlands of north west Guatemala, I saw listless, silent, apathetic infants; passive, quiet, timid three year olds; but active, gay, intellectually competent eleven year olds. There is no reason to believe that living conditions in this village have changed during the last century. So it is likely that the alert eleven year olds were, a decade earlier, listless, vacant-staring infants. That observation has forced me to question the strong form of the continuity assumption.

Take passivity as an example. Very few of the young children in this Indian village tried to establish dominance over other children. They kept this passivity until they were five or six years old. However, by eight, some of the children had begun to dominate. These dominant children's early disposition was less important in determining their behaviour than their physical size, strength and competence in valued skills.

Thus, it seems that the continuity of the psychological disposition does not stem from some neurological structure within the individual, separate from external pressures. The group of scientists who have championed stability — I have been among them — envisage a small box of different coloured gems in the brain, with names like 'intelligent', 'passive', 'irritable' or 'withdrawn', engraved upon them. This belief in a distinct and unchanging mosaic of core traits — an identity — is fundamental to western thought and is reflected in the psychological writings of Erik Erikson and the novels of popular western writers. Only Herman Hesse, among the more gifted modern western novelists, fails to make out the

57

case for personal identity. The heroes of his *Siddartha*, *Magister Ludi* and *Narcissus and Goldmund* are not trying to discover 'who they are', but are seeking serenity. Each appreciates the relevance of setting in that journey. Hesse's prejudice for the philosophy of the east is probably one reason why he gives the theme of identity secondary status.

My own observations were made in various settings in Guatemala. One location was three subsistence-farming villages in eastern Guatemala inhabited by Ladinos (i.e. Spanish speaking people of mixed Indian and Spanish parentage). The villages are fairly isolated, with between 800 and 2,500 inhabitants. The families live in small thatched huts of bamboo or adobe, with a dirt floor and no separate sanitation. Children rarely have books, pencils, paper or pictures before going to school. Even in school, the average child has no more than a thin notebook, with ruled pages, and a stub of pencil.

The second location was the more isolated Indian village of San Marcos. This is on the shores of Lake Atitlan, in the north west mountainous region of Guatemala. It had 850 inhabitants. The Indians of San Marcos have no easy access to a city, and are psychologically more detached than the inhabitants of the three other villages. Their isolation is due not only to geography, but also to the fact that few of the women, and no more than half of the men, speak reasonable Spanish.

During his first ten to twelve months, the San Marcos baby spends most of his life in the small, dark interior of his hut. Women do not work in the field. So the mother usually stays close to the home and spends most of her day preparing food — typically tortillas, beans and coffee — and perhaps doing some weaving. If she travels to a market to buy or sell, she usually leaves her baby with an older child or relative. The baby is close to the mother — held on her lap, enclosed on her back in a coloured cloth, sitting on a mat, or sleeping in a hammock. The mother rarely allows the baby to crawl on the dirt floor of the hut. She feels that the outside sun, air and dust are harmful.

The baby is rarely spoken to or played with. The only objects available for play, besides his own clothing and his mother's body, are oranges, ears of corn and pieces of wood or clay. These babies differ from American children of the same age by their extreme fearfulness, minimal smiling, and, above all, extraordinary quietness. Some, with pale cheeks and vacant stares, were almost like tiny ghosts. Many would not respond to tape-recorded speech, or smile or babble when I spoke to them. They would hesitate for over a minute before reaching for an attractive toy.

An American woman who lived in the village made separate 30-minute observations in the home on twelve babies of eight to 16 months old. On average, the babies were spoken to, or played with, 6 per cent of the time. The maximum was 12 per cent. Colleagues of mine found the comparable average for American middle class homes was 25 per cent, with a maximum of 40 per cent. The sounds the Guatemalan babies made (which lasted about 6 per cent of the time) were usually grunts, going for less than a second, and not the prolonged babbling typical of middle class American homes. The babies cried very little, because the slightest irritability led the mother to nurse her child at once. Nursing was the single, universal therapeutic treatment for all infant distress, whether caused by fear, cold, hunger, or cramps. Observations of homes in the other three villages confirmed those in San Marcos.

One reason why the Guatemalan mothers behave this way may be that it is abundantly clear to every parent that all their children begin to walk by 18 months, to talk by age three, and to perform some adult chores by age ten — despite the listless, silent quality of infancy.

We could not do any formal laboratory testing of the San Marcos children. But we could in the three Ladino villages. Though infants in the Ladino villages were slightly more alert than the Indian children of San Marcos, living conditions and rearing practices were so similar that I assume the San Marcos infants would have behaved rather like the Ladino children. In these laboratory experiments, the Guatemalan mother and child came to a special laboratory equipped with a chair and a stage. This simulated the setting in our Harvard laboratories. We were therefore able to give tests to cross-cultural groups of 84 American and 80 Guatemalan babies, who were aged five and a half months, seven and a half months, nine and a half months and eleven and a half months. There were ten to twenty-four infants from each culture at each age-level.

The first test was of cognitive growth. We wanted to establish concretely what the difference at these ages was between American middle class children and Guatemalan village children.

Each child was shown a two-inch wooden orange block for six or eight successive trials, followed by three or five trials in which a one and a half inch orange block was presented. Three of the original two-inch blocks were then presented. In a test with lights, the child was shown eight or ten repetitions of a sequence in which a hand moved an orange rod in a semicircle, until it touched a bank of three light bulbs. These were lighted on contact between the rod and the bulbs. In the next sequence, of five repetitions, the hand appeared, but the rod did not move, and the lights lit after a four-second interval. Following this, the original light-bulb sequence was repeated three times.

During the tests, two observers noted how long the infant attended to the event; whether it made any sound or smiled; and if it fretted or cried. The Guatemalan infants were less attentive than the Americans on both tests. The differences between them were greater at the two older, than at the two younger ages. We concluded that since the Ladino infants appeared somewhat more mature than the San Marcos children, it is possible that the American infants were three or four months advanced in cognitive function over the San Marcos children during the first year and a half of life.

But we needed to check to see if the apparent slowing of cognitive growth in the Guatemalan child is stable or whether he recovers. When the San Marcos Indian child starts to move around, at about 15 months, he leaves the dark hut, plays with other children, and *provides himself* with cognitive challenges that demand answers. All the San Marcos children have this marked break in experience between their first and second birthdays. How does this make a difference to older Guatemalan and American children?

We gave memory, perception and conceptual tests to children in San Marcos and in the Ladino villages, and two different groups of the children from Guatemala City. One of the Guatemala City groups was at a day-care centre for very poor children. The second group were middle class children attending nursery school, who resembled middle class Americans in both family background and opportunity.

We gave a recall test with twelve objects to two of the samples of Guatemalan children: 80 from a Ladino village, and 55 from San Marcos. The Ladinos were between five and seven years old, equally balanced for age and sex. The 55 Indians were aged between five and twelve years old (26 boys and 29 girls).

The twelve miniature objects to be recalled were common to village life — a pig, a hat, a knife, for example. And they could be clustered conceptually (animals, clothing, utensils). Recall and conceptual clustering both increased with age. Yet no five or six year olds in the Ladino village went to school. School for the others consisted of little more than semi-organised games. Moreover, none of the children in San Marcos had ever left the village, and the five and six year olds usually spent most of the day within a 500 yard radius of their homes. Hence, *school attendance, and contact with books and a written language, do not seem to be prerequisites for recall and conceptual clustering in young children.*

The recall and cluster scores in Guatemala closely resembled those reported for middle class American children by L.F. Appel and his colleagues in 1971. The cultural similarity in recall tests also held for tests of recognition memory. In a separate study, children aged five, eight and

Table 4.1: Percentage of Correct Responses in Recognising Pictures after Delays

Age	Americans			Guatemalans		
	5	8	11	5	8	11
Delay	%	%	%	%	%	%
0	92.8	96.7	93.3	58.4	74.6	85.2
24 hours	86.7	95.6	96.7	55.8	71.0	87.0
48 hours	87.5	90.3	93.9	61.4	75.8	86.2

eleven from the Ladino villages, and from Cambridge, Massachusetts, were shown 60 pictures of objects, some familiar and some unfamiliar. After delays of various lengths, each child was shown 60 pairs of pictures, one of which was old and the other new, and asked to decide which one he had seen. The five and eight year old Americans performed no better than the Guatemalans. But there was no cultural difference for the eleven year olds (see Table 4.1). Thus, recall and recognition seem to be basic cognitive functions that, in fact, mature in a regular way in any natural environment.

In perception tests, the rural five and six year olds were about three years behind the middle-class Guatemala City children. But no five or six

Figure 4.1: Perceptual Inference Test

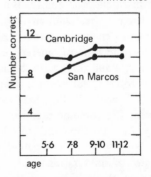

year old was completely incapable of solving any of these problems. The differences reflected the fact that the rural children had difficulty with two or three of the harder items. This was the first time, we think, that many rural children had ever seen a two-dimensional drawing. Nonetheless, these children solved seven or eight of the twelve test items.

The perceptual competence of the San Marcos children is confirmed by their performance on a test administered in both San Marcos and Cambridge, called Perceptual Inference. The children (60 Americans and 55 Guatemalans, from five to twelve years of age) were shown a schematic drawing of an object and asked to guess what that object might be if the drawing were completed. The child was given a total of four clues for each of 13 items. Each of the clues added more information. The child had to guess an object from an incomplete illustration, and to make an inference from minimal information.

Figure 4.1 shows how this worked out in the case of a fish. Though the San Marcos children did slightly worse, the difference for the children over seven was not significant. Figure 4.1 shows the results.

Familiarity with the test objects governed the child's success. All the San Marcos children had seen hats, fish and corn, and these items were rarely missed. By contrast, the American children often failed these items. No San Marcos child not attending school, and therefore unfamiliar with books, correctly guessed the book-related items. The majority of those children who did go to school guessed them correctly.

These findings, of course, have marked implications for educational problems in such countries as America (or Britain). There is a tendency to regard the poor test performances of badly-off minority-group six year olds in the United States as a sign of a permanent, and perhaps irreversible, defect in intellectual ability. But our findings, and others that confirm them, suggest that children differ in the age at which basic cognitive competences emerge; and that 'experience' − not necessarily schooling − influences the time of emergence. Poor city or country children may be between one and three years behind middle class children in some of the problem-solving skills which Piaget has characterised as the stage of 'concrete operation'. But these skills eventually appear by the age of ten or eleven. The common practice in the United States of arbitrarily setting seven years − the usual time of school entrance − as the age when children are to be classified as competent or incompetent, confuses differences in the rate of maturation with permanent, qualitative differences in intellectual ability. This practice is as logical as classifying children as permanently sexually fertile or infertile, depending on whether or not they have reached physiological puberty by their thirteenth birthday.

Our Guatemalan data are not the first of their kind to be reported. Their importance lies in the fact that the San Marcos eleven year olds performed so well, considering the poverty and extreme isolation of their environment. There is a message, therefore, not only for those who set too much store by IQs, but also for those who expect too much from environmental factors, as opposed to biological maturation.

Early environmental experiences have an important influence on intellectual development. But that influence seems to be more reversible and more temporary than many have surmised, if the child is put in a facilitating environment. Support for this comes from recent studies by Harlow and his colleagues. Several years ago, Harlow's group demonstrated that though monkeys reared in isolation for the first six months displayed abnormal, and often bizarre, social behaviour they could, if the experimenter were patient, solve the complex learning problems normally administered to monkeys born normally in the wild. The prolonged isolation did not destroy their cognitive competence.

From Locke's *Essay on Understanding* to Skinner's *Beyond Freedom and Dignity*, we in the west have seen the perfectibility of man as vulnerable to the vicissitudes of the objects and people who block, praise, or push him. We have resisted giving the child any compass of his own. The mind, like the nucleus of a cell, has a plan for growth and can transmute a new flower, and odd pain, or a stranger's unexpected smile, into a form that is comprehensible.

We need not speak of joy in this psychological mastery. Neither walking nor breathing are performed in order to experience happiness. The maturation I have written about occurs because each physiological system or organ naturally exercises its primary function. The child explores the unfamiliar and attempts to match his ideas and actions to some previously acquired representation because these are basic properties of mind. The child has no choice.

References

1. L.F. Apel *et al.*, 'The development acquisition of the distinction between perceiving and memory' (unpublished manuscript, 1971).
2. H.F. Harlow, K. A. Schlitz and M.K. Harlow, 'The effects of social isolation on the learning performance of rhesus monkeys', in C.R. Carpenter (ed.), *Proceedings of the Second International Congress of Primatology*, vol. 1 (New York: Karger, 1969).

5 CULTURAL ASPECTS OF CHILDREARING IN THE ENGLISH-SPEAKING WORLD

John and Elizabeth Newson

Source: M.P.M. Richards (ed.), *The Integration of a Child into a Social World* (Cambridge University Press, 1974), pp. 53-68.

If anthropologists from centres of learning in New Guinea or the Congo were to turn the tables on us and publish studies of the behaviour patterns found among the English-speaking peoples of Great Britain and the United States, one phenomenon to which they would surely pay special attention would be the cult of Child Psychology. The demand of an ever more literate population for books, pamphlets and magazines on parenthood is met by a stream of material which surpasses itself each year, not only in volume, but in the seductive, indeed sumptuous, way in which it is produced. Commercial firms marketing goods for the infant consumer hand out subsidised baby books as part of their advertising policy; others run advisory services or distribute regular magazines in which child care is discussed. In the publishing world as a whole, periodicals concerned with the family become more and more specialised: quite apart from the dozens of magazines addressed to women generally, we find some catering for the interests of parents in particular, some especially for the 'mother-to-be', and others for parents of individual age-groups or of children with special characteristics or handicaps. Books about childhood appear on every level, from those in which specialist communicates only with specialist, through all types of handbook for readers with a vocational interest in children, to those in which the expert and the less expert, with equal show of authority, make parents the target of their beliefs (substantiated or not) on how children 'should' be brought up. And, in support of the printed word, television and radio move in with their advice and discussion programmes, educational bodies run courses in psychology for parents, parent-teacher associations organise lectures, and one can even learn from a gramophone record how to teach one's children about sex.

Seen in historical and anthropological perspective, perhaps the most interesting aspect of the contemporary preoccupation with childrearing is that today we are self-consciously concerned with the possible *psychological* consequences of the methods which we use in bringing up our children. This attention to the total psychological development of the child is indeed a new phenomenon, in that earlier generations of parents have been chiefly preoccupied by the related themes of physical survival and moral growth, rather than with concepts of mental health or social and emotional adjustment. So massive a change of emphasis must be of fundamental significance, not only to the anthropologist and the social historian, but to the child psychologists, psychiatrists and psychotherapists whose very existence as a group depends upon the climate of opinion which regards their professional skills as valuable and necessary, and which places them on an equal footing in social esteem with the more anciently respected callings of the paediatrician and the pedagogue. In this chapter, we intend briefly to survey some of the cultural and technological correlates of a society's attitudes towards child upbringing generally; and, more specifically, to examine a few of the ways in which the individual methods which parents adopt in the handling of their small children are defined or modified by the intricate pattern of cultural pressures to which they find themselves subject. We would ask the reader to bear in mind from the outset, however, that we write from the viewpoint of the English urban sub-culture, in which we are not only field-workers and observers but life members; nevertheless, we believe that the English and American complexes of parental experience show very many points of coincidence, both historically and contemporaneously, both in the things that parents do and in the reasons for which they do them: and that, therefore, a discussion in these terms will have a validity for parent-child behaviour on both sides of the Atlantic.

From the physical point of view, the human child is at its most vulnerable during and just after birth, and it remains 'at risk', in the actuarial sense, throughout early childhood, particularly during what our society thinks of as the preschool years. For the whole of human history up to the turn of the present century, simple physical survival has been the dominant issue in child upbringing: a question not of 'How shall I rear my child?' but of '*Will* I rear him?' In the middle of the eighteenth century, the mortality rate for children under five in England and Wales has been estimated as seventy-five for every hundred births.[1] In 1865, the infant mortality rate was 154 per thousand live births; a hundred years later it is 21.8 per thousand (Registrar General, 1963). Even today, of course, whether the child will survive at all is still the overriding consideration for millions of mothers in the underdeveloped areas of the world. There are still countries in which a mother can expect one in three of her children to die before reaching the age of five (UNICEF, 1964). If we take the 'developing countries' as a group, compared with the 'more developed countries', infant mortality (in the first year) is more than five times as high in the first group as it is in the second: but during the years from one to four — that is, after weaning — the mortality rate in the developing countries is *forty times* as high as elsewhere: forty deaths for every thousand children surviving their first year, compared with one per thousand in the more developed areas (Pate, 1965). These statistics expressed in terms of expectation of life testify even more vividly to the distance Western society has travelled in being able to take the survival of our children almost for granted. At birth, a baby in India has an expectation of life of 32 years; in Mexico, 39 years; in the United Arab Republic, 38 years. The United States baby can expect a life span of 70 years, and in the United Kingdom this rises to 71 years. Once a child has survived his vulnerable first five years, his expectation of life naturally increases, but this increase will vary in direct proportion to the dangers which he has so far evaded: thus the United Kingdom 5-year-old can now expect to live until he is 75, the American until he is 72. The Indian child, however, once he is five, increases his expectation from 32 to 46 years; the Mexican, from 39 to 55 years; and the 5-year-old of the United Arab Republic can now expect to live to the age of 59, having added 21 years to his total expectation of life by virtue of having survived the 'preschool' period (UNICEF, 1964).

The ability to view infant care practices in any other light than whether they help the infant in his basic struggle to live is, then, something peculiar to our own century and, within this century, to the technologically advanced countries in which infant and child mortality rates have now been reduced to comparatively insignificant proportions. Briefly, child psychology is a luxury which only a small section of the world's parents can afford to consider: mothers need a respite from the most urgent problems of hunger, sickness and exposure before they can give much attention to questions of personal adjustment and maladjustment. And this factor of priorities is reflected in the literature directed towards parents, which, though it may often be out of touch with individual parental needs and circumstances, is written within a total social context and expresses closely enough prevailing social trends. Thus what is interesting about the women's magazines in England during the first years of the twentieth century is not the content of the advice given on childrearing, but the fact that so little advice is given at all; sometimes, from one year to the next, children are barely mentioned, save for the occasional appealing illustrations, the pattern for a christening bonnet or the recipe for a nursery pudding. For the literate group of women who might be expected to read magazines, this was in fact a transitional period: freed to a greater extent than ever before from the shadow of death, this was not yet the time of the educated lay interest in infant psychology which was soon to be aroused by Montessori, Froebel, Susan Isaacs and the Freudians generally; nor had the hygienist movement yet got under way. Future historians may one day look back on this short period as a golden guilt-free age for parents!

The Religious Morality

It is true that much was written about the moral upbringing of children during the eighteenth and nineteenth centuries; but this topic was itself clearly linked with the expectation of death, rather than with the hope of a balanced and integrated life. The Evangelical movement, despite its minority status, cast its influence far more widely than the actual numbers of its adherents might suggest; it is of especial interest to students of child-rearing attitudes, in that its followers were so prolific in their writings that their beliefs (or watered-down versions of their beliefs) dominated both the advisory literature available to parents and the children's own reading matter for upwards of two centuries. For the Evangelicals, the prospect of heaven or hell was a major source of motivation in their attempts to 'form the minds' of their children. Susanna Wesley herself, mother of John and Charles, puts this plainly enough in a letter to John:

I insist upon conquering the wills of children betimes; because this is the only foundation for a religious education . . . religion is nothing else but the doing of the will of God, and not our own . . . Heaven or hell depends on this alone. So that the parent who studies to subdue [self-will] in his children, works together with God in the saving of a soul: the parent who indulges it does the devil's work; makes religion impracticable, salvation unattainable; and does all that in him lies to damn his child, soul and body, for ever! . . . This, therefore, I cannot but earnestly repeat, − Break their wills betimes; begin this great work before they can run alone, before they can speak plain, or perhaps speak at all. Whatever pains it cost, conquer their stubbornness; break the will, if you would not damn the child. I conjure you not to neglect, not to delay this! Therefore (1) Let a child, from a year old, be taught to fear the rod and to cry softly. In order to do this, (2) Let him have nothing he cries for; absolutely nothing, great or small; else you undo your own work. (3) At all events, from that age, make him do as he is bid, if you whip him ten times running to effect it. Let none persuade you it is cruelty to do this; it is cruelty not to do it. Break his will now, and his soul will live, and he will probably bless you to all eternity. [Wesley, 1872] [2]

'Break the will, if you would not damn the child' — and damnation was a very present and real risk, in an age when most families would have lost at least one infant and often several. Passages from the catechisms devised for small children by the many child-orientated members of this movement show very clearly the emphasis upon death as a part of normal experience:

Q: When must you repent and believe, children?
A: Now, Sir, in childhood.
Q: Why must you do it now, children?
A: Because we may soon die, Sir.

The famous and vastly influential *Token for Children* (1753) by John Janeway was even more explicit:

Are you willing to go to hell, to be burned with the devil and his angels? . . . O! Hell is a terrible place . . . Did you never hear of a little child that died . . . and if other children die, why may not you be sick and die? . . . How do you know but that you may be the next child that may die? . . . Now tell me, my pretty dear child, what will you do?

Isaac Watts' much loved and quoted hymns (1842) include many verses such as these:

Why should I say, ' 'Tis yet too soon
To seek for heav'n, or think of death?'
A flow'r may fade before 'tis noon,
And I this day may lose my breath.
    [From Song XIII, *The Danger of Delay*]

There is an hour when I must die,
Nor do I know how soon 'twill come;
A thousand children, young as I,
Are call'd by death to hear their doom.
    [From Song X, *Solemn Thoughts of GOD and Death*]

The pious and happy deaths of good little boys and girls, with, for variety, the occasional frightful deaths of irreligious children[3] who were assumed to have passed straight to the eternal fires of hell, are continually described and lingered over in children's books of the eighteenth and nineteenth centuries, from Janeway onward. The *Child's Companion* of 1829, a well-illustrated little volume of stories and poems, contains no fewer than thirteen improving deathbed scenes, together with one discourse on death and two poems inspired by gazing on children's graves. The headstone of a 2-year-old moves the poet to observe:

> Two years! oh happy little life
> We cannot weep its early end;

and he concludes with the familiar warning:

> The grave may open next for *you*!
> You may not see another Spring.
> Keep death, and *heaven*, and *hell* in view;
> Begin the present year, *anew*.

The combined effect of the religious beliefs of the Evangelicals and the historical facts of childhood mortality upon trends in child upbringing is clear enough. Given a society in which death is a familiar occurrence and in which most children will have experienced the loss of a sibling through death; given, too, a belief in a highly authoritarian God with unlimited powers of reward or punishment through heaven or hell: the logical consequence is to prepare children as carefully for death as for life; to ensure above all else that the child shall be 'saved' at least spiritually, if not physically, and indeed to avoid tempting the deity by any suggestion that life is preferable to a happy death. Charles Wesley (1868) wrote a number of hymns for the use of parents; he himself lost his first two children.

> I ask as with my parting breath,
> To each allotted be
> A holy life, or early death;
> But which, I leave to thee.

Moreover, the likelihood of death at a tender age leaves no time for a gentle, patient, permissive approach to child upbringing; the lesson must be learnt by the child early and certainly: 'Break his will *now*, and his soul will live.' The all-powerful God is consciously represented within the family by the almost equally powerful father: 'Vengeance is mine' saith the Lord, but meanwhile vengeance is Papa's. In the sort of conflict situation in which Benjamin Spock (1946) would suggest 'distracting him to something interesting but harmless' or 'give him a graceful way out' (from a temper tantrum), or where Susan Isaacs in 1932 tells the mother 'not to be too ready to treat any momentary defiance as an immediate occasion for a pitched battle of wills', the Evangelicals and their followers were, on the contrary, eager to seize upon such an opportunity, since their battle was with the devil himself, and the child's spiritual salvation at stake; distraction was the last thing they would have advised, for it was their urgent intention to rouse in the young child a vivid appreciation of his own shortcomings, as being the quickest and most effective means of subjugating his will to higher authority.

The Medical Morality

Curiously enough, the Evangelical concern to eradicate the devil in the child finds many echoes in the hygienist movement which dominated the twenties and thirties of our own century. Martha Wolfenstein (1955) has brilliantly analysed the changing pattern of advice given in succeeding editions of *Infant Care*, the bulletin for parents published by the United States Children's Bureau; a close parallel in the United Kingdom is found in the *Mothercraft Manual* (Liddiard, 1928). Although not a Government publication, this book, first published in 1923, achieved considerable popularity before the Second World War and has run to twelve editions, all revised by the original writer, the most recent being that of 1954; in England it was the main vehicle for the principles of Sir Truby King and his Mothercraft Training Society. The passage that follows (very similar to advice given during this period in *Infant Care*) comes from the 1928 edition, and might well be subscribed to by Susanna Wesley: the emphasis may be different, but the spirit is the same. The italics are ours, and mark the parts which had been deleted by the time the twelfth edition was reached in 1954; the word *trained* was replaced by *rightly guided*. There are several signs in the twelfth edition that the writer still hankers for the old methods, despite the necessity for tempering some of the more repressive advice, and the book remains far more authoritarian in tone than more recently written baby-books.

> Self-control, obedience, the recognition of authority, and, later, respect for elders are all the outcome of the first year's training, as emphasised in preceding chapters. The baby who is picked up or fed whenever he cries soon becomes a veritable tyrant, and gives his mother no peace when awake; while, on the other hand, the infant who is fed regularly, put to sleep, and played with at definite times *soon finds that appeals bring no response, and so* learns that most useful of all lessons, self-control, and the recognition of an authority other than his own wishes. If parents and nurses would only realise how much easier it is for the

child to bend to the social and moral laws in later life, when *trained* from infancy, how much sorrow might be saved. *To train an infant for the first year is comparatively easy, but after that the child begins to resent authority, and the conscientious mother has to be prepared to fight and win all along the line, in matters small and great.*

In many ways, the hygienists can be seen as the heirs of the Evangelicals; here again, this trend of social attitudes towards infant care must be set in its broader context. In the twenties, both in England and in America, we have a situation in which the infant and child mortality rates are fast declining, mainly owing to new advances in medical knowledge; at the same time, the world's values have been shaken by the First World War, writers and journalists have both more freedom and more inclination than ever before to discuss religion from an agnostic point of view, and the vengeful God of heaven and hell no longer impresses in quite the old way. For middle-class parents at least, however, a new power is taking his place: the equally authoritarian medical expert. The morality of aseptic rationalism has superseded that of spiritual regeneration.

It was indeed clear in the twenties that the medical profession had something important to say to mothers. The infant death rate was still high enough, especially among the poor, for parents not yet to have become complacent; meanwhile, the promise was held out, and for the first time could be kept, that babies could be successfully reared *provided* that medical advice was faithfully followed. This was an inducement not to be ignored; most parents, given the choice, would prefer the expectation of earthly survival for their children to the hope of heavenly reward. The time was in fact ripe, not only for a secession from religion (which, after all, had never given parents anything very tangible), but for a transfer of allegiance from the other traditional reference groups of parents: away from the methods prescribed by folklore, custom and the baby's grandmother, and towards the new blessings held out by scientific mothercraft.

Medical hygienism was quite obviously a necessity, nor is it likely to become completely unfashionable; the consequence of this interest to the student of child care was that the enthusiasm justifiably generated by its successes led to an assumption that *mental* hygiene, applied on the same principles, would be equally beneficial. Without, apparently, a single doubt as to the validity of this premise, the advice was laid down, the warnings given.

The leading authorities of the day – English, foreign and American –

all agree that the first thing to establish in life is *regularity of habits*. The mother who 'can't be so cruel' as to awake her sleeping baby if he happens to be asleep at the appointed feeding-time, fails to realize that a few such wakings would be all she would have to resort to . . . The establishment of perfect regularity of habits, initiated by 'feeding and sleeping by the clock', is the ultimate foundation of all-round obedience. Granted good organic foundations, truth and honour can be built into the edifice as it grows. [Truby King, 1937]

Never play with or excite a baby before bedtime . . . Half the irritability and lack of moral control which spoil adult life originate in the first year of existence. The seeds of feebleness and instability sown in infancy bear bitter fruit afterwards. [Truby King, 1937]

Masturbation — This is a bad habit . . . The great thing is to recognise the condition early . . . Untiring zeal on the part of the mother or nurse is the only cure; it may be necessary to put the legs in splints before putting the child to bed. He must never be left in such a position that he can carry on the habit, he must be made to forget it; this sometimes takes three months, or longer in the worst cases . . . This habit, if left unchecked, may develop into a serious vice. The child's moral nature becomes perverted; one such child has been known to upset a whole school. [Liddiard, 1928]

Thumb Sucking — If this is done frequently and perniciously it must be taken in hand and treated as a bad habit. Sometimes it is enough to put on cotton gloves; if not, the best plan is to make a splint of corrugated cardboard [illustrated in original]; this allows free movement of the arms from the shoulder joint but prevents the hand from getting to the mouth. These splints should be taken off twice daily and the arms exercised and rubbed. [Liddiard, 1928]

There is a sensible way of treating children. Treat them as though they were young adults. Dress them, bathe them with care and circumspection. Let your behaviour always be objective and kindly firm. Never hug and kiss them, never let them sit in your lap. If you must, kiss them once on the forehead when they say good night. Shake hands with them in the morning. Give them a pat on the head if they have made an extraordinarily good job of a difficult task. Try it out. In a week's time you will find how easy it is to be perfectly objective with your child and at the same time kindly. You will be utterly ashamed of the mawkish, sentimental way you have been handling it. [Watson, 1928]

It seems extraordinary to today's parents in England and the United States that women of the twenties and thirties should have been prepared to accept either the content of these pronouncements or the authoritarian tone in which they were made: yet accepted they were, in that innumerable women made valiant efforts to stifle their natural desire to cuddle their babies and to feed them when they were hungry, or were wracked with guilt and shame when they 'mawkishly' rocked the child or sentimentally eased his stomach pangs in the small hours with a contraband couple of ounces. For the educated mother in particular, it took a great deal of courage to reject a system of upbringing which combined quasi-religious appeals to 'duty' and 'rightness' and 'goodness'[5] with a claim to be based on the rational attitudes which she herself, as a 'modern' woman, was supposed to have embraced. During the last few years, we have begun to learn something of these mothers' true feelings from the women who suffered the regime at first hand: what stands out in such accounts is the emotion which is still generated in the mother by her own memories. The quotations that follow are both from personal letters to the present writers, commenting on a published suggestion that those who give advice to parents often do not pay enough attention to the parents' own views. The first correspondent holds a distinguished position in the highest ranks of the nursing profession; the second is the author of books on social work with children.

I am so in agreement . . . that I feel quite emotional. My daughter was born during the Truby King period, and it took a month of untold agony for myself and the child before I threw every book I had out of the house and all my well meaning and Truby King obsessed relatives with them. From then on, mother and child progressed happily, and since those early and terrible days I have treated advice with cautious courtesy. As for breast feeding, I feel so strongly about this that I can hardly express myself! For the mother who finds breast feeding terribly difficult — and there are so many of these — the solemn pronouncements she will hear from her own parents and from health visitors, obstetricians and other professional people can lead to real emotional and mental suffering. I well remember the long watches of the night when I and my baby struggled to overcome a physical incapability on my part, and I cannot begin to tell you the relief on both sides when I strode out of the house, bought the largest tin of baby food I could find, and gave her the first square meal she had had since birth.

I was caught up in the Truby King Mothercraft doctrine of 1935 . . .
The health visitors prated and bullied; one's baby screamed and tears
splashed down one's cheeks while milk gushed up through one's jersey.
But one must *never* pick the baby *up* — it was practically incestuous to
enjoy one's baby, so I gathered, young, obedient, motherless, indoctrin-
ated mother that I was. I made up my mind then that *next* time I had
a baby I would *love* it. But that baby never came . . . In my day, we
were instructed that frost never hurt a baby yet, and if the baby cried it
must be *mastered*. Working-class women cuddled their babies up in the
warm as women had done for millions of years. We, the young graduate
law-abiding wives of the thirties, cried *ourselves* as our babies went blue
with cold . . . See Mary McCarthy's novel *The Group* . . . She speaks for
us all.

'The young, graduate, law-abiding wife' is indeed exemplified in Mary
McCarthy's Priss, whose situation is exacerbated by being married to a
paediatrician. We cannot quote here more than a short paragraph, but the
whole of chapters 10 and 14 of *The Group* should be required reading for
those whose profession it is to advise parents (McCarthy, 1963).

The nights were the worst. There were nights when, hearing him start at
three or four in the morning, she would have welcomed anything that
would let him stop and rest — paregoric, a sugar-tit, any of those
wicked things. During her pregnancy, Priss had read a great deal about
past mistakes in child rearing; according to the literature, they were the
result not only of ignorance, but of sheer selfishness: a nurse or a
mother who gave a crying child paregoric usually did it for her own
peace of mind, not wanting to be bothered. For the doctors agreed it
did not hurt a baby to cry; it only hurt grown-ups to listen to him.
She *supposed* this was true. The nurses here wrote down every day on
Stephen's chart how many hours he had cried, but neither Sloan nor
Dr Turner turned a hair when they looked at that on the chart; all they
cared about was the weight curve.

Moralities of Natural Development and Natural Needs

Meanwhile, from the direction of the psychoanalysts and the nursery
educationalists, another school of thought had been arising. In some ways
not altogether opposed to the hygienist school (they did not very much
approve of cuddling, although as early as 1932 Ian Suttie had protested
against the 'taboo on tenderness'), nevertheless a basic interest in the
child's natural intellectual and social development,[6] together with a less

inhibited approach to sexual function, opened the door to greater permissiveness generally. In her enlarged edition of *The Nursery Years* (1932), when the Children's Bureau was still advising mechanical restraints for thumbsucking, Susan Isaacs preferred extra play and companionship, and − incredible immorality − *'substitute pleasure*, in the shape of a good boiled sweet'. Where the Children's Bureau had now advanced from restraint to diversion as a treatment for masturbation, Isaacs was giving a brief account of Oedipal conflict and advising parents that they were 'far more likely to do harm by rushing in to scold or correct than by leaving the child to deal with it himself − in a general atmosphere of calm goodwill', and was citing Dr Ernest Jones in her support. Perhaps of especial importance for the liberating influence of the educationalists was their emphasis upon natural play and its functional status in the child's development.[7] Natural play was good − it was also messy and dirty. It was functional − but it was also enjoyed by the child. And if adults were to learn about child development by observing free play, there must also be free communication. At last, the dirty, happy, noisy child could be accepted as a good child.

Martha Wolfenstein (1955) points out the distinction which has long been made 'between what a baby "needs", his legitimate requirements, whatever is essential to his health and well-being, on the one hand, and what the baby "wants", his illegitimate pleasure strivings, on the other'. The hygienists considered only physical needs as legitimate − and even hunger, if expressed at an unsuitable time, was excluded. The wish for companionship was very definitely in the category of illegitimate pleasure strivings: 'We now come to the *treatment*, as it were, for a baby who cries simply because he wants attention, which is: "Baby must cry it out." '[8] In general, the baby's wishes had tended in the past to be suspect, and the mother had been expected to look for some non-permissible motive behind them, in the form either of dangerous (probably erotic) impulses or of a rebellious determination to dominate the mother; in either case, constant control of the child was called for, and only the baby who had submitted himself completely to the mother's control could be called a good baby. Now that virtue could be acknowledged in the toddler as he freely followed his own natural[9] pursuits and interests − not excluding the exploration of his own body − the ground was finally prepared for an acceptance of babies' desires as needs in themselves: 'Babies want attention; they probably need plenty of it' (Children's Bureau, 1945). In Wolfenstein's words (1955): 'What the baby wants for pleasure has thus become as legitimate a demand as what he needs for his physical well-being, and is to be treated in the same way.'

Hygienist theories were in any case too stress-provoking to the mother to have lasted very many years; the only group who did seem to derive satisfaction from them were some who, standing in an advisory role to the parents, found in such an authoritarian regime a source of power. There are still such personalities in advisory positions today; fortunately for parents, as we shall see, this attitude is out of fashion. The final reversal came with the publication of two seminal books, an article and a film; and again it was from the direction of psychoanalysis that the change came. In the United States, Margaret Ribble (1943) published *The Rights of Infants*; in England John Bowlby (1952) followed up his earlier studies of maternal deprivation as an antecedent of what he had called 'the affectionless character' (1946) with his report for the World Health Organisation, *Maternal Care and Mental Health*; and in the opening volume of the journal *Psycho-Analytic Study of the Child*, Rene Spitz (1945) published his paper on hospitalised infants and the effects of lack of mothering, and supported this with the widely circulated documentary film, *Grief: a Peril in Infancy*. All these writers brought dramatic evidence (some of which has since been more critically appraised (Pinneau, 1950; Ainsworth, 1963)), that babies and young children *need* mothering – not only the mother's presence, but the rocking, cuddling and lap play which had been so expressly forbidden – and that to deprive the baby of the natural expression of maternal warmth could prevent normal development of social relationships and permanently mar his personality. According to Margaret Ribble (1943), indeed, for the newborn baby 'the need for contact with the mother is urgent in order to keep the reflex mechanisms connected with breathing in operation as well as to bring the sensory system into functional activity'. While statements such as this invited the charge that factual evidence was becoming confounded with too-hasty interpretation, the basic thesis survived and has been strengthened by other workers not of the psychoanalytical school: notably the ethologists and zoologists, as well as child psychologists (Lorenz, 1952; Harlow, 1961; Schaffer and Emerson, 1964).

The effect of these works can hardly be overestimated: it was immediate, and still continues. Bowlby's report was abridged and published as a paperback (1953), thus becoming widely available to the lay public; in the year of publication and the five years following, more than seventy-five thousand copies were sold, and nearly as many in the next five years: an exceptional sale in Britain for a book not intended as a baby book for parents. Theories of maternal need rapidly found a place in countless training courses for workers with children. In England, James Robertson (1953, 1958), a colleague of Bowlby's at the Tavistock Clinic, started a campaign to persuade children's hospital wards to admit mothers together with their children, or at least not to restrict visiting in any way;[10] some hospitals welcomed the idea, others resisted it, but meanwhile a Government committee was set up which in 1959 published the 'Platt Report' on the welfare of children in hospital, recommending 'that all hospitals where children are treated will adopt the practice of unrestricted visiting, particularly for children below school age', that 'it is particularly valuable for the mother to be able to stay in hospital with her child during the first day or two', and that 'children should not be admitted to hospital if it can possibly be avoided'. Parents themselves thereupon set up a pressure group of their own (Mother Care for Children in Hospital, now the National Association for the Welfare of Children in Hospital), which, with all the enthusiasm of maternal solicitude that has the acknowledged right on its side, and with the help of a sympathetic press, is gradually altering the atmosphere of children's hospital care. Anna Freud (1943, 1960), who had been one of the first to call attention to the emotional difficulties of small children separated from their mothers, attacked from yet another angle, affirming the emotional need, not only in the baby but in his mother, to be together during the first weeks of the child's life, and criticising maternity hospital practice that separated the two. Clearly, parents generally must welcome the news that cuddling is not only nice but necessary; perhaps, however, we should spare a compassionate thought once more for the intellectual mothers of the thirties, whose sufferings as they tried to be 'good' mothers are now repeated in the knowledge that all their efforts only led them to be 'bad' mothers: as one of our correspondents added, 'Here is Bowlby, still out to make us feel guilty — about our rejection of the children we loved but were not *allowed* to love'.

Individualism and the 'Fun Morality'

The widespread influence of Ribble, Bowlby and Spitz, although it was supported by new, more permissive baby books such as Benjamin Spock's *Baby and Child Care* (1946), cannot be entirely explained in terms of parents' reaction against the rigours of aseptic mothercraft. Once again the trend must be seen in historical and sociological perspective. Babies were not the only people whose rights were being demanded at the end of the Second World War; other groups, too, submerged in anonymous poverty through years of unemployment, had in wartime received for the first time their fair share both of work and of food, and were now making it clear that neither malnutrition nor the grinding degradation of worklessness could any longer be tolerated by the 'lower classes' of the victorious nations. Perhaps, too, the final horrors of the war — Hiroshima, Nagasaki and the discovery of the concentration camps – shocked ordinary people, for a time at least, into a more humanitarian frame of mind: and perhaps, combined with this, was a determination to enjoy family life after the unhappy experience of war separations and before the more dreadful possibilities with which all mankind now has to live. Both in Britain and in America, especially marked during the later fifties and early sixties, the voices of dissent began to rise – against McCarthyism, against the Bomb, against any established authority that tells individuals what to do and how to do it – voices that said, and continue to say, 'They shan't push us around any longer'. The protest of the human individual against the massive forces which control him is indeed a theme which can be seen in contemporary art, literature, music and drama,[11] in the struggles against racialism, poverty and war, in the popular movements of Western youth and in the renewed campaign for women's emancipation; so we can hardly be surprised if parents too begin to question the authority of the experts.

The beginning of this trend, in which the fundamental need of parents is to be happy in parenthood, can be seen in two ways. In the first place, the tone in which advice is given changes from the strictly authoritarian to the friendly, neighbourly, perhaps big-sisterly approach. The old bullying manner is completely gone; we now find a persuasive, informal atmosphere, supported by illustrations which reflect the text in their message that bringing up babies is hair-raising, maybe, but lots of fun for everyone – just as the clinical photographs and chaste drawings of the old baby books reflect their atmosphere of stern duty.[12] Where in the thirties the mother was given solemn warnings as to what *would* happen if she disobeyed the rules, the mode now is to refer her, with continual reassurances however, to what *might possibly* result from some mistaken handlings: 'Here's what happens once in a while when the needs of the child aren't recognized' (Spock, 1946, chapter on 'The Two Year Old'). Where formerly she was told that 'the leading authorities of the day all agree . . .', now it is no more than suggested that 'many doctors feel . . .'. Spock is the supreme example of the friendly, conversational approach: just paternalistic enough to give confidence and reassurance, he is otherwise prepared to talk to the mother on equal terms. He probably has no serious rival on either side of the Atlantic, though to a much smaller audience of discriminating parents the English psychoanalyst, the late D.W. Winnicott, speaks (1964) with a similar skill (as does Dr Hugh Jolly to readers of *The Times*).

The second way in which this trend can be seen is in the context of advice given. That it is more permissive goes without saying: permissive both to the child and to the parents. But it is changed too in that it is not so much the details of infant care that are laid down as the principles which should be followed in deciding the details. Parents are no longer told what methods to adopt, but rather the *frame of mind* in which to adopt them. Flexibility is the keynote. *Infant Care* (1958 edition) shows many examples. On the baby's sleeping place: 'Do whatever way disturbs your sleep least'; on his clothing: 'Some mothers prefer ... others think ... ...'; on genital play: 'This is a common thing, and can go unnoticed. But sometimes it is disturbing to mothers, so if you feel uncomfortable about it you can try giving him a toy to hold while he's on the toilet seat'; and in general: 'If you take it easy in caring for your baby, you will be doing him a great service.' Flexibility serves one major aim: to allow parents to enjoy their role. 'When you both feel light-hearted enough to enjoy your baby, you are making a good start' says *Infant Care* on its second page, and Spock uses the same injunction, 'Enjoy Your Baby', as a subheading in his chapter 'The Right Start'. In Martha Wolfenstein's words (1955), 'Fun has become not only permissible but required'; the modern mother is already a creature whose 'feelings of inadequacy are matched only by her undying efforts', according to Johnson and Medinnus (1965), and 'fun morality' now ensures that 'her self-evaluation can no longer be based entirely on whether she is doing the right and necessary things but *becomes involved with nuances of feelings which are not under voluntary control*' (Wolfenstein, 1955, our italics).

Notes

1.   Sangster (1963) gives this figure, which he obtained from Bready's (1938) history of England 'before and after Wesley'. Sangster points out (private communication) that the Wesleyans were especially interested in death and regularly quoted mortality statistics in their journals. Rousseau in *Emile* (1762, p. 325) more optimistically presumes 50 per cent of persons not living to childbearing age: but he is speaking in the context of people of his own class, not the population as a whole.
2.   This letter, and the two quotations that follow it, are taken from Sangster (1963), a most useful source-book on the Evangelists.
3.   Typical in content, but outstanding in its setting, is the story of the death of Augusta Noble, which forms one chapter ('Fatal Effects of Disobedience to Parents') of Mrs Sherwood's extremely popular *History of the Fairchild Family*, first published in 1818 and reprinted many times throughout the nineteenth century.
4.   The father's situation as God's vicar is explicitly stated in many books. Mrs Sherwood (1818) gives Mr Fairchild a speech to his 6-year-old son which is worth quoting in its entirety; the situation is that the child has refused to learn his Latin grammar, despite punishments so far of bread and water for three meals and a flogging with a 'small horse whip'. 'Mr Fairchild got up and walked up and down the room in great trouble; then turning to Henry, he said "Henry, listen to me; when wicked men obstinately defy and oppose the power of God, He gives them up to

their own bad hearts, He suffers them to live, perhaps, and partake of the light of the sun and of the fruits of the earth, but he shows them no marks of his fatherly love or favour; they have no sweet thoughts, no cheerful hours, no delightful hopes. I stand in the place of God to you, whilst you are a child; and as long as I do not ask you to do anything wrong, you must obey me; therefore, if you cast aside my authority and will not obey my commands, I shall not treat you as I do my other children. From this time forward, Henry, I have nothing to do with you; I will speak to you no more, neither will your mamma, or sisters, or John, or Betty. Betty will be allowed to give you bread to eat, and water to drink: and I shall not hinder you from going to your own bed to sleep at night; but I will have nothing more to do with you; so go out of my study immediately." ' (Mrs Sherwood, 1818.)

5.   Many examples could be given. One will suffice: 'There is no doubt whatever as to the duty of mother and nurse in this matter' (Truby King, 1937, p. 16). He is referring to the need to wake the infant if he is asleep when the clock says that it is feeding time. He also has a section on 'The Destiny of the Race in the Hands of its Mothers', and refers the reader to the state of motherhood during the decline and fall of the Roman Empire.

6.   Of especial interest in this context are Susan Isaacs' two seminal works (1930, 1933), which recorded at great length the actual play and conversation of children in the nursery environment; the second volume begins uncompromisingly: 'This book is addressed to the scientific public, and in particular to serious students of psychology and education.' Piaget, too, was beginning to arouse interest in young children's conceptual development: *The Child's Conception of the World* was published in England in 1929, and his next two books appeared in 1930 and 1932.

7.   Obviously the roots of these educational ideas go back to Rousseau (1762), but, although a continuous chain of interest can be traced right through the nineteenth century, it was not until the late 1920s that such theories were communicated in practical terms to a substantial body of parents.

8.   This statement comes from a work entitled *Cries of the Baby*, by Dr Theron Kilmer, which is quoted by Truby King (1937, revised and enlarged edn.) as being 'full of ripe wisdom'.

9.   The history of the cult of 'nature' in all its aspects is itself of great interest to historians of child psychology and child nutrition; we cannot explore this topic here, however.

10.   Robertson's scientific film, *A Two-Year-Old goes to Hospital* (1953), was designated by the British Film Institute as a film of national and historic importance, and a print is preserved in the National Archives.

11.   Some representative names from Great Britain are Francis Bacon for art; Alan Silitoe for literature (Silitoe, 1959); Osborne and Beckett, followed by Pinter and Hopkinson, for straight drama; and Jonathan Miller and his 'Beyond the Fringe' group paving the way for a whole era of satirical revues; and the folk·song-pop movements for music. American readers will easily provide their own examples.

12.   In Truby King's *Feeding and Care of Baby* (1937), the only illustration in which anybody seems to be having fun is one entitled chillingly 'Nurse Imitating a Fond Relation' – from which is drawn the moral that babies should not be over-stimulated.

References

Ainsworth, M.D., Andry, R.G., Harlow, R.G., Lebovici, S., Mead, M., Pough Dane, G. and Wootton, B. (1963), *Maternal Deprivation: a Critical Assessment*. Geneva, WHO.

Bowlby, J. (1946), *Forty-Four Juvenile Thieves*. London, Baillière, Tindall and Cox.

Bowlby, J. (1952), *Maternal Care and Mental Health*. Geneva, WHO.

Bowlby, J. (1953), *Child Care and the Growth of Love*. London, Penguin.

Bready, J.W. (1938), *England before and after Wesley*.

Children's Bureau, US Department of Health, Education and Welfare (1945, 1958), *Infant Care*.

Freud, A. (1943), *Infants without Families*. New York, Internat. Univ. Press.

Freud, A. (1960), Series of four talks for World Mental Health Year on BBC programme, *Parents and Children*, May-June.

Harlow, H. (1961), 'Development of affectional patterns in infant monkeys', in Foss, B.M. (ed.), *Determinants of Infant Behaviour*, 1. London, Methuen.

Isaacs, S. (1929, 1932), *The Nursery Years*. London, Routledge and Kegan Paul.

Isaacs, S. (1930), *Intellectual Growth in Young Children*. London, Routledge and Kegan Paul.

Janeway, J. (1753), *A Token for Children*.

Johnson, R.C. and Medinnus, G.R. (1965), *Child Psychology: Behavior and Development*. New York, Wiley.

Liddiard, M. (1928, 1954), *The Mothercraft Manual*. London, Churchill.

Lorenz, K. (1952), *King Solomon's Ring*. London, Methuen.

McCarthy, M. (1963), *The Group*. London, Weidenfeld and Nicolson.

Pate, M. (1965), Introduction to Gyorgy, P. and Burgess, A. (eds.), *Protecting the Pre-School Child*. London, Tavistock.

Piaget, J. (1929), *The Child's Conception of the World*. London, Routledge and Kegan Paul.

Pinneau, S. (1950), 'A critique on the articles by Margaret Ribble', *Child Development*, 21, 203-28.

Registrar General (1963), *Statistical Review of England and Wales*. London, HMSO.

Ribble, M. (1943), *The Rights of Infants*. New York, Columbia Univ. Press.

Ribble, M. (1944), 'Infantile experience in relation to personality development', in Hunt, J. McV. (ed.), *Personality and the Behaviour Disorders*, 2, New York, Ronald Press.

Robertson, J. (1953), *A Two-Year-Old Goes to Hospital* (film). London, Tavistock Child Development Research Unit.

Robertson, J. (1958), *Going into Hospital with Mother* (film). London, Tavistock Child Development Research Unit.

Robertson, J. (1958a), *Young Children in Hospital*. London, Tavistock.

Robertson, J. (1958b), *Hospitals and Children*. London, Gollancz.

Rousseau, J. (1762), *Emile* (Everyman edn). London, Dent.

Sangster, P. (1963), *Pity My Simplicity*. London, Epworth Press.

Schaffer, H.R. and Emerson, P. (1964), 'Development of social attachments in infancy', *Monogr. Soc. Res. Child Developm.*, 29, no. 3, 1-77.

Sherwood, Mrs M. (1818), *The History of the Fairchild Family*. London, Ward Lock.

Silitoe, A. (1959), *The Loneliness of the Long-Distance Runner*. London, Allen.

Spitz, R. (1945), 'Hospitalism', *Psychoanal. Study Child*, 1, 53-74.

Spock, B. (1946, 1957), *Baby and Child Care*. New York, Duell, Sloan and Pearce.

Spock, B. (1970), *Decent and Indecent*. London, Bodley Head.

Suttie, I. (1935), *The Origins of Love and Hate*. London, Routledge and Kegan Paul.

Truby King, F. (1937), *Feeding and Care of Baby* (revised edn). London, Oxford

Univ. Press.

UNICEF (1964), *Children of the Developing Countries*. London, Nelson.

Watson, J.B. (1928), *Psychological Care of Infant and Child*. New York, W.W. Norton.

Watts, I. (1842), *Divine Songs, attempted in easy language for the use of children*. 'New Edition', London, SPCK.

Wesley, J. (1872), *Works*. London, Wesleyan Conference Office.

Wesley, J. and Wesley, C. (1868), *Poetical Works* (ed. G. Osborn).

Winnicott, D.W. (1964), *The Child, the Family and the Outside World*. London, Penguin.

Wolfenstein, M. (1955), 'Fun morality: an analysis of recent American child-training literature', in Mead, M. and Wolfenstein, M. (eds), *Childhood in Contemporary Cultures*. Chicago, Chicago Univ. Press.

6 CULTURAL VARIATION AND COMMONALITY IN COGNITIVE DEVELOPMENT

Neil Warren

Source: Specially written for this volume. Copyright © 1978 The Open University.

Introduction

This paper discusses various aspects of the thesis that cognitive development may vary significantly across cultures. It is not in itself a systematic review of the literature. Certain surveys and discussions are available elsewhere: in particular fine reviews of the cross-cultural Piagetian literature by Dasen (1972, 1973, 1977); and general articles by Goodnow (1969), Greenfield and Bruner (1969), Price-Williams (1976) and Glick (1975).

This is not a topic which allows cut-and-dried generalisations. Any conclusions drawn must be of a more tentative and interim nature than usual. Although the amount of cross-cultural research conducted by psychologists has expanded greatly in the last decade, there is still too little, and much of what there is is unsatisfactory. Cross-cultural research has peculiar difficulties, most of which are obvious. And a suspicion that the methods or even the concepts employed may be inappropriate to an alien culture, though not to be raised in cavalier or ideological fashion, can rarely be expunged altogether.

It is inevitable that some emphasis be given to Piagetian research. Piaget's is the major theory of cognitive development that psychology has so far produced and has inspired more cross-cultural research of any kind than any other theory. The relative simplicity and 'naturalness' of Piagetian procedures of investigation (short of formal operations) seem, on the face of it, to make them appropriate for use in different cultures. Their materials are pebbles, sand, water, clay, and so on; and one may usually introduce a substance from the local culture without altering the import of the Genevan procedure. They assess what seems to be an only slightly formalised sample of the child's cognitive commerce with his environment — in contrast with the Western schoolroom flavour of conventional intelligence tests. And Piaget's measures do not have age built into them by age norms — again in contrast with intelligence tests, whose IQ is an age-related metric. However, I do not mean to imply that many aspects of Piaget's theory are not controversial; and I shall also draw on other approaches to cognition and intelligence.

Cultural Differences and Commonalities

Lévi-Strauss once prophesied that cultural differences will sometime in the twenty-first century disappear in favour of a single humanity. As the world shrinks, it is already much more difficult than it was for our grandfathers to identify any cultures which we might dare to call 'primitive'. We still accept that there are *cultural* differences; but not necessarily that those cultural variations result from, or result in, fundamental *psychological* differences. Cultural differences may be — I would say obviously are to some extent — an overlay on psychological universals.

If there are psychological universals, this is of course not to say that all people are exactly the same. People vary; and *vive la différence*! If we say that they are really all the same, we mean it in some fundamental, generative sense: they are variations on a common theme or common set of principles. In non-Western or traditional cultures individuals also vary greatly one from another, although this is often obscured by ethnographic reports. Thus in considering psychological universals we are thinking of the *fundamental* ways in which people may be the same, the themes on which all are variations. An old expression for it is 'the psychic unity of mankind'.

It is the same psychological *processes* which will be universal, if at all, and so it is successful comprehension of these processes which can specify the limiting cultural conditions for both similarities and differences. There is in fact a new emphasis today on psychological universals; and it begins to look as if we are all more alike in certain fundamental respects than an earlier generation of social scientists, stressing plasticity, thought (not to speak of those who have linked surface differences with race). Part of this new look consists in pointing out the extent of commonality required to conduct a cross-cultural study at all. This observation will apply even to those studies which take the commonality for granted and emphasise cultural *differences* in their reports. It may be that you need an awful lot of commonality to pin down a difference — between individuals or between cultures.

Let me give an example. The investigation of colour perception is a very good instance. Even the common form of human colour blindness was not identified until the very end of the eighteenth century. (Even today most pet-lovers assume that their cats and dogs see the world in colour, which is almost certainly not true.) In the nineteenth century reports filtered back to the West that various 'primitives' lacked many colour names, and the view was formed that such people had defective colour vision. This view was eventually scotched by some of the earliest cross-cultural research. In the twentieth century an alternative position (often identified with the linguist Whorf) was taken up: colour vision is everywhere the same but the colour spectrum is variously and arbitrarily categorised by the colour terms of different languages. This thesis has in turn been dismissed by a spate of recent research inspired by Berlin and Kay (1969): there appear to be eleven universal foci of perceptual salience within the colour solid, these are named by basic colour terms in a certain sequence, and cultures differ in how many their languages have named, from two to eleven. But within this universality there *do* now seem to be differences in colour *vision*, reflecting differences in retinal pigmentation, which acts as a kind of filter (Bornstein, 1973).

Berlin and Kay (1969), in beginning their research on colour terms, noted the ease with which they and others had been able to learn the usage of colour terms in various cultures – in spite of the host of reports of cultural differences in colour terminology. Berlin has also had to revise an initial assumption (Berlin *et al.*, 1966) that folk taxonomies of botanical and zoological classification would vary greatly from each other and from Western taxonomies (Berlin, 1972; Berlin *et al.*, 1973). Rosch (1977), who has made remarkable psychological contributions to the cross-cultural study of colour categories and to a general theory of human categorisation, observes:

> The facts about a new culture which are most likely to be observed and noted by a naive observer are the ways in which the strange culture differs from the familiar. Thus, we do not find reports of other cultures which tell us that the people chew their food, or that they smile, or that it was possible to learn their words for familiar objects or for colours. All such facts are taken for granted and . . . tend to be overlooked. [p. 4]

Cole and Scribner, in conclusion of their fine survey of culture and cognition (1974), point to the small likelihood of finding cultural differences in 'basic component cognitive processes'.

Child Development

The point about taken-for-granted commonality applies equally well to child development. There is some indication from baby-test data, for instance, that African infants develop a little more rapidly in certain – mostly locomotor – respects of the first year and a half than the Western babies who comprised the standardisation examples for these tests (v. Warren, 1972, 1973). This may also be so for non-Western or pre-industrial infants in general (Warner, 1972). Or rather a certain precocity may be a feature of infants in less 'modern' environments, as suggested, for instance, by African difference by social level (Warren, 1972) or by the early precocity of Moroccan-Jewish infants in Israel in comparison with European-Jewish babies (Smilansky, Shephatia and Frenkel, 1976). Bovet, Dasen and others (summarised by Dasen, 1977) have approached this same issue in the Piagetian manner, studying the sensori-motor development of African village infants in the Ivory Coast, and also find certain specific advances over Parisian norms — though not an overall precocity. The matter has been further and well elucidated by Super (1975) in Kenya: he studied both infant development over time and infant care and stimulation in several cultural groups, and his complicated results indicate the role of both biological and cultural influences in promoting African development in certain motor elements of behaviour. Because the groups which manifest infant precocity seem also to be those whose intelligence test performance falls below average in later years, some authors (e.g. Jensen, 1969, 1973; Eysenck, 1971) have used the earlier African findings to draw large theoretical inferences in support of their contentions about racial differences in intelligence. I believe their arguments to be extremely tendentious, given our ignorance of the causal relations between infant and adult performances. The long-term developmental import of small, specific and inconsistent differences in infant growth rates is certainly unknown, and may plausibly be nil.

Whatever differences there may be, however, rest on a remarkable and usually unacknowledged base of commonality. The same elements of infant development emerge wherever studies are conducted. To take an example relevant to the above precocity issue, Warren and Parkin (1974) found few differences between African and European newborns: these differences were small, not clinically obvious, and did not indicate the precocity of either group. Much more striking was the fact that exactly the *same* set of 45 responses and reflexes was observed in both groups. Only two reflexes were difficult to elicit — in either group. Konner (1972) also noted that the reflex repertoire of Bushman newborns (possibly a distinct race) corresponds precisely with their European counterparts.

And similarly for behaviour later in infancy. Dasen (1977) considers that the most important conclusion from African sensori-motor studies may be obscured by attention to cultural differences in developmental rate:

It is, in fact, that the qualitative characteristics of sensori-motor development are quite similar or even identical in French and African infants, in spite of vast differences in their cultural environment. Not only are the structural properties of the sub-stages, and therefore their order of appearance, identical in both groups, but even the actions and schemes, and the way these are slowly built up into more complex action-patterns which eventually enable the infant to solve rather difficult problems, seem to be identical. [p. 165]

Dasen gives a remarkable example. Around twelve months of age, when given a plastic tube and a chain of paper clips, almost every infant, African or European, looks for some way of making the chain pass through the tube. The African village baby has never seen such things before, and yet he combines them exactly as Parisian infants do: he makes the same errors, and follows the same sequence of progressively adaptive solutions. He also, as it happens, can do this at a slightly earlier age, on the average — there again is the small quantitative difference resting on a huge and impressive commonality. Many other examples could be given. The sub-stage 4B of object permanence, when babies search for an object behind a first screen even though they have seen it moved so as to be behind a second screen, is exactly duplicated by African children (again, a little earlier). It may well be that our received conceptions of scientific method give the wrong bias, for cross-cultural and for developmental problems: we are taught to respect quantitative over qualitative approaches, and that is clearly mistaken here; and our research designs and statistics are sensitised to differences and often ignore commonalities (cf. Meehl, 1967).

The topic of language affords similar observations. Of course people of different cultures speak of different things to some extent, just as they think about different things — this is part of what we mean by distinguishing cultures at all, and it is part of the reason why communication between cultures and translation between languages are sometimes difficult. But again the differences could obscure the commonalities. The phenomenon of universality in colour terminology was noted above. Other studies have documented striking generalities across language-families and cultures in the use of physical terms as metaphors for psychological attributes (Asch, 1958), in the affective connotations of colour terms (D'Andrade and Egan, 1974) and of a large range of adjectival dimensions (Osgood, 1962; Osgood, May and Miron, 1975). Phonetic symbolism — a correspondence between the sound of a word and its meaning — is another curious but documented cross-language phenomenon (Brown, 1958; Brown, Black and Horowitz, 1955).

A large range of purely linguistic universals has been identified (Greenberg, 1966), and Miller (1970) has suggested that they reflect universal psychological processes. Rosch's (1977) theory shows how they may do so, for perceptual and semantic categories. Chomsky's (1968) well-known contention was that a universal deep structure of language and a corresponding universal mental competence underlies all language acquisition. Chomsky initially had little cross-cultural evidence on language acquisition to draw on. As the relevant evidence accumulates, empirical indications of a universal sequence of language acquisition emerge, both for grammar and syntax and for communicative competence (Slobin, 1971; Ferguson and Slobin, 1973; Bowerman, 1973; Sanches and Blount, 1975). Such unrelated languages as Finnish, Samoan, African Nilotic, Mexican Indian, American English (black and white) and Japanese are included in these studies, which also point to the dependence of language acquisition on the prior establishment of cognitive-semantic principles or heuristics, which again would be universal. It is possible that, in the long run, investigations of language development — especially semantics and communicative competence — will contribute as much to the cross-cultural study of cognitive development as will conventional psychological approaches to cognition. These are as yet very early days.

Piagetian theory of cognitive development, while not incompatible with latter-day findings concerning language acquisition, has not especially addressed itself to language development and grants no role to language as an external shaper of the child's cognition. Piaget's theory clearly posits universals of ontogeny — not, as some seem to think, by reference to heredity but as the necessary outcome of the sequential interaction between an intact and maturing human organism and the successive environments he is able to construe. I have mentioned sensori-motor development above; but the bulk of cross-cultural Piagetian work is on conservation, and thus the transition to concrete operations. As for the infancy stage, it seems clear that measures of conservation can be widely used in different cultures and probably identify similar phenomena. Formal operations are much more problematic, and have scarcely been studied cross-culturally.

Because Piaget's is a stage theory, we may ask if the same sequence of stages is found in all cultures. It was noted above that the detail and sequence of sensori-motor sub-stages is precisely paralleled in Africa. And, though longitudinal studies following the same children over many years have simply not been done in non-Western cultures, it is reasonable to conclude tentatively that the same broad sequence is followed everywhere as far as the transition to concrete operational thought. But for this transition, or at any rate for the much-studied conservation concepts, the picture is so confused that it is not profitable to analyse it in detail here. The reader is referred to Dasen (1972, 1977). Suffice it to say that the

Genevan sequence (*décalage*) of conservation concepts — such as quantity → weight → volume — appears to vary cross-culturally, but the variation is not obviously systematic. There are some instances of apparent 'regression' in development or of 'pseudo-conservation'. Another problem is that the sequence of conservation concepts has usually not been analysed for each child individually. Piaget's theory in any case gives no real explanation of *décalages*. But it remains that with the acquisition of conservation and the move to operational thought we can no longer see neat cross-cultural parallels in ontogeny.

Standardised psychometric tests of intelligence and ability are currently in almost total disrepute among cross-cultural researchers. In the past, outrageous conclusions have been drawn from the facile administration of intelligence tests to non-Western groups. Cross-cultural psychometricians are these days much more careful (e.g. Irvine, 1969; Vernon, 1969); but they are also scarce — outside the 'applied' field of educational and occupational selection in third-world countries. Even so, one occasionally sees findings which reinforce the point I have been emphasising above, of a remarkable but unremarked commonality across cultures. Moreigne and Senecal (1962) and Massé (1969) tested Senegalese children aged three to six with a slightly modified version of the Stanford-Binet (Terman-Merrill) test. IQs were below the American average — as one might reasonably expect for various reasons, including the purely methodological. But the correlations of IQ from year to year compare nicely in size with American Terman-Merrill data for these ages and show the entirely usual trend of an increasing correlation with age and a decreasing one as the interval between testings is lengthened. Thus, measured intelligence in Senegal shows the same stability over this age range as in the United States. Further, there is a slight superiority of girls over boys at this early age which is precisely replicated in the Senegalese sample. I suggest that these commonalities, which are independent of mean level of intelligence quotient, are far more substantial than putative differences in mean level across cultures.

Universality and Difference

I hope I have been making clear that the issue is only very superficially one of commonality *versus* difference: it is ultimately one of commonality *and* difference. To quote Rosch (1977) again:

> In so far as psychology is to be a science whose statements are of some interest and some beauty, it must attempt to formulate principles of the mental and behavioural functions of humans which are general and

universal. That is not to say that theory must focus only on the ways in which humans are the same; rather, the universality of theory comes from its ability to encompass and predict differences as well as universals in human thought and behaviour. [p. 1]

To return briefly to the elegant example of colour, cultures differ in the number of basic terms they have available for naming the universal eleven colour foci, which can be scaled into a single sequence.

There is an old Western idea of a 'primitive mentality' or 'savage mind', which supposedly holds that the thought and consciousness of 'primitives' is essentially different from our own (we seem to be condemned by our very consideration of the issue to reside in the non-primitive camp, whether we like it or not — though see Price-Williams (1975) for a fine new twist to this). The notion of a Primitive Mentality is repeatedly repudiated in these egalitarian and culturally relativist times; but it dies an astonishingly hard death. In fact it keeps arising in muted form, even, as we shall see, from premises of universality, and is clearly not to be put to rest by fiat. There is a renewed scholarly interest in the writings of Lévy-Bruhl, the philosopher-sociologist who first characterised and analysed Primitive Mentality in several volumes — without setting foot outside Europe. Lévy-Bruhl referred Primitive Mentality to primitive culture (*représentations collectives*), not to primitive neurology; and towards the end of his life he appears to have retracted his position. The American anthropologist Boas is often cited today (1911, 1935) as having put Lévy-Bruhl in his place; and true, Boas successfully demolished the 'race' concept as an explanation of cultural differences. But this was not Lévy-Bruhl's thesis in any case; and the extent to which Boas's actual statements seem clearly to endorse a notion of cultural differences in mentality is remarkable (I am grateful to Webb (1977) for drawing my attention to this feature). It is as if both Lévy-Bruhl and Boas were compelled to equivocate between the two sides of the same coin of commonality and difference — because they could not take it as a single coin.

Influential recent discussions of this same issue, which set out with some charity so as not readily to raise *us* above *them*, come to draw a distinction none the less. Lévi-Strauss (1966) finds primitive thought restricted to tangible attributes in categorisation and to the form of creative thinking he calls *bricolage*. Horton (1967) finds traditional cultures 'closed' in the sense that they have no developed awareness of alternatives to their basic beliefs. Gellner (1973) lists four distinguishing features of the Savage Mind. Hallpike (1976) we shall come to below.

Approaches from developmental psychology splay this issue along two dimensions, those of age and culture. And again difference is thought to arise out of universality: now, it is the developmental sequence which is universal, as emphasised above; but the rate and extent of developmental progression which may differ by culture, to be taken up here. Werner (1940) characterised both children's and primitives' thinking as lacking abstract and differentiated modes of thought. The now eminent Russian psychologist Luria was involved in a research expedition to remote villages in Soviet Central Asia in 1931-2, some details and conclusions of which have recently been published in English (Luria, 1971, 1976). Luria's account purports to show how new forms of work organisation and short literacy courses transformed the consciousness of the villagers to a higher level of mentality, including a move from the concrete and situational to more abstract, analytic and generalising thought processes. Both Werner and Luria refer to Lévy-Bruhl, and their accounts of the less developed forms of consciousness contain very strong echoes of his account of Primitive Mentality. More recent cross-cultural studies have led their prime mover, Bruner (Bruner, Olver and Greenfield, 1966; Greenfield and Bruner, 1969) to conclude that cognitive development in some cultures may be adequate for concrete tasks but not for matters involving abstract conception:

> some environments 'push' cognitive growth better, earlier and longer than others. What does not seem to happen is that different cultures produce completely divergent and unrelated modes of thought . . . [Our biological] heritage makes it possible for man to reach a form of intellectual maturity that is capable of elaborating a highly technical society. Less demanding societies — less demanding intellectually — do not produce so much symbolic embedding and elaboration of first ways of looking and thinking. [Greenfield and Bruner, 1969, p. 654]

There is something of a consensus: *we* are abstract, |*they*|concrete thinkers; and this because we have been carried further along a common developmental course. The hubris of this stance is of course too much for many to bear; and it is opposed, most notably by Cole (e.g. Cole and Scribner, 1974). Even Bruner may be thought to have tempered the position cited above (v. Cole and Bruner, 1971). But Piaget can be counted as within the consensus: he has suggested more than once that in many cultures adult thinking may not proceed beyond the level of concrete operations (Inhelder and Piaget, 1958; Piaget, 1966, 1971). In referring above to cross-cultural Piagetian research, I attended only to the striking commonality of qualitative and sequential aspects. It is time to turn to the issues of developmental rate and the completion of the sequence.

In doing so I shall not dredge the literature. There has now been a good deal of non-Western Piagetian work, and one necessarily relies on Dasen's (1972, 1973, 1977) excellent surveys. Certainly, non-Western infants do not appear to lag behind Western infants (unless, perhaps, they be severely malnourished): there are in fact some indications to the contrary, as mentioned above. The real interest, however, is as usual in the acquisition of conservation, which marks the transition to fully operational thinking at the concrete level. A few reports — notably the early and influential study of Tiv children in Nigeria by Price-Williams (1961) — show unschooled non-Western children achieving the conservation concepts at something like the Genevan ages. But it is now clear that these few studies are exceptions. Non-Western samples typically show a marked 'lag' in the development of conservation. Whatever this means, the fact of it is inescapable.

Slowness of development would matter little if the sequence were eventually completed. But this seems not to be the case for all cultures. A fair number of non-Western samples — even some including adolescents and adults — do not approach 100 per cent success in conservation tasks or other indices of concrete operations. This should mean that the concrete level of operativity — not to speak of formal thought — has not been fully mastered by many members of certain cultures. The most striking examples seem to be from aboriginal Australian and Papua New Guinean cultures. True, operational thought could perhaps mature later than the ages studied; but it seems increasingly unlikely with greater age.

It should also be mentioned that developmental studies using standardised tests in non-Western cultures, suspect though they must be, similarly show a systematically increasing deficit with age from early childhood onwards. The Senegalese study mentioned above to illustrate commonality (Moreigne and Senecal, 1962; Massé, 1969), for instance, reported a mean IQ of 95 at age 3, 93 at age 4, 88 at age 5, 87 at age 6. The most painstaking longitudinal study to date has been conducted by Holtzman, Diaz-Guerrero and Swartz (1975), comparing large numbers of children in Mexico City and Austin, Texas, over 12 grades of schooling. The findings are immensely complex; but in the early grades there were similar levels of cognitive ability in the two groups, while with increasing age the Mexican children, schooled, literate and urban, steadily fell behind.

The cultural correlates of such differences in cognitive development should provide clues to potential causes. However, although we have some information, it hardly contains surprises, and the independent variables are gross. Contact with Westerners and the consequent acculturation improves operational development, at least as indexed by the display of conservation. So does urbanisation. Schooling of the Western type appears to make a striking difference in some cases but not in others – a curiosity which I shall return to below. The real problem is that these 'modernising' variables are generally compounded together in any case, and are difficult to isolate one from another. They are also not truly psychological variables, and thus cry out for 'unpacking', so that we may know what they actually mean in terms of the organisation of children's knowledge and experience. I cannot do that here except speculatively; and so I shall concentrate my attention on one variable, that of literacy, which is coming to be of major interest to developmental and cross-cultural researchers.

Primitive Mentality, Ontogeny and Literacy

The first article by an anthropologist which takes Piaget and developmental psychology seriously in consideration of the issue of Primitive Mentality is Hallpike's (1976) 'Is there a Primitive Mentality?'. Hallpike chastises his fellow anthropologists – in my view, quite rightly – for the neglect of developmental psychology. (Social anthropology, at least in Britain, has traditionally been hostile to any but common-sense versions of psychological approaches and explanations.) I believe Hallpike overestimates the role granted to the social environment by Piaget's theory of ontogeny. He also seems unaware that the differences between Piaget's and Bruner's approaches to cognitive development (which he treats as more or less reinforcing each other) have been and remain a matter of sharp controversy: in particular, Piaget does not grant a major causal role in cognitive growth to language; Bruner of course does; and so does Hallpike.

Hallpike argues that the difference between 'primitive' thought and the thinking of members of modern industrial societies reflects the developmental level at which cognitive growth stabilises in a culture – this point is consonant both with Piaget's position and that of Bruner in the 'sixties. He further identifies schooling and particularly literacy as a crucial influence on cognitive growth – which takes him into some good company, as we shall see, but cuts him off from orthodox Piagetians. Hallpike finds it astonishing

that anthropologists, and for that matter philosophers, trying to explain the difference between European and primitive thought, have not considered the obvious point that people who go to school for a number of years and acquire literacy and numeracy, are likely to think in rather different ways from those who have never had this experience. [1976, p. 263]

I have mentioned several psychologists whose views and findings are consonant with Hallpike's position. Luria (1971, 1976), in association with Vygotsky, extensively documented the differences in forms of consciousness that appeared to result from collectivisation and crash courses in literacy in Soviet Uzbekistan. The change is characterised as 'developmental' in both the individual-ontogenetic and the cultural-historical senses, each partaking of the other. Bruner (1966) identified literacy and formal schooling as the most important shaping forces in culture that produce crucial differences in cognitive growth. There is actually an oddity, mentioned above, about the effects of schooling on operational development: it makes a great difference in some cultures but not in others. It makes some sense to suppose that schooling, including literacy, makes a difference when it is a major source of cultural stimulation of a novel, 'modern' kind for a basically non-literate culture. Otherwise, as in Hong Kong (Goodnow, 1962; Goodnow and Bethon, 1966), schooling is not a primary lever of cognitive growth. If correct, this supposition will also apply to Western societies (cf. Mermelstein and Shulman, 1967): thus the 'deschooling' of society (Illich, 1971) can seem plausible to some, Western culture having been brought − in large part by the institution of universal schooling − to a general level of stimulation of its young which ironically lessens the direct function of formal schooling.

There is probably something very important about the consequences of literacy. Certainly, after a long period when literacy was to social scientists as water to the fish, there has been a recent quickening of interest in the topic. Goody, an anthropologist, has done most to stimulate this interest (Goody and Watt, 1962; Goody, 1968). He stresses, for instance, that a true sense of the past as distinct from the present depends on annals and records; and points out that the first great civilisation of the world had, in the ancient Greek alphabet, the first comprehensibly phonetic and easily learnable system for transcribing speech. The idea of 'logic' − an impersonal mode of reason − arose in classical Greece; as probably did the idea of objective 'history'. Lévy-Bruhl's thesis of the 'pre-logical' mentality of primitives survives its numerous repudiations to find new ground in Goody's account:

there may . . . exist general differences between literate and non-literate societies somewhat along the lines suggested by Lévy-Bruhl. One reason for their existence . . . may be . . . that writing establishes a different kind of relationship between the word and its referent, a relationship that is more general and more abstract, and less closely connected with the particularities of person, place and time, than obtains in oral communication. [Goody and Watt, p. 331]

These ideas have become pervasive in recent discussions. A literate society stresses telling out of context rather than showing in context, so that learning becomes an art in itself (Bruner, 1965). Reading and writing foster context-independent speech and thought; and linguistic contexts can be manipulated, transmuted and juxtaposed far more readily than real ones (Greenfield and Bruner, 1966). The utterances of an oral language are one symbolising step removed from concrete reality; the texts *and the speech* of a written language are likely to be two steps removed, and that greater independence of distance facilitates generalisation and abstraction (Greenfield, 1972). Greenfield also takes the consequences of the difference between oral and written language/speech to characterise social class differences in the USA in maternal teaching styles (Hess and Shipman, 1965) and in linguistic codes as characterised by Bernstein (1961). Olson (1975) extends the argument – utterance is to text as common sense is to theoretical knowledge:

> writing turns utterances as descriptions into propositions with implications. Sentences may be treated in either way; and while our children treat them as descriptions of events, our adults treat them as logical propositions. This jump is fundamental to development in a literature culture but it is achieved, I suggest, primarily through the reflection on statements made possible by writing systems. [p. 39]

Cogent though the arguments may be, these things are very hard to study in a systematic fashion. For one thing, the very large majority in a Western society – above a certain age – is literate, and the few illiterates are probably atypical in many other ways also. Many non-Western countries, however, contain a high proportion of illiterates; and it therefore falls to cross-cultural psychology to tease out the cognitive consequences of literacy. The problem there is that literacy is normally compounded with other influences, such as urbanisation, modernisation and whatever effects formal education may have on children over and above teaching literacy. So that it is difficult precisely to single out the cognitive effects of literacy from the modernising imbroglio which renders literates different from illiterates in many correlated respects.

None the less, the professional concern with research design which psychologists bring to anthropological studies is already producing refinements. Cross-culturally, Cole and Scribner have led the way. Extensive earlier research among the Kpelle of Liberia reported by Cole *et al.* (1971) found that the really large qualitative differences in performance on cognitive tasks resulted from literacy and Western-style education; in contrast, between younger and older non-literate Kpelle there were only small and negligible quantitative differences. A further Kpelle study by Scribner found various effects of schooling on classification and the explication of criteria for classification: in particular (and this is borne out by other studies), schooling seems to promote the search for a principle or rule, the awareness of possible alternative principles and the ability to explain one's own mental operations. Well aware that schooling provides more than literacy, and that psychological changes can occur without schooling, Cole and Scribner have more recently turned their research attention to another Liberian tribe, the Vai, among whom literacy for one script is not compounded within the imbroglio of acculturation. The Vai have their own Vai script, evolved within the tribe; though not all are literate in Vai.

Vai is a Mande language spoken in northeast Liberia, and the Vai people rank among the few societies in the history of the world to have invented their own script. Vai culture is now multiliterate, for the international written languages of Arabic and English have found their way to Vai country. Vai literacy is not taught in schools, rather being learned from a friend or relative; so that one encounters here the truly rare phenomenon of literacy without education. Scribner and Cole (1977) are at pains to point out, however, that literacy in Vai, whose most common use is in letter-writing, is not profound. In fact, Scribner and Cole found no marked differences between unschooled Vai literates and complete non-literates on logical and classificatory tasks. However, Vai literates were better than both non-literates and Arabic literates in explaining, out of context, a simple board game to another person. This kind of thing, i.e. communication of detail and sequence in an orderly manner without reliance on mutual perception, has frequently been observed to be painfully difficult for non-literates (e.g. Cole *et al.*, 1971) — more difficult, in fact, than educated moderns can easily credit. Vai literates tended to give a general characterisation of the game before going into rules of play and other details. Vai literates were also better than non-literates in verbal learning, though here Arabic literates (who learn the Koran by rote) were superior. These are preliminary findings, pending the eventual full report from Scribner and Cole. One also wonders how Vai non-literates, partaking of a somewhat literate culture of long standing, may compare with historically non-literate tribes nearby.

Olson (1975; Olson and Hildyard, in press) has approached the design problem in another way. Though considering the consequences of literacy in a broad cross-cultural and historical fashion, Olson has chosen to study the differences between Western — in this case, Canadian — children and adults in the drawing of implications from sentences. It is likely that the experiments can be fruitfully transposed to another cultural context in which literacy can be varied independently of age. The general conclusion of the studies is that young children do not calculate the logical implications of propositions as many adults do, but rather take sentences as potential descriptions of events about which they have knowledge and expectations. When these modes conflict, children get their inferences wrong — or so it appears to adults. If it is literacy rather than stage of development which transforms the analysis of implications, Olson expects non-literate adults to be cognitively similar to his Canadian children, and he points to Kpelle evidence from Cole *et al.* (1971) which conforms to his expectations. Neither Cole nor Olson, therefore, takes cognitive epigenesis *per se* as the basis for differences in mentality, and thus they are both somewhat at variance with Piaget and Piagetians and with any epigenetic stage theory of development.

Culture as Institutionalised Operativity

It was suggested above that literacy and schooling may have different consequences for cognitive development in different cultures; but also that the cultural differences in question depend in large part on literacy and schooling. In case this seems madly paradoxical, let me stress that there is a twofold level of analysis involved: *cultural* difference or change on the one hand, and *individual* change or development on the other. A traditional oral culture is one whose children may be cognitively transformed by schooling, in comparison with the remaining unschooled children and adults. When, however, schooling is institutionalised and literacy widespread, not only does speech take on the less context-dependent and more abstract forms of a written language, but the other social and technological changes of 'modernisation' tend to occur at the same time. Modernisation, whatever its prime movers and channels of diffusion, is an evolution of social, economic, psychological and linguistic dimensions all rolled into one. Schooling is a critical change agent for a *traditional* society not only because of its cognitive consequences but because it breaks the cultural continuity between the generations, perhaps for the first time ever. Lack of schooling and illiteracy for an individual in a *modern* society will obviously have great social consequences for that person but may no longer restrict his cognitive development in any fundamental way. For the modern world he lives in is itself a 'school' for his thought: operativity has been institutionalised in the external environment.

Institutionalised operativity confronts children in any man-made environment, *par excellence* in a modern city, and in particular in the prosthetic environment of machines, appliances and instruments. The principles – and errors – in the work of man are therefore to be inferred, in the concrete reality itself, so to speak. They are also there to be talked about, and the attention of children can be drawn to them by the explicit speech of literate adults. A modern man-made environment is both complex and diverse, and therefore presents contrasts and conflicts of understanding so as to provoke thought and explanation. Society, too – social and economic organisation – is in part the work of man; and 'pluralisation' within it (cf. Berger *et al.*, 1974) offers similar invitations to thought. Eventually, even the media of understanding themselves – language, culture, thought itself – may become objects of knowledge: the process is reflexive, and may never end. Riegel (1973) believes it may extend beyond formal operations, developmentally.

If one thinks only of individual ontogeny, one may note the common lag and the not uncommon arrest in cognitive development observed in non-literate cultures, and conclude that primitive children are first of all like Western children but that primitive adults may be no more developed intellectually than older Western children. It would, however, be a mistake. I have stressed the cultural level of institutionalised operativity in order to put the comparison into proper perspective. It is rather that, as Hallpike (1976) puts it, in primitive societies 'cognitive skills appropriate to the pre-operatory and concrete operations stages are selected for development to a very high degree of expertise' (p. 260). Thus in the artefacts and techniques of those cultures there will be little or no built-in invitation to more complex or formal modes of thought. The point is that the degree of refinement of skills based on concrete thought may surpass anything that Western children and Western adults are ordinarily capable of. This is unfortunately obscured by cross-cultural research (including all that in the Piagetian vein) which simply examines the supposedly critical indicators of developmental level. And it is doubly obscured by the cross-cultural use of standardised intelligence tests.

The most beautiful example is Trukese navigation (Gladwin, 1964, 1970). Truk is a small island in the Pacific. Gladwin and Sarason (1953) had commented on the strikingly concrete level of the thinking of the Trukese. Gladwin (1964) describes Trukese thought as a sort of *bricolage*, as relying on 'the cumulative product of the adding together of a great number of discrete bits of data, summed together in accordance with pre-determined parameters, to arrive at a desired conclusion'. Gladwin is also of the opinion that the Trukese would perform poorly on even an appropriate intelligence test; and observed that they could not master the principles required to locate a fault in an internal combustion engine which they could take apart and reassemble almost blindfold.

The Trukese, however, are very great navigators. They voyage in small canoes over astonishing distances of open ocean, without instruments and without sight of land. Destinations are tiny islands, invisible from the ocean surface unless one comes very close, i.e. unless navigation by dead reckoning is perfectly accurate. Navigation is by stars and wind direction and wave pattern. On a dark and starless night, by the sound of the waves and the feel of the boat. The navigator can accomplish feats of steering involving long and complex tacking which on theoretical grounds are possible only with advanced navigational equipment, nowadays electronic. But the Trukese does it in his head, in an automatic routine. He survives, with no need to tell the tale.

As Gladwin describes the navigation, it combines the information of a large number of discrete observations, each concrete and factual. The navigator always knows where he is in relation to every island and reef in his total ocean world. Each move is successively determined on an *ad hoc* basis. The Trukese cannot give a verbal account of all that he is doing, although he can always point to where his destination will be. The European navigator can typically give a logical account of what he is doing. But strip him of his technical aids, put him in the Trukese situation, *mutatis mutandis*, and he would almost certainly perish. His knowledge is another ocean, and he too would probably perish. His knowledge is contingent, and the contingencies would differ.

Allow the European his techniques and instruments, however, and he could do the job. He uses deductive principles which are highly abstract and will thus serve him anywhere. This is not to say, none the less, that the European navigator himself necessarily has those abstract principles firmly sedimented in his own head. It is likely that he understands them to some extent through his navigational training and by his experience of their use. But he need not (cf. driving a car). He too could be a concrete thinker *vis-à-vis* navigation, and vastly inferior as such to the Trukese. For formal operativity is built into his techniques and instruments, and he need only know how to use them, mechanically. The scientific culture which lies behind him has taken care of formal thought: *somebody* has had to understand fully those abstract principles and their implementation in planning and monitoring navigation. This is institutionalised operativity.

Piaget (1971, pp. 116-17) criticises Lévi-Strauss for his assumption, in *The Savage Mind*, that the 'logic' of social and cultural institutions in a given society gauges the logical level of its members' thought. Kinship systems and language structures, however complex, are the products of cultural and sometimes biological evolution, not of the creative thought of individuals. They depend on institutions, and their power surpasses the resource of individuals:

> the real problem is to make out how the ensemble of these collective instruments is utilised in the everyday reasoning of each individual. It may very well be that these instruments are of a level visibly superior to that of Western logic — Lévi-Strauss reminds us that there are plenty of natives who can 'calculate' the implicit relations of a kinship system exactly. But the kinship systems are finished systems, already regulated, and of limited scope. What we want to know about is individual inventions. [Piaget, 1971, p. 117]

Beginnings have now been made, as if in accord with Piaget's advice, in studying the development in children of an understanding of kinship systems (in Nigeria — Levine and Price-Williams, 1974) and of dreams (Schweder and Levine, 1976). A remarkable (if poorly documented) study by Kohlberg (1969) may represent the extreme case in which culture not only arrests but may dissipate or even reverse the ontogenetic course of development. Kohlberg investigated the dream concept among the Atayal, a Formosan aboriginal people. He found that the dream concept develops in Atayal children exactly as for Genevan children studied by Piaget. That is, the child first of all conceives of dreams as real and coming from outside himself; but by middle childhood he has come to think of dreams as unreal and internally generated. However, by late childhood or early adolescence the Atayal are introduced to the fundamental lore of the society: this is a 'dream culture', taking dreams as of great significance and viewing them as real and externally generated. Thus the child, in preparing to be an Atayal adult, has to learn what he has 'grown out of'. It seems plausible that his conceptions of reality and causality are perturbed by this cultural learning, and Kohlberg reports that conservation responses become uncertain as Atayal children are initiated into the dream culture. The report of this research is very sketchy, and this is most unfortunate: for it relates not only to my present concern to distinguish the operativity of cultural institutions from the developmental level of individual cognition; it could also provide a rare and dramatic test of a problematic aspect of Piagetian theory, that of the role of 'learning' as opposed to 'development'.

There is no need to restrict the point of Piaget's comments on Lévi-Strauss to primitive or traditional cultures. As is often said, most thought of individuals in modern, Western society is not particularly abstract or principled. As with the example of modern navigation above, this can easily be so when the techniques utilised and thus the total operation conducted incorporate formal, abstract principles. When it comes to dealing with people and managing social relations (the human sciences being what they are) modern Western thought is probably comparable with that of Trukese navigation — at its very best, a refined *bricolage* of discrete adhocisms. 'Bureaucracy' is one institutional attempt to transcend incompetence in the social sphere: bureaucrats need not (but can) grasp the principles of bureaucratic organisation.

Modern culture, however, is by definition different from primitive culture. Somebody has had to formulate the abstract principles, others have tested, accepted and refined them, others have implemented and maintained them in institutional operativity. And of course, most principles will be rejected as wrong — formal thought is no guarantee of validity or utility. Formal thought is going on somewhere all the time, and to a noticeable minority it is a vocation. The principles are taught to children, and some of it sticks. And the man-made environment in all its aspects is both concrete fact and semiotic invitation to the principles of its creation and functioning.

In this way modern society lifts itself by its own bootstraps. The process is epigenetic and evolutionary, involving both the cognitive evolution of the child and adult and the historical evolution of the culture. It is not that ontogeny recapitulates phylogeny — that seductive error has long been exposed. It is rather that individual ontogeny and cultural phylogeny stimulate and partake of each other: the institutionalised operativity of culture both enhances and is enhanced by the level of cognitive development of individuals. This complex conception of the dynamic interdependence of the changing individual and a changing society is extensively discussed and illustrated by Riegel (1975, 1976). There have been many precursors, including Luria and Vygotsky (1930), who, before organising their expedition to Central Asia, published a monograph, *Essays in the History of Behaviour*, arguing parallels and connections between their psychological principles of individual development and the process of sociocultural development.

Epigenetic evolution, of course, is not necessarily 'progress'; or, at any rate, it is so only by the tautological yardstick of its own developmental progression. An example comes from the study of word associations: this began early in experimental psychology, and systematic changes in word association norms of American adults are analysed by Jenkins and Russell (1960) for 1910-52, and for children, 1916-63, by Koff (1965). In brief summary, the historical change in word associations over this period was in the direction of 'maturity' — maturity being objectively defined by age differences in the earliest studies. The conclusion that Americans have grown more mature in their thinking is tempered, however, by further inspection of the kinds of associations involved. This 'maturity' contained more automatic, stereotyped responses and fewer associations based on logical connections. Progress indeed!

Concluding Remarks

It was emphasised at the outset that the survey and discussion presented here are an interim stocktaking and by no means a final account. That of course must always be the case; for science and scholarship flow on submerging those who pronounce on their contemporary state. Physicists are unlikely ever again to err as they did in the nineteenth century by considering physics to be virtually a finished enterprise, little more than a mopping-up job. Psychologists and social scientists are only too well aware that their reach exceeds their grasp; and with this topic, culture and cognitive development, one can even feel that the ground is moving under one's feet. The fields I have spanned above are all moving fast. Cross-cultural work is expanding exponentially. So is the study of cognition and language in child development; and the impact of psycho-linguistic and socio-linguistic approaches on the cross-cultural field is due to be felt. Literacy is being studied as I write, and present efforts are just beginnings. Conceptions of primitive and modern mentalities are no longer shunned as ethnocentric. The idea of 'culture' is perhaps coming to be articulated in a way that makes sense for psychologists; and the tricky problem of relating individual development and cultural-historical change or evolution is being addressed.

Research to date indicates a remarkable correspondence across cultures in cognitive development in infancy and early childhood. From middle childhood on, variations become manifest in three important respects. First, qualitative similarities across cultures are no longer so clear-cut. Second, non-Western children appear frequently to lag behind Western children in so far as the same qualitative sequence of development can be observed. Third, there is reason to believe that literacy and formal schooling may powerfully affect the development of children's thought. I would add that if literacy and schooling turn out to be as important as certain psychologists (Cole, Scribner, Olson) and anthropologists (Goody,

Hallpike) persuasively hold them to be, Piaget's basically epigenetic conception of cognitive growth will have to be modified. I have also suggested, however, that literacy, schooling and the other trappings of modernity do not operate simply as the 'independent variables' beloved of psychologists reared on experimental designs. Individual ontogeny and cultural change are to some extent in dialectical relation each with the other, and a culture may include forms of institutionalised operativity the effects of which mimic and therefore render partially dispensible the direct impact of schooling and literacy on the cognition of the individual child and adult. This last is my most tentative suggestion, and may be taken with pinches of salt.

All in all, it appears likely that cognitive development can *potentially* be much the same in all cultures, both in its processes and its products. If there are inherent biological differences, such as in colour vision or in African infant motor precocity, they operate to a tiny or negligible extent in influencing the course of cognitive growth. Cultural differences, for example, in schooling and in the institutionalisation of operativity in the man-made world, are obviously the important influences. With modernisation (however desirable or undesirable it may be), cognitive development in all cultures is likely eventually to follow the same course at much the same rate. Lévi-Strauss' vision of a single world culture will then be well on the way to fulfilment. If people react to the prospect of homogenisation, as I suspect they will, by increasingly setting up communities and subcultures deliberately to foster chosen cultural and personal ideals, there may then be great variation in what people know and how they behave, but little variation in the process of knowing and the development of that process.

References

Asch, S.E. (1958), 'The metaphor: a psychological inquiry', in R. Tagiuri and L. Petrullo (eds.), *Person Perception and Interpersonal Behaviour*. Stanford, California: Stanford University Press.

Berger, P.L., Berger, B. and Kellner, H. (1974), *The Homeless Mind*. Harmondsworth: Penguin.

Berlin, B. (1972), 'Speculations on the growth of ethnobotanical nomenclature', *Language in Society, 1*, 51-86.

Berlin, B., Breedlove, D.E. and Raven, P.H. (1966), 'Folk taxonomies and biological classification', *Science, 154*, 273-5.

Berlin, B., Breedlove, D.E. and Raven, P.H. (1973), 'General principles of classification and nomenclature in folk biology', *American Anthropologist, 75*, 214-42.

Berlin, B. and Kay, P. (1969), *Basic Colour Terms: Their Universality and Evolution*. Berkeley: Univ. of California Press.

Bernstein, B.B. (1961), 'Social structure, language and learning', *Educational Research, 3*, 163-76.

Boas, F. (1911; revised edn, 1935), *The Mind of Primitive Man*. London: Macmillan.

Bornstein, M.H. (1973), 'Colour vision and colour naming: a psycho-physiological hypothesis of cultural difference', *Psychological Bulletin, 80*, 257-85.

Bowerman, M. (1973), *Early Syntactic Development: A Cross-Linguistic Study with Special Reference to Finnish*. London and New York: Cambridge University Press.

Brown, R. (1958), *Words and Things*. New York: The Free Press.

Brown, R., Black, A.H. and Horowitz, A.E. (1955), 'Phonetic symbolism in natural language', *Journal of Abnormal and Social Psychology, 50*, 388-93.

Bruner, J.S. (1965), 'The growth of mind', *American Psychologist, 20*, 1007-17.

Bruner, J.S., Olver, R. and Greenfield, P.M. (eds.) (1966), *Studies in Cognitive Growth*. New York: Wiley.

Bruner, J.S. (1966), 'On cognitive growth 2', in Bruner *et al.*

Chomsky, N. (1968), *Language and Mind*. New York: Harcourt.

Cole, M. and Bruner, J.S. (1971), 'Cultural differences and inferences about psychological processes', *American Psychologist, 26*, 867-76.

Cole, M., Gay, J.H., Glick, J.A. and Sharp, D. (1971), *The Cultural Context of Learning and Thinking*. London: Methuen.

Cole, M. and Scribner, S. (1974), *Culture and Thought: A Psychological Introduction*. Wiley.

D'Andrade, R.G. and Egan, M. (1974), 'The colours of emotion', *American Ethnologist, 1*.

Dasen, P.R. (1972), 'Cross-cultural Piagetian research: a summary', *Journal of Cross-Cultural Psychology, 3*, 23-39.

Dasen, P.R. (1973), *Canadian Psychologist, 14*, 149-66.

Dasen, P.R. (1977), 'Are cognitive processes universal? A constribution to cross-cultural Piagetian psychology', in N. Warren (ed.), *Studies in Cross-Cultural Psychology*, vol. 1. London and New York: Academic Press.

Eysenck, H.J. (1971), *Race, Intelligence and Education*. London: Temple Smith.

Ferguson, C.A. and Slobin, D.I. (eds.) (1973), *Studies of Child Language Development*. New York: Holt.

Gay, J., Lloyd, B.B. and Bruner, J.S. (eds.) (in press), *Psychological Universals in Africa*.

Gellner, E. (1973), 'The savage and the modern mind', in R. Horton and R. Finnegan (eds.), *Modes of Thought*. London: Faber.

Gladwin, T. (1964), 'Cultural and logical process', in W.H. Goodenough (ed.), *Explorations in Cultural Anthropology*. New York: McGraw-Hill.

Gladwin, T. (1970), *East is a Big Bird*. Cambridge, Massachusetts: Harvard University Press.

Gladwin, T. and Sarason, S.B. (1953), *Truk: Man in Paradise*. New York: Wenner-Gren Foundation.

Glick, J.A. (1975), 'Cognitive development in cross-cultural perspective', in E.M. Hetherington *et al.* (eds.), *Review of Child Development Research*, vol. 4. Chicago: Univ. of Chicago Press.

Goodnow, J.J. (1962), 'A test of milieu effects with some of Piaget's tasks', *Psychological Monographs, 76* (36), whole no. 555.

Goodnow, J.J. (1969), 'Cultural variations in cognitive skills', in D.R. Price-Williams (ed.), *Cross-Cultural Studies*. Harmondsworth: Penguin. (Also in *Cognitive Studies*, vol. 1.)

Goodnow, J.J. and Bethon, G. (1966), 'Piaget's tasks: the effects of schooling and intelligence', *Child Development, 37*, 573-82.

Goody, J. (ed.) (1968), *Literacy in Traditional Societies*. Cambridge: Cambridge

University Press.

Goody, J. and Watt, I. (1962), 'The consequences of literacy', *Comparative Studies in Society and History, 5*, 304-45.

Greenberg, J. (1966), *Universals of Language*. 2nd edn. Cambridge, Massachusetts: MIT Press.

Greenfield, P.M. (1972), 'Oral or written language', *Language and Speech, 15*, 169-78.

Greenfield, P.M. and Bruner, J.S. (1966), 'Culture and cognitive growth', *International Journal of Psychology, 1*, 89-107.

Greenfield, P.M. and Bruner, J.S. (1969), 'Culture and cognitive growth', in D.A. Goslin (ed.), *Handbook of Socialisation Theory and Research*. New York: Rand McNally.

Hallpike, C.R. (1976), 'Is there a Primitive Mentality?', *Man, 11*, 253-70.

Hess, R.D. and Shipman, V. (1965), 'Early experience and the socialisation of cognitive modes in children', *Child Development, 36*, 869-86.

Holtzman, W.H., Diaz-Guerrero, R. and Swartz, J.D. (1975), *Personality Development in Two Cultures: a Cross-Cultural Longitudinal Study of School Children in Mexico and the US*. Mexico: University of Texas Press.

Horton, R. (1967), 'African traditional thought and Western science', Part I: *Africa, 37*, 50-71; Part II, *37*, 155-87.

Illich, I.D. (1971), *Deschooling Society*. London: Calder and Boyars.

Inhelder, B. and Piaget, J. (1958), *The Growth of Logical Thinking from Childhood to Adolescence*. London: Routledge and Kegan Paul.

Irvine, S.H. (1969), 'Factor analysis of African abilities and attainments: constructs across cultures', *Psychological Bulletin, 71*, 20-32.

Jenkins, J. and Russell, W.A. (1960), 'Systematic changes in word association norms: 1910-1952', *Journal of Abnormal and Social Psychology, 60*, 293-304.

Jensen, A.R. (1969), 'How much can we boost IQ and scholastic achievement?', *Harvard Educational Review, 39*, 1-123.

Jensen, A.R. (1973), *Educability and Group Differences*. London: Methuen.

Koff, R.H. (1965), 'Systematic changes in children's word association norms, 1916-1963', *Child Development, 36*, 299-305.

Kohlberg, L. (1969), 'Stage and sequence: the cognitive-developmental approach to socialisation', in D.S. Goslin (ed.), *Handbook of Socialisation Theory and Research*. New York: Rand McNally.

Konner, M.J. (1972), 'Aspects of the developmental ethology of a foraging people', in N.G. Blurton-Jones (ed.), *Ethological Studies of Child Behaviour*. London: Cambridge University Press.

Levine, R.A. and Price-Williams, D.R. (1974), 'Children's kinship concepts: cognitive development and early experience among the Hausa', *Ethnology, 13*, 25-44.

Lévi-Strauss, C. (1966), *The Savage Mind*. London: Weidenfeld and Nicolson.

Luria, A.R. (1971), 'Towards the problem of the historical nature of psychological processes', *International Journal of Psychology, 6*, 259-72.

Luria, A.R. (1976), *Cognitive Development*. Cambridge, Massachusetts: Harvard University Press.

Luria, A.R. and Vygotsky, L.S. (1930), *Essays in the History of Behaviour* (untranslated from the Russian; mentioned in M. Cole's introduction to Luria, (1976).

Massé, G. (1969), *Croissance et Développement de l'Enfant en Dakar*. Paris: Centre Internationale de l'Enfance.

Meehl, P.L. (1967), 'Theory-testing in psychology and physics: a methodological paradox', *Philosophy of Science, 34*, 103-15.

Mermelstein, E. and Schulman, L.S. (1967), 'Lack of formal schooling and the acquisition of conservation', *Child Development, 38*, 39-52.

Miller, G.A. (1970), 'Linguistic communication as a biological process', Herbert Spencer Lecture, Oxford University, 13 November 1970. Cited by Cole and Scribner (1974).

Moreigne, F. and Senecal, J. (1962), 'Résultats d'un groupe d'enfants africains au Terman-Merrill', *Revue de Psychologie Appliquée, 12*, 15-32.

Olson, D.R. (1975), 'The language of experience: on natural language and formal education', *Bulletin of the British Psychological Society, 28*, 263-73.

Olson, D.R. and Hildyard, A. (in press), 'Literacy and the specialisation of language', in N. Warren (ed.), *Studies in Cross-Cultural Psychology*, vol. 2. London and New York: Academic Press.

Osgood, C.E. (1962), 'Studies on the generality of affective meaning systems', *American Psychologist, 17*, 10-28.

Osgood, C.E., May, W.H. and Miron, M.S. (1975), *Cross-Cultural Universals of Affective Meaning*. University of Illinois Press.

Piaget, J. (1966), 'Nécessité et signification des recherches comparatives en psychologie génétique', *International Journal of Psychology, 1*, 3-13.

Piaget, J. (1971), *Structuralism*. London: Routledge and Kegan Paul.

Price-Williams, D.R. (1961), 'A study concerning concepts of conservation of quantities among primitive children', *Acta Psychologica, 18*, 297-305.

Price-Williams, D.R. (1975), 'Primitive mentality – civilised style', in R. Brislin, S. Bochner and W. Lonner (eds.), *Cross-Cultural Perspectives on Learning*. Sage Publications.

Price-Williams, D.R. (1976), 'Cross-cultural differences in cognitive development', in V. Hamilton and M.D. Vernon (eds.), *The Development of Cognitive Processes*. London and New York: Academic Press.

Riegel, K.F. (1973), 'Dialectic operations: the final period of cognitive development', *Human Development, 16*, 346-70.

Riegel, K.F. (1975), 'From traits and equilibrium towards developmental dialectic', in W.J. Arnold (ed.), *Nebraska Symposium on Motivation 1975*, Univ. of Nebraska Press.

Riegel, K.F. (1976), *The Psychology of Development and History*. Plenum Press.

Rosch, E. (1975), 'Universals and cultural specifics in human categorisation', in R. Brislin, S. Bochner, and W. Lonner (eds.), *Cross-Cultural Perspectives on Learning*. Sage Publications.

Rosch, E. (1977), 'Human categorisation', in N. Warren (ed.), *Studies in Cross-Cultural Psychology*, vol. 1. London and New York: Academic Press.

Sanches, M. and Blount, B.G. (eds.) (1975), *Sociocultural Dimensions of Language Use*. London and New York: Academic Press.

Scribner, S. and Cole, M. (1977), 'Unpackaging literacy'. Paper presented to the National Institute of Education Conference on Writing, June 1977.

Shweder, R.A. and Levine, R.A. (1976), 'Dream concepts of Hausa children', in T. Schwartz (ed.), *Socialisation as Cultural Communication*. Berkeley: University of California Press.

Slobin, D.I. (1971), *Psycholinguistics*. Glenview, Illinois: Scott Foresman.

Smilansky, S., Shephatia, L. and Frenkel, E. (1976), *Mental Development of Infants from Two Ethnic Groups*. Research report no. 195, Henrietta Szold Institute, Jerusalem, Israel.

Super, C. (1975), 'Environmental effects on motor development: the case of African infant precocity'. Paper presented to American Academy for Cerebral Palsy, New Orleans.

Vernon, P.E. (1969), *Intelligence and Cultural Environment*. London: Methuen.

Warren, N. (1972), 'African infant precocity', *Psychological Bulletin, 78*, 353-67.

Warren, N. (1973), 'African infancy in psychological perspective'. Invited paper for the Burg Wartenstein Symposium on *Cultural and Social Influences in Infancy and*

Early Childhood.

Warren, N. and Parkin, J.M. (1974), 'A neurological and behavioural comparison of African and European newborns in Uganda', *Child Development, 45*, 966-71.

Webb, A. (1977), *The Psychic Unity of Mankind*. BA Honours Dissertation, University of Sussex.

Werner, E. (1972), 'Infants around the world: Cross-cultural studies of psychomotor development from birth to two years', *Journal of Cross-Cultural Psychology, 3*, 111-34.

Werner, H. (1940), *The Comparative Psychology of Mental Development*. New York: Follett.

SECTION TWO: PERCEPTUAL ABILITIES

Introduction

From the preceding considerations of cultural setting, this section turns to the abilities that the infant brings to the initial stages of cognitive development. This is a field in which great advances have been made in recent years, mainly through the invention and discovery of powerful new experimental techniques. Most research has concentrated on the visual and auditory senses, and the papers in this section deal with this.

Harry McGurk's review of the visual perception research picks out the main developments in this area, showing how judicious choice of stimuli displays and careful observation of infants' gaze direction has added greatly to what we know of the world as an infant sees it. Philip Morse reviews another intriguing area: that of the perception of speech and speech-like sounds. This area has recently created a great deal of interest, as it is beginning to look as if infants are born with a very specific perceptual mechanism for dealing with speech, that is unlike that used for other sounds. Here again, it is a new experimental technique that has produced the breakthrough. The final paper, a brief research report by Laurent Demany *et al.* supplements the previous review by presenting persuasive evidence that the perception of rhythm, which is highly relevant to speech-perception, is also apparently well-developed very soon after birth.

7 VISUAL PERCEPTION IN YOUNG INFANTS

Harry McGurk

Source: B. Foss (ed.), *New Perspectives in Child Development* (Penguin Modern Psychology, 1974), pp. 11-29. Copyright © Brian Foss and Contributors, 1974. Reprinted by permission of Penguin Book Ltd.

The Infant's Visual System

At birth, the human eye is about half the size and weight of that of the mature adult (Mann, 1964). The infant eye is anatomically identical to the adult eye in that all the parts are there, but the relation of the parts to each other is different from that in adulthood, and not all parts develop at the same rate; for example, at birth the cornea is much closer to its final developmental status than is the iris. The retina — the light sensitive surface at the back of the eye — is fairly well developed at birth. At one time it was thought that the retina of the human newborn was sensitive only to changes in the brightness and intensity of light and not to changes in colour. However, recent anatomical and physiological evidence has demonstrated this view to be mistaken. Horsten and Winkelman (1962, 1964; Winkelman and Horsten, 1962) found that rods and cones were clearly differentiated in the retina of the human foetus from the seventh month of gestation (rods are sufficient for the mediation of brightness differences or for so-called scotopic vision, but cones are essential for colour, or so-called photopic vision). Moreover, the same investigators observed that electroretinographic[†] (ERG) recordings from human newborns contained the same photopic and scotopic components as are observed in the ERG records of human adults. This is not to say that no retinal development occurs after birth. For example, the macula, the small yellow area in the centre of the retina which contains the fovea and which, in adults, is the area of clearest vision, is only partially developed at birth. Fovea and macula are structurally differentiated by about four months, but macular development continues into early childhood. However, the systems which mediate brightness and colour vision both appear to be functional at birth.

The optic tract — the bundle of nerve fibres which carry impulses from the retina to the visual centre of the brain — is partially myelinated at birth. In the process of myelinization, a protective sheath grows around the axon of the nerve cell. This sheath serves to insulate the axon from surrounding tissue and enhances its conductivity. In the absence of myelinization, conductivity of the nerve fibres is considerably reduced and

111

electrical activity disperses to surrounding tissue. Myelinization of the optic tract is essential for effective vision, for without the myelin sheath it is probable that the organism may be capable of experiencing only diffuse flashes of light. Compared with adults, however, the myelin sheath around the optic tract of the human newborn is relatively thin. If brief flashes of light are presented to the human eye, changes occur in the pattern of electrical activity, recorded by means of surface electrodes, at the occipital region of the cortex. These changes are called evoked responses. In newborns, the latency between actual presentation of the flash of light, and the occurrence of the evoked response, is longer than is the case with adults (Hrbek and Mares, 1964a, 1964b). Conductivity in the adult optic tract is enhanced by its thicker myelin sheath. Accordingly, information from eye to brain is transmitted relatively more rapidly in adults than in newborns. Myelinization of the infant's visual fibres is almost complete by about four months of age.

It would appear, therefore, that anatomically and physiologically, the visual system of the human infant, although immature, is in a functional state at birth and is capable of responding to stimulation. Thus, a necessary condition for extracting information from the environment is fulfilled. But it is not a sufficient condition. In order for there to be efficient extraction of environmental information, the organism has to be capable of simultaneously orienting both eyes towards the source of stimulation, of focusing upon that source, of resolving the detail of the stimulus, of controlling the amount of light entering his eyes, of making compensatory eye movements for any movement of the stimulus. These are all adjustments which the mature adult achieves spontaneously. It is towards their development in infancy that we now turn.

Ocular Control in Infancy

It has long been known that from the earliest days of life the human infant is capable of making gross postural movements of the head both to avoid excessively bright visual stimuli and to bring into view light stimuli of lower intensity (Preyer, 1888). Early investigators (Sherman, Sherman and Flory, 1936) were also able to establish that the pupillary reflex – the mechanism which regulates the amount of light entering the eye under conditions of variable brightness – was functional from shortly after birth and matured rapidly during the first few weeks of life.

Thus, the young infant seems capable of making gross orientations towards a source of visual stimulation and of controlling the amount of light entering his eyes from that source. The question arises, however, as to whether the infant is capable of simultaneously orienting both eyes towards the same stimulus source. Such convergence is necessary if clear vision is to result. Otherwise each eye would obtain different images, a rather confusing state of affairs, to say the least. Moreover, if the stimulus source moves, then, for clear vision to be maintained, both eyes must move together, must move conjugately, to keep the stimulus in view. Hershenson (1965) has demonstrated that convergence occurs from as early as two days in the human infant. He photographed his subject's eyes whenever it was deemed that one eye was directed towards a target stimulus. A record of the corneal reflections of the target was thus obtained and when the reflections from the cornea of the observed eye were compared with those of the unobserved eye, an almost complete overlap was obtained. This could only have occurred if both eyes had converged on the same point. Hershenson, who employed pairs of stationary targets, also observed that the newborn's eyes moved conjugately from one target to another. Evidence for conjugate tracking of a moving target has been reported by Dayton and his colleagues (Dayton and Jones, 1964; Dayton, Jones, Steele and Rose, 1964). Although such tracking was relatively inefficient at birth and involved much back-tracking, there was marked improvement during the first three months of life.

In order to focus upon targets at different distances, the lens of the human eye bends and changes shape, thus accommodating to differences in distance. The development of accommodation of the lens has been investigated by Haynes, White and Held (1965). They employed a technique called dynamic retinoscopy. Under this procedure a sharply focused spot of light is projected into the subject's eye from different distances, through the pupillary opening. Modifications in the reflected image, quantitatively assessed by lenses of known power, are employed as an index of the refractive state of the eye. The principal finding was that at birth the human eye operates much like a fixed-focus camera and no accommodation of the lens occurs to targets presented at different distances. The ideal focal distance for the newborn is around eight inches. Stimuli presented at greater or lesser distances result in blurred retinal images. This state of affairs persists for the first few weeks of life. Thereafter there is a rapid period of development in the accommodative power of the lens and by four months accommodation in the infant is comparable to that in adult subjects.

Two techniques have been employed to study the acuity of the infant's visual system. One of these involves a reflexive response known as optokinetic nystagmus (OKN). If a stimulus of black and white stripes is placed in front of the visual field and the eyes are fixated on the stimulus then, if the stimulus is moved, the eyes deflect in the direction of movement as if in compensation. Such reflexive following is evident from birth onwards. Employing this reflex, infant visual acuity has been studied by Gorman, Cogan and Gellis (1957). Stimuli comprising stripes of various widths are presented to infant subjects and it is noted which elicit OKN and which do not. It is reasoned that striped stimuli which do not elicit OKN cannot be discriminated by the subject. Using this technique, Gorman *et al.* concluded that newborn infants could discriminate stripes which subtended about thirty-three minutes of visual arc.[1]

Fantz and his colleagues have used a different technique to study visual acuity in infancy (Fantz, 1966; Fantz, Ordy and Udelf, 1962). They objected that reflexive following of a moving pattern, which is under neural control, may yield a misleading picture of infant acuity compared with that when visual exploration is under voluntary control. Accordingly, they presented their subjects with pairs of stimuli one of which was always a plain grey while the other was composed of black and white stripes of equal overall brightness. They had previously observed that infants preferred to look at a patterned stimulus than at a plain one. The stripes, and the spaces between them, varied systematically across stimulus pairs and it was reasoned that as long as the infants could discriminate the stripes from the background, they would look more at the striped (i.e. patterned) stimulus than at the plain grey one. Whenever the stripes become so thin as not to be resolved then, of course, the striped stimulus would be indistinguishable from the grey one and both should be fixated equally. In this way Fantz established that infants of less than one month could resolve stripes one eighth of an inch in thickness at a distance of ten inches. Now, this is equivalent to a visual angle of about forty minutes of arc and this bears close correspondence to the data reported by Gorman *et al.* Fantz further observed that by two months or so infants could resolve stripes of only twenty minutes of arc and by six months they could discriminate stripes of one sixty-fourth of an inch, a visual angle of only ten minutes.

The picture, then, that emerges from our discussion so far is one wherein the young infant is seen to have a visual system which is anatomically and physiologically intact and which, though quite immature by adult standards, fulfils the necessary conditions for the mediation of sensory information. We have seen, too, that the infant, from his earliest days, is able to orient towards a source of visual stimulation, has the necessary muscular control to converge upon a stimulus and to maintain his image of the stimulus even when it is moving, and can do this with both eyes in a coordinated fashion. His accommodative capacity, although initially limited, rapidly improves, as does his ability to resolve increasingly fine detail. In short, from a relatively early stage, the infant is endowed with a visual apparatus which is in good working order and although much development remains to take place, he has the potential to embark on a visual voyage of discovery of the world around him. We now turn to a consideration of what he does with that potential and to a discussion of the nature of the visual world in which the young infant lives.

Perceptual Discrimination in Infancy

Many of the techniques currently used to investigate the perceptual ability of the human infant have been developed only relatively recently; for example, those employed by Winkelman and Horsten (1962) and by Hershenson (1965) require fairly sophisticated electronic and photographic apparatus not readily available to earlier generations of researchers. Much of what was accepted as fact in an earlier era was based on casual observation and anecdotal report, and such reports tended to stress the immaturity and insensitivity of the infant's visual system. James' (1890) description of the infant's condition as being 'assailed by eyes, ears, nose, skin and entrails at once', feeling it all as 'one great blooming, buzzing confusion' was a persuasive and widely accepted one. The infant was largely regarded as a relatively insensitive organism who had to grow up before he became worthy of serious investigation. A few developmental studies of infant perception were undertaken but such studies were the exception rather than the rule and studies of perceptual development in infancy were relatively few and far between. For example, in a review of *developmental* studies of perception by Wohlwill (1960) covering the period from about 1900 to 1959, fewer than 10 per cent of the 170 or so references cited involved subjects younger than two years.

Since the mid-fifties and early sixties there has been an upsurge in the study of the perceptual world of the infant. For example, an extensive investigation of infant responsiveness to facial and face-like stimuli was carried out by Ahrens (1954). The stimuli which he presented to his subjects included various dot and angle arrangements drawn on round and oval contours, a crossbar on an oval contour, partial and complete drawings of faces, and 3D facial models, as well as actual, live faces. A most interesting finding concerned the amount of facial detail required to elicit smiling from infants at different ages. At six weeks, for example, a crude, two-dot representation of the eyes was most effective; contour was unimportant. Between six weeks and three months, the eye-like pattern was still most effective, but realistic as opposed to schematic representation became important with increasing age. By four months of age, the presence of eyes was still necessary to elicit smiling, but was no longer sufficient; now other facial detail, such as nose and mouth, had to be present, though subjects may not have fixated these directly. At this age also, an actual, live face was most effective in eliciting smiling, followed by a realistic facial drawing, followed, in turn, by a schematic drawing of a face.

Ahrens' work establishes that the eyes are the most salient facial feature for the young infant. Just why this should be the case is not immediately obvious. That the eyes are also a primary focus of attention for older subjects is probably attributable, at least in part, to their mobility. However, Ahrens found that immobile, schematic representations of the eyes were most efficient in eliciting smiling during the beginning months of life. It may be that, as others have suggested, the eyes serve as an innate releasing mechanism (IRM) for the smiling response during early infancy.

Much of the increased interest in the study of infant perception since the mid-fifties is attributable in no small measure to the work of Fantz (1958, 1961). Fantz's procedure was elegantly simple and was one which overcame an earlier reluctance to use infants as experimental subjects due to their limited response repertoire. He was interested in determining the age at which infants first became capable of form and pattern discrimination and reasoned that if a subject looked significantly longer at one than at the other of two forms or patterns, then this could be regarded as evidence that the subject was discriminating between the two stimuli in terms of the dimension in which they differed. Accordingly, he presented his infant subjects, aged between one and fifteen weeks, with pairs of stimuli and recorded how long they spent fixating each member of the pair. The babies lay on their backs within an observation chamber and the stimuli were presented from above. Through a peep-hole in the roof of the chamber the experimenter could observe which stimulus the subject was fixating, such fixation being reflected in an image of the stimulus from off the cornea, above the pupil. By such means Fantz was able to demonstrate that from an early age infants looked longer at circular bull's eyes than at striped squares, more at checkered squares than at plain squares and so on. Thus, he concluded that infants could perceive both form and pattern and that there was an innate preference for complex as opposed to simple stimuli. The procedure employed by Fantz became known as the spontaneous visual preference technique and, as we have already seen, it was later used in a study of infant visual acuity (Fantz, Ordy and Udelf, 1962). The procedure was also employed to demonstrate an early preference for 3D over 2D stimuli of equivalent shape (Fantz, 1961).

One of the more dramatic findings reported by Fantz (1961) concerned what appeared to be an innate preference for facedness in human infants.

Subjects between four days and six months were presented with all possible pairs from the following three stimuli:

1 a schematic representation of a human face, with the features drawn in black on a pink background;
2 a form with the same detail as in 1 but with the facial features randomly scrambled;
3 a similar form to the two others but with a solid patch of black at the top equal in area to that occupied by the features in the other two stimuli.

Fantz reported that at all age levels infants looked more at the 'real' face than at the 'scrambled face' and largely ignored the control pattern. Although the differences in preference between the 'real' and 'scrambled' faces were slight, Fantz suggested that the results indicated a primitive, unlearned preference for facedness in human infants. Fantz regarded such preference as an important precursor of later social responsiveness.

Subsequent investigators have not always been able to replicate the results reported by Fantz in his early studies. This is especially true of his finding of a preference for facial stimuli among very young infants. For example, Hershenson (1965) presented newborn infants with all possible pairs of three stimuli, one depicting a female face and the others representing lesser degrees of organization of the same face: a 'distorted' face retained the outline of head and hair but altered the position of other features, and a 'scrambled' face altered the facial contour in addition to scrambling the features. Hershenson reported that the three stimuli did not elicit differential responding. Koopman and Ames (1968) argued that, in the original Fantz (1961) study, infants may have been responding to the symmetry of the realistic face rather than to its facedness *per se*. Accordingly, they presented ten-week-old babies with all possible pairs from a realistic face, an asymmetrical scrambled face, and a scrambled face in which the features, though wrongly located, were symmetrically distributed about the vertical axis. No differences were observed between looking times for the three stimuli. In a further experiment, in which only the realistic and asymmetrically scrambled faces were compared, negative results were again obtained. Wilcox (1969) also found no differences between infant responsiveness to realistic and scrambled facial stimuli in subjects between four and sixteen weeks of age. At sixteen weeks, however, infants manifested a preference for a photograph of a female face over a realistic facial drawing. A well-conducted study by Haaf and Bell (1967) also demonstrated that four-month-old infants show a distinct preference for more face-like over less face-like stimuli. These authors presented their subjects with all possible pairs from four stimuli which were ordered in their degree of facedness. Infants fixated most on the most face-like stimulus, least on the least face-like, with the other two placed intermediate in terms of their facedness. Although earlier, the Haaf and Bell study was methodologically superior to the one by Wilcox in that the former included a control for complexity. In the Wilcox study the more realistic photograph may also have been the more complex stimulus and could have been preferred on this basis (see below).

It is important to note that in the studies by Hershenson (1965), Koopman and Ames (1968) and Wilcox (1969), all of which yielded negative results concerning young infants' preferences for more face-like as opposed to less face-like stimuli, the conclusion to be drawn is *not* that these subjects could not *discriminate* between the various stimuli, but rather that they showed no *preference* for one stimulus over another. This is an important distinction and one which serves to draw attention to a frequently remarked weakness in the spontaneous visual preference procedure employed by Fantz and his colleagues. The spontaneous preference procedure affords data which can be unambiguously interpreted only when significant differences are observed between duration of fixations upon the two stimuli. In the absence of such differences, though the conclusion that the subject has failed to manifest a *preference* for one stimulus over the other may be justified, one is not entitled to conclude that the subject does not *perceive* differences between them. Such differences may be discriminated but the subject not care enough about them to look at one stimulus more than the other. For example, employing the visual preference procedure, Fantz (1958) reported no preference among three-month-old babies for a circle as against a cross, or vice versa. However, Saayman, Ames and Moffett (1964) firstly presented subjects of the same age with a circle (or a cross) for a relatively prolonged familiarization period, before presenting both forms together. It was recorded whether subjects now attended more to the familiar or to the novel stimulus, regardless of its form. Results indicated that three month olds could discriminate circles from crosses, a conclusion which could not be reached on the basis of the Fantz (1958) data. Thus, by itself, the spontaneous visual preference procedure may be a relatively insensitive one for assessing infant capacity to discriminate perceptually between stimuli.

A further problem which confronts the researcher who employs the spontaneous preference procedure is that of controlling adequately for infant position preferences. When exposed to two stimuli, one to the right and one to the left, many infants have a tendency to look more to one side than to the other. It is easy to see how such a tendency, if not controlled for in the experimental design, might have a confounding influence on experimental results. The usual control is to present each pair of stimuli twice and to reverse the relative positions of the two stimuli on each presentation. Duration of fixation to each member of the pair is then summed across the two presentations. Thus, a subject who looked only to the right during both presentations would receive the same score for each number of the pair of stimuli and that is how it should be, for he had shown no stimulus preference, only a position preference. However, Watson (1965) has argued that this procedure may be a counter-productive one. Suppose of two stimuli, A and B, A is likely to be preferred over B by a particular subject and suppose also that, on first exposure, A is presented to the right and B to the left. By scanning back and forth between A and B, the subject learns the location of A and subsequently fixates more upon A. In order to ensure that this is not a case of position preference, we now present the pair again, this time with A to the left and B to the right. Where will our subject look? Watson argues that since A is the preferred stimulus and since A was at the right position on the first exposure, the subject has effectively been reinforced for looking to the right. Thus, when the stimuli are again presented, the subject will continue to look to the right, at least initially. Watson has presented convincing evidence that such conditioning of direction of regard can occur within the relatively brief time spans occupied by the usual spontaneous preference experiment. If such a response does become conditioned then, of course, it will have to extinguish before the subject can change his direction of regard to the left and look again at A; until then, of course, he will be looking at B, the less preferred stimulus. Thus, the effect of controlling for side preference may be to reduce the probability of observing real differences, as indexed by fixation duration, between subjects' preferences for A and B. Despite these acknowledged limitations of the visual preference procedure, it continues to be widely used. Care has to be exercised, therefore, when interpreting the results for such studies, particularly when negative results are reported.

Despite the fact that other investigators have not always been able to replicate findings originally reported by Fantz and despite the methodological weakness inherent in the procedures employed in his early studies, the innovative nature of his work cannot be overstressed. Prior to Fantz, infant perception was a topic of only sporadic interest to psychologists. The enormous upsurge of interest in infant perceptual development that has taken place over the past fifteen years is in no small measure attributable to his pioneering efforts in this field.

The studies which have followed since the early Fantz work fall into two broad categories: those related to what might be called visual *activity* and those related more to perceptual *discrimination*. Perhaps the best known work on infant perceptual activity is that of Salapatek (Salapatek, 1969; Salapatek and Kessen, 1966), who has carried out extensive investigations of newborn and infant scanning of visual stimuli. In an early study, Salapatek and Kessen presented a sample of ten newborn subjects with a black triangle on a white field whilst a control group of ten newborns were shown a homogeneous black visual field. From photographs of eye positions taken at a rate of one per second during each exposure, the investigators were able to reconstruct the scanning pattern of newborns to these kinds of stimuli. Infants exposed to the homogenous field showed widely dispersed scanning patterns with a marked horizontal component. Infants exposed to the triangle showed much less dispersion of scanning. Instead, most subjects tended to focus on a single feature of the triangle, usually a vertex, and to exercise slight, mainly horizontal, excursions about this point. These findings obtained regardless of the orientation of the triangle, though the preferred vertex varied from subject to subject. Salapatek and Kessen interpreted their data to mean that newborns do not respond to figures as wholes but rather orient towards preferred elements in the visual field. In terms of what mediates newborns' preference for vertices in the present instance, they suggested three alternatives:

1 that newborns respond to transitions in brightness and that orientation towards a vertex is directed by the occurrence of two brightness changes;

2 that newborns have a specific analyser mechanism tuned to angles, analogous to the neurophysiological coding mechanisms for visual stimuli proposed by Hubel and Wiesel (1962);[2]

3 following Hershenson (1964), Salapatek and Kessen suggested that newborns may respond to an optimal level of brightness which, in the present instance, is to be found only near a vertex.

In a subsequent study Salapatek (1969) reported that between one and two and a half months of age infants showed a shift from fixation of only a limited portion of a visual stimulus towards scanning a more substantial area. Other investigators have shown that changes in visual scanning strategies occur across the whole developmental spectrum. Zaporozhets (1965) reported that three- to four-year-old children spent more time focusing upon the centre as opposed to the contour of a complex form whereas five- and six-year-old children began tracing the outline of the figure. By seven years this pattern of scanning was well established, as if the children were reconstructing or modelling the figure. Older children showed more discrete eye movements than younger children but the actual duration of their fixations was shorter. Across a much wider age span Mackworth and Bruner (1970) observed marked differences in the scanning patterns of six-year-old children compared with young adults. Adult subjects tended to relate important areas of visual displays by long, leaping movements of the eyes whereas children lacked adequate coverage and tended to have many short eye movements about small regions of detail, not necessarily the most informative regions. In a study involving children aged six to nine years, Nodine and Steuerle (1971) observed a comparable developmental trend. When required to make same-different judgements between briefly exposed pairs of letters, six year olds required more fixations, longer fixation durations and more cross-pair comparisons than older children. Also, six year olds showed less tendency to fixate upon distinctive feature (Gibson, 1969) areas of the letters than did the older children.

What, then, can be concluded on the basis of these visual scanning studies? Clearly, developmental changes occur in the eye-movement strategies which subjects employ when exposed to visual stimuli. It is clear also that such changes are in evidence from infancy, through childhood into adulthood; always, it seems, in the direction of increasing efficiency. In all the data, however, there is no necessary justification for Salapatek and Kessen's view that young infants are capable of responding only to parts of forms rather than to whole forms, on the grounds that their fixations on stimuli tend to be clustered about single units. As Bond (1972) has pointed out, such a view is tenable only if a strict motor copy theory of visual perception is adopted. This position maintains that sufficient information for stimulus recognition is acquired only through active scanning of all its parts (Zaporozhets, 1965). Charlesworth (1968) has argued that there is no necessary reason why an infant has to scan the edges of an object many times in an active fashion before its form will be perceived, and has suggested that such information can be extracted just by 'looking or staring with minimum of eye movement'. Nodine and Simmons (1972) have some relevant data here, albeit concerning older children. They observed that in a paired-comparison discrimination task involving letter-like stimuli, several subjects fixated briefly at a point midway between the two stimuli but were still able to give accurate judgements; such subjects had clearly become proficient in the use of peripheral as opposed to foveal vision. The relative importance of central and peripheral vision during early infancy has never been clearly established. Moreover, it is uncertain whether the response index employed by

Salapatek and Kessen reflected central or peripheral perceptual activity. It is known that among newborns a fine beam of light passing through the cornea and the centre of the lens will not strike the fovea, the retinal area of maximum sensitivity. Now, Salapatek and Kessen used corneal reflections as their primary data and employed deviations of images from the centre of the cornea to determine which part of their triangular stimulus was being fixated at a given moment. Exactly what such data mean, therefore, in terms of what was actually being processed by the infants is not at all clear.

Rather than focus upon visual activity as evidenced by scanning patterns, a number of investigators have examined the ways in which infants discriminate and respond to various stimulus dimensions. Doris and Cooper (1966) examined sensitivity to brightness in infants between four and sixty-nine days and observed that discrimination of brightness increased rapidly during the first two months of life. Hershenson (1964) employed a sample of newborn infants to investigate their preferences for different intensities of brightness. He compared fixation preferences to three levels of brightness, 3.56 (dim), 35.6 (medium) and 356 (bright) foot-candles. In a paired-comparisons design, the subjects fixated the medium stimulus more than the other two and fixated the bright stimulus more than the dim one. Hershenson (1964, 1967) makes the important methodological point that before concluding that subjects are responding to a particular stimulus dimension it should be demonstrated that a transitive relationship exists among different values on that dimension, as far as subject responsivity is concerned. Thus, if value A is preferred over value B and B is preferred over C, then A should be preferred over C. If subjects' responses to different dimensional values do not constitute such an ordered set then it cannot be unambiguously concluded that they are responding to the dimension in question. It is clear from Hershenson's data that a transitive relationship was observed among subjects' responses to different levels of brightness and the conclusion is therefore justified that newborns can perceive differences in brightness.

Complexity is another stimulus attribute that has attracted a great deal of attention from psychologists interested in the study of perceptual development. Complexity is one of the many concepts which psychologists have taken over from the common language and attempted to refine for technical usage. Intuitively, we all seem to know what we mean when talking about complexity and we could probably reach a fair level of agreement if asked to classify a group of stimuli into those that were more and those that were less complex. However, we might find it difficult to specify what the criteria were which we employed to determine the complexity level of a particular stimulus, for complexity is not a unitary concept. Similarly, psychologists have experienced great difficulty in agreeing upon an acceptable and viable operational definition of the term. As Schaffer (1971) has pointed out, most definitions have treated complexity in terms of the total quantity of information transmitted by stimuli or 'as the variety or diversity of distinguishable elements contained within the stimulus'. Even so, there have been many diverse definitions; thus Fantz (1966) seemed to equate complexity with the number of stimulus elements, Munsinger and Weir (1967) with the number of turns in the stimulus, McCall and Melson (1970) with the randomness versus the regularity of the stimulus configuration. Not surprisingly a number of conflicting results have been reported on the basis of these differing definitions. One approach which has yielded fairly consistent results has been to equate complexity with the amount of internal contour in a stimulus and to manipulate contour by employing black and white checkerboards of a constant size but of differing densities (2 x 2 *v.* 4 x 4 *v.* 8 x 8 checkerboards, and so on). This procedure controls for brightness since the black-white ratios are always constant. However, Hershenson (1967) has cautioned that the control for brightness may be vitiated if subjects do not scan the entire stimulus surface (cf. Salapatek and Kessen, 1966).

An initial finding from a study employing the above approach was reported by Berlyne (1958) who reported that infants preferred the most complex stimulus offered. Hershenson (1964), however, reported that newborns showed a distinct preference for a 2 x 2 as against a 4 x 4 or a 12 x 12 checkerboard, that is, they preferred the least complex stimulus. The apparent contradiction between these results was partly resolved by a report by Brennan, Ames and Moore (1966) who found that among infants of three, eight and fourteen weeks, the youngest preferred 2 x 2 checks, the middle preferred 8 x 8 checks, and the oldest preferred 24 x 24 checks. Thus, complexity preference was shown to be a function of age. This view was further substantiated by Karmel (1969) who found that between thirteen and twenty weeks there was an inverted U-shaped function between complexity (as indexed by the square root of the amount of contour) and stimulus preference. Moreover, the older infants preferred more complex stimuli so that the peak of the inverted U-curve shifted upwards with increasing age.

Attentional Processes in Perceptual Discrimination

It will have occurred to the reader that a large number of the studies already referred to have regarded differential attention to different stimuli as the primary means of determining whether subjects are capable of discriminating between pairs of stimuli. As we have noted previously, a frequent strategy is to determine whether the subject fixates more upon one member of a stimulus pair than upon another; if the subject does show differential attention in this manner it is reasoned that he has manifested a preference and, *ipso facto*, has discriminated between the stimuli. The role of attention in perceptual discrimination is clearly an important one and it is to a consideration of this topic that we now turn.

Just as Fantz's early experiments provided the impetus for a closer study of infant perception so did they also provide the motivation for a renewed interest in infant attentional processes. He had suggested that infants attend to the more complex of two stimuli. Subsequent investigations directed themselves to the question of what was going on during the attentional process itself. A number of researchers, notably Kagan and Lewis (1965) and their associates, approached this question from the point of view of an oft-noted decline in overt infant attention towards a repeatedly exposed stimulus. In a typical experiment, infant subjects would be presented with the same stimulus over and over again for several trials and attention towards the stimulus would be recorded. Attention was assessed in a number of ways — visual fixation upon the stimulus, changes in heart-rate upon stimulus onset, changes in respiration rate. These measures are usually highly interrelated and in this discussion we will consider only the visual fixation measure. Under the conditions just described it has regularly been observed that the duration of infant fixation on a stimulus declines systematically with each successive presentation. A rather simple and perhaps obvious explanation for such a phenomenon is that the infants' eyes become fatigued and that they therefore look increasingly less at the stimulus as time goes on. However, it is readily demonstrated that such an account is inadequate for, if, after a series of trials with a constant stimulus, a new stimulus of less intensity is now presented, there is almost invariably a recovery of attention to the level observed during initial trials. Such recovery is sufficient to demonstrate that the previously noted decline could not have been due to fatigue.

The procedure just described has come to be known as the violation of expectancy paradigm (Lewis and Goldberg, 1969). The interpretation of results from this procedure that is now widely accepted is based on a theoretical framework whereby, due to repeated exposure of a constant (S_1) stimulus, some central representation or scheme of S_1 comes to be established (perhaps through the laying down of a neuronal model, as proposed by Sokolov, 1963). Attentive behaviour (e.g. visual fixation) declines so long as there is a match between external event and internal representation. This is the case so long as S_1 continues to be presented, and the subject thereby develops an expectancy for the appearance of S_1. However, with the introduction of a new stimulus, S_2, the external-internal match no longer obtains; expectancy has been violated and, in order that the resultant discrepancy might be assimilated, there is an increase in attentive behaviour.

The violation of expectancy paradigm, or variations of it, has been widely used to investigate a whole range of problems in the field of infant attentional, perceptual and cognitive development. Thus, Lewis and his colleagues (Lewis, Goldberg and Campbell, 1969) have investig-ated developmental changes in the efficiency of model acquisition; Caron and Caron (1969) have examined differences in rates of decrement when simple and complex stimuli are repeatedly presented; infant response to novelty has been investigated by this means by Schaffer and Parry (1969). A number of these studies have recently been reviewed by Jeffrey and Cohen (1971).

The application of the violation of expectancy paradigm to studies of perceptual development has been highlighted by Lewis and Goldberg (1969). They argued that the rate of attentional decline during repeated presentations of an S_1 stimulus can be regarded as an index of the subject's ability to assimilate or acquire an internal model or schema of that stimulus. They argued also that the magnitude of attentional recovery upon presentation of S_2 can be regarded as an index of the subject's discrimination between S_1 and S_2. Later, Lewis and Baumol (1970) were able to demonstrate the viability of this approach by showing that, follow-ing a series of S_1 trials, differential magnitudes of response recovery were induced by different kinds of stimulus change. It should be noted that this kind of approach to perceptual discrimination moves one away from the traditional stimulus-centred approach, wherein the subject's response is related to variation in some property of the stimulus (e.g. its colour, form, brightness, complexity, etc.) and moves, instead, towards a more subject-oriented approach, wherein behaviour is regarded as the product of a relationship between the cognitive structure of the subject, on the one hand, and certain characteristics of the stimulus (e.g. its familiarity or novelty), on the other.

Notes

1. For comparison purposes, adults with normal vision can discriminate stripes subtending one minute of visual arc.

2.　　Hubel and Wiesel (1962) have observed that, in the cat's visual cortex, there are individual cells which are maximally responsive to particular aspects of stimulus edges or boundaries. For example, one cell may fire maximally to an edge of a particular shape and minimally to an edge of another shape; another cell may only fire when the edge is at a particular orientation; other cells may only fire when edges move in a particular direction. It has been argued that there are cells in the human visual cortex which function analogously.

References

Ahrens, R. (1954), 'Beitrage zur Entwicklung des Physiognomie und Mimikerkennes', *Zeitschrift fur experimentelle und angewandte Psychologie*, vol. 2, pp. 412-544, 599-633.

Berlyne, D.E. (1958), 'The influence of the albedo and complexity of stimuli on visual fixation in the human infants', *Brit. J. Psychol.*, vol. 49, pp. 315-18.

Bond, E.K. (1972), 'Perception of form by the human infant', *Psychol. Bull.*, vol. 77, pp. 225-45.

Brennan, W.M., Ames, E.W. and Moore, R.W. (1966), 'Age differences in infants' attention to patterns of different complexities', *Science*, vol. 151, pp. 354-5.

Caron, R.F. and Caron, A.J. (1969), 'Degree of stimulus complexity and habituation of visual fixation in infants', *Psychonom. Sci.*, vol. 14, pp. 78-9.

Charlesworth, W.R. (1968), 'Cognition in infancy: where do we stand in the mid-sixties?', *Merrill-Palmer Q. Behav. Devel.*, vol. 14, pp. 25-46.

Dayton, A.O. Jr and Jones, M.H. (1964), 'Analysis of characteristics of fixation reflexes in infants by use of direct current electo-oculography', *Neurology*, vol. 14, pp. 1152-6.

Dayton, A.O., Jr, Jones, M.H., Steele, B. and Rose, M. (1964), 'Developmental study of coordinated eye movements in the human infant: II. An electro-oculographic study of the fixation reflex in the newborn', *Arch. Ophth.*, vol. 71, pp. 871-5.

Doris, J. and Cooper, L. (1966), 'Brightness discrimination in infancy', *J. exp. child Psychol.*, vol. 3, pp. 31-9.

Fantz, R.L. (1958), 'Pattern vision in young infants', *Psychol. Res.*, vol. 8, pp. 43-7.

Fantz, R.L. (1961), 'The origin of form perception', *Sci. Amer.*, vol. 204, pp. 66-72.

Fantz, R.L. (1966), 'Pattern discrimination and selective attention as determinants of perceptual development from birth', in A.H. Kidd and J.L. Rivoire (eds.), *Perceptual Development in Children*, International Universities Press.

Fantz, R.L.., Ordy, J.M. and Udelf, M.S. (1962), 'Maturation of pattern vision in infants during the first six months', *J. comp. physiol. Psychol.*, vol. 55, pp. 907-17.

Gibson, E.J. (1969), *Principles of Perceptual Learning and Development*, Appleton-Century-Crofts.

Gorman, J.J., Cogan, D.A. and Gellis, S.S. (1957), 'An apparatus for grading the visual acuity of infants on the basis of optokinetic nystagmus', *Pediatrics*, vol. 19, pp. 1088-92.

Haaf, R.A. and Bell, R.Q. (1967), 'A facial dimension in visual discrimination by human infants', *Child Devel.*, vol. 38, pp. 893-9.

Haynes, H., White, B.L. and Held, R. (1965), 'Visual accommodation in human infants', *Science*, vol. 148, pp. 528-30.

Hershenson, M. (1964), 'Visual discrimination in the human newborn', *J. comp. physiol. Psychol.*, vol. 58, pp. 270-6.

Hershenson, M. (1965), 'Visual discrimination in the human newborn', *Dissert. Abstr.*, vol. 26, p. 1793.

Hershenson, M. (1967), 'Development of the perception of form', *Psychol. Bull.*, vol. 67, pp. 326-36.

Horsten, G.P.M. and Winkelman, J.E. (1962), 'Electrical activity of the retina in relation to histological differentiation in infants born prematurely and at full term', *Vision Res.*, vol. 2, pp. 269-76.

Horsten, G.P.M. and Winkelman, J.E. (1964), 'Electroretinographic critical fusion frequency of the retina in relation to the histological development in man and animals', *Documenta Ophth.*, vol. 18, pp. 515-21.

Hrbek, A. and Mares, P. (1964a), 'Critical evoked responses to visual stimulation in full-term and premature newborns', *EEG clin. Neurophysiol.*, vol. 16, pp. 575-81.

Hrbek, A. and Mares, P. (1964b), 'The development of electrophysiological reactivity of CNS in children', *Activ. Nerv. Sup.*, vol. 6, pp. 92-3.

Hubel, D.H. and Wiesel, T.N. (1962), 'Receptive fields, binocular interaction and functional architecture in the cat's visual cortex', *J. Physiol.*, vol. 160, pp. 106-54.

James, W. (1890), *Principles of Psychology*, Holt.

Jeffrey, W.E. and Cohen, L.B. (1971), 'Habituation in the human infant', in H. Reese (ed.), *Advances in Child Development and Behavior*, vol. 6, Academic Press.

Kagan, J. and Lewis, M. (1965), 'Studies of attention in the human infant', *Merrill-Palmer Q. Behav. Devel.*, vol. 11, pp. 95-127.

Karmel, B.Z. (1969), 'The effects of age, complexity and amount of contour on pattern preferences in human infants', *J. exp. child. Psychol.*, vol. 7, pp. 339-54.

Koopman, P.R. and Ames, E.W. (1968), 'Infants' preferences for facial arrangements: a failure to replicate', *Child Devel.*, vol. 39, pp. 481-7.

Lewis, M. and Baumel, M.H. (1970), 'A study in the ordering of attention', *Percept. mot. Skills*, vol. 31, pp. 979-90.

Lewis, M. and Goldberg, S. (1969), 'The acquisition and violation of expectancy: an experimental paradigm', *J. exp. child Psychol.*, vol. 7, pp. 70-80.

Lewis, M., Goldberg, S. and Campbell, H. (1969), 'A developmental study of information processing within the first three years of life: response decrement to a redundant signal', *Mongr. Soc. Res. Child Devel.*, vol. 34, no. 9.

McCall, R.B. and Melson, W.H. (1970), 'Complexity, contour and area as determinants of attention in infants', *Devel. Psychol.*, vol. 3, pp. 343-9.

Mackworth, N.H. and Bruner, J.S. (1970), 'How adults and children search and recognize pictures', *Human Devel.*, vol. 13, pp. 149-77.

Mann, I. (1964), *The Development of the Human Eye*, British Medical Association.

Munsinger, H. and Weir, M.W. (1967), 'Infants' and young children's preferences for complexity', *J. exp. child Psychol.*, vol. 5, pp. 69-73.

Nodine, C.F. and Simmons, F.G. (1972), 'Development of cognitive strategies for processing distinctive features of letter-like stimuli', Paper presented at meeting of Eastern Psychological Association, Boston, Mass.

Nodine, C.F. and Steuerle, N.F. (1971), 'Development of perceptual-cognitive strategies for differentiating graphemes', Paper presented at meeting of Eastern Psychological Association, New York.

Preyer, W. (1888), *The Mind of the Child: I. The Senses and the Will*, Appleton.

Saayman, G., Ames, E.W. and Moffett, A. (1964), 'Response to novelty as an indicator of visual discrimination in the human infant', *J. exp. child Psychol.*, vol. 1, pp. 189-98.

Salapatek, P. (1969), 'The visual investigation of geometric pattern by one- and two-month-old infants', Paper presented at meeting of the American Association for the Advancement of Science, Boston, Mass.

Salapatek, P. and Kessen, W. (1966), 'Visual scanning of triangles by the human newborn', *J. exp. child Psychol.*, vol. 3, pp. 155-67.

Schaffer, H.R. (1971), *The Growth of Sociability*, Penguin.

Schaffer, H.R. and Parry, M.H. (1969), 'Perceptual-motor behaviour in infancy as a function of age and stimulus familiarity', *Brit. J. Psychol.*, vol. 60, pp. 1-9.

Sherman, M., Sherman, I. and Flory, C.D. (1936), 'Infant behavior', *Comp. Psychol. Mongr.*, vol. 12, no. 91.

Sokolov, Y.N. (1963), *Perception and the Conditioned Reflex*, Macmillan Co.

Watson, J.S. (1965), 'Evidence of discriminative operant learning within 30 seconds by infants 7-26 weeks of age', Paper presented at meeting of Society for Research in Child Development, Minneapolis, Minn.

Wilcox, B.M. (1969), 'Visual preferences of human infants for representations of the human face', *J. exp. child Psychol.*, vol. 7, pp. 10-20.

Winkelman, J.E. and Horsten, G.P.M. (1962), 'The ERG of premature and full-term infants during their first days of life', *Ophthalmologica*, vol. 143, pp. 92-101.

Wohlwill, J.C. (1960), 'Developmental studies of perception', *Psychol. Bull.*, vol. 57, pp. 249-88.

Zaporozhets, A.V. (1965), 'The development of perception in the pre-school child', *Mongr. Soc. Res. Child Devel.*, vol. 30, pp. 82-101.

8 INFANT SPEECH PERCEPTION

Philip A. Morse

Source: D.A. Sanders (ed.), *Auditory Perception of Speech* (Prentice-Hall, 1977), pp. 161-76.

Perhaps the most obvious point at which to begin our discussion of speech perception in infants is the nature of the experimental organism. Anyone who has spent time with babies, either in or out of the laboratory, will readily admit that one- to four-month-old infants are far from ideal subjects. Not only are they unable to verbalize what they know about the world, but also they have a number of behaviors (e.g. sleeping, crying, etc.) which compete quite successfully with our efforts to study them.

To date, two major procedures have been developed to extract linguistic knowledge from the human infant:

1. *the heart-rate (HR) habituation/dishabituation paradigm, or model* (In this procedure a physiological response reflecting the infant's attention to a novel event is seen to decrease in magnitude as the novel stimulus becomes 'familiar' and to reappear if a second novel stimulus is presented.)

2. *the nonnutritive high-amplitude sucking (HAS) paradigm* (This is an operant conditioning procedure that employs as the response the infant's strong sucking on a pacifier.[†] Changes in the infant's sucking to a familiar vs. a novel stimulus are used to index discrimination.)

The HR habituation/dishabituation paradigm was derived from the finding that when a sound is presented to an infant at a comfortable listening level, the infant's heart rate slows down (decelerates) in response to the sound over the course of the next 0 to 20 seconds. This heart-rate deceleration has been shown to be the cardiac counterpart of the general orienting behavior of the individual. Thus, the cardiac orienting response reflects the subject's *attention* to a novel event (Graham and Clifton, 1966). If a sound is presented repeatedly to an infant, he will begin to develop a 'memory' of its characteristics. This eventually results in the infant's ceasing to respond to the sound as 'novel'. Consequently, we should expect to see the heart-rate orienting response gradually become smaller and smaller as the stimulus is repeated. This is in fact what we see in Figure 8.1 which shows both the initial orienting response and its habituation over five trial blocks. If we change the stimulus after the

Figure 8.1: Habituation of the Orienting Response over Successive Trial Blocks (1-5)

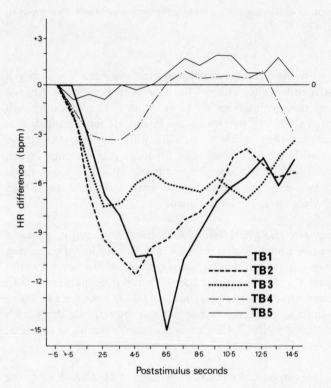

Source: C.L. Miller, P.A. Morse and M.F. Dorman, *Infant Speech Perception, Memory and the Cardiac Orienting Response*, 1975.

orienting response of the infant has become habituated to it, we may observe a further orienting response to the changed stimulus. This is the dishabituation explained in (1) above. If this reoccurrence of the orienting response is observed, we can assume that the infant has discriminated the second stimulus from the first one; in other words, he has responded physiologically to the acoustic change manifest in the shift from the first sound to the second one. This orienting response, habituation/dishabituation paradigm has been employed quite successfully in studying the auditory discrimination of infants four months of age and older (Berg, 1972; Moffitt, 1971). Its use with infants less than four months of age, however, has been rather discouraging (Brown, Leavitt and Graham, in press; Leavitt, Brown, Morse and Graham, in press; Miller, Morse and Dorman, 1975).

The second paradigm for infant testing, the high amplitude sucking procedure, on the other hand, has proven to be extremely useful with infants as young as one to four months of age (Eimas, Siqueland, Juszyck and Vigorito, 1971; Morse, 1972). The logic of this paradigm is quite similar to that of the heart rate procedure, except that the infant is in full control of the stimulus presentation. As the infant sucks on a non-nutritive nipple, he causes a sound to be transmitted through a speaker. The more the infant sucks on the nipple, the more frequently the sound is presented. If the infant is a cooperative subject, he will eventually learn that the sucking turns on the sound. As the experiment progresses the first thing we observe is an increase in the sucking rate (acquisition). Eventually, as the sound loses its reinforcing properties, the infant's sucking rate will drop off (habituation). When the sucking rate meets some predetermined habituation criterion, the sound is changed. If we observe a recovery of the sucking rate relative to a no-change control group, we can infer that the infant has discriminated between the new and the old stimuli. However, each infant sucks with varying degrees of strength and interest. For this reason, in the beginning of this procedure, the experimenter selects the infant's hardest (high amplitude) sucks (HAS) as those which he will subsequently reinforce. The next step is to allow a one-minute silent period to permit the determination of an average, or a baseline, count of the infant's HAS. After this baseline period only the infant's high amplitude sucks are permitted to cause a sound to be presented. A typical experimental result showing the averaged data for the baseline (BL), for the five minutes prior to stimulus shift (-5, -4, -3, -2, -1 mins.), and for the four minutes following shift ($+1$, $+2$, $+3$, $+4$ mins.), is shown in Figure 8.2. A more extensive discussion and a comparison of the heart rate and high amplitude sucking paradigms can be found in an earlier publication (Morse, 1974).

Using these two paradigms, infant speech researchers have begun to ask several different questions about auditory perception in the human baby. Some investigators have sought to determine if infants can discriminate auditorily between different pairs of speech sounds. Positive results from such studies, however, do not necessarily indicate that the infant is treating these sounds as speech, or processing them in a speech mode. This problem has stimulated other researchers to try to answer this particular question; namely: Does the infant utilize the *phonetic* categories of adult speech in organizing his discriminative behavior, i.e. low level

Figure 8.2: Changes in HAS for Baseline (BL) Five Minutes Prior to Stimulus Shift (−5 to −1), and Four Postshift Minutes (+1 to +4)

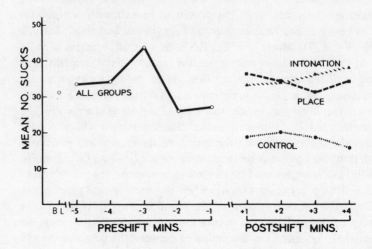

Source: P.A. Morse, 'The discrimination of speech and nonspeech stimuli in early infancy', 1972.

linguistic processing, or is he simply classifying the sounds as acoustically different? As we review the major findings in infant speech perception, we should bear in mind this important distinction between auditory and phonetic discrimination, a distinction which has already been stressed.

The first important study in the recent history of infant speech perception asked whether 4- to 5-month-old infants could discriminate two syllables which differed in *place* of articulation (bilabial, [p/b],[1] vs. velar sounds, [k/g], for example). Moffitt (1971) used a heart-rate habituation/dishabituation paradigm to show that infants at this age could discriminate auditory [ba] vs. [ga] when the only acoustic difference between the stimuli was in the second formant (F2) transition[†] of each. I have also used the HAS procedure to demonstrate that as early as 6 weeks of age infants can discriminate [ba] vs. [ga] when they differ in both F2 and F3 transitions (Morse, 1972). Furthermore, if infants are presented with the F2 and F3 transitions in isolation (these sound like chirps or glissandos), they discriminate them in a manner different from the way they do when the same transitions are presented in the speech contexts [ba] and [ga]. Most recently, Eimas (1974) confirmed the finding that infants can discriminate acoustic cues which signal place of articulation contrasts. In addition, he showed that they can do this not only auditorily, but also phonetically. When 2- to 3-month-old infants were tested with the high-amplitude sucking paradigm, a change between categories ([dae] vs. [gae]) resulted in a large increase in the HAS rate. However, the infants showed no response recovery for either a no-change control or for a comparable acoustic shift within categories (within [dae] or within [gae]). That is to say, an acoustic shift in the F2 and F3 transitions evoked a change in response when it crossed a phoneme boundary, but a shift of equivalent magnitude within the category failed to do so. Since the acoustic differences in the F2 and F3 transitions were identical both in the between- and in the within-category conditions, these results show that the discriminations infants are able to make are constrained by adult phonetic categories. That is, they discriminate place contrasts only when the *phonetic categories are different*. (A study by Miller and Morse (in press) has recently replicated this finding of categorical discrimination for place of articulation using a cardiac orienting response paradigm.) Finally, Eimas (1974) has also observed that if the same F2 transitions signaling the distinction [dae] vs. [gae] are presented in isolation (chirps), infants discriminate not only between categories, *but also within categories*. These transitions, in this case, are processed as continuous rather than categorical stimuli. This provides additional evidence that the infant is capable of phonetically discriminating the acoustic cues for place of articulation.

Similar research has been conducted with the acoustic cues that signal the voicing[†] distinction in stop consonants [p/b, t/d, k/g] in the initial position. Such cues permit differentiation, for example, between [ba] and [pa]. These cues, labeled collectively voice-onset-time (VOT), are definitely discriminated auditorily by infants. Trehub and Rabinovitch (1972), using the HAS paradigm, observed that 4- to 7-week-old infants could discriminate both natural and synthesized [ba] and [pa] syllables. However, Eimas, Siqueland, Juszyck and Vigorito (1971) found that by one month of age (and also at four months) the HAS procedure revealed that infants discriminated these voice-onset-time cues between the categories [ba] vs. [pa] but not within these voicing categories. This finding of *phonetic*, categorical discrimination has been recently replicated by Miller (1974) and extended to the voicing contrast in [da] and [ta] (Eimas, 1975b). Thus, these findings for infant VOT discrimination are in complete accord with the perceptual behavior for place cues already discussed.

In contrast to the finding that both adults and infants *categorically* discriminate stop consonants varying in place of articulation and voicing, vowels are generally perceived continuously rather than categorically (Stevens, Liberman, Studdert-Kennedy and Oehman, 1969; Pisoni, 1971, 1973). Trehub (1973) demonstrated, using the HAS paradigm, that 4- to 17-week-olds could discriminate auditorily the vowel contrasts [i] vs. [a] and [i] vs. [u]. Most recently, Swobodia, Morse and Leavitt (1976) showed that 8-week-olds, like adults, do not discriminate the vowels [i] and [I] categorically. They are able to discriminate equally well between- *and* within-category contrasts. Thus, for both adults and infants the phonetic categories of vowels (at least vowels 200-300 msec in duration) do not preclude the discrimination of within-category differences, thereby yielding continuous rather than categorical discrimination.

Using the high-amplitude sucking paradigm, additional studies of speech cues have revealed that infants are able to discriminate falling vs. rising intonation in the syllable [ba] (Morse, 1972); categorical differences in the liquids [ra] vs. [la] (Eimas, 1975a); and differences in the fricatives [va] vs. [sa], [sa] vs. [ʃa], but not in [sa] vs. [za] (Eilers and Minifie, 1975). Finally, Miller, Morse and Dorman (1975), using a heart-rate paradigm to be described below, found that 3-month-olds could discriminate the very brief burst cue (5 to 30 msec) which occurs at the release of initial stop consonants.

In sum, all of these studies in infant speech perception reveal that infants can discriminate almost every relevant acoustic cue(s) in those speech sounds that have so far been presented to them. Furthermore, research has shown that, as in adults, discrimination between stop consonants is phonetic (i.e. categorical), whereas in vowels it resembles continuous (nonphonetically constrained) discrimination. This research thus supports the position that *some aspects of processing in a speech mode are either a genetically endowed capacity in infants, or they are learned within the first few weeks of life.* Furthermore, it indicates that infants, like adults, process vowels and consonants differently (continuous vs. categorical discrimination).

The data on infant speech perception suggest, therefore, that at a very early age the infant's auditory and phonetic capabilities are quite sophisticated. The findings raise a number of very important issues about the factors that might influence the development of these impressive capabilities. In the remainder of this chapter we shall explore some of the theoretical implications of these findings as they relate to the development of speech perception in human beings.

The Role of Memory Factors

If we were to present an infant with a [ba] sound on Monday and with a

[ga] sound on Wednesday and ask whether he could discriminate them, we should not be too surprised if, when tested, we found that he was unable to do so. Although this example is exaggerated, the point I wish to make is that if we exceed the infant's short-term (STM) or long-term memory (LTM) abilities in our testing procedures, we may fail to determine the infant's true discriminative capacities. Brown, Leavitt and Graham (in press) recently studied the development of the discrimination of triangular wave stimuli (sounds sweeping four times a second between 1,500 and 2,500 Hz or between 150 and 250 Hz) using a 6/2 habituation/dishabituation heart-rate paradigm. In this paradigm, 6 habituation trials of the same stimulus (repeated 5 to 6 times per trial) were followed by 2 trials of a novel stimulus. Each trial was separated by 25 to 35 secs of silence. Six-week-old infants failed to show an initial orienting response to these stimuli (trials 1 and 2) and exhibited no habituation or dishabituation on subsequent trials. Nine-week-old infants did orient to the onset of these stimuli, but failed to show either habituation or dishabituation. Finally, in a subsequent study (Brown, personal communication) twelve-week-old infants showed both orienting and habituation, but no dishabituation to the changed stimulus (trials 7 and 8). A second study by Leavitt, Brown, Morse and Graham (in press) also failed to find auditory discrimination (dishabituation) with a 6/2 heart-rate paradigm in 6-week-old infants. However, when a paradigm was used that completely eliminated the silent intervals between trials, 6-week-old infants evidenced differential responding to a similar acoustic change. In this No-intertrial-interval (No-ITI) paradigm a series of one stimulus was followed immediately (No-ITI) by a series of a novel stimulus.

In marked contrast to the failure to demonstrate auditory discrimination in six-week-old infants with a 6/2 paradigm, Moffitt (1971), Berg (1972) and Lasky, Syrdal-Lasky and Klein (1975) have reported that an habituation/dishabituation paradigm *does* yield successful auditory discrimination in infants four months of age or older. Thus the Leavitt *et al.* study taken together with the findings of Moffitt, Berg and Lasky *et al.* *suggest* that between six weeks and four months of age the short-term memory constraints of the paradigm (i.e. the intervals between the trials) may have important consequences for the assessment of the infant's auditory discriminative abilities. The failure of the younger infants to exhibit auditory discrimination in the 6/2 paradigm may be related to their relatively poor ability to retain the auditory image in short-term memory long enough to permit the necessary discriminative comparison to be made. This is an important consideration if we are to attempt to define the components of auditory perception. Additional evidence for this position derives from the Miller *et al.* (1975) study of burst discrimination, mentioned earlier. In this study, three-month-olds showed orienting and impressive habituation to the syllables [bu] and [gu], but failed to demonstrate dishabituation even though an 8/2 (8 habituation trials/ 2 change trials) paradigm was employed. In contrast, infants of the same age *did* demonstrate discrimination of the burst cue in these stimuli when a No-ITI paradigm was employed. In this particular study infants simply heard 20 presentations of one stimulus followed by 20 presentations of the syllable change with no interval between the two. As in the Leavitt, Brown, Morse and Graham study (in press), heart-rate change was measured at the stimulus shift.

Memory factors in infants affect not only whether discrimination occurs but also the quality of that discrimination. Pisoni (1971, 1973) and Fujisaki and Kawashima (1969) have both suggested that an auditory short-term memory (STM) and a phonetic STM component play an important role in speech discrimination. If the stimuli or the paradigm is such as to permit the subject to retain *an auditory short-term memory* of the fine details of the stimulus, then discrimination within categories will be enhanced. In contrast, a paradigm, which forces the subject to reply primarily on his *phonetic short-term memory* of the stimuli, will make within category discrimination more difficult. Specifically, the extent to which vowels are perceived categorically is influenced by the duration of the stimuli and by the intervals between stimuli in the discrimination task (Pisoni, 1971, 1973). Long vowels tend to be perceived more continuously than short vowels (for which within-category discrimination is reduced). Following this logic, we could ask about the human infant: Does the extent to which auditory short-term memory is available for vowels (short vs. long stimuli) affect the categorical-continuous nature of the infant's discrimination? As was indicated earlier, Swoboda, Morse and Leavitt (1976) found that when the stimuli had a 240 msec duration, 2-month-old infants discriminated [i] and [I] continuously. If the duration of the stimuli is reduced to 60 msec, reliable between-category discrimination remains but within-category discrimination is not significant. The difference between the between- and within-category conditions also is not statistically significant (Swoboda, Kass, Morse and Leavitt, in preparation). The failure of these two conditions to be statistically significant from each other is not surprising since Pisoni observed that shortening the duration of vowels for adults made perception relatively more categorical, but not as impressively categorical as observed for consonants. These results suggest that the infant's discrimination of vowels, like the adult's, can be made more categorical or more continuous as a function of stimulus duration. Presumably, this effect is related to the extent to which auditory short-term memory for vowels is available to the infant. Reducing the stimulus duration apparently compels infants (and adults) to rely more on their categorical, phonetic short-term memory of the stimuli, thus yielding more categorical-like discriminations.

How 'Phonetic' is 'Phonetic'?

In reviewing the literature on infant speech perception, we stressed at the outset the difference between primary acoustic discrimination and linguistic discrimination. Some studies examined the infant's ability to discriminate *auditorily* various speech contrasts (e.g. Moffitt, 1971), whereas other studies have investigated the *phonetic* quality of this discrimination (Eimas, 1974). However, those studies which have examined the phonetic capabilities of infants have done so within a very restricted definition of 'phonetic'. In the case of stop consonants, they have looked at categorical discrimination of a particular acoustic cue(s) under conditions in which the vowel is held constant (Eimas, 1974; Eimas *et al.*, 1971). We have already seen, in our examination of studies on adult speech perception, that the acoustic cues for consonants vary as a function of vowel context and position in the word. Figure 8.3 illustrates, for example, that the critical cue for the place of articulation of the alveolar dental consonant [d] may be radically different in [di] and [du]. Similarly, the bilabial consonant 'p' may be cued by voice-onset-time cues as in 'pit' vs. 'bit', by silence as in 'split' vs. 'slit', or by vowel duration as in 'sip' vs. 'sib'. In other words, the 'phonetic' category 'p' is much more than the voice-onset-time category examined in studies of categorical perception. It is quite plausible that these more 'abstract' phonetic categories do not emerge in linguistic development until much later than the categorical discrimination observed in 1- to 3-month-old babies.

To date, we know very little of the infant's ability to organize these more abstract phonetic classes. This is primarily due to the fact that both the heart-rate and sucking paradigms are designed to study discrimination. What is needed is a paradigm which contains two different responses and permits us to study the infant's generalizations or identifications *among* stimuli. Recently, Fodor, Garrett and Brill (1975) have reported the success of a head-turning paradigm in studying this very problem. They examined the infant's learning of a head-turning response to natural speech syllables such as [pi], [ka] and [pu]. Their results indicate that 4-month-olds find it easier to associate syllables (learn to turn their heads to the same side) that have the *same* (e.g. [pi] and [pu]) rather than different (e.g. [pi] and [ka]) initial consonants. If we assume there were no invariant

Figure 8.3: A Simplified Acoustic Representation of the Syllables [di] and [du]

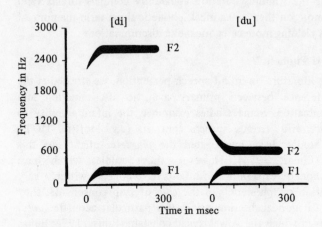

Source: Mattingly (1972). © The Society of the Sigma XI, New Haven, Conn.

acoustic cues in the natural [pi] and [pu] stimuli used, cues which might have aided infants in learning this task, then these findings do provide some indication that infants are able to classify very different acoustic stimuli into the same abstract, phonetic class. Obviously, much more research with synthetic and natural speech stimuli is necessary before we fully understand the infant's acquisition of the many levels of 'phonetic' classification.

Is Speech Special?

If infants do have the ability to discriminate speech sounds in an adult-like manner at such an early age, they may also be equipped to process speech in a special mode; this may be a consequence of the evolution of uniquely human capabilities for speech (Lieberman, 1974). Recent studies have begun to examine this problem in infants in three different ways:

1. hemispheric differences for speech vs. nonspeech;
2. the categorical discrimination of speech vs. nonspeech;
3. the attention (orienting) that the infant pays to speech and nonspeech stimuli.

Before we explore some of these findings, a word of caution is in order regarding the differences between speech and nonspeech stimuli. It is virtually impossible to produce a nonspeech control stimulus perfectly equated (acoustically) with a speech stimulus which is *not* perceived by listeners as speech. You will recall from earlier discussions that the auditory system must make an early decision concerning whether a signal is to be analyzed as speech or nonspeech. Providing a stimulus meets the minimal criteria for classification as speech, it will be processed and perceived as speech regardless of whether or not it is speech. Consequently, all of the studies to be discussed must be viewed as exploring differences between responses to particular types of nonspeech and speech stimuli.

Studies dealing with the specialized role of the two hemispheres of the brain suggest that young infants may perceive speech better in the left hemisphere and nonspeech better in the right hemisphere. Molfese, Freeman and Palermo (1975) observed that when infants averaging approximately 5 months of age were exposed to speech stimuli ([ba], [dae], 'boy', 'dog') they exhibited the strongest cortical responses over the left hemisphere, whereas the greatest responses to nonspeech (C major chord, 250 Hz to 4 kHz noise burst) occurred over the right hemisphere. Entus (1975) has recently reported related findings using the high-amplitude sucking procedure with the two ears receiving competing stimuli. She demonstrated that infants between 2 and 4 months of age discriminated a speech change better in the right ear than in the left ear, whereas a nonspeech change was discriminated better in the left ear. Although both of these findings need to be replicated, they do suggest that at a very early age the infant's brain may be responding to speech sounds in a special (lateralized) way.

Research on the discrimination of speech vs. nonspeech stimuli has shown that the transitions of the second formant (F2) in a speech context ([ba/da]) are discriminated categorically by infants 2 to 3 months of age, whereas the F2 transitions presented in isolation are discriminated *continuously* (Eimas, 1974). On the other hand, a recent study by Juszyck, Rosner, Cutting, Foard and Smith (1975) has revealed that nonspeech stimuli varying along a continuum of rise-time (that is, stimuli with varying rates of onset buildup) are discriminated *categorically* (as is the case for adults). *These findings suggest, at the very least, that young infants can discriminate speech and nonspeech stimuli in a manner similar to adult listeners.* Whether the infant (or adult) necessarily discriminates all nonspeech stimuli differently from speech stimuli remains to be determined.

Finally, Leavitt, Brown, Morse and Graham (in press) observed that 6-week-old infants pay attention (orient) to *pulsed* (with silent interval between stimuli) speech ([ba], [ga]) and nonspeech (sine wave) stimuli. However, when these same speech stimuli were presented nonpulsed (continuously, with no silent interval between stimuli), infants continued to pay attention to them (Morse, Leavitt, Brown and Graham, in press) but failed to orient to the nonspeech triangular wave stimuli of the Brown, Leavitt and Graham (in press) study. Although these results may not necessarily be valid for other types of nonspeech stimuli, they do suggest that under some conditions speech stimuli may be attended to more than other auditory stimuli. In sum, these three types of research offer some *suggestive* evidence that under some conditions infants respond to speech stimuli in a 'special' manner.

Role of Experimental and Innate Factors

Certainly one of the most interesting questions posed by this research is: How does the infant acquire phonetic categories in the development of speech perception? Of particular interest is the fact that the development of these perceptual categories precedes the infant's production of these phonetic contrasts (e.g. Kewley-Port and Preston, 1974). Although we do not yet know exactly to which sounds the infant is exposed in the first few months of life, the development of these categories does not appear to depend entirely on the infant's experience with his parents' language. This is suggested by the work of Streeter (1976), Eimas (1975b) and Lasky, Syrdal-Lasky and Klein (1975), who have shown that during the first few months of life infants can discriminate differences in the voicing of languages foreign to their home environments. These cross-language findings suggest that perhaps these voicing categories are not acquired ontogenetically (i.e. within the developmental stages of the individual infant), but phylogenetically (i.e. within the development of the human species). Since the production of the full range of speech sounds is unique to the human species (Lieberman, 1974), it may be that human beings have evolved special auditory perceptual capabilities that are optimally correlated with their categories of speech sound production. Behavioral research with adult subjects using an adaptation paradigm (e.g. Eimas and Corbit, 1973; Cooper, 1975; Diehl, 1975) has suggested that special auditory, and perhaps even phonetic, feature detectors may be operative in the human auditory system. Eimas (1975b) has further proposed that these feature-detector mechanisms, together with similar adaptation processes, may be responsible for the infant phonetic discrimination data discussed above. However, recent discrimination findings in the rhesus monkey (Morse and Snowdon, 1975; Waters and Wilson, 1976) suggest that categorical discrimination of stop consonants may not be limited to human adults or infants. If further research with nonhuman species continues to yield similar results, then we may wish to conclude that, rather than being an ability limited to the human species, some of these discriminative capabilities may be a general property of the primate or mammalian auditory system. Perhaps extending to infants and other species the use of the adaptation procedure employed in human adults may shed more light on the viability of a feature-detector explanation for the ontogenetic[†] and phylogenetic[†] development of some 'phonetic' categories in speech perception (Morse, in press).

Individual Differences

Our overview of the literature on infant speech perception suggests that infants with 'normal' medical histories are able to grasp many of the important basics of the human speech code at a very early age. The language development literature, on the other hand, indicates that premature infants or those who have experienced a variety of stresses during pregnancy or delivery have a greater chance of later developing problems in language acquisition (Braine, Heimer, Wortis and Freedman, 1966; Ehrlich, Shapiro, Kimbal and Huttner, 1973). Consequently, an interesting question is whether or not infants with stressful neonatal histories already exhibit language development problems in their early speech perception capabilities. To date, very little is known about the speech perception of this population of infants. One study, perhaps the only one in this area to date (Swoboda, Morse and Leavitt, 1976) obtained some suggestive evidence of differences in the within-category vowel discrimination of normal vs. 'at-risk' infants. Although the Swoboda *et al.* study represents an important first step in studying infants at risk for later language development problems, we have only begun to scratch the surface in terms of our knowledge of speech perception difficulties in 'at-risk' infants. We must consider not only the wide range of auditory discriminations that the normal infant can make, but also the importance of memory factors, innate and experiential factors, the scope of the 'special' nature of speech perception, and the 'phonetic' complexities of the speech code. Only after we have assessed these factors, can we begin to comprehend the multitude of ways in which 'at-risk' infants may reveal deficiencies in infant speech perception. Hopefully, in the development of the organization of the speech code in the 'normal' infant, we shall move closer to detecting problems in the very early language development of infants who are at risk for later developmental problems. Such research will be of paramount importance to those who seek not only to understand the complexities of auditory problems in language processing but also to develop effective strategies for early detection and early intervention.

Notes

1.   Elsewhere slashes have been used to describe speech sounds in terms of *phonemic* classes (for example, /ba/). However, since it would be premature to argue that young infants perceive speech sounds according to minimal differences in the meaning of words (phonemically), brackets (e.g. [ba]) have been employed throughout most of this chapter to describe speech sounds of *phonetic* categories.

References

Berg, W.K., 1972, 'Habituation and dishabituation of cardiac responses in 4-month-old alert infants', *J. Exp. Child Psychol., 14*, 92-107.

Braine, M.D.S., C.B. Heimer, H. Wortis and A.M. Freedman, 1966, 'Factors associated with impairment of the early development of prematures', *Monogr. Soc. Res. Child Dev., 31* (7).

Brown, J.W., L.A. Leavitt and F.K. Graham, 'Response to auditory stimuli in six and nine week old human infants', *Develop. Psychobiology*, in press.

Cooper, W.E., 1975, 'Selective Adaptation to Speech', in *Cognitive Theory*, vol. 1, eds. F. Restle, R. Shiffrin, N. Castellan, B. Landman and D. Pisoni. Potomac, Md.: Erlbaum, pp. 23-54.

Diehl, R.H., 1975, 'The effect of selective adaptation on the identification of speech sounds', *Perception and Psychophysics, 17*, 48-52.

Ehrlich, C.H., E. Shapiro, B.D. Kimbal and M. Huttner, 'Communication skills in five-year-old children with high-risk neonatal histories', *J. Sp. Hrg. Res., 16*, 524-9.

Eilers, R. and F. Minifie, 1975, 'Fricative discrimination in early infancy', *J. Sp. Hrg. Res., 18*, 158-67.

Eimas, P.D., 1974, 'Auditory and linguistic processing of cues for place of articulation by infants', *Perception and Psychophysics, 16*, 513-21.

Eimas, P.D., 1975a, 'Auditory and phonetic coding of the cues for speech: Discrimination of the [rl] distinction by young infants', *Perception and Psychophysics, 18*, 341-7.

Eimas, P.D., 1975b, 'Developmental Studies of Speech Perception', in *Infant Perception*, vol. II, eds. L.B. Cohen and P. Salapatek. New York: Academic Press, pp. 193-231.

Eimas, P.D. and J. Corbit, 1973, 'Selective adaptation of linguistic feature detectors', *Cognitive Psych., 4*, 90-109.

Eimas, P.D., E.R. Siqueland, P. Juszyck and J. Vigorito, 1971, 'Speech perception in infants', *Science, 171*, 303-6.

Entus, A.K., April 1975, 'Hemispheric asymmetry in processing of dichotically presented speech and nonspeech sounds by infants'. Paper presented at the meetings of the Soc. for Res. in Child Dev., Denver, Colo.

Fodor, J.A., M.F. Garrett and S.L. Brill, 1975, 'Pi ka pu: The perception of speech sounds by prelinguistic infants', *Perception and Psychophysics, 18*, 74-8.

Fujisaki, H. and T. Kawashima, 1969, 'On the modes and mechanisms of speech perception', *Ann. Rep. Engin. Res. Inst.*, Faculty of Engineering, Univ. of Tokyo, 28, 67-73.

Graham, F.K. and R.K. Clifton, 1966, 'Heart-rate change as a component of the orienting response', *Psychol. Bull., 65*, 305-20.

Juszyck, P., B. Rosner, J. Cutting, C. Foard and L. Smith, April 1975, 'Categorical perception of nonspeech sounds in the two-month-old infant'. Paper presented at the meetings of the Soc. for Res. in Child Dev., Denver, Colo.

Kewley-Port, D. and M.S. Preston, 1974, 'Early apical stop production: a voice onset time analysis', *J. Phonetics, 2*, 195-210.

Lasky, R., A. Syrdal-Lasky and R. Klein, 1975, 'VOT discrimination by four- to six-month-old infants from Spanish environments', *J. Exp. Child Psych., 20*, 215-25.

Leavitt, L.A., J.W. Brown, P.A. Morse and F.K. Graham, 'Cardiac orienting and auditory discrimination in six-week infants', *Develop. Psychol.*, in press.

Lieberman, P., 1974, 'On the evolution of language: a unified view', *Cognition, 3*, 59-94.

Mattingly, I.G., 1972, 'Speech signs and sign stimuli', *American Scientist, 60*, 327-37.

Miller, C.L., P.A. Morse and M.F. Dorman, 1975, 'Infant speech perception, memory, and the cardiac orienting response'. Paper presented at Society for Research in Child Development, Denver, Colo.

Miller, C.L. and P.A. Morse, 'The "heart" of categorical speech discrimination in young infants', *J. Sp. Hrg. Res.*, in press.

Miller, J., 1974, *Phonetic Determination of Infant Speech Perception.* Unpublished doctoral dissertation, University of Minnesota, Minneapolis, Minn.

Moffitt, A.R., 1971, 'Consonant cue perception by twenty- to twenty-four-week-old infants', *Child Dev., 42*, 717-31.

Molfese, D.L., R.B. Freeman and D.S. Palermo, 1975, 'The ontogeny of brain lateralization for speech and nonspeech stimuli', *Brain and Language, 2*, 356-68.

Morse, P.A., 'Speech perception in the human infant and rhesus monkey. Proc. of "Conference on Origins and Evolution of Language and Speech" ', *Annals of the New York Academy of Sciences*, in press.

Morse, P.A., L.A. Leavitt, J.W. Brown and F.K. Graham, 'Discrimination of continuous speech in six-week-old infants', in preparation.

Morse, P.A., 1974, 'Infant speech perception: A preliminary model and review of the literature', in *Language Perspectives – Acquisition, Retardation, and Intervention*, eds. R. Schiefelbusch and L. Lloyd. Baltimore: University Park Press, 19-53.

Morse, P.A., 1972, 'The discrimination of speech and nonspeech stimuli in early infancy', *J. Exp. Child Psychol.* (© Academic Press, Inc.), *14*, 477-92.

Morse, P.A. and C.T. Snowdon, 1975, 'An investigation of categorical speech discrimination by Rhesus monkeys', *Perception and Psychophysics, 17*, 9-16.

Pisoni, D.B., 1973, 'Auditory and phonetic memory codes in the discrimination of consonants and vowels', *Perception and Psychophysics, 13*, 253-60.

Pisoni, D.B., 1971, *On the Nature of Categorical Perception of Speech Sounds.* Unpublished doctoral dissertation, University of Michigan, Ann Arbor, Mich.

Stevens, K.N., A.M. Liberman, M. Studdert-Kennedy and S.E.G. Oehman, 1969, 'Cross-language study of vowel perception', *Lang. Speech, 12*, 1-23.

Streeter, L., 1976, 'Language perception of 2-month-old infants shows effects of both innate mechanisms and experience', *Nature, 259*, 39-41.

Swoboda, P.J., J. Kass, P.A. Morse and L.A. Leavitt, 'Memory factors in infant vowel discrimination', in preparation.

Swoboda, P.J., P.A. Morse and L.A. Leavitt, 1976, 'Continuous vowel discrimination in normal at risk infants', *Child Development, 47*, 459-65.

Trehub, S.E., 1973, 'Infant's sensitivity to vowel and tonal contrasts', *Develop. Psych., 9*, 91-6.

Trehub, S.E. and M.S. Rabinovitch, 1972, 'Auditory-linguistic sensitivity in early infancy', *Develop. Psychol., 6*, 74-7.

Waters, R.S. and W.A. Wilson, Jr, 1976, 'Speech perception by Rhesus monkeys: The voice distinction in synthesized labial and velar stop consonants', *Perception and Psychophysics, 19*, 295-9.

9 RHYTHM PERCEPTION IN EARLY INFANCY

L. Demany, B. McKenzie and E. Vurpillot

Source: *Nature*, 21 April 1977, vol. 266, pp. 718-19.

The chief characteristic of rhythm is the subjective grouping of objectively separate events. In a rhythmic sequence of identical tone-bursts, adults do not perceive the repetition of a single sound, but a recurring configuration which has temporal form. Such a sequence is organised according to the Gestalt law of proximity.[1],[2] Organisation of temporal form has never been studied systematically in pre-verbal infants. We present here results suggesting a precocious achievement of this function and contrasting with previous research,[3] which failed to demonstrate organisation of spatial form by babies in accordance with the proximity law.

We adopted an habituation paradigm in which infants received auditory reinforcement contingent upon their visual fixation on a simple patterned-figure: a black outline-square on a white background. The infants themselves initiated the presentation of sound by looking at the figure and terminated it by looking away. After several such fixations, the auditory reinforcement was changed from one sound sequence to another. Any resulting increase in time of fixation on the visual stimulus was an index of discrimination.

Sequences of tone-bursts were presented by a loudspeaker placed directly behind the stimulus figure at a distance of 40 cm from the infant. The tone-bursts, 40 ms in duration, were derived from a tape-recording of a consonant chord produced by an electronic organ, with 270 and 1,620 Hz as dominant frequencies; intensity was 63 dB, about 25 dB above the ambient noise level. The stimulus figure subtended a visual angle of $8°$ and was positioned $20°$ to the left of midline. Fixation, as assessed by the corneal reflection technique,[4] was observed from directly in front of the infant, through a small hole in the screen containing the figure. The infant was judged to be fixating when, his eyes being turned to the left, the stimulus reflection was clearly observable over the right of the pupillatory opening. Duration of fixation, to the nearest tenth of a second, was recorded manually by a switch which simultaneously operated sound-emission and an event-recorder. In previous research, a high inter-observer reliability has been obtained for this measure.[5]

The first experiment was designed to demonstrate discrimination between the rapid, quite different sequences, S1 and S2, shown in

Figure 9.1: Sound Sequences

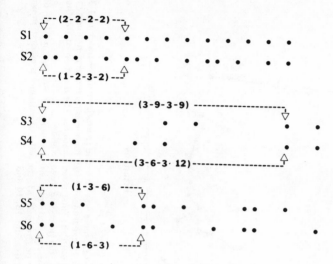

Each dot represents a 40-ms tone-burst. The shortest onset-to-onset interval was calibrated as 97 ms. All intervals were multiples of this unit. Their relative magnitudes in each sequence are given in brackets. Arrows delimit the period of each sequence. For example, the period of S2 is a succession of 1, 2, 3 and 2 time units (that is 97, 194, 291 and 194 ms). A sequence started always at the beginning of its period, and terminated when visual fixation ended (experiment 1) or after completion of the period in progress at that instant (experiments 2 and 3). Scale bar represents 1 s.

Figure 9.1. A regular pulse of tone-bursts, S1, was changed to an irregular sequence, S2. The two sequences had the same mean density of sound. We tested two samples, each of 10 infants, with mean ages of 71 d (s.d. 12) and 107 d (s.d. 6) respectively. Three fixations without sound reinforcement were followed by 12 fixations reinforced by S1 and then three fixations reinforced by S2. Median fixation times are shown in Figure 9.2a. A significant increase in fixation time followed the change in reinforcement ($F = 10.37$, $P < 0.005$), indicating discrimination of the two sequences. No main or interaction effect was associated with age.

In a second experiment, we studied discrimination of slower rhythms, using the sequence S3 and S4 depicted in Figure 9.1. The visual fixations of 10 infants (mean age 69 d; s.d. 18) were contingently reinforced nine times by S3 and then three times by S4. Fixation time increased ($t = 3.72$,

Figures 9.2a and 9.2b: Median Time of Fixation in Experiments

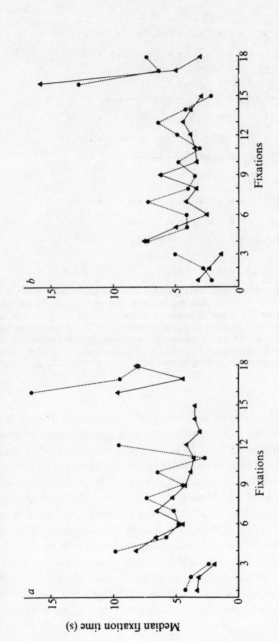

Figure 9.2a. Median time of fixation in experiments 1 and 2. In experiment 1 (▲), there was no sound reinforcement for fixations 1-3. S1 was presented contingently with fixations 4-15, and S2 with fixations 16-18. In experiment 2 (●), there was no sound reinforcement for fixations 1-3, S3 was presented contingently with fixations 4-12, and S4 with the final three fixations. The duration of the first fixation after change of reinforcement was compared with the mean duration for the preceding three fixations.

Figure 9.2b. Median time of fixation in experiment 3. No sound reinforcement was associated with fixations 1-3. For Group 1 (●), S5 was presented contingently with fixations 4-15 and S6 with fixations 16-18. For Group 2 (▲), the order of sequence presentation was reversed. The duration of fixation 16 was compared with the mean duration for fixations 13, 14 and 15.

$P < 0.005$) when S4 replaced S3 (Figure 9.2a). Thus, the 6-unit intervals of S4 were discriminated from the 12-unit intervals of S4 or from the 9-unit intervals of S3; alternatively, a new ratio of intervals was detected in S4. In any case, we conclude that infants are able to perceive intervals of six units (582 ms) as subjective links between sounds.

The aim of the third experiment was to examine perception of temporal form in sequences differing only in the order of their intervals. In the preceding experiment, discrimination might be attributed solely to the detection of a new interval. In experiment 3, however, the same intervals were used in both sequences, and the minimum segment for distinguishing between them was composed of a pair of successive intervals. Thus, the grouping of three consecutive sounds into a perceptual configuration was mandatory if discrimination was to occur. The longest interval appearing in S5 and S6 (Figure 9.1) had already been shown to be perceptible in experiment 2. Therefore, within each reinforcement, all the sounds may have been linked in a temporal continuum. The first interval in each sequence was the same in order to ensure that discrimination was not based solely on a difference in this first interval, without further grouping. To adults, the sequences sound like recurring groups of three pips, the groups (●● ●) in S5 being perceived as the inverse of the groups (● ●●) in S6. In all emissions of S6, however, the first and final groups were incomplete (see Figure 9.1). We tested two samples, each of 10 babies. Group 1 (mean age 69 d; s.d. 12) was tested in the order S5 followed by S6, and Group 2 (mean age 70 d.; s.d. 18) was tested in the reverse order. Median fixation times are shown in Figure 9.2b. An increase in fixation time followed the change in sequence ($F = 11.81, P < 0.005$); order of testing was associated with no reliable main effect or interaction. Since the differentiating of these new sequences entails the grouping of three successive sounds, we infer that they were perceived as recurring 'rhythmic groups' organised in temporal form according to the Gestalt law of proximity. In addition, it may be noted that, following the first half-second, the rhythms can be distinguished only by the order of the within-group intervals. The magnitude of the novelty response suggests that, rather than perceiving only a single, very brief change, the infants have also noted the repetitive difference in within-group structure.

A succession of several sounds was apprehended by babies as a psychological unit. This phenomenon of temporal grouping is, of course, not peculiar to rhythm perception. Language comprehension, for example, requires a similar process, since a semantic unit must be grasped as a whole, despite its sequential character. In the results reported here, perceived structure rests on a purely temporal variable: the relative values of the intervals between sounds. These results indicate that skills of temporal analysis and synthesis, prerequisites for operating with the sequential dimension of language, are present well before the stage of speech, and suggest that the early experience of time is more complex than is generally assumed.

We thank the staff and mothers of the infant centres: 'Enfance et Famille', Paris, and 'P.M.I. Georges Braque', La Courneuve. D. Demany designed and constructed the electronic equipment.

Notes

1.   Koffka, K., *Principles of Gestalt Psychology* (Harcourt, Brace and World, New York, 1963).
2.   Fraisse, P., *Les Structures Rythmiques* (Publications Universitaires de Louvain, Louvain, 1956); *Psychologie du Rythme* (Presses Universitaires de France, Paris, 1974).
3.   Bower, T.G.R., *Psychon. Sci.*, *3*, 323-4 (1965); *Percept. Psychophys.*, *2*, 74-6 (1967).
4.   Maurer, D., in *Infant Perception: From Sensation to Cognition, 1* (eds. L.B. Cohen and P. Salapatek), 1-76 (Academic, New York, 1975).
5.   McKenzie, B. and Day, R.H., *J. exp. Child Psychol.*, *11*, 366-75 (1971).

SECTION THREE: THE OBJECT CONCEPT

Introduction

This section goes more deeply into one particular aspect of the infant's perceptual world, and samples the research that has been carried out into the permanency, or lack thereof, of objects in that world. Jean Piaget's hypothesis that the concept of enduring objects takes a long time to develop in infants is a topic of much debate. Tom Bower, who is joint author of the majority of the papers in this section, has given a continuing contribution to this research, and has made a number of experimental observations that suggest modifications to the Piagetian descriptions. The more important of these are represented in the papers here. The papers have also been chosen to give a feel for the way in which these experiments have continued to build on previous research.

10 DEVELOPMENT OF THE OBJECT CONCEPT AS MANIFESTED IN CHANGES IN THE TRACKING BEHAVIOUR OF INFANTS BETWEEN 7 AND 20 WEEKS OF AGE

T.G.R. Bower, J. Broughton and M.K. Moore

Source: *Journal of Experimental Child Psychology*, 1971, vol. 11, pp. 182-93.

Piaget (e.g. Piaget and Inhelder, 1969) has described in considerable detail how the concept of a permanent object develops in infancy. Bower (1967) presented data which was interpreted as showing that there is a perceptual precursor of conceptual permanence and that, under appropriate conditions of stimulation, infants as young as 7 weeks of age may manifest a belief in the continued existence of vanished objects. Piaget (personal communication) has rightly objected that the methods used were insufficient to demonstrate that the infants were responding to objects as such, rather than to a perceptual configuration which contained the object as an undifferentiated element. The object presented in these displays was static. It is thus possible that a physical object could be seen, not as an object in itself but as a portion of a total array, with no independent existence of its own. However, Gardner (1969) has shown that infants in the same age range will anticipate the reappearance of an object which has moved behind a screen. This experiment does not seem susceptible to Piaget's objection unless either (a) movement itself is seen as a configurational element rather than as a change in position of an object, or (b) the infants have learned that a movement on one side of a screen will be followed by a movement on the other. If the infant interprets translatory movement of an object behind a screen in either of these ways, then this anticipatory behavior — which seems to indicate object permanence — in fact must indicate something quite different. The experiments here described were designed to discover which interpretation the infant actually adopts.

The first experiment compared the infant's response to translatory movement of an object behind a screen under two conditions: (1) the object moved behind a screen and stopped there; (2) the object moved towards the screen and stopped 15 cm from the screen, in sight, without going behind the screen. All three hypotheses about the way the infant sees translatory movement — the object movement, configurational

151

movement, and movement-movement contingency hypotheses — would predict that the infant should look over to anticipate in Condition 1. The object movement hypothesis predicts that he should not look in Condition 2; the other two hypotheses predict that he should look as much in Condition 2 as in Condition 1.

Experiment I

Method

A pink dome 6 cm wide by 10 cm high moved along a 1-m track at 10 cm/sec. A 15-cm-wide screen occluded the center of the track. The track was of natural wood, the background of black velvet, and the screen of white styrofoam. Forty movement cycles were presented. Eight stop trials were randomly interspersed during the last 37 cycles. Stops in sight (Condition 2) were systematically alternated with stops out of sight (Condition 1), i.e. 1 2 1 2 . . ., 1 1 2 2 . . ., 1 1 1 1 . . ., 2 2 2 2 . . ., and the reverse. Stop duration was 6 sec in both cases. Direction of movement at stop was randomly chosen.

The subjects sat upright 75 cm from the screen. Two observers positioned behind the black background on either side of the screen recorded the infant's looking behavior on stop trials. Six 8-week-old infants served as subjects. The observers made no attempt to judge anticipation or following during continuous movement of the object. On stop trials they recorded whether or not during the 6-sec stop the infants' gaze line moved on to that half of the movement path which the object would have reached had it not stopped. Interobserver reliability was very high. In only two cases was there disagreement. Cases of disagreement were treated as failures of anticipation.

Results

The results for individual infants are shown in Figure 10.1. Briefly it appeared that these infants were as likely to anticipate the reappearance of the object on the other side of the screen after it had stopped in sight as they were when it had stopped behind the screen.

Discussion

These results would seem to rule out the idea that infants of this age interpret translatory motion of an object behind a screen as movement of an object. It would seem that they must perceive the event in one of the two other ways described above. However, one might object that both the appropriate and inappropriate anticipations shown in this experiment

Figure 10.1: The Frequency of False Anticipations (Condition 2) Plotted Against Valid Anticipations (Condition 1) for Individual Infants in Experiment I. (Three infants had the same score.)

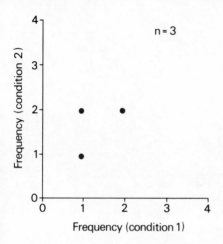

merely reflect the infants' poor control of their head and eyes, an inability to inhibit an ongoing pursuit movement. Such an objection seems plausible in the case of linear translatory movement. The experiment was therefore repeated using a rotary path of movement.

Experiment II

Method

A red foam rubber sphere was moved cyclicly through 240° on a black wire by a variable speed sweep generator. The speed used was 0.25 cps.

Six infants aged 8 weeks, naive to tracking situations, served as subjects. They sat upright 50 cm away from the center of the display.

The stop in sight was made at the 0 or 180° position, depending on the direction of movement at the stop. Stops were made in upward movements only. The stop out of sight was made at the 90° position. The remainder of the procedure was as in Experiment I.

Results

The results, shown in Figure 10.2, were similar to those found in Experiment I. The infants were as likely to make false anticipations as valid anticipations.

Figure 10.2: The results of Experiment II, plotted as in Figure 10.1

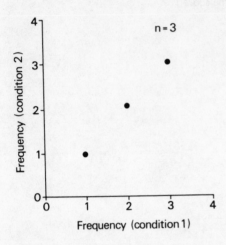

Discussion

The results of Experiment II definitely rule out the poor head control hypothesis mentioned above. Were poor head control involved, the path of head and eye movements on stops in sight would have been tangential to what was actually observed. Both observers agree that the path of head and eye movements matched the path of the object, even including the invisible topmost segment of the path. For what it is worth, this observation would also seem to run counter to the movement-movement contingency hypothesis, since there is no reason on that hypothesis why the infants should interpolate the invisible segment of the trajectory.

Be that as it may, these two experiments would seem to rule out any idea that the infant, in his own umwelt,[†] is tracking a moving object when presented with a moving object to track. The tracking continues when the object stops, something which could not happen were the moving object perceived as a moving object. The second experiment also seems to rule out failure of head and eye control as an explanation. It therefore was necessary to test the two other interpretations to discover whether either was a valid description of the way infants perceive events involving moving objects.

If the inappropriate and appropriate anticipations seen here reflect movement-movement contingency detection, learning that a movement in one place will be followed by movement in another, two consequences would seem to follow: the spatial and temporal relationships between the two movements should not matter, nor should the identity or lack of identity of the object(s) which carry the movement. Thus, if an infant perceives translatory movement of an object behind a screen as two movements whose only connection is contingent, then it should not matter to him if the object which reemerges from behind the screen is different from the one which went in; likewise, it should not matter if the speeds are different or if the dwell time behind the screen is inappropriate to the speed of the object. By contrast, if the infants are responding to the object movement as a movement *per se*, then anything which disrupts or changes the specifications of the movement should be extremely disruptive.

Experiment III

Method

A schematic of the apparatus used is shown in Figure 10.3. The carriers on the two track segments were driven by two independent separately controlled motors. Two solid state timers provided precise control of the intervals between movements. The center segment was screened by a 15-cm-wide white screen. The background was black velvet. Two objects were used, a white 5-cm-high faceless manikin made of styrofoam, and a 90cm-high red rubber toy lion. Two basic movement cycles were used. They are shown in Figure 10.4. One is 'impossible' in the sense that no single object could make such a movement. Only one object was ever visible at a time.

Four presentation conditions were used: (A) possible movement – same object on both sides of screen; (B) impossible movement – same object on both sides of screen; (C) possible movement – different object on one side of screen from other; (D) impossible movement – different object on one side of screen from other. Condition A was essentially a repetition of the presentation condition used in Experiment I. The presentation procedure used with each condition was the same as that used

Figure 10.3: A Schematic of the Apparatus used in Experiment III

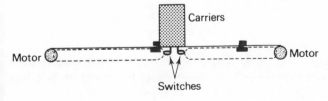

Figure 10.4: The Two Movement Events presented in Experiment III

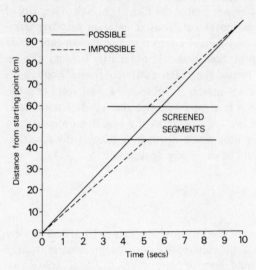

in Experiments I and II save that sequences 11112222 and 22221111 where 1 refers to stop out of sight and 2 refers to stop in sight were not used. Six pairs of conditions were used: A-B, A-C, A-D, B-A, C-A, D-A. There was a 7-day interval between the presentation of each condition in a pair. Two infants served as subjects in each condition pair. Mean age of the subjects was 60 days. The observers scored anticipation as before and also assessed the frequency of tracking, whether anticipatory or pursuit, during simple nonstop cycles.

Results

The results are shown in Figure 10.5. Conditions A and C were essentially equivalent and totally different from the impossible motion conditions; B and D produced virtually no anticipations; they also elicited rather little simple tracking behavior, the typical response to the accelerated re-appearance being a rapid checking back and forth between moving object and screen edge.

Discussion

This last experiment shows how insensitive infants are to changes in the featural characteristics of a moving object, which is yet another point against the idea that infants apprehend object movement as such. The failure of the impossible movement conditions to produce anticipation

Figure 10.5: Results of Experiment III

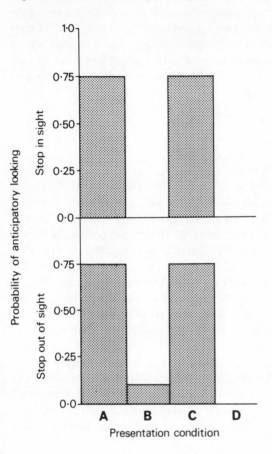

weighs against the movement-movement contingency detection hypothesis. Rather it would seem that they apprehend movement of an object as movement in a specified direction at a specified speed and that they are capable of anticipating and following that movement but become disrupted if another movement is introduced (hence the checking back and forth mentioned above) and that, while they can detect and use the parameters specifying movement, they either cannot or do not use the featural properties to the movement properties. The infant, far from tracking a moving object, is merely 'pursuing . . . the trajectory delineated by the immediately preceding perception' (Piaget, 1954, p. 18); note that it is the trajectory rather than the object carrying it which is tracked. It seems that when the object stops in plain sight it becomes dissociated from its prior trajectory. Infants will continue to track the trajectory, ignoring the stationary object. A stationary object and a moving object, even the same object, are apprehended as quite different by infants of this age. A moving object which becomes stationary, in a place, is not seen as the terminus of a trajectory, but as something completely different, bearing no relation to the prior trajectory.

Experiment IV

It seemed worthwhile at this point in the research to assess the pattern of performance on these tasks developmentally.

A total of 24 infants, eight 12-week-old, eight 16-week-old, and eight 20-week-old infants, served as subjects in the experiment. All were naive to tracking experiments. All were run through a replication of Experiment II (Experiment IVR). Two infants at each age level were run through one of the conditions of Experiment III (Experiments IVA, IVB, IVC, IVD). Half of the infants saw IVR first, half saw it second. In IVA, IVB, IVC, and IVD twice as many trials were presented as had been presented in Experiment III. There was a 3-day interval between conditions. Thus at each age level one infant saw IVR then IVA, one infant saw IVA then IVR; one infant saw IVR then IVB, one saw IVB then IVR, and so on.

The design of this experiment was dictated by the small number of subjects available. The restriction on numbers available was known ahead of time. It meant that if all conditions were to be studied, not even two subjects at each age group could serve in each condition, as naive subjects. We therefore decided to run all subjects through IVR and one other condition, since IVR was on the surface maximally different from the other conditions, and could be expected to produce minimal interaction with these conditions.

We had no *a priori* hypotheses about the nature of development in these situations.

Results

The basic results are shown in Figure 10.6. In the simple tracking tasks, IVR and IVA, the probability of anticipation following a stop out of sight was high at all ages and did not change with age; the probability of anticipation following a stop in sight, by contrast, declined steadily with age.

The pattern of development in the other conditions was quite different. In condition IVB the probability of in sight and out of sight anticipations both increased with age, in a similar fashion (r out of sight/in sight = .98, $t = 9.8$, $df = 4$, $p < .001$). Similar results were obtained in IDV (r out of sight/in sight = .9, t = 18.9, df = 4, p < .001). There was a larger total number of anticipations in IVD than IVB (t = 2.6, df = 5, p < .05).

Condition IVC produced a different pattern of development from either IVR and IVA or IVB and IVD. Anticipations in the stop in sight case declined to one at 20 weeks. However, anticipations in the out of sight case declined and then recovered, producing a curvilinear relationship between the two stop conditions (η = .90, r = .16, p < .001).

Figure 10.6: Results of Experiment IV

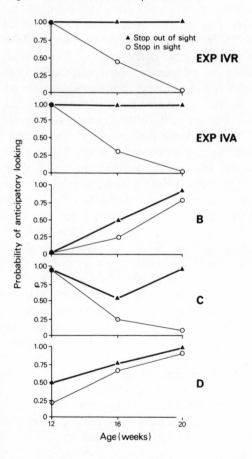

Probability of anticipatory looking in the two stop conditions is plotted against age.

Discussion

How is one to comprehend the pattern of these results? What has been acquired between 7 and 20 weeks to account for the observed change in behavior? The first acquisition may best be expressed as a coordination of response to moving objects with response to stationary objects, so that stationary objects are seen as termini of movements. Such a development could account for the dropping out of false anticipations between 12 and 20 weeks of age in simple rotary and Condition A linear tracking. How can one then account for the increase in both false and valid anticipations in Condition B and D of the linear tracking task? These two conditions involve an impossible trajectory, that is, two movement components which cannot be seen as a single movement unit. The development of false anticipations may be taken as indexing the development of the ability to see the impossible trajectory as two independent or temporally contingent movements which may terminate or begin in an invisible location, behind the screen. Some comfort for this speculation may be found in the fact that Condition D, where the objects seen in the two movement segments were completely different, led Condition B in frequency of false anticipations. One might expect that the object difference would facilitate the interpretation of the presented event as two independent events. What then are we to make of the infant's response to Condition C, where the two movement segments were continuous but the objects in the two segments different. At 20 weeks, this presentation elicited but one false anticipation and that invariably on the first stop trial. This condition differs from B and D in that the featural information points in one direction and the trajectory information in another.

The objects seen in the two track segments were different, a cue which is interpreted as indicating the presence of two objects, as in IVD: the movement segments seen were extensions of one another, making up a continuous whole, a cue which seems to be interpreted as indexing the presence of one object, as in IVR and IVA. Here the featural information and the trajectory information contradict one another. The youngest infants seem to handle this by suppressing the featural information. The age pattern indicates suppression does not continue as the resolving mechanism. How do the 20 week old infants perceive this event, if they do not simply suppress the object difference? They could perceive the event as involving a single object which changes behind the screen, or they could perceive it as a causal sequence, involving two objects. The key question is whether one object or two objects are perceived. Experiments to answer this question are currently in progress.

The important segment of development is the change in conception of he object which occurs between 8 and 20 weeks. At the beginning of this period, stationary objects and moving objects bear no relationship to one another. One might say that for an 8-12-week-old infant an object may exist in a place or an object may move continuously, but an object cannot move from stationary place to stationary place; for the 16-20-week-old infant an object can move from stationary place to stationary place, even to invisible termini. The coordination of place and movement is the essence of this developmental change. Mundy-Castle and Anglin (1969) have recently demonstrated a similar coordination occurring at about the same age. What is the mechanism which generates the coordination? One possibility is that the data rate of the infant visual system increases to allow multiple object dimensions to be handled simultaneously. This hypothesis seems appropriate to one part of the development, the registration of the featural properties of a moving object. It seems rather strained as an account of the developing coordination between place and movement. A more appropriate hypothesis might start from the limited data rate of the infant visual system which constrains the speed of movement which the infant can register as movement (Bower, 1967; Trevarthen, 1968). On many occasions, the infant is faced with objects changing position at a rate high enough that he cannot register their trajectory. Mundy-Castle and Anglin (1969) have shown that in this kind of case infants quickly learn where an object moving from place to place is likely to reappear, and they show a kind of place-to-place tracking which is independent of trajectory. This place-to-place tracking contrasts with the trajectory tracking mostly observed here. In many real life situations, the two styles of tracking must come into conflict with one another. That they do was shown in an experiment of ours which was unrelated to the present series. In this experiment, the infants viewed a screened track with three open ports in it. The object moved from center to left and back cyclically eight times, then moved to the right, followed by a reverse presentation. Pause duration in each port was 3-5 sec. Speed of movement was 25 cm/sec. Tracking behavior in this situation showed trajectory responses where the infant would track past the object once it had stopped. Place-to-place tracking was also observed, the infants on the 9th catch trial looking to where the object had previously gone rather than in its current direction. Both types of tracking were observed in the same session in the same infant. More interestingly a number of infants around 14 weeks of age showed both types of tracking in conflict. Thus on the catch trial where the object changed direction the infants would track the object in its new direction and then flip back rapidly to the port where it had previously reappeared. This conflict behavior suggests that the coordination of place and movement may arise as an equilibration between two partially adaptive responses which are in conflict. The aim of tracking is to maintain contact with a moving object. Both place-to-place tracking and trajectory tracking can attain only partial success in this aim. It seems likely that situations like the three-port tracking task are frequent enough that the infant could become aware of the incomparability and maladaptive nature of both strategies. He would thus be in a classic state of disequilibrium (Piaget, 1954) which could only be resolved by the coordination of the two systems of response.

These speculations could be confirmed or infirmed by an acceleration experiment. If the development described here does result from resolution of a conflict, then frequent presentation of situations which induce the conflict, such as the three-port tracking task, should speed development of the mature behavior.

References

Bower, T.G.R., 'The development of object permanence: some studies of existence constancy', *Perception and Psychophysics*, 1967, 2 (9), 411-18.

Gardner, J., *Two aspects of identity*. Unpublished research, Center for Cognitive Studies, Harvard University, 1969.

Mundy-Castle, A.C. and Anglin, J., 'The development of looking in infancy'. Paper presented at Annual Conference of the Society for Research in Child Development, Santa Monica, California, April, 1969.

Piaget, J. and Inhelder, B., *The psychology of the child*. New York: Basic Books, 1969.

Piaget, J., *Construction of Reality*. New York: Basic Books, 1954.

Trevarthen, C.B., 'Co-ordination of head and eye movements'. Research reported in Eighth Annual Report of the Center for Cognitive Studies, Harvard University, 1968.

11 THE EFFECTS OF MOTOR SKILL ON OBJECT PERMANENCE

T.G.R. Bower and J.G. Wishart

Source: *Cognition*, 1972, vol. 1 (2/3), pp. 165-73.

Piaget (1954) found that if one presents a six-eight month old infant with an attractive toy that is then covered with a cloth or a cup before the infant can grasp it, the infant will make no attempt to remove the obstacle to get at the toy. This observation has been interpreted as showing that such infants think that an object that is no longer visible no longer exists; out of sight is, allegedly, out of mind at this stage of development. Other investigators, by contrast, have found that infants of twenty weeks or less do seem to believe that objects that are out of sight still exist in a localizable place. Thus, Bower, Broughton and Moore (1971) found that infants of twenty weeks were able to anticipate the reappearance of an object that had moved out of sight behind a screen. Mundy-Castle and Anglin (1970) found that even younger infants were able to do this and in addition to follow the invisible path of the object while it was out of sight, even when that path was complex (Figure 11.1). These experiments would thus seem to show that out of sight is not out of mind for infants of twenty weeks or more.

The standard interpretation of Piaget's classic observations is in contradiction with the more recent observations described above. Bower (1967) argued that the contradiction was more apparent than real. Bower *et al.* (1971) and Mundy-Castle and Anglin (1970) used eye movements as indicator behaviors to make manifest the infants' knowledge about objects. Piaget, by contrast, used hand movements, manual search behavior, as an indicator. Manual search behavior is a far more complex task for an infant than is visual search behavior. Control of the hand develops much later than control of the eyes. Bower (1967) thus argued that the apparent contradiction between Piaget and the other authors cited was simply a matter of experimental method: The infants in the Piagetian manual search situation knew that the toy was under the cup, but they did not know how to remove the cup to get at the object.

Bower presented data in support of this hypothesis gathered in an informal experiment in which 5-6 month old infants were presented with a toy that was covered, before they could reach it, with a transparent cup. Since an object under a transparent cup is fully visible all the time, a

Figure 11.1: Apparatus Used by Mundy-Castle and Anglin

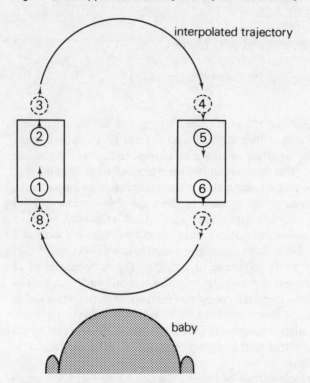

Mundy-Castle and Anglin found that, after the object disappears in one window, prior to its reappearance in the other, infants of 16 weeks will interpolate an eye-movement trajectory corresponding to the invisible path of the object.

failure with it could not be put down to out of sight meaning out of mind. Failure with a transparent cup could only result from lack of manual skill, and the same lack of manual skill could explain failure with an opaque cup, without thereby suggesting that the infants did not know that an object they had seen hidden under a cup was under the cup.

The results gathered from what was an extremely unsystematic experiment favored the hypothesis that 5-6 month old infants fail the standard Piagetian test because they lack the motor skill to pick up a cup; the infants failed with both transparent and opaque cups. The data was gathered very unsystematically and, indeed, was not reported as an experiment. Yonas (personal communication) and Gratch (personal communication) have performed more systematic replications, finding the opposite result, that infants who failed with opaque cups could remove transparent cups. Since the result is important for theories of the development of the object concept, it seemed worthwhile performing the experiment with more control of conditions than had been employed before in any of these studies. The first experiment was thus a systematic replication of the observations reported by Bower (1967).

Although at first sight there would seem to be few methodological problems involved in testing whether or not an infant knows there is an object under a cup, this first impression would be very misleading. Object permanence experiments are done under somewhat relaxed conditions with a heavy emphasis on rapport between subject and experimenter. Given the need for rapport, it is essential to have very precise definitions of what constitutes a passing response or a failing response. The mere fact that a child finishes up with the object that was hidden in his hands is not a scorable piece of information. The following considerations must be borne in mind in devising criteria for a pass or fail response in an object permanence situation. First of all it must be certain that the subject can pick up an object from a foreplane surface. If the baby cannot pick up any object at all, there is little point in checking whether or not the subject can pick up an occluder to get at another object. If the subject can pick up an object, then it follows that he can pick up an occluding object, provided the occluder is not too large. However, picking up an occluding object is not the same thing as picking up an occluding object in order to get at an object that had been hidden underneath the occluder, and it is the latter action that we wish to consider criterial in this situation. Piaget has certainly never denied that infants who do not have object permanence can nevertheless pick up objects. The special characteristic of picking up an occluder in the object permanence situation is that the occluder is not picked up for its own sake but is removed to allow the infant to get at the object that has been occluded. It is this ability to conjoin actions rather than the mere ability to pick up an occluder that Bower (1967) thought was lacking in the infants who failed the standard object permanence test. The problem is thus to decide whether an infant who picks up an occluder is picking it up for its own sake or in order to get at the object inside the occluder. The criterion was as follows. Prior to the beginning of object permanence testing the infants were presented with a toy placed on the table top before which they sat. The time from presentation up to successful capture of the object was recorded; this time interval will be referred to as free capture time. It was determined that if an infant removed an occluder and then picked up the object that had been under the occluder, with the time from removal of the occluder to picking up the object less than that infant's free capture time, the infant would be recorded as having picked up the occluder to get the object, a successful response. Picking up an occluder without getting the object that had been occluded or only getting it after an interval longer than free capture time was scored as a failure.

Subjects

Sixteen twenty-one week old infants served as subjects, 8 male, 8 female.

Procedure

Subjects sat at a plain brown wooden table, facing the experimenter. A stylized manikin 4.0 cm high, painted day-glo pink, by 1.5 cm in diameter was used as a toy. Previous work had found this to be a desirable enough toy. The transparent occluder was a plastic cup 6 cm high by 3 cm in diameter, with a transmission ratio of .7, so that an object within it could be clearly seen while the cup itself was clearly visible. The opaque occluder was a white plastic cup 6 cm high by 3 cm in diameter, that was perfectly opaque.

The infants were presented with the toy, placed within reach, and their free capture time recorded. After 15 seconds the toy was taken away from the baby. In its original location was placed one of the occluders, the opaque to 8 babies, the transparent to the remainder. Free capture time was recorded. The occluder was then taken away and the toy replaced in its original location. Before the baby could take the toy again the opaque occluder was placed over the toy. The baby was then given three minutes to remove the occluder before the trial was terminated. At the end of the trial the occluder was removed revealing the object which the infant was allowed to pick up and retain for 15 seconds. At the end of this time the toy was removed and replaced in its original location, this time being covered by the transparent occluder. Trial duration was again three minutes, save that if an infant had a hand on the occluder at the end of three minutes he was given a further two minutes to complete his response. At the end of this period, if the infant had the toy, it was taken away, replaced and recovered by the opaque occluder, with a trial duration equal to that given with the transparent occluder. If the infant did not have the toy at the end of the transparent occluder trial, the occluder was removed, and the infant allowed to take and retain the toy for 15 seconds before the second opaque occluder trial was begun.

Results

The results are summarized in Table 11.1. As can be seen there, the

Table 11.1: Results of Manual Search Task

Condition	N. picked up occluder	Mean time to pick up occluder	N. picked up toy	Mean time to pick up toy	N. within free capture time
Opaque 1	0	—	0	—	—
Transparent	14	115 secs	10	40	8
Opaque 2	2	125 secs	2	35	2
Mean free capture time for object		45			
Mean free capture time for occluder		55 secs			

hypothesis that there is no difference between an opaque and a transparent occluder as obstacles in a manual search task can be clearly rejected. The opaque occluder was far more difficult than the transparent occluder. On the other hand, it cannot be concluded that the transparent occluder offered no difficulties at all. Only eight infants were clearly able to pick up the occluder to get at the toy. The latency of picking up the transparent occluder when there was a toy inside it was far greater than the latency to pick up the occluder alone, indicating that the conjoined response was more difficult.

Discussion

The result of this experiment reopens the issue of the apparent contradiction between the eye movement results cited above and the classic Piagetian manual search task. The transparent occluder did pose problems but not enough to account for the difficulties shown with the opaque occluder. Part of the problem in the classic situation is behavior sequencing but it is obvious that the opaque occluder, with the toy out of sight, produced yet more serious problems, seemingly implying that out of sight is out of mind in the manual search situation. Since out of sight is definitely not out of mind in eye tracking situations, this raises the theoretically interesting possibility that there is a process of decalage operating between the eye movement control system and the hand movement control system; with, at this stage of development, the eye movement control system knowing that out of sight objects still exist while the hand movement control system has not yet incorporated this information. As Piaget normally uses the term decalage it is applied to extension of information from one situation to another that resembles the initial one formally if not in detail. One can thus speak of decalage between conservation of volume and conservation of weight since the situations are formally similar and developmentally asynchronous. It would not be doing violence to the concept to use it in the context of an asynchrony between an ability to find objects that have gone out of sight by eye and the ability to do this with the hand. However, the statement 'out of sight is out of mind' is a very broad one. The data of the experiment described above do not unambiguously support such a statement. The transparent occluder did produce difficulties, so that the resulting non behavior might have resulted from a summation of occluder effects with effects of the out of sight condition, without the latter being so severe that the infant thought that the occluded toy no longer existed. To test this hypothesis it is necessary to have an out of sight condition that imposes no behavioral problems or only very minimal ones. If out of sight is out of mind for the hand the absence of behavioral problems will not help the infant. If, on the other hand, out of sight is simply a problem, then the absence of the additional behavioral problems posed by the classic situation might allow the babies to succeed. The next experiment was designed to test this hypothesis.

Subjects

Twelve twenty-week old infants, 6 male, 6 female, served as subjects.

Procedure

The subjects were given a standard Piagetian object permanence test as described in experiment 1. All of them failed to do anything with the occluder. They were then given a different out of sight condition. The table used before was removed. The manikin was presented on the end of a string, dangling in front of the baby. Before the baby could reach out for the toy, the room lights were extinguished. Since the room was light tight, this left the baby in total darkness. The toy was thus out of sight, as was everything else in the environment. The babies' behavior was observed and recorded with an infra-red TV system, the vidicon of which was sensitive to light between 850 and 875 millimicrons. Illumination in this spectral band, which is totally invisible to the human eye, was provided by a specially constructed light source. The babies were left alone in darkness for three minutes. At the end of this time the standard object permanence test was repeated.

Results

None of the infants passed the standard object permanence test on either presentation. All of them were able to reach out to obtain the object out of sight in darkness. The reaching in the dark was accurate. The hands went straight to the object locus even after initial periods of distress lasting as long as 90 seconds.

Discussion

It thus seems that out of sight is not necessarily out of mind, not even that part of the mind that controls hand movements, provided the transition to out of sight is accomplished by plunging the room into darkness. One could infer from this that out of sight is not out of mind in the standard test situation either, the difficulties of the motor task simply summing with difficulties created by the fact that the object is no longer visible. On the other hand, one should beware of equating all the changes in stimulation that result in disappearance of an object. The psychophysics of disappearance has been studied (Michotte, 1962; Bower, 1967; Gibson *et al.*, 1969) and it is clear that some disappearance sequences result in perception of the continued existence of the object that has disappeared while others have just the opposite result, the vanished object seeming no longer to exist anywhere. It is possible that disappearance under a cup or a cloth is a disappearance transformation of the latter sort, for infants of 5-9 months. More careful psychophysical work will be required to decide the issue.

References

Bower, T.G.R. (1967), 'The development of object permanence: Some studies of existence constancy', *Percept. Psychophys.*, 2 (9), 411-18.

Bower, T.G.R., Broughton, J.M. and Moore, M.K. (1971), 'Development of the object concept as manifested in changes in the tracking behavior of infants between 7 and 20 weeks of age', *J. exper. Child Psychol.*, 11, 182-93.

Gibson, J.J., Kaplan, G.A., Reynolds, H. and Wheeler, K. (1969), 'The change from visible to invisible: A study of optical transitions', *Percept. Psychophys.*, 5, 113-16.

Michotte, A. (1962), *Causalité permanence et réalité phenomenales*, Louvain, Publications Universitaires, Belgium.

Mundy-Castle, A.C. and Anglin, J. (1970), 'The development of looking in infancy', paper read at Society for Research in Child Development, Santa Monica, California, April 1970.

Piaget, J. (1954), *The Construction of Reality in the Child*, New York, Basic Books.

12 STAGES IN THE DEVELOPMENT OF THE OBJECT CONCEPT

T.G.R. Bower and J.G. Paterson

Source: *Cognition*, 1972, vol. 1 (1), pp. 47-57.

The development of the mature object concept is generally reckoned to be one of the most significant steps in intellectual development in infancy (Piaget and Inhelder, 1969). The main outlines of this segment of development were initially described by Piaget over thirty years ago (Piaget, 1954). Subsequent work has merely amplified and extended his description without materially changing it (Bower, Broughton and Moore, 1971; Bower, 1971; Escalona and Corman, 1969). In all of that time the validity of the problems has never been questioned. No one has ever asked for evidence that there is an object concept that develops. This is not an idle question, but rather a specific instance of a problem that bedevils all of developmental psychology. The development of the object concept spans the period from birth to about 18 months. The responses used to index the level of the concept change drastically in this period; eye movements, heartrate, operant responses, overt grasping, locomotor movements, have all been used to gauge the stage of concept attainment. The stimulus presentations used to elicit these indicator behaviors also change markedly, from simple movement of an object to fairly elaborate versions of 'find the lady'. What justification do we have for saying that these various S-R situations are all markers for a unitary concept? To take a specific example, how can we say that the stage of development that ends around five months with the ability to track a visible object following it when it moves, wherever it moves, regardless of where it has moved in the past, stopping when it stops (Bower *et al.*, 1971; Bower and Paterson, in press), is the ancestor of the stage of development that ends nearly a year later with the infant able to find an object hidden in any location, regardless of where it has previously been hidden? The problem is particularly acute here since the older infant apparently repeats, at a formal level, many of the mistakes made and overcome by the younger infants.

The techniques used by embryologists are of interest in this connection, although they are obviously not directly applicable. We cannot stain a behavior as we can stain a cell, using the presence of the stain to make manifest the descendants of the original cell. Nor can we destroy a behavior as we might destroy a cell to identify its descendants by their absence in the developed organism. However, we can seek to accelerate the appearance of a behavior. If the acceleration succeeds in speeding the appearance of one behavior, and also — without further intervention — the appearance of a later behavior, we might with some justice conclude that behavior *one* is causally connected with behavior *two*, subject of course to many obvious qualifications. The first experiment to be reported here was directed only at establishing the presence or absence of a long-term causal connection between three substages in the development of the object concept, with long-term acceleration effects as criteria for causation.

Two of the three phases of behavior under investigation were briefly alluded to above. The first phase concerns the development of accurate visual tracking of objects, and terminates between four and five months of age. The second phase concerns the development of accurate, visually guided search for hidden objects, and terminates between nine and twelve months of age. The characteristics of the development of visual tracking in early infancy have been described elsewhere (Bower, 1971). Briefly, the infants of 12-20 weeks of age display two characteristic errors in tracking tasks. When tracking a moving object that suddenly stops, these infants will continue to track along the path on which the object was moving, ignoring the visible, stationary object. This error may be described as the result of an inability to identify a moving object with itself when stationary. The complementary error resulting from an inability to identify a stationary object with itself in motion, has also been demonstrated, although with a somewhat more complex experiment. If infants of 12-14 weeks are presented with an object that moves from place 1 to place 2 and back again cyclically, stopping in both places, they can learn to track the object back and forth between the two places. The error described above occurs initially but drops out, so that the infants simply track the object from place to place. If, however, the object moves to a new place going from place 1 to place 3, the infants will look for the object in place 2, the place where they have usually seen the object, ignoring the fully visible object at place 3. The infants will then look for an object in a familiar place, ignoring it as it moves to a new place. Both of these errors decline to zero frequency of occurrence by the age of 23 weeks in cross-sectional samples.[†]

The second phase of development studied here was the transition from stage 4 to stage 5 of the object concept. When a child is in stage 4 he can retrieve an object that has been hidden under a cloth or in a container. However, if allowed to retrieve the object from one place, A, more than once, the child will search for the object at A after seeing it hidden at B, a different place. In stage 5 the child does not commit this error, and can find an object that he has seen hidden, regardless of his and its past history of hidings and findings. It is noteworthy that the error characteristic of stage 4 is persistence of search for an object at a place where the object has been found before, ignoring the new place where the object has just been seen to be hidden. At one level of description at least, this error seems identical to the error described above as characteristic of the tracking behavior of young infants; they look for an object where they have seen it before, ignoring the place where the object has just been seen to move to. The formal similarity between these behaviors would seem to argue against a causal connection between them, since it seems improbable that the same error should have to be overcome twice at different times in the development of the same concept, while there is adequate precedent for the same problems having to be overcome twice in the development of different behaviors (Bernstein, 1971).

The third phase of the behavior investigated was the transition from stage 5 to stage 6 of the object concept. In stage 5 the infant makes errors that can be explained as an inability to track visible displacements of an object. The way we assess this inability was devised independently by Aronson and McGonigle (personal communication). The child is presented with two cups or cloths under one of which a toy is placed so that it is out of sight. The stage-5 child has no problem in finding the object under such circumstances, no matter what the sequence of hidings is. If, however, the two cups or cloths are transposed so that the cup or cloth containing the object is in the place that was occupied by the other cup and vice versa, the stage-5 child will pick up the wrong cup. The transposition is done in full view of the child who nonetheless fails to take the transposition into account in choosing which cup to pick up.

Subjects

Sixty-six infants served as subjects. They were divided into an experimental and a control group, matched for birth order, sex, and parental occupation.

Procedure

The tracking task (Bower and Paterson, op. cit.) was as follows. The object to be tracked was a 10 cm diameter bullseye, painted in day-glo pink, white and orange. It was mounted at the end of an arm 30 cm in length, driven by a sweep generator at .24 cycles per sec, through an arc of $180°$. The infant sat one meter from the display. Object position was monitored by a TV camera mounted behind the infant. Head and eye movements were monitored by a TV camera mounted behind the display. The output of the two cameras was combined and fed into a VTR;[†] providing a simultaneous record for subsequent analysis of object position and head and eye position.

The object was set in motion before the infant was brought in. The presentation 'began' when the infant first looked at the display. From this point, twenty movement cycles were presented. The last cycle and a random three others incorporated a stop in which the object stopped moving for ten seconds. Stops were always made in the central $90°$ of the arc. Records were scored for frequency of tracking on all trials. Behavior on the stop trials was scored for the following features.

1. Did the infant stop and fixate the stopped object?
2. If yes, for how long?
3. If no, did the infant continue to track the trajectory of the object?
4. If no to both 1 and 3, did the infant (a) return to starting point of movement, or (b) look away?
5. If yes to 1, did the infant then after the time given in 2, (a) continue to track the trajectory of the object, or (b) look back to starting point or (c) look away?

Records were scored by two observers.

The experimental group was given weekly exposure to the tracking task from 12 weeks until 16 weeks. The control group was given an equivalent number of laboratory visits that did not involve tracking and then tested on tracking at 16 weeks.

After this test no further tracking experiments were carried out. However, all of the infants were brought in ten times to participate in experiments on reaching before the object-permanence testing was begun and repeated weekly. It was originally intended to continue the object-permanence testing until all of the infants had reached stage 6. However, financial considerations forced us to stop before this point was reached.

The object-permanence testing was always begin with a simple stage 4 test. An object was covered by a cloth in view of the infant. If the infant succeeded in obtaining the object, the stage 4-5 transition testing was begun. Two cloths were placed on the table, and the object hidden under one of them, A. After retrieval and recovery from the infant, it was again hidden under the same cloth, A. After retrieval and recovery from the infant, it was hidden under the other cloth, B. After this, new cloths and a new toy were introduced, and the procedure repeated. After each AAB sequence toys and cloths were changed. The side chosen as the A side varied randomly from trial block to trial block. Six AAB sequences were run through. When the child reached the criterion of six errorless B trials, the stage 5-6 testing sequence was begun. On each week thereafter the infant was given one AAB trial, as described above, before the testing proper began. The testing procedure was as follows. Two cloths were placed on the table. An object was placed under one cloth, with the baby watching. The positions of the two cloths were then transposed. Six trials were given. Testing was discontinued after two sessions without errors.

Results

The results are summarised in Table 12.1. As can be seen there, the accelerated group maintained and even increased its lead over the whole experiment. It will be seen there that the results as presented are a hybrid of measures, with number of errors at a particular age used in one place, and age of attainment of zero errors used elsewhere

Table 12.1: Development of Stages of the Object Concept in Experimental and Control Groups of Infants

	Accelerated	Control
Probability of errors in tracking at 16 weeks	0	.51
Mean age of attainment in weeks of Stage 5	39.3	46.6
Number reaching Stage 6	.8	.6
Mean age of attainment in weeks of Stage 6	43.7	59.5

We had originally intended to treat our results in terms of errors at a particular age only. However, the developmental changes in errors were such that a measure of that sort would be necessarily misleading. The use of such a summary depends on the assumption that performance improves continuously from zero correct responding to zero errors. In the course of the experiment it became obvious that such an assumption would be entirely erroneous in this context. Figure 12.1 shows the performance of one infant in the weeks up to and including the last error in the stage 5-6 transition test. This profile was not uncharacteristic of all of the infants and certainly does not suggest any continuous decline in errors. The distribution of errors for all of the infants on the last day on which they made an error in the stage 4-5 transition test in shown in Table 12.2 which also gives the expected distribution on the assumption of random responding. As can be seen there the difference between the two distributions is

Figure 12.1: Performance of One Infant

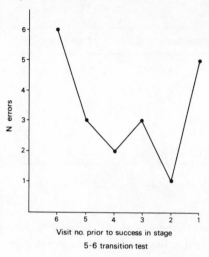

Table 12.2: Expected and Obtained Distributions of Errors on Last Error Trial of Stage 4-5 Transition Test

N errors	f expected	f obtained
6	0	1
5	5	6
4	13	14
3	18	14
2	13	12
1	5	7

chi-square = 2.09; $.90 > p > .75$

not significant. Table 12.3 shows expected and observed distributions of errors on the last error trial of the stage 5-6 transition test, for those infants that reached stage 6. The difference is again not significant.

Discussion

The results described above support the hypothesis that there is an object concept developing from birth onwards and that facilitatory intervention at one point will speed development at later points. However, results like this tell us nothing unless we can devise a plausible theory to link the

Table 12.3: Expected and Obtained Distributions of Errors on Last Error Trial of Stage 5-6 Transition Test

N errors	f expected	f obtained
6	1	3
5	3	1
4	7	6
3	9	12
2	7	6
1	3	2

chi-square = 6.9; $.25 > p > .10$

various stages. That is beyond the capacities of the present writers. However, we will outline some of the questions such a theory would have to answer, and some of the answers the theory might come up with.

The theory would have to be able to describe the infant's concept of an object at each stage of development. This is not such an easy task as one might suppose, since there are apparent circularities and reversals in the course of development. For example, there is evidence that a 12-week-old infant expects that a stationary object will remain in place after it has been covered by a screen (Bower, 1971). There is evidence that a 12-week-old infant expects an object that moves behind a screen to reemerge from behind the screen. By around 20 weeks these two bits of information are coordinated. Why then does the 24-week-old infant, presented with an object covered by a cloth or a cup, act as if the object was no longer obtainable? The hypothesis that this results from lack of motor skill (Bower, 1967) has been disproved (Yonas, personal communication). Bower (1967) suggested covering objects with transparent covers; if motor skill hindered success with opaque covers, it should equally well hinder success with transparent covers. Yonas found that this was not so; infants who were successful with transparent covers were not successful with opaque covers. Perhaps the answer lies in the object concept, or perhaps it lies in the concept of a cover. Certainly the covers used at 24 weeks to elicit manual search are different as stimuli from the screens used at 12 weeks to elicit visual anticipation.

A similar problem arises with the latter stages of looking behavior and manual search. By around 20 weeks the average infant will look for an object where he has seen it move, ignoring the place where he has been accustomed to see it. Why then does the infant some months later search for an object where he has been accustomed to find it, ignoring the place where he has just seen the object hidden. Is this error a result of conceptual development or does it represent lack of transfer of information from the eye-movement control system to the hand-movement control system? There is some evidence favoring the latter interpretation in an unpublished study by Heinowski (personal communication) who found that infants who were in stage 5 as far as their hand movements were concerned were still in stage 4 when required to crawl to a hidden object. That is to say, they would crawl to the place where they had been accustomed to find the object, rather than the place they had seen it hidden. If what we are observing here is lack of transfer of information between motor control systems, then it is not a problem for a theory of development of the object concept. This explanation, however, runs into difficulties with the experiment described here, since it is hard to see how motor skill could transfer between motor systems as diverse as those of the eye and the hand.

These then are some of the descriptive problems that must be solved before a theory of the development of the object concept can even begin to consider the processes that produce the development.

References

Bernstein, N. (1967), *The Coordination and Regulation of Movement*. New York, Pergamon Press.

Bower, T.G.R. (1967), 'The Development of Object Permanence: some studies of existence constancy', *Percept. Psychophys.*, 2, 411-18.

Bower, T.G.R., Broughton, J.M. and Moore, M.K. (1971), 'Development of the object concept as manifested in changes in the tracking behaviour of infants between 7 and 20 weeks of age', *J. exp. Child Psych.*, 11/2.

Bower, T.G.R. (1971), 'The object in the world of the infant', *Scient. Amer.*, pp. 30-8.

Bower, T.G.R. and Paterson, J.G. (in press), 'The separation of place, movement and object in the world of the infant', *J. exp. Child Psych.*

Escalona, S.K. and Corman, H.H. (1969), 'Stages of sensorimotor development: a replication study', *Merrill-Palmer Quart.*, 15/4.

Piaget, J. (1954), *The Construction of Reality in the Child*. New York, Basic Books.

Piaget, J. and Inhelder, B. (1969), *Psychology of the Child*. New York, Basic Books.

13 INFANTS' SHORT-TERM PROGRESS TOWARD ONE COMPONENT OF OBJECT PERMANENCE

Keith Nelson

Source: *Merrill-Palmer Quarterly*, January 1974, vol. 20 (1), pp. 3-8.

The human infant acquires only slowly one of the most basic human concepts, the concept of objects as permanent entities with enduring and predictable characteristics. By the end of the first year, the infant's substantial progress toward this concept provides a cornerstone for referential language, for social attachment, and for conceptual growth generally. A general outline of object permanence acquisition provided by Piaget (1952, 1954) has been largely confirmed and somewhat elaborated in recent work (Gouin-Decarie, 1965; Charlesworth, 1969; Grath and Landers, 1971; Wachs, Uzgiris and Hunt, 1971).

In contrast to an established outline of the infant's major successive achievements toward object permanence, only sparse evidence is available concerning how the infant achieves transitions between the successive developmental levels. Piaget suggests that change occurs gradually as the result of repeated accommodations of action patterns to encountered details of the world, but provides little elaboration — theoretically or empirically — of this assumed process. In Piaget's work and in most contemporary research, changes across age have been examined rather than changes across closely-spaced observations. In one recent study (Nelson, 1971), however, 3- to 9-month-olds rapidly changed their responses across repeated observations in a way which paralleled long-term developmental changes toward object permanence. The subjects in this study initially reacted to the disappearance of a moving toy train into a tunnel by watching the point at which the train disappeared. As repeated cycles of train appearance and disappearance were presented these infants learned instead to respond to this one train movement pattern in the same way that one-year-olds (and older children and adults) respond to similar events in general — they looked for the object, after its disappearance, along the extension of its trajectory. Generalization of this learning was tested for only one new condition, the train running in reverse direction around the same track and tunnel layout. No evidence of generalization was obtained.

In the present investigation, as in the study just cited, young infants were shown repeated instances of real object movement-disappearance-reappearance. Across a number of learning trials, infants were expected to learn to anticipate reappearances of the object from behind a screen. Changes in spatial-temporal trajectory and object were introduced to test generalization.

Method

Subjects

Infants ranging in age from 6 months, 15 days to 8 months, 15 days participated. Mean age of the 28 infants was 7 months, 13 days.

Procedure

Each infant was seated in a highchair. The infant's mother and an observer stood behind the highchair. By slightly leaning forward the observer could determine where the infant was looking. Directly in front of the infant, at a distance of 36 inches was a large screen (54 in. wide, 78 in. high). One of two 'objects' — an unfamiliar toy truck (6 x 12 x 12 in.) or an unfamiliar man (height = 68 in.) appeared on each trial. The object traveled laterally within view and then disappeared behind the screen to continue traveling at a constant speed and reappear at the opposite end of the screen. Trials presenting right-to-left movement and trials presenting left-to-right movement were alternated throughout the experiment. On each trial the observer recorded where the infant was looking at the instant of object reappearance from behind the screen; at the location on the edge of the screen where the object disappeared, at the location on the opposite edge of the screen where the object reappeared, between these two positions, or the extreme right or extreme left beyond these two positions. Two observers made identical judgements in 139 (90.3 per cent) of 154 trials examined. An 'anticipation' was scored on each trial in which the infant was looking in the appropriate location to see the object as soon as it reappeared. Experimental effects were assessed in terms of number of anticipations.

Two contrasting trajectories were employed. In a short-slow movement pattern the object began a trial 43 inches from one screen edge, moved laterally across the field at a rate of 29 inches per second, and stopped 43 inches beyond the screen's opposite edge. In a long-fast movement pattern, the object's initial and final positions were 113 inches from the screen's edges and the rate of lateral movement was 58 inches per second.

Infants were first presented 6 pretest trials, then a 12-trial learning series, and finally two 4-trial generalization tests. Relative to stimulus conditions in the learning series, the first generalization test introduced trajectory change and the second generalization test introduced object change. Two trials of the type presented to the infant in the learning series were introduced between the two generalization tests, so that both tests would be immediately preceded by the same type of movement pattern.

In the first two pretest trials, the toy truck was presented in the short-slow movement pattern. The man was presented in the final four pretest trials, the learning series, and the first generalization test. Half the infants watched the man in short-slow movement patterns for the final four baseline trials and the learning series, and in long-fast movement patterns for the first generalization test. The remaining subjects were assigned the complementary sequence of fast-long for the final four baseline trials and the learning trials, and short-slow for the first generalization test. Thus, for all subjects the first generalization test was designed to determine if anticipatory behavior established with one trajectory during the learning series would generalize to a new trajectory. And for all subjects the second generalization test assessed generalization of learning (based on the man's movements) to a new object, the toy truck presented in a short-slow movement pattern.

Results

Infants averaged .125 anticipations per trial on the two 'truck' pretest trials as well as on the four 'man' pretest trials. As these two rates were comparable, as expected, performance on the four pretest trials with the man as object was used as a single baseline for comparison with performance in subsequent four-trial periods.

Anticipations per trial averaged .241 on the first four learning trials, .241 on the next four learning trials, and .313 on the final four learning trials. Mean anticipations in the first generalization test, .268, and means for the learning periods did not differ significantly (in each case, t [27] < 1). But anticipations in each of the 4-trials learning periods as well as in this first generalization test were significantly more frequent than anticipations in the pretest baseline (mean = .125), as Table 13.1 documents. In short, infants achieved significant levels both of learning and of generalization to a new trajectory.

In the second generalization test the toy truck was presented for four trials. Anticipations averaged .214. This score was significantly lower than the number of anticipations (.313) achieved on the final four learning trials (t [27] = 1.86, $p < .05$) but significantly higher than the score (.125) for the baseline (t [27] = 2.03, $p < .03$). The increase over baseline demonstrates clear generalization of anticipatory responding established during learning trials to an object not presented during the learning trials. Although the lower frequency of anticipations observed in this

Table 13.1: Anticipations per Trial in Each Four-Trial Period and Comparisons of Baseline with Each Subsequent Period

Period	Mean	t[a]	p
Baseline period (4 trials)	.125	—	—
Learning trials 1-4	.241	2.29	.02
Learning trials 5-8	.241	2.55	.01
Learning trials 9-12	.313	2.88	.01
First generalization test (trajectory change)	.263	3.29	.01
Second generalization test (trajectory change)	.214	2.03	.03

[a] df = 27 in each comparison

generalization test with the toy truck than in the final four learning-series trials could reflect fatigue, it may instead indicate that the infants discriminated the man and the toy truck. Thus, their response patterns to object movement and disappearance may have been based not only upon spatial-temporal trajectory information, but to some extent upon the infants' prior learning experience with the particular object involved.

Further analyses support the conclusion that variations in spatial-temporal factors had little effect on the acquisition or extension of anticipatory responding. Subjects who received short-slow movement patterns and subjects who received long-fast movement patterns in the baseline and learning series, did not differ significantly in terms of number of anticipations in any of the periods compared — baseline, either generalization test, learning trials 1-4 or 5-8 or 9-12 (in each case, t [26] ≤ 1.30, $p < .20$). Similarly, in each of these 4-trial periods only minor differences in mean anticipations were observed for trials of left-to-right (½ the trials) versus right-to-left (½ the trials) movement; in the only difference which reached significance, for trials 9-12 of the learning series, anticipations were more frequent for the left-to-right direction of movement (t [27] = 1.88, $p < .05$). Within-subject analysis also documents the similar distribution of anticipating for left-to-right and right-to-left directions: among the 27 (of 28) Ss who made two or more anticipations in learning and generalization trials, the median proportion of anticipating to the left (and also to the right) was .50.

Discussion

The concept of object permanence encompasses broad knowledge of the predictable characteristics of objects. This knowledge is reflected in diverse behaviors, including the widely-studied manual recovery of objects hidden within reach but obscured by other objects. Visual anticipation of the reappearance of a moving object from behind a screen is another component of the general concept. For this component the young infants of the present study rapidly accommodated — in terms of increased rates of visual anticipation — to the reappearances of one object in a regular pattern of movement-disappearance-reappearance. Then they generalized this learning to new stimulus conditions in terms both of objects and spatial-temporal movement parameters. I assume that infant's progress toward a general concept of object permanence is based upon frequent instances of gradual learning and transfer much like the present instance. But evidence relevant to this assumption is presently lacking for other components of object permanence. More generally, it is assumed that the young human infant possesses the ability to construct complex general concepts — including object permanence as just one example — through gradual accommodations of response patterns to encountered patterns of events. Although the detailed theoretical account of such accommodation largely remains to be worked out, one important contrast with other viewpoints is apparent. In the present approach the key changes in early cognitive development are seen to rest primarily upon the infant's gradual adaptation of old responses through encounters with new events — rather than upon the acquisition of essentially new responses through either maturation or learning.

A differing viewpoint taken by T.G.R. Bower requires special comment. In numerous studies (Bower, 1967; Bower, Broughton and Moore, 1971; Bower, 1971) he has stressed the role played by maturationally-related and inborn structure in the infant's relationships with objects. For certain components of object permanence, Bower presents observations which indeed suggest innately programmed structure. In several of these studies, however, many trials of object movement were presented to infant subjects but no analyses of responses across trials were reported. Such failure to distinguish initial responses and subsequent learning clouds interpretation of the studies. This is true especially if the rapid learning observed in the present study typically occurs when infants encounter repetitive patterns of object displacement.

References

Bower, T., 'The development of object-permanence: Some studies of existence consistency', *Perception and Psychophysics*, 1967, vol. 2, 411-18.

Bower, T., 'The object in the world of the infant', *Scientific American*, 1971, vol. 225 (4), 30-7.

Bower, T., Broughton, J. and Moore, M., 'Development of the object concept as manifested in changes in the tracking behavior of infants between 7 and 20 weeks of age', *Journal of Experimental Child Psychology*, 1971, vol. 11, 182-93.

Charlesworth, W., 'The role of surprise in cognitive development', in D. Elkind and J.H. Flavell (eds.), *Studies in Cognitive Development: Essays in Honor of Jean Piaget*. New York: Oxford University Press, 1969.

Gouin-Decarie, T., *Intelligence and Affectivity in Early Childhood*. New York: International Universities Press, 1965.

Gratch, G. and Landers, W.F., 'Stage IV of Piaget's theory of infant's object concepts: A longitudinal study', *Child Development*, 1971, vol. 42, 359-72.

Nelson, K.E., 'Accommodation of visual-tracking patterns in human infants to object movement patterns', *Journal of Experimental Child Psychology*, 1971, vol. 12, 182-96.

Piaget, J., *The Origins of Intelligence in Children*. New York: International Universities Press, 1952.

Piaget, J., *The Construction of Reality in the Child*. New York: Basic Books, 1954.

Wachs, T., Uzgiris, I. and Hunt, J., 'Cognitive development in infants of different age levels and from different environmental backgrounds: An explanatory investigation', *Merrill-Palmer Quarterly*, 1971, vol. 17, 283-317.

14 ON LEVELS OF AWARENESS OF OBJECTS IN INFANTS AND STUDENTS THEREOF

Gerald Gratch

Source: *Merrill-Palmer Quarterly*, 1976, vol. 22 (3), pp. 157-76.

A wise friend provided a point of departure for this paper about the studies my students and I have conducted on infants and Piaget's object concept notion. He reacted to my struggling to tell him what we have been about by saying, 'Oh, it's like the situation of the British anthropologists of the early 20th century'. In other words, we have been on a long trip into the jungle, have seen many interesting things, and now have to find a way of giving common meaning to the exotica we have experienced. My pretentious title signifies my struggle for meaning. It would be appropriate for a paper I discovered I was not ready to write. Instead, I'll primarily dwell on the two types of phenomena that I have worked with in terms of a notion of levels. You will find me sometimes using levels in a Piagetian sense, levels of mindedness; sometimes you'll find me using levels like the Gibson's (1966, 1969), levels of information in the stimulus array. However, I'll leave it to you, or to others, to reflect on the nature and virtue of a notion of levels. I primarily will try to convince you that the phenomena we have been working with are interesting.

I started off my trek almost 15 years ago. It was an exciting time. The importance of infancy was being trumpeted on every side, headlined by such phrases as 'imprinting', 'early experience', 'critical periods'. The principal things to be discovered in the 'far-off-land' seemed to be the origins of social feeling and thinking, those distinctive characteristics that make us human. I, like Burton White in his address to a conference a number of years ago (1969), felt that Piaget's account of infancy, particularly his story of the development of the object concept, was the best available 'ethnography' to build upon. Most simply put, Piaget seemed to say that one cannot love others or think about them unless one knows them as distinctive permanent objects. One cannot relate objects to one another spatially, temporally, or causally unless one has a sense of an object. To quote Piaget, 'As Mr Brunschvig says, "to conceive of space consists first of all in furnishing it".' (1954, p. 183)

The Piaget (1951, 1952, 1954) of the infancy books appealed to me. He made infants very real. A given observation enabled me to see a detailed relation between the infants' acts and the situations in which they were acting. I often felt as if I could literally re-enact the infants' attempts to make sense of the situations and thereby know their experience. The observations took in a broad compass of settings and issues of adaptation. Further, he brought a sense of proportion to the period of infancy. Perhaps it was my fault — I don't really think so — but I sensed something magical about the banners of that time. They seemed to say that an answer to some large question of adult life was contained either in infantile experience or in the congenital make-up of infants. Piaget took a much more modest stand. Each period of life has its function. Like such American pragmatists as John Dewey and George Herbert Mead, Piaget has a view of development in which each period results in an achievement that sets the stage for re-achieving the goal in a larger context, the idea of vertical decalage. Like Dewey and Mead, he rejected both empiricism and nativism and yet tried to use the wisdom of both. Before there can be experience, there must be an idea in some sense. But the idea is small, a limited one. In growing up, one does more than concretize the pre-formed competence, one enlarges and transforms the idea. While identifying and giving clear meaning to the periods of life is easier said than done, the endeavor promised order and sense to me.

One way of looking at Piaget's (1954) approach to formulating the key achievement of infancy, the attainment of the object notion, is to focus on three age-graded observations Piaget made. Two of the observations have been commonly made. The third one is a relatively uncommon one to which Piaget attributed great importance and was my own starting point.

The first common observation is the 'out-of-sight, out-of-mindedness' of the 6-month-old. The observation is interesting because such babes can sit up and reach for what they see more or less well. Even more to the point, if they see a desirable object that is partially obscured by a cloth, they can remove the cloth and gain the object. Yet despite their apparent possession of all the requisite skills, they will not retrieve the object if it is completely covered by the cloth. Piaget's analysis of this event is quite radical. He chooses to believe that it indicates that infants at this and earlier ages are not aware of objects. If they were aware of objects, then they would perceive them as 'disappearables' and would have no trouble removing them from under the cover. What they do perceive are 'pictures'. They can recognize and follow forms, but only when they are in view. Such infants only *appear* to anticipate the reappearance of an object that moves behind a screen; they only *appear* to relocate the position of an object they previously turned away from. What joins the successive moments of an object are the infants' recurrent actions. The infants have no basis for knowing whether they have observed the same object over time or simply many different but similar objects — they live in a world of sensed similarities, not in a world in which things remain identical to themselves.

The second common observations have to do with pretending, deferred-imitation, and search for objects which cannot be located at their place of disappearance. To treat a present-thing as different than it is, to re-enact a non-present event, to imagine possible locations, these indicate that the child is re-presenting, is unequivocally thinking about an object or event. Such clear signs of object knowledge appear in the second year of life. To Piaget, they indicate that *only then* do infants perceive and think of objects, enduring invariant forms which exist independently of the infant. When we observe infants act in such a manner, *then* we can assume that they know objects much as we adults do. Such knowledge marks the principal intellectual achievement of infancy, the goal of that period of life. The infant has the basis for joining the human community — he can engage in symbolic communication and form mutual attachments.

To this point, I seem to have characterized Piaget as one of many theorists who have argued that infants initially are aware of objects on a sensory level and eventually become aware of them on a symbolic level. The radical aspect of Piaget's position has only been implicit in what I have said until now. Let me make it explicit. While most theorists have identified the problem of early object knowledge in terms of how proximal sensory information is perceived as information about a definite distal form, Piaget made awareness of the object context the chief issue. The problem is how the infant becomes aware that the successive 'pictures' are tied together in a spatio-temporal framework. The creation of the framework is responsible for the infant being able both to see objects as such and to symbolize them. Symbolization is not something that follows from the perception of objects. The two events are conjoint.

The third observation serves further to bring out the uniqueness of Piaget's view. The observation, in Piaget's eyes, indexes an intermediate level of development. It shows the infant beginning to work on the problem of locating 'pictures' in an 'objective' context, and the observation indicates the mechanism for this achievement.

The observation is a relatively uncommon one. Piaget was fascinated by the fact that when his own three infants were first able to uncover an object hidden within their view they then would search at that first location when the object was subsequently hidden in plain view at a second location. Piaget could have interpreted their initial success as the critical phenomenon. He could, like Hunter (1913) and others, have assumed that the infants were able to symbolize, were able to guide their search in the absence of the object by some kind of image of the object. He could have dismissed the subsequent error by assuming that the infants simply had trouble keeping places in a limited memory store.

He chose not to reason in this way. Instead, he saw the observation as strongly supporting his hypothesis that the infant constructs a notion of object through action. In his view, the observation indexed the first sign in the infant of a sense of object permanence, a level that was no longer 'pictorial' but was not yet 'objective'. The infant committed the error because he interpreted the object egocentrically, 'a reality at disposal in a certain context, itself related to a certain action' (Piaget, 1954, p. 65). The egocentricity of this level, stage 4, in Piaget's six stages, is a distinct advance over the egocentricity of stage 3.

The stage 3 infant is unable to unconfound act from thing, in so far as he follows or grasps a disappearing object, it is only because he extends the act of following or reaching. If the act is interrupted, the infant repeats the act or loses all sense of the absent object. The stage 4 infant has some sense of the object independent of the act. He attends to the obstacle of the cover without losing track of the object sought. But he as yet has no clear sense of the object as 'disappearable', as an object which is imaged when out of view. Rather, the screen is an index of the object. 'The screen is perceived as related to the subject and not as related to the object . . .' (Piaget, 1954, p. 192). In other words, the infant senses that an act on the screen will produce the object. The successful retrieval of the object leads the infant to perceive it as the object of that particular place, and therefore, when he sees it disappear at a second place, he codes the event as a disappearance of the object-of-the-first-place and searches there.

Thus, Piaget interprets the error as indicating a level of mindedness in which the infant has a sense of enduring, 'permanent', objects relative to his actions. The objects have no individual identity. They are not known as independent entities locatable at many possible places, but rather the object exists as multiple similar entities. Piaget hypothesized that he was known at that time as 'daddy-of-the-window', 'daddy-of-the-study', etc. (Piaget, 1954, p. 63).

I now more or less have brought you to the place where I was when I began my investigation of infants. I wasn't too clear what an object concept was or what action was nor how the two were related. But I was clear that Piaget thought that something very special was indexed by the developmental concordance of the ability to uncover a hidden object at one place and search at that place when the object was subsequently hidden at a second place, what from now on I'll call the AB̄ error. If Piaget was right, therein lay the origins of object knowledge. I could ignore babies less than six months of age and study the AB̄ phenomenon.

Further, I sensed that the virtue of Piaget's stage claims lay not in the discovery of age-graded sequences of performance but in the discovery of counter-intuitive intermediate steps in the sequence. Piaget invariably identifies three stages. There is a preliminary, a preconceptual, phase in which the child acts on but has no sense of the problem. There is a final phase in which the solution to the problem usually is immediately obvious, e.g. 'perception' of the conservation of one-to-one correspondence. The intermediate phase marks the beginning of a sense of what is the problem. In this phase, the child seems to perform much like the child of the final phase, but often when seemingly minor variations on the task are introduced, the intermediate child's performance is strikingly inappropriate and differs systematically from that of the child of the final phase. Such errors indicate that such a child is only into the problem, that he does not really understand the problem. His systematic errors give indications of the processes which underlie the course of development.

The AB̄ error was counter-intuitive. It occurred when the baby first succeeded at A, and Piaget described the baby as alertly watching the disappearances at A and B. The baby's manual act of finding the toy at A was supposed to determine its nature and location; the phenomenon was supposed to reveal the critical role of action in the construction of the concept of object.

My search of the literature revealed that only Piaget had claimed to have made this developmental observation. My path was clear. I would attempt to confirm Piaget's observation. If I was successful, then I would attempt to confirm his explanation of the phenomenon.

I decided to do a short-term longitudinal study in which I would begin at a point where the infants could not find an object hidden under a cover and would stop when they could easily find it wherever they saw it disappear. A student, Bill Landers, and I set up a series of tasks. We would first test to see if the baby could find the toy at A. If he could find it twice in a row at A, we would hide it at B. If he could find it twice in a row at B, we would then hide it more or less randomly at A or B 10 times to see if the babe could find it wherever it disappeared. When the infant could do all these things in two successive sessions, we'd stop. If the infant failed to find the toy at A then we would follow Piaget and first partially hide the toy and then hide the toy completely just before the infant grasped it. We eventually studied 13 infants, with each infant being tested every two weeks. Typically, we started when the infants were about

6 months of age and stopped when they were about 11 months of age.

The upshot of this study (Gratch and Landers, 1971) was that we confirmed Piaget's A$\overline{\text{B}}$ observation and made a number of discoveries of our own which were relevant to Piaget's theme. In the first sessions, the infants would fail to find the object hidden at A, but then would find the partially-hidden object by pulling it out from under the cover. We then went on to the task of covering the toy while the infant was reaching for it. However, sometimes we were slow and dropped the cover only *after* the infant had grasped it. The infants did not remove the cover. 'A toy in the hand did not seem to equal even one in the bush.' That seemed worth pursuing and we changed our procedure so that we consistently dropped the cloth only after the infant grasped the toy. We continued to discover that they would retrieve the object if they saw a portion of it but would not retrieve it if they had it in hand while their hand and the toy were covered.

I note, as an aside, that in a subsequent study (Gratch, 1972), I documented that the covering as such was not responsible for this phenomenon. When the cover was transparent, 6-month-old infants would retrieve the toy. When the cover was opaque, they were far less likely to do so.

Thus, from the very outset of our attempt to follow Piaget, we seemed to be finding evidence that infants who had relatively well-developed abilities to reach and grasp for what they saw and who could deal with obstacles did not seem to be able to cope with an object once it disappeared from view. Having the object in hand, while certainly providing the infants with some kind of information, did not appear to be providing information about objects as such. There was nothing about the touched object that implied its 'seeableness' and there was nothing about the disappearance of the object from sight which implied its 'touchableness' or 'seeableness'.

To give you some sense of the time course of some of the phenomena found in our longitudinal study, I shall now describe the *median age* at which certain events *first* appeared. Almost all infants found the partially-covered object in the very first session, 6 months, 20 days (6-20). Infants then found the object when it was covered after they grasped it (7-18). Then, they made the A$\overline{\text{B}}$ error (8-02). Later, they would take both sides into account when the object was hidden at B. They would either look at both B and A when the object was out of sight or they would touch one cover and then pull off the other cover (8-15). Still later, they would search directly at B (9-08).

The A$\overline{\text{B}}$ error occurred often in a session and occurred in many sessions. The infants only gradually learned to take the B side into account. When, in the early sessions, they made the AB̄ error, they would not try to correct themselves by searching at B. When they first successfully searched at B, hiding the toy at A would then lead them to search at B. They were learning a new special place, as opposed to learning to search where the toy disappears.

Thus, I have made the point that infants often make the mistake and that it has a developmental course. There are two points that I would like to add about the circumstances surrounding it. One is so obvious that you may think me simplistic for mentioning it. When the toy is hidden, the examiner must be sure that the infant is attending to it and its disappearance. I make the point because only under such circumstances can one feel that the infant who fails to search or who searches in the wrong place does so because he may understand objects in a different way than we do. While I do not know how other infant researchers deal with the infants they study, Fletcher (1965) has amply documented that a long line of infra-human primate researchers failed to keep this elementary idea in mind. The second point is that when one has the infants' 'eye on the ball' of the particular game, then a host of potentially distracting events can occur which do not interfere with the game. In the course of our study procedure, we often talked to the mothers, to the babies, to people behind partitions, all without distracting the infants from their task. This is not to say that infants will not be distracted. For example, like Charlotte Buhler (1930), we found that the examiner could talk back and forth with observers sitting behind a partition when we worked with 9-month-olds, but 12-month-olds were very likely to be concerned about those distant voices. Rather, the point I am trying to make is that one need not be overly concerned with strict, standardized procedures. The key issue is not standardization, but methods that are sensitive to whether the infant is in fact doing what he is being asked to do. In any case, Landers and I confirmed Piaget's observation of the AB̄ error.

Given the existence of the AB̄ phenomenon, my students and I set off to evaluate Piaget's explanation of it. It was a painful process because we did not feel we understood what he was claiming. We understood some explanations he rejected and we understood some particularities of his explanation. These became our focus.

Piaget claimed that the phenomenon was not a matter of forgetting but rather had to do with the failure of the infant to register the information that the object had disappeared at B. If forgetting explains the error, then its likelihood should vary directly with the length of time the object is out of sight. We might not be able to show Piaget was right, but he did give us the possibility of showing he was wrong, a decided virtue in so grand a theorist. We studied infants around 9 months of age. The toy was placed in the well and covered and then the infants waited either 0, 1, 3 or 7 seconds before the tray was slid within their reach. Different groups were exposed to each of the delay conditions. They did not differ in their ability to find the toy when it was hidden at A. Table 14.1 shows what happened when the toy was hidden at B.

Two things are very clear. The O-second group did not err. As you can see, 11 of 12 infants had an O-run score, indicating that they searched at B on the first B trial. Second, the great majority of the infants in the 1, 2, and 7 second conditions searched at A on at least the first B trial. The pattern of results both provides support for Piaget's claim and doesn't. The support comes from the fact that a seven second period, which is really quite long, as well as a 3 and 1 second period were equally likely to lead to error. Further, patterns of attention and gazing during the delay periods conformed with Piaget's notion. Younger infants were likely both to err and to look at A almost as soon as the object disappeared, holding that orientation during the delay period. Older infants were less likely to show such a gazing pattern and were likely to err only when they were somewhat inattentive during the delay period. Thus, the younger infants seemed to be erring because they failed to make sense of the disappearance of the object at B.

Table 14.1: Relation of Delay Length and Length of Run of B Trials in which Subject Searches at A: Number of Subjects

| Delay | Length of run (begins with first B trial) | | | | | | |
	0	1	2	3	4	>5	Total
0 seconds	11	0	0	0	0	1	12
1 second	4	1	3	0	0	4	12
3 seconds	3	3	1	0	0	5	12
7 seconds	3	1	0	4	1	3	12
Total (seconds)	21	5	4	4	1	13	43

Piaget's theory also predicts that the O-second infants should err. We initially thought that the failure to err might be an artifact of our hiding procedure. We induced reaching toward the place where the toy was being hidden. We thought such reaching plus the sliding tray might freeze the babes on the B side. However, changing the procedure by restraining the reach and not sliding the tray did not lead O-second infants to err. On balance, we don't think this result invalidates Piaget's hypothesis. We find it easier to believe that success in the O-second condition is based on a stage 3 levels process, an extension of the visual and bodily point that is set in motion by the hiding. We don't want to push the interpretation but do note that Harris also has pursued the forgetting hypothesis. In his first study (1973), he believed he showed Piaget was in error. In a subsequent study (1974), he has come to believe in the merit of the idea that infants of this age are perceiving the displacements of objects in a way very different than we adults do.

Piaget's account of the AB̄ error places great stress on the action of manually finding the toy at A. He has repeatedly emphasized that this manual act determines the infant's failure to register the hiding at B. Landers (1971) took up this point by attempting to compare active search at A with observation of toy disappearance and reappearance at A. However, the observational group actively searched at A on the first two trials and only then began a series of observational trials. His study therefore is inconclusive, since both the observational and the active-condition infants engaged in active search at A.

Evans (1974) took up the same question in a more direct fashion. He compared 4 groups. Two actively searched at A, one twice, the other 5 times. The others watched the toy disappear and reappear at A either 2 or 5 times. The number of subjects who erred in each group was approximately the same. Thus Piaget's emphasis on the role of active search seems misplaced. The key event that seems to determine the error is the observation of the disappearance and reappearance of an object at A. Again, we don't think this invalidates Piaget's central thesis, but we think it calls for a greater emphasis on the role of the stimulus displays the infant sees than Piaget's provides. I'll return to this point later.

As I have tried to indicate, these studies were very 'stimulus bound'; Piaget's observations and arguments dominated our efforts. We gradually began to 'de-center', since we began to wonder more and more about what kind of object was leading our infants to be so spatially disoriented.

Appel (1971) did the first of these studies. He wondered whether the searches we observed in infants around 9 months of age had anything to do with an object being hidden. In other words, he got to thinking on a decidedly non-Piagetian line. He reasoned that infants must come to our situation with a long history of discovering that if you pull on a cover you might find something interesting underneath it. He decided to see what would happen if he hid 'no toy'. One group of 9-month-olds saw a toy hidden in a box which then was pushed in front of them. Another group saw 'no toy' hidden. Half saw a covered box. He rapped on the front of it and pushed it toward them. The others saw him 'hide' his empty hand and withdraw it. Appel was wrong. The 'no toy' groups did not search on

5 trials and the toy group searched on all 5 trials. Our babies searched only when a toy was hidden. But then he reversed the conditions. The no toy/toy infants searched on the toy trials. But 8 of 12 toy/no toy infants attentively watched 'no toy' hidden and then searched. If babies search for the disappearing toy, we should not have found that result. The AB̄ phenomenon might be the same kind of event, i.e. the experimenter's action of hiding the toy at B may have no more bearing on the search at A than the hiding of 'no toy' at A. Before examining this question, Appel observed 12-month-olds. The results were quite different. Twelve-month-olds searched only when the toy was hidden and did not search when 'no toy' was hidden; they really seemed to have their 'eye on the ball'.

Appel then extended the study to the two-position case. Nine- and 12-month-old infants saw a toy hidden at A five times. All found it. Then half saw a toy hidden at B. Half simply saw Appel rap on the front of the covered B well.

The study produced a mixture of clear and peculiar things. The 9-month-olds who saw a toy hidden at B were far more likely to search at A than were the 9-month-olds who did not see a toy hidden at B. Thus hiding a toy at B was important in the AB̄ error: the activity of hiding a toy at B was more than diffuse signal to the infant to pull the A cover. Further, 12-month-olds who saw a toy hidden at B searched at B. So much for clarity — because the 12-month-old 'no toy' infants searched (as did the 9-month-olds), sometimes at A, sometimes at B, sometimes at A and B. They did not refuse to search. The seemingly simple complication of introducing two places made the 12-month-olds less than 'clear-eyed'. While the result is very generally consistent with Piaget's account and a recent study by Harris (1974) of children in this age range, we are less than clear why the 12-month-old 'no toy' infants searched and why the 9-month-olds were far less likely to search at A simply because 'no toy' was hidden.

We did not pursue those interesting leads. Instead we did another study keyed to an aspect of Piaget's reasoning. Piaget seems to argue that finding a toy at A marks it as the toy of that place. Evans and I (1972) reasoned that if we hid a discriminately different toy at B, it would not be seen as the toy of the A-place and the infants would not be likely to err. Alternatively, if hiding the same or a different toy at B are equally likely to lead to the AB̄ error then one would have to conclude that the error had to do with spatial difficulties rather than object-conceptual difficulties as such. The result of this investigation of 9-month-olds was that infants were equally likely to err under the two conditions, even though the infants in the different toy condition appeared definitely to notice that a new toy was hidden at B.

While this result seems to indicate that the infants are having difficulties with spatial locations rather than with the problem of knowing that one-and-only-one toy is being moved from place to place, the issue is unresolved. Shortly, more information on this point will be presented, but for the present, I would like to point out that we have seen infants who uncovered the toy at B then remove the cover at A. In their case, they certainly searched where the toy disappeared but did not seem to appreciate that they were dealing with only one toy. Moore (1973) has been actively pursuing this issue, claiming that the $A\bar{B}$ error is indeed a result of a failure to understand the identity of objects. We eagerly await a full reporting of his findings.

At this point, I hope I have convinced you that the $A\bar{B}$ phenomenon is a real developmental event and that study of how infants keep track of objects in space must be an integral part of any investigation of the development of object awareness. I don't think the investigations I have reported on clearly confirm or deny Piaget's ideas about the lack of awareness of object identity in 9-month-olds or the role of action in the development of object notions.

I am now ready to consider the second type of phenomenon we have been working with. Off of our work, my students and I decided to approach the question of levels by another route. We chose to examine the kind of relation infants perceive between the specific object that disappears and the specific object that reappears, an issue that Piaget never attacked in a concerted manner. LeCompte and I (1972) did this in a simple, direct fashion. We observed the reaction of 9-, 12- and 18-month-old infants to repeated cycles of the following situation. On three occasions, a toy was hidden in a box and the infants found it. Then the toy was hidden, but the infants found a grossly different toy. We assumed that the ages chosen corresponded roughly to Piaget's stages 4, 5 and 6. We developed a way of thinking about this little world which we used to code what happened.

We reasoned that an adult sees the disappearance of a toy into a box and the subsequent reappearance of the toy in the box as a single event. The adult has the idea that what goes into the box will remain there in the same form. The disappearance of the object sets in motion the subsequent phases of that unitary expectation. Therefore when the adult uncovers the well and sees a different object, he'll be surprised, i.e. he will react suddenly and intensely to the missing step in the invariant sequence of events. He'll then react to the new object by wondering where the other one is and what accounts for the appearance of the unexpected object. He may search for the missing object, ask the experimenter what he did, search the box for a false bottom, etc.

Given Piaget's characterization of stage 6, we felt that such infants would react much like the adults I have described. Further, Piaget's theory also indicates that there should be two other gross, and lower, levels of reaction to the trick. The second level should be one in which the infant is not aware of a unitary disappearance-reappearance sequence. The child should only have a contingent sense of the two events (they usually belong together) and no sense of why they are united. Such a child should not be surprised. He should slowly become puzzled as he assimilates the fact that the new toy is different than the one he was set to see. Further, because he has no basis for imaging the missing object, he should not search for the missing one but instead should focus confusedly on the new toy. In other words, these were the kinds of reactions we expected from infants Piaget would characterize as being in stage 4 or 5. We visualized the third and lowest level as one in which the child would have an appreciation that the two 'pictures' were different but no sense that they had to belong together. Such infants should attend to the new object as a novel event. They should stare at the toy prolongedly, examine it, but *not* be distressed by its presence.

Given these hypotheses, we constructed two scales. One, the puzzlement scale (see Table 14.2), is an attempt to describe the infants' initial reaction to the sight and perhaps touch of the toy. It consists of 6 categories. 6 is surprise, 5 is definite puzzlement, 4 is mild puzzlement. Categories 6 through 4 all imply that the infant has some sense that a violation of the connection between the toy that disappeared and the toy that reappeared has occurred. 3 is definite noticing, the novel reaction I described earlier. 2 is recognition, a short definite look at the object, and 1 is an automatic look, a quick casual glance at the toy. Category 3 implies a sense of change of object but no sense of violation, and the other two categories imply no sense of change.

The instrumental scale (see Table 14.3) describes what the babies then went on to do about the toy in front of them. It has 8 categories, only 6 of which are relevant to our purpose. 6 involves a questioning focus on both the experimenter and the missing toy, as if the infant were looking for a cause. 5 involves a focus on the missing toy. Both 5 and 6 directly imply some form of representation of the missing toy. 4 is a transitional category, the infant neither accepts nor rejects the toy in the box, implying the infant is troubled but has no sense of the missing toy. 3 refers to examination of the toy, 2 is appropriate use of the toy, and 1 is

Table 14.2: Levels of Puzzlement Scale

6 — Surprise	A stunned look appears on the subject's face. Eyes widen, eyebrows move up, face relaxes, and mouth falls open. These facial expressions are coupled with such behaviors as a freezing of the body, hand stopping in mid air, and sudden vocalization changes.
5 — Definite puzzlement	A strong persistent frown appears on the subject's face. The eyebrows knit, the face sobers up, a tightness appears in the mouth and cheeks. The body and the hand may also respond with a momentary freeze, but this would not be as intense and prolonged as in the case of surprise.
4 — Mild puzzlement	A weaker, and more fleeting puzzlement. A very slight frown appears on the subject's face and a sobering occurs. There is no freezing of the body or the hand and the intensity of stare at the toy is lower. (This category has a sub-category which is rated when subject shows no frowning but a vague, confused, baffled look, with a loosening of the face rather than a sobering up.)
3 — Noticing toy only	Subject looks at toy carefully with a long, decided stare. He may show pleasure or displeasure, but no indication of bafflement, puzzlement or surprise.
2 — Recognition	Subject looks at toy with a short stare of recognition. He spends some time to recognize what is in the box, but not as long as in scale point 3.
1 — Automatic look	Subject takes a very quick, casual, automatic look at the toy. He either hardly sees the toy before he takes it out of the box, or does not even bother to look until he has it out of the box.

stereotyped play with it.

Figure 14.1 presents, in graphic form, the general result that we found in the study. It presents, on the ordinate, the puzzlement scores, our judgements of the children's initial reactions. On the abcissa you can see that the infants on the non-trick trials — trials 1, 2, 3, 5, 6, 7 and 9 — tended to get scores of 2 and 3, i.e. they tended to stare, briefly or at great length, at the toy. However, on trials 4 and 8, the trick trials, infants of all ages reacted differently. The mean score for the 18-month-olds was about 5 on the first trick and the score for the 9- and 12-month-olds was about 3.5. Comparable trends were present on the second trick, with the 12-month-olds scoring higher than they did before. We had expected that the infants, at least the older ones, would be distressed on the trials after the trick, perhaps even being puzzled over not being tricked again. While a few infants did react to the trick on the subsequent non-trick trials, Figure 14.1 indicates that most quickly acted as if the trick had never occurred. The trends for the instrumental reactions paralleled those of the puzzlement reactions. I'll not report them because I would only be

Table 14.3: Levels of Instrumental Reaction

8	— Solving the puzzle	Subject actually finds the knob and works it to make toys appear and disappear.
7	— Eyes on the mechanism of the game	Subject takes box, and turns it around in a variety of ways, and systematically searches for a mechanism.
6	— Focus on toy box and experimenter	Subject includes both the box and the experimenter in his attempts to determine what has happened. He searches in the box persistently and looks at the experimenter repeatedly in a questioning and suspicious manner.
5	— Focus on lost toy	Subject searches in and around the box, in washcloth, on the floor for the missing toy. He may look at the experimenter, but this is either a sociable glance, or a complaining look, as opposed to a questioning, suspicious one, as in scale point 6.
4	— Questioning the toy found	Subject acts as if he cannot accept or reject the toy he finds in box. He persistently picks up and puts down the toy, questioning its presence in the box. He may look at the toy and the experimenter in bafflement, and treat the toy as if it has some 'eerie' quality.
3	— Examining the toy	Subject recognizes he is faced with a different toy, and actively explores the properties of this thing.
2	— Appropriate treatment of the toy	Subject treats the toy in a manner appropriate for that toy. If he likes the toy, he plays with it; if he doesn't like it, he refuses to take it or gives it to the experimenter, or throws it on the floor.
1	— Stereotyped play with the toy	Subject takes toy and either mouths it or bangs it, or he simply holds the toy in his hand doing nothing with it.

presenting more means, and a better way to indicate how the results of this study conformed to Piaget's description of levels is to talk about individuals. Ten of the twelve 18-month-olds, on at least one of the two trick trials, reacted with surprise or deep puzzlement, scores of 6 or 5, and then searched for a cause or the missing toy, scores of 6 or 5. Nine-month-olds also acted as if they had a notion of the connectedness of the disappearing and reappearing toy but their sense of the connection seemed more diffuse. Eight of the twelve 9-month-olds, on at least one trick trial, either reacted with mild puzzlement, a score of 4, or subsequently questioned the toy they found, a score of 4. Finally, the responses of the 12-month-olds were both intermediate and more variable. Thus, looking at infants' reactions to the trick in terms of our rating scheme led to results which generally conform to Piaget's account of the development of the object concept.

Saal (1975) set out to examine the phenomena I have just presented

Figure 14.1: Mean Puzzlement Scores of the Age Groups on Each Trial

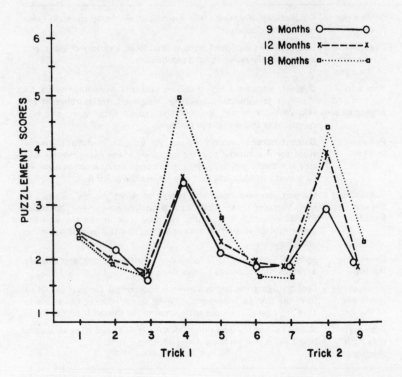

in two ways. On the one hand, she chose to extend the age range, studying 6-month-olds as well as 9-, 12- and 18-month-olds. On the other hand, she varied the nature of the object change. In the LeCompte and Gratch study, toy 1 and toy 2 were different toys. Saal replicated this condition, using a small drab plastic horse and a relatively large colored block which contained a bell. The other condition involved a change in the color of the block. She had a number of hypotheses, one of the more entertaining being the possibility that the gross change would be interpreted as an object exchange whereas the color change would be interpreted as a transformation of the same object. I'll not elaborate here her various hypotheses because to her disappointment the two change conditions did not produce differences in responses to the tricks.

Table 14.4 presents the results of her study, where the two toy conditions are collapsed. There are two interesting trends, both statistically significant. If you look at the puzzlement heading and the third column under it, the mean of the two tricks, you'll note that the scores for the

Table 14.4: Mean Puzzlement and Instrumental Reactions

Age (months)	Puzzlement			Instrumental		
	Trick 1	Trick 2	Mean	Trick 1	Trick 2	Mean
6	3.00	2.83	2.92	2.67	2.50	2.58
9	3.17	2.83	3.00	3.42	3.33	3.37
12	3.83	3.92	3.88	3.58	3.42	3.50
18	4.83	4.83	4.83	4.58	4.33	4.46

6- and 9-month-olds are about 3 and these scores differ from the scores of the 12- and 18-month-olds. In other words, only the 12- and 18-month-olds tended to react to the trick with puzzlement when they first looked at the toy. On the other hand, looking at the comparable mean column under the instrumental reaction heading reveals a different picture. Only the 6-month-olds tended not to show signs of distress over the new toy. The 6-month-olds tended to have scores of 3 or less whereas the 9-month-olds were more likely to get scores of 4, behaving much like the 12-month-olds. In other words, once the 9-month-olds took the toy in hand, they often were distressed by the change. But looking alone did not provoke the distress. This is an intriguing result, one much like that reported by Schaffer, Greenwood and Parry (1972) in another context. In each session of longitudinal study, those investigators repeatedly gave the infant the opportunity to see and handle an object. Then the infant was given a different colored copy of the toy. There was a substantial change in the infants' reactions at around ages 8 and 9 months. At younger ages, the infants would stare longer at the new toy than the old toy, but they would quickly snatch it up, as if the novel object were more interesting than the old one. At 8 and 9 months, the infants would stare even longer at the new toy than they did at younger ages, but more importantly, they would reach far more slowly for it. Thus, the sudden appearance of a new toy led them to be wary: they gave the toy a different meaning than did the younger infants.

Saal discovered two other things I'd like to mention. She tricked a few babies at each age on the very first trial of the game and got comparable age trends. In other words, the reactions I have described do not appear to be a function of the particular sequence of trials we used in the LeCompte and Gratch (1972) and Saal studies. The infants appear to come to the game with a set, a scheme, that determines how they will react to the trick. Second, at the end of her trial series, Saal played one last trick with some of the babies. She hid a toy and the infants found nothing. The infants' reactions to finding nothing were comparable to their reaction to finding a different toy.

I have now ended my trip and return to my original metaphor of the jungle. I have repeatedly emphasized the phenomenal because I feel clear at that level, and I think an important virtue of Piaget's approach to the problem of object knowledge lies in what phenomena he chose to study and how he studied them.

Piaget studied the problem in a direct way. What the examiner does, what the infant does, what the situation is, all tend to be in plain view. The events are not obscured from the subject, the examiner, or the observer by elaborate machinery or complicated indices of the events.

Piaget sensed that the task of the infant is not so much that of object recognition as that of keeping track of objects. We seldom get a clear view of things, either because we or they are on the move. While some forms stay put — are the walls and furniture of our 'boxes' — something usually is in front or beside or behind them. Other forms, particularly animate ones, are on the move. The problem for the infant is one of keeping track of such things, in-sight, out-of-sight, in space-time. In this, the problem for the infant, and for us, is somehow to determine whether what we see now was different, similar, or the same as what we once saw and, comparably, will be the same, similar, or different from what we will see.

So much for clarity. While the phenomena I have discussed are orderly, their meaning remains to be determined. I'll close by presenting some provisional thoughts on how to interpret what I have presented to you.

I would like to think that I have given you reason to believe in the viability of Piaget's hypothesis that somewhere between 6 and 9 months infants come to a new level of awareness of objects — the successive appearances in time and space of objects are seen as connected albeit diffusely. The LeCompte and Gratch (1972) and Saal (1975) studies show that 9-month-olds have a real but confused sense that the specific toy that disappears in one place should reappear in that place. The AB̄ studies suggest that the sense of connectedness also involves spatial confusions. The Schaffer, Greenwood and Parry study (1972) seems to support this generalization. At 8 and 9 months of age, infants treated the suddenly appearing new object warily, implying that they had a sense of what was to be expected and that it was violated. But what does Piaget's hypothesis really entail? And isn't there strong contrary evidence provided by Bower's (1974) many studies of much younger infants?

As to the contrary evidence, I don't think it is compelling. I had hoped to come before you to talk about a study by a student, Muriel Meicler. She intends to examine the reaction of 5- and 6-month-old infants to a trick in a visual tracking situation much like that employed by Bower and his group. Unfortunately, she has run into an unspeakable apparatus problem. Therefore, I have no direct evidence that infants of that age and younger do not know about the permanence of objects when they simply watch objects track behind a screen. However, I can say that there is reason to doubt the evidence that young infants do know about the permanence of objects on a visual level and somehow lose it when they have to coordinate vision and touch. In particular, one major study, that of Bower, Broughton and Moore (1971), had major procedural flaws which I have detailed elsewhere (Gratch, 1975). Gardner (1971) also reported that young infants will be distressed and will search for the missing object when they are tricked in a tracking situation. Her study does not suffer from the procedural flaws of the prior study, but her observations were not made in such a manner that one can demonstrate that the infants were not simply reacting to, in Piaget's terms, 'picture changes'.

The issue is an important one and has to be settled by direct investigation. Further, the controversy serves to focus attention on the role of action. Smillie (1972) has ably pointed out that Piaget of the infancy books certainly underestimated the amount of event structure that very young infants are able to attend to visually. But even if we grant the possibility that Piaget is right in asserting that infants move from a 'pictorial' to a pre-object-conceptual to an object-conceptual level of awareness, is the elaboration and coordination of action schemes the mechanism responsible for this course of development? Clearly action has something to do with the course of development. The great increase in infants' sensorimotor resourcefulness that appears around 6 to 9 months of age clearly puts them in a position to know very different things about objects than they could have known previously. But the key issue is whether the actions are constituitive of knowledge, as Piaget would argue, or whether 'the acts of picking up and reaching *reveal* certain facts about objects; they do not create them' (Gibson, 1966, p. 274).

I have no answers. The study by Evans (1974) of the AB error, in which he compared observing the toy disappear and reappear at A with finding it at A, clearly suggests that Piaget is wrong in a limited sense. The specific act of finding at A does not appear to determine the error. Rather noting the appearance-disappearance sequence seems to mark A as the special place. On the other hand, Piaget seems to be trying to use the theme of action to explain something larger than particular objects and places. He talks of these as specifics, figurative matters, matters highly determined by particular sensory displays. Piaget is trying to use the notion of action to account for how we order particularities, how we get at generalities, initially of a sensorimotor sort – the object in an ordered context – ultimately of a logical sort. I presently cannot do more than to say that Piaget, for all of his vagaries of at least expression, serves us well by keeping our attention focused on this key issue – the developmental relation between the particular and the general.

I shall close by commenting upon what I see as a salutory trend, sparked by Piaget's focus on levels of object awareness. Piaget came to focus on the particular paradigm of playing hiding games with infants from a rich context of observations of infants in many settings. My own work, and that of others, by sticking very closely to the hiding game paradigm, contains the seeds of creating a world of its own, falsely hailed by the phrase 'object concept'. Thus, I would like to note the efforts of Keith Moore (1974) and Kessen and Nelson (1974). They have begun to map out the kinds of placements of animate and inanimate objects in time-space that infants are exposed to at different times of life. Such an ecological mapping is the necessary counterpart to the attempt to map out the growth of the mind and contains the basis for reconciling the wise but conflicting positions of constructionists such as Piaget and realists like E.J. and J.J. Gibson.

References

Appel, K.J., *Three Studies in Object Conceptualization: Piaget's Sensorimotor Stages Four and Five*. Unpublished dissertation, University of Houston, 1971.

Bower, T.G.R., *Development in Infancy*. San Francisco: Freeman, 1974.

Bower, T.G.R., Broughton, J.M. and Moore, M.K., 'Development of the object concept as manifested in the tracking behavior of infants between 7 and 20 weeks of age', *Journal of Experimental Child Psychology*, 1971, vol. 11, 182-93.

Buhler, C., *The First Year of Life*. New York: John Day, 1930.

Evans, W.F., *The Stage IV Error in Piaget's Theory of Object Concept Development: An Investigation of the Role of Activity*. Unpublished dissertation, University of Houston, 1974.

Evans, W.F. and Gratch, G., 'The Stage IV error in Piaget's theory of object concept development: Difficulties in object conceptualization or spatial localization?', *Child Development*, 1972, vol. 43, 682-8.

Fletcher, H.J., 'The delayed response problem', in A.M. Schrier, H.F. Harlow and F. Stollnitz (eds.), *Behavior of nonhuman primates* (vol. 1). New York: Academic Press, 1965, pp. 129-65.

Gardner, J.K., 'The development of object identity in the first six months of human infancy'. Paper presented at the meeting of the Society for Research in Child Development, Minneapolis, Minnesota, 1971.

Gibson, E.J., *Principles of Perceptual Learning and Development*. New York: Appleton-Century-Crofts, 1969.

Gibson, J.J., *The Senses Considered as Perceptual Systems*. New York: Houghton-Mifflin, 1966.

Gratch, G., 'A study of the relative dominance of vision and touch in six-month-old infants', *Child Development*, 1972, vol. 43, 615-23.

Gratch, G., 'Recent studies based on Piaget's view of object concept development', in L. Cohen and P. Salapatek (eds.), *Infant Perception: From Sensation to Cognition* (vol. 2). New York: Academic Press, 1975, pp. 51-99.

Gratch, G., Appel, K.J., Evans, W.F., LeCompte, G.K. and Wright, N.A., 'Piaget's Stage IV object concept error: Evidence of forgetting or object conception?', *Child Development*, 1974, vol. 45, 71-7.

Gratch, G. and Landers, W.F., 'Stage IV of Piaget's theory of infants' object concepts: A longitudinal study', *Child Development*, 1971, vol. 42, 359-72.

Harris, P.L., 'Perseverative errors in search by young infants', *Child Development*, 1973, vol. 44, 28-33.

Harris, P.L., 'Perseverative errors in search by young infants', *Journal of Experimental Psychology*, 1974, vol. 18, 535-42.

Hunter, W.S., 'The delayed reaction in animals and children', *Behavioral Monographs*, 1913, vol. 2, no. 1 (Serial no. 6).

Kessen, W. and Nelson, K., 'What the child brings to language'. Paper presented at the Fourth Annual Symposium of the Jean Piaget Society, Philadelphia, Pennsylvania, 21 May 1974.

Landers, W.F., 'The effect of differential experience on infants' performance in a Piagetian Stage IV object-concept task', *Developmental Psychology*, 1971, vol. 5, 48-54.

LeCompte, G.K. and Gratch, G., 'Violation of a rule as a method of diagnosing infants' level of object concept', *Child Development*, 1972, vol. 43, 385-96.

Moore, M.K., 'The genesis of object permanence', paper presented at the meeting of the Society for Research in Child Development, Philadelphia, Pennsylvania, 1973.

Moore, M.K., 'The genesis of object permanence'. Paper presented at the meeting of the Society for Research in Child Development, Philadelphia, Pennsylvania, 1973.

Moore, M.K., 'The genesis of object permanence'. Chapter 1 of unpublished dissertation.

Piaget, J., *The Origins of Intelligence in Children*. New York: Norton, 1952.

Piaget, J., *The Construction of Reality in the Child*. New York: Basic Books, 1954.

Saal, D., *A study of the development of object concept in infancy by varying the degree of discrepancy between the disappearing and reappearing object*. Unpublished dissertation, University of Houston, 1975.

Schaffer, H.R., Greenwood, A. and Parry, M.H., 'The onset of wariness', *Child Development*, 1972, vol. 43, 165-75.

Smillie, D., 'Piaget's constructionist theory', *Human Development*, 1972, vol. 15, 171-86.

White, B.L., 'Child development research: An edifice without a foundation', *Merrill-Palmer Quarterly*, 1969, vol. 15, 49-79.

SECTION FOUR: INFANT LEARNING

Introduction

When behaviourist psychologists first turned their attentions to forms of learning in infancy, considerable confusion and doubt arose as to whether the conditioning of responses was possible in children of this age. Part of the problem was undoubtedly that not enough care was taken over the choice of responses to be used. For example, early experiments tried to use the salivary response (as did Pavlov) or limb movements (again based on Pavlov's approach). However, once more appropriate responses were used, progress began to be made. Hanus Papousek's paper, the first in this section, describes in detail the study of conditioning in infants using head-turning as a conditioned response. This particular response has proved to be one of the most useful to experimenters (along with sucking) and Papousek's work reported here was instrumental in showing the possibilities to subsequent researchers.

The other response of interest, sucking, is the subject of the second paper, by Siqueland and DeLucia. This describes how they were able to establish control by infants over the presentation of projected pictures, in which strong sucking by the infants on a special nipple caused the picture to appear.

From the very detailed studies in the first two papers, the third, by Burton White, moves to a much broader consideration of the role of learning in the development of basic competences in the cognitive and social areas. White's paper sets out categories of competences in these areas, how these were studied longitudinally over a period of three years, and relates the course of development of these to various factors in the children's experience.

The final paper in this section, by Rheingold, Gewirtz and Ross, picks up a further specific area that has been studied by experiment in the behaviourist tradition: that of the conditioning of vocalizations. Working with three-month old children, they found (in two parallel experiments) that it was possible to increase the frequency with which infants vocalize by reinforcement which consisted of a smile, a touch of the baby's stomach and 'tsk' sounds. The authors see this conditioning as highlighting what may be an important component in the normal course of language development.

15 EXPERIMENTAL STUDIES OF APPETITIONAL BEHAVIOR IN HUMAN NEWBORNS AND INFANTS

Hanuš Papoušek

Source: H.W. Stevenson, E.H. Hess and H.L. Rheingold (eds.), *Early Behaviour: Comparative and Developmental Approaches* (Wiley, 1967), pp. 249-77. Copyright © 1967. Reprinted by permission of John Wiley & Sons, Inc.

Probably every parent has a similar experience when seeing his newborn baby's behavior for the first time: The monotonous crying that is the only vocal manifestation and the diffuse mass activity that is often elicited by inadequate stimuli are so strikingly different from the behavior of adults that they seem to be completely incomprehensible. Yet most parents are soon able to find clues for understanding the basic meaning of the neonate's behavior and to learn to detect even the very early manifestations of developing integrated patterns of voluntary activity.

The author of this report sought to find a pattern of behavior that under experimental control might be used to study the learning abilities of newborns, and that would represent a model for the analysis of the development of intentional behavior. The motor components of appetitional behavior seemed particularly advantageous for this purpose because the need for food is a factor that is both effective and controllable. Inborn responses associated with feeding have therefore been repeatedly applied in studies of such basic learning processes as conditioning or conditioned discrimination.

Conditioning methods were first used for the systematic study of higher nervous functions in immature human subjects soon after Pavlov's basic experiments in dogs (Krasnogorskii, 1907). But until the last two decades the studies of infants dealt more often with the problems of the onset of conditioning or with the capacity for sensory perception than with the development of learning processes. Recent surveys by Rheingold and Stanley (1963) and by Lipsitt (1963) have called attention to the fact that most studies of learning in infants have merely described the occurrence

The author wishes to thank his research assistants Jormila Melicharová and Svatava Sýkorová, as well as the staff of the research unit, for their devoted and skillful assistance in both nursing care and research investigation. Thanks are due also to our statistical consultant Dr J. Vondráček, Institute of Mathematics, Czechoslovak Academy of Sciences, Prague, for his suggestions.

of the phenomenon; and the authors suggest that there is a need for additional studies of the processes underlying infant learning.

In the comparative physiology of infrahuman infants, attempts to analyze the development of the conditioning process have already appeared. Comparative data recently summarized by Sedláček (1963) indicated that the form and adaptive significance of temporary connections depended on the development of the CNS[†] in individual species, and that the three main types of connections — the summation reflex (Wedenskii in 1881), the dominant center reflex (Ukhtomskii in 1911), and Pavlov's conditioned reflex — can be considered different evolutionary degrees of the same general process of synthesis in the CNS. Orbeli (1949) explained the ontogenetic development of central nervous functions by means of a similar evolutionary view. He hypothesized a genetic relation between inherited, unconditioned responses and acquired, conditional responses, with an intermediate continuum of various transitory forms. Sedláček (1962; 1964) made a serious attempt to prove this hypothesis through studies of prenatal conditioning in relatively mature newborns, such as chickens and guinea pigs.

In man, prenatal conditioning has been studied either directly in the human fetus during pregnancy (Ray, 1932; Sontag and Wallace, 1934; Spelt, 1938; 1948), or in premature infants (Kasatkin, 1951; Irzhanskaia and Felberbaum, 1954). These studies have shown evidence of conditioned responses before the expected date of birth, but were not concerned with the mechanisms of temporary connections or with their development.

The lack of information about the earliest development of higher nervous functions in human infants stimulated the team to which the present author belongs to undertake a developmental study of individual differences in conditioning abilities. Unlike similar studies in the Pavlovian literature on typological differences in children (Ivanov-Smolenskii, 1953; Krasnogorskii, 1958) and infants (Volokhov, 1959), individual differences were defined by us in a much broader sense than the limits imposed by typological parameters. In order to maximize the generalizability of our conclusions, the same infants were exposed to several different conditioning methods — aversive, appetitional and orientational — and to the analysis of sleep and waking, emotional and social behaviors, and EEG[†] patterns.

Here we shall be concerned mainly with the data on learned appetitional responses and with the models for complex patterns of intentional behavior. Although the classical conditioning method of salivary response has been used with children, it is not appropriate for infants

(Krasnogorskii, 1958). Therefore the analysis of conditioned sucking movements that was recommended by Bekhterev and Stshelovanov (1925) has been preferred by most authors. The first natural conditioned sucking was reported during the third week of life by Denisova and Figurin (1929), and Ripin and Hetzer (1930). The conditioning of sucking in infants to acoustic stimuli during the second or third month and to visual stimuli during the third or fourth month was reported by Kasatkin and Levikova (1935). Conditioned discrimination with vestibular stimulation[†] was first reported by Nemanova (1935) in her study of infants 2 to 4 months old. Marquis (1931) reported much earlier conditionability; in 8 or 10 newborns she obtained conditioned oral responses to a buzzer at the age of 4 or 5 days, but her study lacked necessary controls for pseudoconditioning. On the other hand, Wenger (1936) could not establish conditioned responses before the tenth day of age with either appetitional or aversive techniques.

The problems of early conditioning continued to engage the attention of later investigators who used newer techniques and larger samples of infants (Kasatkin, 1964). Lipsitt and Kaye (1964) confirmed appetitional conditionability in 3- to 4-day-old newborns. Sucking movements were also used for testing the influence of hunger on conditioning (Kantrow, 1937), for detecting neonatal brain injuries (Dashkovskaia, 1953), and for studying premature infants (Polikanina, 1955; Polikanina and Probatova, 1957).

Until recent years, methods using other motor components of appetitional behavior were not employed adequately; Irwin (1930) discussed general motor activity, and Kriuchkova and Ostrovskaia mentioned head-turning (1957).

For the purposes of our studies, the sucking method appeared inconvenient, particularly because of the regressive changes in sucking movements that are in contrast to the progressive development of higher nervous functions (Papoušek, 1969). With increasing age, anticipatory sucking movements gradually disappear, perhaps because they are nonfunctional or nonadaptive.

Head-turning, therefore, was chosen by the author as another conditionable motor component of infantile appetitional behavior. As an inborn response, head-turning has been studied by many neurophysiologists since the first observations published by Darwin (1886) and Preyer (1895). According to Minkowski (1928), head movements appear in the human fetus by the third postconceptional month and are fully functional at birth. They can be elicited by various stimuli and during periods of hunger occur without any discernible stimulation (Prechtl,

1953). According to Babkin (1953), an inborn rooting reflex, probably coordinated in the diencephalon, should be differentiated from the purposive movements that develop gradually, probably under cortical control, into various learned behavioral patterns such as orientational, aversive, or appetitional movements.

Natural conditioning of head movements to a visual (bottle) stimulus by the first month of life was described by Peiper (1958). After satiation, both conditioned and unconditioned food-seeking activity was suppressed.

For several reasons, head-turning seemed advantageous for conditioning studies. The movement matures earlier than do movements of the extremities, and its intensity and latency can be more easily quantified. It can be used with different kinds of reinforcement: appetitional or aversive, incidental or intentional. Thus it is suitable for molding a simple inborn reflex movement into a complex purposive or voluntary response. Finally, because head-turning involves bilateral response, and differential reinforcement can be applied for responses to the left or right, it can be used for the simultaneous study of two symmetrical responses in a single subject.

A method was devised for appetitional conditioning with milk reinforcement (Papoušek, 1959; 1961a; 1961b). For orientation conditioning with visual reinforcement the method was modified by another member of our team (Koch, 1962) and, within an operant framework, has been successfully explored by Siqueland (1964) and Siqueland and Lipsitt (in press).

Method

Subjects

For our investigations infants up to 6 months of age were reared in a special unit under relatively standard conditions. As far as possible, we tried to keep their life conditions comparable, at the same time meeting the demands of individual infants. Between 1956 and 1965, more than 130 infants were observed. They were healthy, full term, and without any evidence of pathology in the mothers' pregnancies or deliveries. The infants were cared for by their mothers and by specially trained nurses who could substitute for the mothers if necessary. Our team included a pediatrician who watched over the infants' health, nutrition and somatic development, and a psychologist who was concerned with their mental development and educational care. If an occasional break in experimentation exceeded five days, the procedure being investigated during the period was eliminated from consideration.

The infants were also used by other members of the team for other experimental conditioning studies, such as conditioned eye-blinking (Janoš, 1965) and orientational head-turning (Koch, 1962).

Stimuli and Apparatus

The sounds of an electric bell (CS_1) or a buzzer (CS_2) were the conditioning stimuli. The unconditioned reinforcement (UCS) was milk presented from one side or the other through a rubber nipple connected to a thermos bottle.

Electronic equipment enabled the experimenter to program the kind and duration of both conditioning and reinforcing stimuli and to operate them and the timing mechanisms by a single button, thus freeing the experimenter to make detailed observations of the infant's behavior.

A seven-channel polygraph recorded the presentation of the stimuli and the infant's head-turning, breathing, and general motor activity. On a protocol, the experimenter recorded, by means of codes, intensity and latency of head-turning, changes in general behavior, and vocal, facial, and oral responses.

The infant lay in a stabilimeter crib, partially immobilized, in order to eliminate any disturbing activity of his upper extremities. An elastic pad oscillated with the infant's movements; the oscillation was transmitted to the polygraph through a pneumatic system. This system also included a special calibrator allowing actograms of infants of different body weights to be compared. Breathing movements were recorded by means of a pneumatic pick-up.

The infant's head was placed in a plastic head cradle lined with plastic foam. The cradle's rotations on a horizontal axis changed the potential in a two-potentiometer circuit, and these changes were recorded as deflections from the baseline on the polygraph (Figure 15.1).

The attachment of the head cradle to the axis could be shifted vertically to balance the cradle and eliminate the influence of head weight, enabling even a newborn to turn his head or keep it in a central position without difficulty.

Thus information was gathered not only on the specific response — head-turning — but also on concomitant changes in general activity (decrease or increase in general motor activity), vocalization, facial responses, eye movements, and breathing. Records of such changes were essential for estimating the general state of wakefulness during the experiment and the inhibitory or excitatory effects of the experimental stimuli.

Figure 15.1: Polygraph Recordings from an Experimental Session

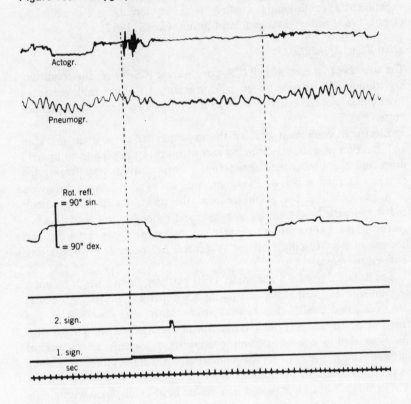

Procedure and Measures

Infants were tested in the late morning, approximately 10 minutes after their regular sleep in the fresh air. The routine schedule of feeding and sleep in the sequence of sleep, feeding, and waking enabled us to examine the subjects in comparable states of hunger and wakefulness.

First, a baseline measure of head-turning prior to experimental stimulation was recorded. Then, all Ss received five pre-experimental trials of CS_1 and CS_2 without reinforcement. The source of the stimuli was in the midline behind the infant's head so that the sounds by themselves did not elicit head-turning. The first presentation of milk occurred prior to the conditioning trials and from the midline so that Ss might adapt to the experimental situation. Interruptions in feeding did not result in problems, particularly if the interruptions followed spontaneous breaks in the infant's sucking.

The development of the conditioned reflex to the bell (CR) was then initiated with the milk (UCS) being presented from the left side. The UCS was presented by the assistant, who sat screened behind S's head. If S responded to the bell and turned to the left, milk was offered to him immediately. The bell continued ringing until S started sucking the milk. If S did not respond to the presentation of the CS within 10 seconds, the assistant (nurse) tried eliciting the head-turn by tactile stimulation, touching the left corner of his mouth with the nipple. If this stimulation was ineffective, she turned his head to the left and placed the nipple in his mouth. At the end of reinforcement the nurse turned his head back to the middle, leading it with the nipple, and then took the nipple from his mouth.

Ten such trials occurred during one session, which covered one normal feeding period of 10 to 15 minutes. The intertrial interval was one minute, on the average, but was intentionally changed to avoid temporal conditioning. A head-turn of $30°$ or more from the central position was considered a positive response. The criterion of conditioning was five consecutive positive responses in the 10 trials of one daily session.

There was, therefore, considerable biological significance to head-turning under this procedure. The hungry infant had to rotate his head to obtain milk, and the sooner he did so, the sooner he was fed. Under these conditions, the gradual shortening of the latency of response could be considered a parameter of the process of conditioning.

Extinction was the next procedure. CS_1 was presented without the UCS for 10 seconds; as in the conditioning procedure, 10 trials were given in one session. After the criterion of five consecutive negative responses was reached, reconditioning took place. The process was the same as the first conditioning procedure.

Next, the Ss were trained to discriminate between the two stimuli; CS_1 (bell) was reinforced from the left and CS_2 (buzzer), from the right. In any one session, five CS_1 and five CS_2 were presented in random order. Six consecutive correct responses (three bell and three buzzer CRs in random order) represented the criterion of learning for this phase of the procedure. After reaching criterion, the signals were reversed: CS_1 was reinforced from the right, CS_2 from the left. The criterion for concluding this portion of the procedure was analogous to that employed in the trials for the first discrimination.

In addition to these basic procedures, other experiments were designed for the analysis of stimulus influence and for the shaping of more complex forms of learned behavior, such as the conditioned emotional behavior or the development of intentional behavior. These experiments are discussed later.

Studies of Basic Learning Abilities

The data given first demonstrate the early development of learning abilities in infants, their age pecularities, and the individual differences among them. These data were gathered from the basic six conditioning procedures that were studied with three independent groups of *S*s: newborns (A), 3-month-old infants (B), and 5-month-old infants (C). The variability of initial age within each group was reduced to a minimum. The results for the 44 infants in the three groups are summarized in Table 15.1. In this table are presented the means and standard deviations for initial age, rapidity of learning as measured by the number of trials necessary to achieve criterion, and latency of CRs.

In addition to the analysis of these data, attention was also paid to the appearance of typical phases in the course of learning and to the various concomitant patterns of behavior. In these observations the group of newborns deserves more attention, particularly in comparison with group B, because a marked qualitative change in the development of higher nervous functions occurs during the first three months of life (Janoš, Papoušek and Dittrichovà, 1963).

Conditioning in Newborns

In newborns we had a rare opportunity to study experimental motor learning before spontaneous natural learning substantially interfered. Slow conditioning permitted an easier analysis of its phases that in older infants often passed too quickly and could be interpreted as accidental deviations.

In newborns the baseline before conditioning usually showed no head movements. Even tactile stimulation with the nipple elicited head-turning only in three of the 14 newborns on the first reinforcement, whereas three to 22 trials were necessary for the remaining 11 *S*s (mean = 6.57). In group B the tactile stimulation itself elicited head-turning more quickly, usually after one or two trials (mean = 1.23). This difference was highly significant $(p < 0.001)$.[1]

The rate of conditioning, as shown in Table 15.1, was very slow in newborns. On the average, 32.21 trials preceded the first conditioned head turn in group A, whereas only 9.43 trials were necessary in group B. Such a significant decrease $(p < 0.001)$ indicates a rapid development of conditionability during the first three months of life. A similar decrease of the mean number of trials to criterion also supported this conclusion; the difference between groups A and B was highly significant $(p < 0.001)$,

Table 15.1: Means and Standard Deviations of Responses of Three Groups of Infants to the Six Basic Conditioning Procedures

Groups of infants	N	Initial age in days Mean	SD	Trials to criterion Mean	SD	Latency in seconds CR 1 Mean	SD	CR 2 Mean	SD
Conditioning:									
A	14	3.42	1.01	177.14	93.40	4.95	0.74		
B	14	85.78	1.76	42.28	18.38	3.92	1.08		
C	16	142.50	2.63	27.75	13.70	3.55	1.29		
Extinction:									
A	12	31.83	13.89	26.83	12.90	5.49	1.01		
B	14	94.14	4.58	25.07	10.39	3.70	0.94		
C	16	149.06	4.07	27.31	15.29	3.25	0.99		
Reconditioning:									
A	12	37.25	13.34	42.83	29.88	4.90	0.93		
B	14	100.35	1.45	31.64	19.84	2.73	0.65		
C	16	153.93	3.43	22.37	11.88	3.28	0.85		
Discrimination:									
A	11	43.90	15.68	223.54	99.23	4.00	0.58	3.90	0.63
B	13	105.92	6.48	176.23	82.52	2.62	0.66	3.03	0.71
C	14	159.92	5.46	68.14	28.72	2.10	0.77	2.66	0.87
Reversal 1:									
A	11	76.36	18.68	195.18	86.85	3.43	0.65	3.47	0.81
B	12	135.58	11.57	120.00	66.01	2.58	0.66	2.48	0.60
C	10	170.00	4.81	79.40	79.83	2.83	1.01	2.56	0.83
Reversal 2:									
A	11	107.54	23.81	94.63	35.51	3.29	0.91	2.91	0.74
B	12	155.51	19.08	82.41	37.74	2.34	0.91	2.15	0.74
C	10	182.80	13.50	77.60	63.60	2.29	0.97	2.72	0.97

A = newborns   B = 3-month infants   C = 5-month infants

whereas the difference between groups B and C was significant at the .05 level. The mean number of 177 trials for the group A represented approximately three weeks of conditioning, and shows that during the 28 days of the neonatal period most newborns can achieve even a relatively severe criterion of conditioning. But wide individual differences in the newborns were apparent; the fastest conditioners needed only 7, 10, 11, or 12 days, the slowest ones, more than a month.

The latency of the CR is here considered in the behavioral sense, rather than in the physiological. Latency was defined as the interval between the onset of CS and a head turn of 30° or more. It depended, therefore, not only on the interval preceding the onset of CR, but also on the rate at which the head was turned. An analysis of variance showed significant age differences for the three groups ($p < 0.005$), indicating that newborns carry out the CRs more slowly than older infants. For newborns, there was also a significant correlation during conditioning between latency and speed of conditioning, indicating longer reaction times in slower conditions ($r = 0.68, p < 0.01$).

Several different stages could be distinguished during the course of conditioning. To a certain degree they were comparable to the four stages of conditioned sucking described by Kasatkin (1948): indifference to the CS, inhibition of general activity, unstable CR, and, finally, a stable CR.

During the first phase the CS usually elicited nonspecific orientational behavior (wider opening of the eyes, inhibition of other activities, changes in breathing) that was quickly extinguished. After a period of indifference to the CS, this phase was succeeded by one during which partial responses and later the first CRs were manifested. In newborns this phase was relatively long and had several features that should be noted. Its main features were gradual coordination of individual components of CR, such as head-turning and unilateral mouthing or eye turning, increased general motor activity, and concomitant vocal and facial responses that are generally accepted as signs of distress. Before a good coordination developed, the newborn could be seen to be upset, fussing, and grimacing, turning his eyes and contracting his mouth to the left, but not yet turning his head. Marked signs of such an insufficient coordination were present in 50 per cent of the Ss in group A, but only in .7 per cent of the Ss in group B.

The next phase was that of unstable conditioning. The frequency of correct responses increased, but the responses were isolated or appeared in small groups with fluctuating intensity and latency. Insufficient coordination was still evident in two characteristic features: (a) a generalized form of CR (the S responds with the whole body), and (b) an increased frequency of unilateral or bilateral intertrial head turning. The first feature, considered a sign of increased irradiation of central nervous processes in immature organisms, was more frequent in group A. The second feature, indicating central dominance, usually appeared only in the unilateral form in group A and was less frequent (50 per cent) than in group B (71 per cent).

The gradual consolidation of the CR, that is, the increasing ability to carry out more CRs consecutively, also appears to be a function of age. The analysis of the first 10 CRs (Table 15.2) showed that in group A,

Table 15.2: Grouping of Conditioned Responses of Three Groups of Infants, in Percentages

| Group of infants | N | The first to positive conditioned responses | | |
		Isolated	In groups 2	3 or more
		%	%	%
A	14	60.7	32.9	6.4
B	14	34.9	17.2	47.9
C	16	18.7	20.6	60.6
		A:B $p < 0.001$	A:B $p < 0.01$	A:B $p < 0.001$
		B:C $p < 0.025$	B:C $p > 0.05$	B:C $p > 0.05$

A = newborns   B = 3-month infants   C = 5-month infants

60.7 per cent of the responses were isolated, whereas in group C, 60.6 per cent appeared consecutively in groups of three or more. It is evident that the main development of this ability again occurs during the first three months of life.

Three main types of cumulative curves appeared to characterize the course of conditioning in the infants: (a) relatively constant increase of percentage in CRs, (b) increase of percentage with several gross waves, and (c) increase of percentage after a retarded onset. The second type may indicate a functional lability† of the CNS, typical of immature organisms, and the third, a phasic maturation of the CNS (Janoš, 1965). It can be seen in Table 15.3 that the relative frequency of the three types differed in the three age groups, and that the last two types were more characteristic of the newborn.

The final phase is that of stable conditioning. The frequency of CRs approaches 100 per cent, and the CRs are stronger, faster, well coordinated, and carried out economically with shorter and more regular latencies. They were no longer accompanied by emotional signs of distress; on the contrary, the older infants often showed vocal or facial patterns of pleasure. In this phase the *S*s reached the criterion of 5 successive correct CRs and, at the same time, the average number of CRs in three successive days usually exceeded 50 per cent.

Even in this phase, the stability of conditioning was only relative, particularly in the younger groups in which a sudden decrease sometimes appeared after a period of consistent responses. Alternation between

Table 15.3: Frequency of Occurrence of Different Types of Conditioning
Curves in Individual Age Groups

Types of acquisition curves	Age groups		
	A	B	C
Relatively constant percentage increase	6	12	16
Several gross waves	6	2	—
Retarded onset	2	—	—
Total	14	14	16

increased excitation and inhibition seems typical for newborns and probably caused the limited occurrence of consecutive CRs. Polygraphic
records of breathing and general motor activity provided more sensitive
indications of increased excitation or inhibition than the apparent state
of wakefulness.

No relation was found in newborns between the occurrence of the first
CR and the number of trials to criterion, but there was a significant correlation between the occurrence of the first group of two CRs and the
criterion ($r = 0.71$, $p < 0.01$) or between the first group of three consecutive CRs and the criterion ($r = 0.86$, $p < 0.01$).

All these indices of age characteristics in the higher nervous functions
of newborns confirm the hypothesis that the immaturity of the CNS
manifests itself in the functional lability of higher centers and in the
weakness of the basic central nervous system processes of excitation and
inhibition. A similar conclusion was drawn from the analysis of developmental changes of sleeping and waking states in these infants (Dittrichová,
1962; Dittrichová, Janoš and Papoušek, 1962). Even under conditions
involving relative immaturity of the CNS, it is apparent that a basic
pyramidal response can be learned which, in later weeks and months,
develops into a more complicated pattern of behavior. Our data suggest,
in fact, that learning does occur in humans within the first days of life.

Further Development of Conditioning Capacity

In the older infants, as compared with the newborns, developmental
changes were observed of both a quantitative and a qualitative nature. The
significant increase with age in the speed of conditioning was discussed
in the preceding section on newborns. This finding is important for developmental studies since experimental evidence, in spite of many ontogenetic studies, is still equivocal. As shown recently (Janoš *et al.*, 1963),

during the first half-year of infancy an age difference of one month may produce significant differences in both aversive and appetitional conditioning.

With increased speed of conditioning, the individual phases in the conditioning process that are characteristic of newborns become shorter, and often such phases are detected only fleetingly, particularly in fast conditioners. Nevertheless, several qualitative differences could still be observed in groups B and C. Incoordination of partial components of the CR, associated with the appearance of the first CRs in newborns, was absent or appeared in a slight form only in a few trials. The generalization of the CR, observed in the phase of unstable conditioning, was also different. In newborns the CR was preceded or accompanied by increased movements of the whole trunk and extremities, and by changes in breathing and vasomotor responses, etc. These changes can be considered the result of nonspecific diffuse irradiation of the central excitatory process. It was observed that older infants showed more specific generalization, which was expressed in the specific vocal or facial signs of emotional arousal frequently shown by older children or adults in solving difficult problems.

An increase in the number of head turns during the intertrial intervals was more frequently found in older infants during the phase of unstable conditioning, and, unlike what is found in newborns, here the bilateral form of the intertrial head turns prevailed. It is difficult to estimate the proportion of maturation and extraexperimental learning in the qualitative differences found between newborns and older infants.

Extinction and Reconditioning

The main purpose of our extinction and reconditioning procedures was to confirm the critical feature of the CR — its temporary character — and thus to differentiate it from pseudoconditioning. According to previous experience (Papoušek, 1961a; 1961b) and to analogous findings in aversive conditioning (Janoš, 1965), we did not expect to gain as much information about the development of learning abilities from the study of extinction and reconditioning as we found in the use of other procedures.

Table 15.1 shows that extinction occurs more quickly than conditioning but no significant difference in the speed of extinction was found among the three groups. This finding is difficult to explain. The experiments dealing with extinction may have involved an age span different from that in which the main development of extinction ability occurs; or the role of age may have been obliterated by the level of conditioning necessary to achieve the relatively severe criterion of conditioning employed. It is interesting that in group A, a negative correlation between trials to conditioning and trials to extinction was found ($r = -0.66, p < 0.05$), indicating faster extinguishing in slower conditioners. Moreover, the newborns had a significantly longer latency of the CR ($p < 0.001$) than did groups B and C.

To a certain extent, the course of extinction is a mirror image of conditioning. The CRs gradually cease to be made and their latencies become longer. The negative responses appear first as isolated events and later in consecutively larger numbers. The individual components of the CR do not extinguish simultaneously, particularly in younger Ss. For example, in response to the CS_1, the S may stop turning his head to the left but may continue to turn his eyes to the left or contract the left corner of his mouth for some time. A negative response to the CS still does not mean that the CS is totally indifferent to the S. Particularly during the phase of unstable extinction, the CS obviously exerts an inhibitory influence upon the S's behavior, sometimes to such an extent that it can elicit a catatoniclike state in the S for several seconds.

Reconditioning may be considered a repetition of the first conditioning process. Here, however, the differences between individual age groups were at the limit of significance, according to a Kruskal-Wallis analysis of variance ($p < 0.05$).

Only in younger groups is reconditioning significantly faster than conditioning. The difference in speed between conditioning and reconditioning can be the effect of either maturation or relearning. The first seems more plausible since the difference was highly significant in group A ($p < 0.001$), in which the Ss were 34 days older during reconditioning than they were during conditioning, but was at the limit of significance in group B ($p < 0.05$), and nonsignificant in group C ($p < 0.05$), in which the Ss were only 15 and 11 days older. Within the total sample (but not within individual age groups), the correlation between trials to conditioning and trials to reconditioning was significant ($r = 0.38, p < 0.01$).

Discrimination

There is a lack of data in the literature on the development of discriminative abilities in man. It was not the goal of this study to answer the question of the age at which human infants begin to discriminate different acoustic stimuli. The Ss had to proceed through several other procedures before the discrimination tests were begun. But even under these conditions evidence was found that in the fastest conditioners the ability to discriminate was functional as early as the second month of life. In group A, the mean age at which the Ss reached the criterion of discrimination between bell and buzzer was 2½ months.

During the following months of the first half year of life the ability to discriminate improves substantially and the speed of differentiation increases. An analysis of variance among groups A, B, and C, showed significant differences dependent on age ($p < 0.005$). Furthermore, the latencies of response to both CS_1 and CS_2 were significantly lower ($p < 0.005$) for group A than for groups B and C.

Individual variability in the speed of acquisition of prior procedures results in a gradual increase of the variability in the age at which Ss begin subsequent procedures. Ranking according to age is in this case identical with ranking in order of decreasing speed in the preceding procedures; within individual groups the slower the Ss were in preceding tests the older they were in succeeding tests. Therefore, the correlation between age and speed of discrimination or its reversals was not significant within individual groups, although in some procedures the span of the initial age exceeded one month. It has been reported by Janoš *et al.* (1963) that such an age difference may be associated with significant differences in the speed of conditioning.

Several main phases may be distinguished in the course of discrimination and particularly in the reversal of discrimination. There is first a disintegration of the previously learned ability that is followed by a gradual adaptation leading to successful acquisition of the new discrimination. Secondary phases were also present, such as alternating dominance of left or right CRs in Ss' responses to both kinds of CSs. The frequency, sequence, and expressiveness of these secondary phases were, however, less constant.

Developmental differences were evident in the course of discrimination. In group A, a marked decline in both CRs was observed in 6 of the 11 Ss soon after CS_2 was introduced. After the period of decline, a gradual increase in both CRs occurred simultaneously, with gross waves as the dominant type of acquisition curve. In groups B and C, such a general decline was never observed. A gradual increase in responses to CS_2 usually occurred with a stable or only a transitory decrease in the level of responses to CS_1. The periods of alternating dominance of left or right responses were less frequent in groups B and C. In all groups the stability of discrimination was only relative even after reaching criterion; a marked decline could be easily produced by various interfering factors.

Reversals of Discrimination

In the last two procedures included in Table 15.1, the variability of the age at which the procedures were introduced increased to such an extent that the group limits overlapped, but the differences between mean ages still remained highly significant.

The speed of learning significantly increased from discrimination to the second reversal in groups A and B, but not in group C. It appears that by 6 months of age further improvement based upon age alone was not in evidence. For the first reversal, a one-way analysis of variance showed a reliable age trend reflecting a decrease in the number of trials to criterion ($p < 0.005$). In the second reversal, however, this trend was no longer significant. Similar relations were observed in the latency data. Within individual age groups there was no significant correlation between age and speed of the reversals. A possible interpretation was discussed in the previous section on discrimination. The speed with which the first reversal was acquired was positively related to the speed of discrimination ($r = 0.37, p < 0.025$).

The first reversal was established, on the average, in group A by the third month of life, and the second reversal by 3½ months. We may conclude, therefore, that during the first trimester there has developed not only the capacity to discriminate but also the capacity to reverse a discrimination.

Determinants of Individual Differences

Individual differences in addition to those based upon age were found in all groups and in all of the quantitative and qualitative indices. The literature contains different opinions on the detectability of differences in higher nervous function during early infancy. Chesnokova (1951) and Krasuskii (1953) assumed that differences in higher nervous activity continued to develop until adulthood and could not be assessed definitely at earlier ages. Troshikhin (1952) and Volokhov (1953), on the other hand, recommended that they be studied as early as possible. Kriuchkova and Ostrovskaia (1957) and, in a project similar to ours, Kaplan (1963) reported stable individual differences in higher nervous function from the first months of life through later infancy.

In the present study, marked individual differences were found to be present in newborns according to all indices. As an illustrative example, acquisition curves of conditioning for groups A and B are presented in Figure 15.2. Whether or not the observed differences represent permanent characteristics of individual Ss cannot be answered because our studies have not yet been oriented toward this problem. It should be noted, however, that studies on aversive conditioning in the same infants have also shown marked individual differences in learning abilities at early ages (Janoš, 1965).

In Table 15.1, the standard deviations for the trials-to-criterion measures of conditioning and discrimination decreased from group A to group C, indicating a developmental change in the variability of these functions. The *F* tests comparing groups A and C indicated that the decrease in variability was significant in both instances ($p < 0.001$).

Other determinants of the individual differences found in learning abilities were also investigated, for example, sex differences, nutrition, somatic differences, seasonal influences, etc. A preliminary analysis of our data showed no significant sex differences in any procedure between 19 girls and 25 boys of the present example. Seasonal difference was not significant either when performances were compared for the first and second halves of the calendar year, or for the spring through the summer with the autumn through the winter.

It did not appear that the individual differences in learning ability that were found could be attributable to somatic or constitutional factors

Figure 15.2: Acquisition Curves of Conditioning for Groups A and B

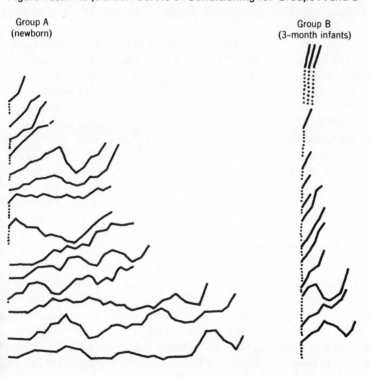

Group A
(newborn)

Group B
(3-month infants)

studied, such as birth weight and birth length, head and chest circumference, or gain in weight or length during the first trimester. Only in newborns did some parameters of learning abilities seem to be related to some of the mentioned determinants. A significant correlation was found, for example, between the CR latency and chest circumference ($r = -0.67$, $p < 0.05$), indicating that a conditioned head turn was carried out more quickly in stouter newborns.

Since appetitional behavior can be substantially influenced by nutritional factors, the mean caloric quotient (daily intake in calories per kilogram of body weight) was calculated during each experimental procedure and was correlated with the conditioning parameters. In groups A and B, significant correlations of .59 ($p < 0.05$) and .63 ($p < 0.02$), respectively, indicated that conditioning proceeded more quickly in infants with a lower daily intake of milk, that is, they indicated an excitatory effect of a mild degree of hunger that can appear in younger infants during, for example, the period of additional feeding when a supplementary formula is kept slightly reduced in order to maintain adequate sucking at the mother's breast.

Similarly, a breast-to-cow-milk ratio was calculated during conditioning to test the influence of breast feeding and, indirectly, also of mother's presence, since mothers usually stayed at our unit as long as they could nurse. No significant correlation was evident between this ratio and the parameters of conditioning. It was the practice, however, to compensate for the mother's absence by providing substitute mothering and adequate emotional stimulation.

Thus, in general, we can conclude that this preliminary analysis of the potential determinants of individual differences in performance during the procedures employed did not contradict the hypothesis that with the conditioning procedures considered here, we were testing differences in higher nervous functions.

Role of Environmental Stimulation

In the preceding sections it has been shown that various indifferent external stimuli may play an important role if they become conditioned stimuli, particularly in connection with a significant form of reinforcement such as that used in these studies of appetitional conditioning. Acoustic signals can elicit striking changes in general motor activity, in the general state of excitation or inhibition, and in emotional and other forms of behavior. Although the effect sometimes can be too slight to be observed in general behavior, it can still be detected during the process of conditioning.

Such an example is illustrated in Figure 15.3. In a 5-month-old infant

Figure 15.3: Latencies of Responses after Presentation of Inhibitory Stimuli

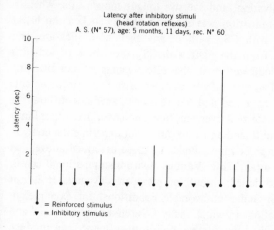

with an established discrimination between the bell, reinforced with milk from the left, and the buzzer, reinforced from the right, the reinforcement associated with the buzzer was stopped in order to reverse the buzzer to an inhibitory stimulus. After a period of training, the buzzer ceased to elicit the CR, but an inhibitory after-effect appeared in an increased latency in succeeding CRs to the bell. The more inhibitory stimuli were applied consecutively, the greater was the increase in latency.

In infants of the second trimester, further observation illustrated the effectiveness of the CSs, and, in addition, an interesting interrelation between learned and unlearned behavior. For instance, in several Ss, after completing a normal conditioning session with 10 trials and after a normal amount of milk had been presented as reinforcement, another 10 or 20 CSs were applied to test the influence of satiation upon the emission of CRs. Under these conditions the Ss did not stop responding to the CSs, even when they were fully satiated. At every sound of the bell they turned to the left, even though they refused the milk presented. Any attempt to feed them elicited avoiding head turns.

Other experimental situations for studying the interrelation between learned and nonlearned behavior were undertaken by using different tasting fluids. These situations used 15 Ss aged 88 to 201 days, in whom a left-right discrimination in head-turning had already been established. For instance, sweet milk was used as the UCS presented from the left in CS_1, and a weak solution of the quinine tincture was presented from the right in CS_2. Soon the concomitant emotional responses appropriate to the kind of UCS became differentiated, so that the Ss responded to the

CS_1 with quiet sucking and head-turning, but to the CS_2 with arousal, grimacing, increased salivation, and aversive tongue movements. When in this situation the discrimination was reversed, the Ss sucked the bitter solution from the left with CS_1 without any signs of displeasure, and refused the sweet milk from the right with CS_2. For some period, this maladaptive behavior indicated that the effectiveness of conditioning stimuli was stronger than the effects of unconditioned reinforcement. Finally, a readaptation appeared and led to a new, adequate differentiation. These studies indicate that even emotional behavior, like other kinds of behavior, can be conditioned and thus put under experimental control.

Natural conditioning procedures, similar to those described above, can normally occur in the infant's life. Various environmental stimuli can in this way become conditioned stimuli of great effectiveness. It is not difficult to realize that under unfavorable conditions, for example, in various frustration situations in which many CSs remain unreinforced and become inhibitory stimuli, a cumulative inhibitory influence can produce undesirable effects in the infant's behavior.

Models of Voluntary Behavior

We attempted to mold a simple example of voluntary behavior in 12 infants of whom four were newborns aged 4-5 days on the average, and eight were in the second trimester, with an average age of 130.1 days. The Ss were trained in a discrimination and one or two reversals of it with only one kind of CS. The CS was reinforced with either sweetened milk from the left or unsweetened milk from the right. If he did not carry out a head turn himself, tactile stimulation with a rubber nipple was applied with the restriction that equal numbers of tactile stimulations were applied to both sides. Otherwise, the S was allowed to choose the kind of milk himself.

An exact quantitative analysis was not possible since different kinds of stimulation were used, but several general conclusions seem warranted. All Ss preferred the sweetened milk, and this preference gradually developed in a manner similar to the discrimination described in the basic conditioning procedures. The criterion of five consecutive CRs to the same side was reached in an average of 290 trials (ranging from 246 to 390) in the newborns and in 38 trials (9 to 109) in the older infants.

After achieving this criterion, the UCSs were reversed — the sweetened milk was presented from the right side and the unsweetened milk from the left. A gradual reversal in CRs occurred, consequently, and its course was analogous to that of the reversal described earlier. During the disintegration phase of a previously learned ability, accidental head turns to the side

Figure 15.4: Latencies of Responses in Initial Learning and Following Reversal of the UCSs

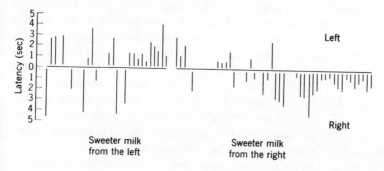

Z.C. (no 51), age: 5 months 22 days, rec. no: 1-8

of sweetened milk helped the *S*s to find the source of the preferred UCS. Concomitant emotional responses, gradual grouping of CRs to the preferred side, and other signs indicated that this simple model of voluntary behavior was learned in the same way as in the basic conditioning procedures. In the younger infants 108 trials (15 to 185) were necessary for achieving the criterion, whereas only 70 (10 to 162) were necessary in the older infants. In a schematic form, one typical case is illustrated in Figure 15.4.

When I speak of voluntary behavior in infants of prelingual age, I do not assume that I am thereby simplifying a difficult problem. I wish only to emphasize that the chosen pyramidal movement, brought under experimental control at a very early stage of postnatal development, can be molded to patterns resembling voluntary behavior. Perhaps it would be better to say that through conditioning processes, the organism can be brought to the beginning of a long and complicated pathway of structuring, at the end of which there are patterns of behavior as highly coordinated as those generally designated as voluntary behavior.

Summary

Head movements were chosen as a conditionable motor complex of infantile appetitional behavior to study the early development of learning abilities and the molding of a simple response to a pattern of intentional behavior.

A method was developed for appetitional conditioning with milk reinforcement in newborns and infants. The basic conditioning procedures

— conditioning, extinction, reconditioning, discrimination and its double reversal — were studied as early forms of learning in three independent age groups of healthy full-term infants (newborns, 3-month infants, and 5-month infants).

Quantitative and qualitative differences among these groups were analyzed with particular attention to the peculiarities of the learning process in newborns, and evidence was found that learning occurs during the first days of life. In the course of investigating various procedures in the study of conditioning in newborns, different phases of learning became apparent. The immaturity of the central nervous system manifests itself in the functional lability and in the infirmity of the basic central nervous processes of excitation and inhibition. The evidence for this appears in the slow grouping of consecutive CRs, gross waves in the acquisition curves, and instability in the percentage, intensity, and latency of CRs.

In several indices the comparison among individual groups indicated that major developmental changes occur during the first three months of life. During this period there develops not only the capacity to discriminate between various acoustic stimuli but also the capacity to reverse such a discrimination.

Marked individual differences are present from the neonatal period on in all parameters of conditioning employed. An analysis of the correlation between these differences and various potential determinants such as sex, somatic development, nutrition, mother-infant interaction, or seasonal influence support the hypothesis of independent variability in higher nervous function as a cause of the observed individual differences.

Further studies helped to elucidate the interrelation between learned and nonlearned behavior, indicating increasing effectiveness of conditioning stimuli in comparison to unconditioned ones. A left-right differentiation of head-turning reinforced by two as different and as emotionally effective taste stimuli as sweet and bitter solutions indicated that even emotional behavior can be put under experimental control and can be conditioned in young infants.

Finally, there is reported the attempt to design experimental conditions under which the learned response can be considered as the earliest precursor of later intentional or voluntary behavior. Here, head-turning was conditioned to one CS, and that CS was reinforced either with sweetened or unsweetened milk, depending on the side to which S turned his head. All Ss appeared to prefer the sweetened milk and to be able to find its source on the opposite side when the two variants of UCS were reversed. Learning of such a response proceeded on the same principles as conditioned discrimination or its reversal.

Note

1.   The following statistical procedures were employed, depending on the particular data being analyzed: the Mann-Whitney U test; the Kruskal-Wallis one-way analysis of variance for k-sample cases; for large samples, the Snedecor F test with logarithmic transformation of scores and, if necessary, with Scheffé's (1959) method of multiple comparison; and Spearman rank-order correlation coefficients.

References

Babkin, P.S. (1953), 'Head-turning reflexes in infants' (Rus.), *Zh. Nevropat. Psikhiat.* 53, 692-6.

Bekhterev, V.M. and Stshclovanov, N.M. (1925), 'The principles of genetic reflexology' (Rus.), *Novoie refleksologii i fiziologii nervnoi sistemy*. USSR: Leningrad-Moscow.

Chesnokova, A.P. (1951), 'Dynamism of higher nervous activity in puppies during their individual development' (Rus.), *Zh. vys. nerv. Deiat.*, 1, 555-65.

Darwin, C. (1886), 'Biographische Skizze eines kleinen Kindes' (Germ.), *Kleinere Schriften* (Leipzig), 2B., 134.

Dashkovskaia, V.S. (1953), 'The first conditioned responses in newborns under normal and pathologic conditions' (Rus.), *Zh. vys. nerv. Deiat.*, 3, 247-59.

Denisova, M.P. and Figurin, N.L. (1929), 'The question of the first associated appetitional reflexes in infants' (Rus.), *Vopr. genet. Refleksol. Pedol.* Mladen, 1, 81-8.

Dittrichová, J. (1962), 'Nature of sleep in young infants', *J. Appl. Physiol.*, 17, 543-6.

Dittrichová, J., Janoš, O. and Papoušek, H. (1962), 'Characteristics of higher nervous activity in newborns' (Czech.), *Sb. čsl. lékař. kongresu.*, Prague, pp. 254-5.

Irwin, O.C. (1930), 'The amount and nature of activities of newborn infants under constant external stimulating conditions during the first ten days of life', *Genet. Psychol. Monogr.*, 8, 1-92.

Irzhanskaia, K.N. and Felberbaum, R.A. (1954), 'Some data on conditioned activity in premature infants' (Rus.), *Fiziol. Zh. SSSR*, 40, 668-72.

Ivanov-Smolenskii, A.G. (1953), 'Studies on the types of higher nervous activity in animals and in man' (Rus.), *Zh. vys. nerv. Deiat.*, 3, 36-54.

Janoš, O. (1965) (Czech.), *Age and Individual Differences in Higher Nervous Activity in Infants*. Prague: SzdN.

Janoš, O., Papoušek, H. and Dittrichová, J. (1963), 'The influence of age upon various aspects of higher nervous activity in the first months of life' (Czech.), *Activ. nerv. super.*, 4, 407-10.

Kantrow, R.W. (1937), 'Studies in infant behavior. IV. An investigation of conditioned feeding responses and concomitant adaptive behavior in young infants', *Univer. Iowa Stud. Child Welf.*, 13, no. 3, 1-64.

Kaplan, L.I. (1963), 'To the question of the development of individual typologic differences of higher nervous activity in infants' (Rus.), *Mater. 6th scient. conf. devel. morphol., physiol., biochem.* Moscow: Izd. APN, p. 354.

Kasatkin, N.I. (1948) (Rus.), *Early Conditioned Reflexes in the Ontogenesis of Man*. Moscow: Medgiz.

Kasatkin, N.I. (1951) (Rus.), *In Outline of the Development of the Higher Nervous Activity during Early Infancy*. Moscow: Medgiz.

Kasatkin, N.I. (ed.) (1964) (Rus.), *From the Simple to the Complex*. Moscow-Leningrad: Izd. Nauka.

Kasatkin, N.I. and Levikova, A.M. (1935), 'On the development of early conditioned reflexes and differentiation of auditory stimuli in infants', *J. exp. Psychol.*, 18, 1-9.

Koch, J. (1962), 'Die Veränderung des Exzitations Prozesses nach der Nahrungsein-nahme und nach dem Schlafe, bei Säuglingen in Alter von 5 Monaten' (Germ.), *Z. artzl. Fortb.*, 55, 219-23.

Krasnogorskii, N.I. (1907), 'An experience with establishing experimental conditioned reflexes in infants' (Rus.), *Russkii vrach. 36*, in (Rus.), *Studies in the Research of Higher Nervous Activity in Man and Animals* (1954). Moscow: Medgiz.

Krasnogorskii, N.I. (1958) (Rus.), *The Higher Nervous Activity in the Child*. Leningrad: Medgiz.

Krasuskii, V.K. (1953), 'Methods of studying the types of nervous system in animals' (Rus.), *Trudy Inst. Fiziol. Pavlov.*, 2, 111-19.

Kriuchkova, A.P. and Ostroveskaia, I.M. (1957), 'Developmental and individual differences of higher nervous activity in infants' (Rus.), *Zh. vys. nerv. Deiat.*, 7, 63-74.

Lipsitt, L.P. (1963), 'Learning in the first year of life', in L.P. Lipsitt and C.C. Spiker (eds.), *Advances in Child Development and Behavior*, vol. 1. New York: Academic Press, pp. 147-95.

Lipsitt, L.P. and Kaye, H. (1964), 'Conditioned sucking in the human newborn', *Psychon. Sci.*, 1, 29-30.

Marquis, D.P. (1931), 'Can conditioned responses be established in the newborn infant', *J. genet. Psychol.*, 39, 479-92.

Minkowski, H. (1928), 'Neurobiologische Studien an menschlichen Früchten', *Abderhalden's Handb. biolog. Arbeitsmeth.* (Berlin), 5, 5b. 511-618.

Nemanova, C.P. (1935), 'The earliest positive and negative aversive and nutritive conditioned responses to vestibular stimuli in infants' (Rus.), *Vopr. Pediat. Okhran.*, 7, 278.

Orbeli, L.A. (1949), 'On the mechanism of the development of cerebrospinal coordinations' (Rus.), in *The Problems of Higher Nervous Activity*. Moscow-Leningrad: Izd. AN SSSR, pp. 7-20.

Papoušek, H. (1959), 'A method of studying conditioned food reflexes in young children up to the age of six months' (Rus.), *Zh. vys. nerv. Deiat.*, 9, 136-40.

Papoušek, H. (1960), 'Conditioned motor alimentary reflexes in infants. I. Experimental conditioned sucking reflexes' (Czech.), *Cesk. Pediat.*, 15, 861-72.

Papoušek, H. (1961), 'Conditioned head rotation reflexes in infants in the first months of life', *Acta Paediatr.*, 50, 565-76. (a)

Papoušek, H. (1961) (Czech.), *Conditioned Motor Nutritive Reflexes in Infants*. Thomayer. Sb., Prague: SzdN, p. 409. (b)

Peiper, A. (1958), 'Unbedingte und bedingte Reflexe der Nahrungsaufnahme' (Germ.), *Kinderaerzt. Prax.*, 26, 507-15.

Polikanina, R.I. (1955), 'Origin and development of a nutritive conditioned response to sound in premature infants' (Rus.), *Zh. vys. nerv. Deiat.*, 5, 237-46.

Polikanina, R.I. and Trobatova, L.J. (1957), 'Development of an orienting response and a conditioned motor nutritive response to color in premature infants' (Rus.), *Zh. vys. nerv. Deiat.*, 7, 673-82.

Prechtl, H.F.R. (1953), 'Die Kletterbewegungen beim Säugling' (Germ.), *Menchr. Kinderhk.*, 101, 519-21.

Preyer, W. (1895), *Die Seele des Kindes* (4th edn.) (Germ.). Leipzig.

Ray, W.S. (1932), 'A preliminary report on a study of fetal conditioning', *Child Development*, 3, 175-7.

Rheingold, Harriet L. and Stanley, W.C. (1963), 'Developmental psychology', *Ann. Rev. Psychol.*, 14, 1-28.

Ripin, R. and Hetzer, H. (1930), 'Frühestes Lernen des Säuglings in der Ernährungssituation' (Germ.), *Z. Psychol.*, 118, 82-127.

Scheffé, H. (1959), *The Analysis of Variance*. New York: Wiley.

Sedláček, J. (1962), 'Functional characteristics of the center of the unconditioned reflex in elaboration of a temporary connection in chick embryos' (Czech.), *Physiol. Bohemoslov.*, 11, 313-18.

Sedláček, J. (1963), 'Problems of the ontogenetic formation of the mechanism of temporary connections' (Rus.), *Acta Univer. Carol. Medica*, 4, 265-317.

Sedláček, J., Hlacáčkova, V. and Svenlova, M. (1964), 'New findings on the formation of the temporary connections in the prenatal and perinatal period in the guinea pig' (Czech.), *Physiol. Bohemoslov.*, 13, 268-73.

Siqueland, E.R. (1964), 'Operant conditioning of head turning in four-month infants', *Psychon. Sci.*, 1, 223-4.

Siqueland, E.R. and Lipsitt, L.P. (in press), 'Conditioned head turning behavior in newborns', *J. exp. child Psychol.*

Sontag, L.W. and Wallace, R.F. (1934), 'Study of fetal activity' (preliminary report on the Fels Fund), *Amer. J. Dis. Child*, 49, 1050.

Spelt, D.K. (1938), 'Conditioned responses in the human fetus in utero', *Psychol. Bull.*, 35, 712-13.

Spelt, D.K. (1948), 'The conditioning of the human fetus in utero', *J. exp. Psychol.*, 38, 338-46.

Troshikhin, V.A. (1952), 'Some tasks in the research of higher nervous activity in ontogenesis' (Rus.), *Zh. vys. nerv. Deiat.*, 2, 561-71.

Ukhtomskii, A.A. (1952), 'The principle of dominant center' (Rus.), in I.M. Sechenov, I.P. Pavlov and N.E. Wedenskii (eds.), *Physiology of the Nervous System*, vol. 1 (3rd edn.). Moscow: Medgiz, pp. 262-6.

Volokhov, A.A. (1953), 'Typologic differences of nervous system in infants' (Rus.), *Med. Rabol.*, 16, 2-3.

Volokhov, A.A. (1959), 'Typologic differences in higher nervous activity in infants and their reflection in some autonomic functions' (Rus.), *Mater. 7th Congr. Soviet. Pediat.*, 77-80.

Wedenskii, N.E. (1952), 'Relationship between rhythmical processes and functional activity of an excited neuromuscular apparatus' (Rus.), in I.M. Sechenov, I.P. Pavlov and N.E. Wedenskii (eds.), *Physiology of the Nervous System*, vol. 2 (3rd edn.). Moscow: Medgiz.

Wenger, M.A. (1936), 'An investigation of conditioned responses in human infants', *Univer. Iowa Stud. Child Welf.*, 12, 9-90.

16 VISUAL REINFORCEMENT OF NON-NUTRITIVE SUCKING IN HUMAN INFANTS

E.R. Siqueland and C.A. De Lucia

Source: *Science*, 1969, vol. 165, pp. 1144-6. Copyright 1969 by the American Association for the Advancement of Science.

The development of learning tasks for the human infant, in which his behavior is made experimentally effective for producing changes in the exteroceptive environment, may provide important tools for studying the ontogeny[†] of exploratory behavior over the first weeks and months of human life. In experiments with infants from 3 weeks to 1 year of age we began to explore the feasibility of using the sucking response as a conditioned operant to assess the infant's response to visual feedback as a reinforcing event. Sucking is a response that can be reliably elicited in most infants during the first days of life, and studies with newborns have suggested that sucking is a functionally adaptive response that may be influenced by nutritive reinforcement contingencies in the feeding situation.[1] We created an artificial environment for the infant in which visual feedback was made experimentally contingent upon his emission of high-amplitude non-nutritive sucking responses.

Our apparatus consisted of a nipple and a pressure transducer which provided both polygraphic recordings of all sucking behavior and a digital record of sucking pressure in excess of 17 mm-Hg. Presentation of the projected visual stimulus was automatically programmed. Criterion amplitude sucks activated a power supply which was designed to increase the intensity of a 500-watt light source in a standard 35-mm slide projector. The reinforcing consequence was the opportunity to view on a rear projection screen a 35-mm slide. Transition from no illumination to maximum brightness of the projected visual stimulus occurred gradually, in direct proportion to the infant's sucking rate ('conjugate reinforcement', Lindsley[2]).

In the first experiment we studied the effects of visual reinforcement on the acquisition of high-amplitude sucking in 4-month-old infants. Groups of ten infants were randomly assigned to one of three experimental conditions. One group (base-line group) provided base-line reference data for spontaneous changes in the frequency of high-amplitude sucking over 10 minutes of testing in the experimental situation. For the other two groups a 15-minute conditioning procedure consisted of 2-minute baseline, 4-minute conditioning, 2-minute extinction, 4-minute reconditioning, and finally a second 3-minute extinction phase. For the sucking reinforcement group (SR group), presentation of the projected visual stimuli was experimentally contingent upon the occurrence of criterion sucking during each of the two 4-minute conditioning phases. For the last group (SW group) the occurrence of criterion sucking resulted in the discrete withdrawal of the projected visual stimuli, and each high-amplitude suck delayed the presentation of the visual stimulus for 5 seconds. For the last two groups, eight 35-mm chromatic slides (geometric patterns, cartoon figures, and human faces) were presented during each conditioning phase with a change of visual stimuli occurring every 30 seconds. During the base-line and extinction phase, infants sucked in the presence of a constant, dimly illuminated projection screen. All subjects were seated facing the projection screen on the lap of a female research assistant who held the nipple to the infant's mouth for the duration of the experimental procedures. A criterion amplitude suck was a positive pressure response of 18 mm-Hg or greater. Base-line reference data obtained from infants of this age had shown that approximately 35 per cent of the infant's normal non-nutritive sucking met our experimental criterion of a high-amplitude suck.

The mean rate of criterion sucks for each of the three groups in 1-minute blocks over base-line, conditioning, and extinction phases are shown in Figure 16.1. The apparent reinforcing effects of visual feedback seen in the performance of the SR group reflect reliable differences ($P < .05$ or less for all comparisons noted; two-tailed tests) between the SR group and the other two groups during the initial 4-minute conditioning and the 2-minute extinction phases. One-way analyses of variance (Kruskal-Wallis) indicated that there were no overall differences between the base-line sucking for the three groups, but highly reliable differences between the sucking rates for these groups were obtained during the initial conditioning and extinction phases. Subsequent individual comparisons between the pairs of groups (Mann-Whitney U-test) indicated that the SR group responded at a higher rate than either of the other two groups during the first conditioning and extinction phases. Reliable differences between the high-amplitude sucking rates of the SR and SW groups were maintained over the reconditioning and final extinction phases of the experiment. A series of Wilcoxon matched-pairs tests were used to determine the statistical reliability of the apparent acquisition and extinction effects for the SR group over the conditioning and extinction procedures. This group demonstrated predictable shifts in sucking rate, indicating response acquisition and extinction effects over each of the two conditioning and two extinction phases of the experiment. Similar statistical

Figure 16.1: Mean Response Rates for the Three Groups of 4-month Infants over Conditioning and Extinction Phases

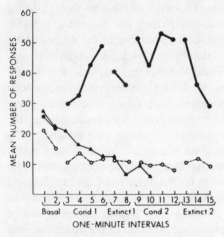

Solid circles, sucking reinforcement group; open circles, stimulus withdrawal group; closed triangles, base-line group.

tests with the SW group indicated negligible shifts in frequencies of criterion sucking over the conditioning and extinction phases.

The sucking data for the three groups were also analyzed with respect to changes in the proportion of criterion high-amplitude sucks relative to the total number of sucks emitted during each minute in the experimental situation. Selective reinforcement of high amplitude sucking should have resulted in progressively higher proportions of the infant's sucking behavior meeting the criterion for the conditioned operant. This analysis provided clear support for the conclusion that visual reinforcement resulted in a rapid conditioned response differentiation by the SR group. While there were negligible differences in the mean response ratios (the number of criterion amplitude sucks divided by the total number of sucks) for the three groups during base-line measures (range from 0.36 to 0.39), by the 4th minute of conditioning 0.70 of all sucks emitted by the SR group met the criterion of high-amplitude sucking. In contrast to this high proportion of criterion sucking for the sucking reinforcement group, mean response ratios for the base-line and SW groups were 0.30 and 0.24, respectively. By the final minute of the reconditioning phase the SR group had a mean ratio of 0.85 as compared with 0.38 for the SW group. Furthermore, extinction of the acquired response was reflected in the ratio measures with the proportions of high-amplitude sucking for the SR group decreasing from 0.70 to 0.49 and from 0.85 to 0.56 over the respective extinction phases. The other groups showed negligible shifts in their response ratios over the extinction phases. It should be noted that the experimental procedure of withdrawing the projected visual stimuli contingent upon sucking (SW group) failed to produce evidence for an acquired suppression of high-amplitude sucking. However, the performance of this group does provide additional control data indicating that the changes in criterion sucking in the SR group were not attributable to either generalized arousal or specific eliciting effects of visual stimulation *per se*. Simply presenting infants with a changing pattern of visual stimulation while they were sucking did not result in their response rates differing reliably from those of the base-line control subjects. Only those infants who were specifically reinforced with visual feedback for emitting high-amplitude sucks (SR group) showed evidence of an acquired response differentiation. The reinforcing effectiveness of the visual feedback is seen in the fact that the learned response differentiation occurred quite rapidly, and by the end of 8 minutes of reinforced training these infants showed marked proficiency in their performance with better than 0.80 of their responses meeting the conditioned response criterion.

Additional evidence for the reinforcing effects of visual feedback on sucking behavior in human infants was obtained in a subsequent experiment with 12-month infants. While the first experiment showed that visual reinforcers could be employed to modify the topography of sucking in 4-month infants, the second experiment was designed to determine whether similar reinforcement procedures could be effectively employed to reestablish sucking in infants for whom non-nutritive sucking was no longer a stable response in their behavioral repertoire. Attempts to obtain base-line reference data on non-nutritive sucking with 12-month infants indicated that better than 60 per cent of the infants actively rejected the experimental nipple prior to completing a 5-minute base-line measure of sucking. The apparent aversiveness of the sucking task for these infants was reflected in the high frequency of such behaviors as 'crying', 'fussing' and attempts by subjects to push away the non-nutritive nipple. Thus, in the second experiment we studied the effectiveness of visual reinforcers in reestablishing sucking with 12-month infants. A second variable studied in this experiment was the effect of varying the amount of redundancy in the array of visual reinforcers on the reinforcing effectiveness of the visual feedback. Studies with infrahuman organisms have indicated that instrumental exploratory behavior increases with increasing amounts of change in the visual reinforcing event.[3,4] Briefly, the second experiment compared the conditional sucking rates for two groups of ten 12-month infants who received visual reinforcers varying in the amount of redundancy. Both groups were presented with conditioning and extinction procedures similar to those employed with the SR group in the previous experiment. One group (high-redundancy group) received three replications of four chromatic stimuli as reinforcers over the two 4-minute conditioning phases (with a stimulus change each 30 seconds). The second group (low-redundancy group) was presented with a single replication of eight visual stimuli as reinforcers over these conditioning phases. The results showed that when sucking was made functional for visual feedback, both groups showed rapid acquisition of conditioned sucking during the initial 4-minute conditioning phase.

In contrast to a base-line reference group of 12-month infants, who averaged less than 15 sucks per minute over a 5-minute sucking measure, both of the experimental groups averaged better than 40 sucks per minute during the 4th minute of the initial conditioning phase. Although the two groups did not differ in their conditioned sucking rates during the initial 4-minute conditioning and 2-minute extinction phases, the effects of stimulus redundancy on the reinforcing effectiveness of the visual feedback was seen during the reconditioning and second extinction phases, with the high-redundancy group sucking at reliably higher levels than the low-redundancy group during both these phases. In contrast to the apparent satiation effects due to reinforcement which are reflected in the decreasing sucking rates for the former group during reconditioning (third and fourth replication of the set of four stimuli), infants receiving only the second replication of the set of eight stimuli during reconditioning (low-redundancy group) maintained highly stable rates of conditioned sucking. These results supported the prediction that the reinforcing effectiveness of visual feedback was reliably influenced by the amount of stimulus redundancy.

Our experiments provide support for the conclusion that effective reinforcement of motivated behavior in the young human infant is not limited to a restricted class of stimuli in his environment. In addition to nutritive reinforcers, there are other classes of stimuli, possibly in each of the sensory modalities, that are effective in strengthening instrumental behaviors in infants. Berlyne[5] has suggested that any stimuli that are effective in 'capturing the subject's attention' can have reinforcing value in suitable circumstances. The important developmental problem is the specification of stimulus parameters which distringuish positive and negative stimuli, and distinguish reinforcing and nonreinforcing stimuli for the developing infant in each of the sensory modalities. In subsequent experiments with infants we have found that visual feedback of the type employed in these experiments was effective in supporting motivated exploratory behavior with infants as young as 3 weeks of age. Furthermore, acquisition of conditioned sucking has been demonstrated when hetero-geneous auditory feedback in the form of music and human voices was employed for reinforcement.

References

1. A.J. Sameroff, *J. Exp. Child Psychol.*, 6, 607 (1968).
2. O.R. Lindsley, *Amer. J. Orthopsychiat.*, 33, 624 (1963).
3. D.E. Berlyne, *Brit. J. Psychol.*, 41, 68 (1950).
4. E.W. Menzel, R.K. Davenport, C.M. Rogers, *J. Comp. Physiol. Psychol.*, 54, 16 (1961).
5. D.E. Berlyne, in D. Levin (ed.), *Nebraska Symposium on Motivation* (Univ. of Nebraska Press, Lincoln, 1967), p. 1.

17 CRITICAL INFLUENCES IN THE ORIGINS OF COMPETENCE

Burton L. White*

Source: *Merrill-Palmer Quarterly*, 1975, vol. 21 (4), pp. 243-66.

The research to be described in this paper focuses on the question of the experiential sources of human competence, a topic I have been performing research on continuously since 1958. Because my field has been psychology, I have been examining the experiential rather than the genetic or nutritional or other roots of competence.[1]

For ten years or so I studied the development of abilities during the first six months of life. I reported on that work at the Merrill-Palmer Institute in 1968 (White, 1969) and summarized its totality in a small book in 1971 (White, 1971). In that research effort, I learned quickly that the scientific study of experiential or environmental factors is considerably more difficult than the study of developmental outcomes such as language or intellectual skills. Plotting changing skill levels is child's play compared to coping with the problem of which aspects of the environment translate into which types of experiences that have substantial effects on the development of skills. I became involved in disputes with people about measurement. My 1969 statement on that issue still expresses my position: 'My policy has always been to measure as well as I can what I believe merits measurement, rather than to measure only what I can measure with unquestionably high precision.' By this statement I do not mean to advocate the demise of the kind of child development research where precise measurement of small elements of human function are the rule. Much of that work is of excellent quality and must be protected and nurtured if we are to have a science of human development. I do mean, however, to point out that very few *practical* issues can be dealt with meaningfully, at this point in history, with strict adherence to the requirements of precise measurement and experimental control. The entire contents of our experimental psychological journals of the last thirty years have given us only modest amounts of information for dealing with problems of compensatory education, effective child-rearing practices, infant education, the mental health of children, etc. (La Crosse, Lee, Litman, Ogilvie, Stodolsky and White, 1970). I would have you bear in

* Harvard University, Graduate School of Education, Roy E. Larson Hall, Appian Way Cambridge, Massachusetts 02138.

mind that Congress, in providing hundreds of millions of dollars of funds for child development research over the years, thought it was supporting work that would help solve the nation's problems.

The Harvard Preschool Project

Since 1965, I have directed a large-scale research attack on the question of the role of experience in the development of abilities during the first six years of life (White, 1972; White and Watts, *et al.*, 1973). This paper is a progress report. The Harvard Preschool Project is an educational psychology research project in its ninth year of existence. In 1965 when substantial funds became available to combat educational underachievement, two major program directions were considered: the rapid creation of preventative or remedial practices for three- and four-year-olds, or a 'back to the drawing board' approach to the larger issue of how to structure the experiences of the first six years of life so as to help each child make the most of his potential. Our project represents the drawing board or long-range approach to the problem.

The steps we have followed in our research, along with what we think we have learned at each phase, will be described. The sequence is as follows:

Step 1. Determine the behavioral characteristics of a well-developed six-year-old.

Step 2. Identify when those characteristics first emerge during the zero- to six-year age range.

Step 3. Create measurement techniques for gathering quantitative data during the one- to three-year age range on: (a) competencies of children; (b) their day-to-day learning situations (the stream of experience); (c) the environmental factors that may influence their day-to-day learning and developing competencies.

Step 4. Conduct a longitudinal natural experiment to generate hypotheses about effective child-rearing practices.

Step 5. Create a training program (experimental treatment) to test those hypotheses.

Step 6. Conduct a longitudinal experiment to test those hypotheses.

Step 7. Refine and test our hypotheses.

We have finished step 5 and are currently planning the comparative experiment.

What is a Well-Developed Six-Year-Old?

In spite of some recent attempts to redefine and broaden the original goals of Project Head Start, it seemed to me that the primary original goal was to prevent educational underachievement by large numbers of our children. The Harvard Preschool Project research goals included the prevention of underachievement, but we also hoped to study the more general question of how to structure the experiences of the first six years of life so as to help each child make the most of whatever potential he was born with. We have worked therefore with the concept of competence. Our use of the term grossly corresponds to that of R. White (1959) and Wenar (1972), and is essentially the same as Lois Murphy's treatment of coping abilities (1956). To deal specifically with the issue of competence, we engaged in extensive, systematic observations of three- to six-year-old children in their natural habitats. We conducted (ethological-ecological) studies of over a hundred children over a two-year period. We observed a varied group at home, at school, on playgrounds, in supermarkets, etc. We became knowledgeable about the lives and habits of children in cities and suburbs. We paid particular attention to children we all considered unusually competent or less competent than average (for more details, see White and Watts, *et al.*, 1973). Emulating Lorenz on the jackdaw or Cousteau on the octopus, we tried to describe the distinguishing behavioral talents of the well-developed six-year-old Eastern Massachusetts human.[2]

Distinguishing Behaviors of the Competent Six-Year-Old

Social Abilities: Labels and Definitions

(1)   To get and maintain the attention of adults in socially acceptable ways.

Definition. The ability to get the attention of an adult through the use of various strategies (e.g. moves toward and stands/sits near A; touches A; calls to A; shows something to A; tells something to A).

(2)   To use adults as resources when a task is clearly too difficult.

Definition. The ability to make use of an adult in order to obtain something by means of a verbal request or demand or a physical demonstration of his need. The object may be to gain information, assistance, or food, and he may demonstrate this by declaring what he wants, making a request, making a demand, or by gesturing, acting out, or pointing. This behavior is to be distinguished from the use of an adult in order to avoid exerting oneself or to manipulate the adult.

(3)   To express both affection and hostility to adults

Definition. The ability to express affection and/or hostility through verbal and/or physical means (e.g. friendly statements, such as, 'I like you', 'You're nice', or hugging A; statements of dislike, such as, 'I hate you', 'You're bad', hitting A, or physically resisting A).

(4)   To lead and follow peers

Definition. The ability to assume control in peer-related activities (e.g. to give suggestions, to orient and direct, to set oneself up as a model for imitation). The ability to follow the lead of others (e.g. to follow suggestions).

(5)   To express both affection and hostility to peers

Definition. The ability to express affection and/or hostility to peers through verbal or physical means.

(6)   To compete with peers

Definition. The ability to exhibit interpersonal competition.

(7)   To praise oneself and/or show pride in one's accomplishments

Definition. The ability to express pride in something he has created, owns or possesses at the moment, or something he is in the process of doing or has done.

(8)   To involve oneself in adult role-playing behaviors or to otherwise express the desire to grow up

Definition. To act out a typical adult activity or verbally express a desire to grow up.

Nonsocial Abilities: Labels and Definitions

(1)   Linguistic competence

Definition. Grammatical capacity, vocabulary, articulation, and extensive use of expressed language.

(2)   Intellectual competence:

(a)   The ability to sense dissonance or note discrepancies

Definition. This is a critical faculty on the part of the child, an ability to indicate one's awareness of discrepancies, inconsistencies and other forms of irregularity in the environment. It is almost always expressed verbally, but occasionally takes nonverbal forms as well. It is observable whenever a child comments upon some noticed irregularity. The effect that generally accompanies it usually involves mild confusion, a look of discovery, or a display of righteousness, in pointing out and correcting the irregularity.

(b)   The ability to anticipate consequences

Definition. This is the ability to anticipate a probable effect on, or sequence to, whatever is currently occupying the attention of the child. It is usually expressed verbally, but also takes nonverbal forms. It can take place in a social context or in relative isolation. It is not simply an awareness of a future event (e.g. 'Tomorrow is Thursday'), but must some-how relate that event to a present condition. The relationship may be either causal (e.g. 'If X, then Y'), or sequential (e.g. 'Now 1, next 2'). The second half of each relationship *must* be an anticipated future outcome. It cannot actually occur until after the child anticipates its occurrence.

(c)   The ability to deal with abstractions (i.e. numbers, letters, rules)

Definition. The ability to use abstract concepts and symbols in ways that require building upon what is concretely present, and showing mental organization of what is perceived. The term *concept* means 'A mental state or process that refers to more than one object or experience'; the term *symbol* means 'An object, expression, or responsive activity that replaces and becomes a representative substitute for another'.

(d)   The ability to take the perspective of another

Definition. The ability to show an understanding of how things look to another person whose position in space is different from the subject's, or to show an understanding of a person's emotional state or mental attitude when they are different from the subject's (the opposite of egocentricity).

(e)   The ability to make interesting associations

Definition. When presented with visible scenes, objects, or verbal descriptions, a person with this ability shows a capacity to produce related kinds of objects or themes from either his own realm of past experience or some imagined experience. These productions are characterized by the ingenuity of the relationships or the elaborateness of the representation. Another form is the ability to build upon these events by assigning new and interesting labels or building coherent stories around the presented elements.

(3)   Executive abilities:

(a)   The ability to plan and carry out multistep activities

Definition. This designation applies largely to self-directed activities, rather than activities in which the child is guided. It would have developed in earlier age levels through gradual refinement of the use of means-ends relationships and of the ability to plan and execute longer sequences.

(b)   The ability to use resources effectively

Definition. The ability to select and organize materials and/or people to solve problems. An additional feature is the recognition of unusual uses of such resources.

(4)   Attentional ability – dual focus

Definition. The ability to attend to two things simultaneously or in rapid alternation (i.e. the ability to concentrate on a proximal task and remain aware of peripheral happenings; the ability to talk while doing).

The Emergence of Competence in Children

We found that a *three*-year-old who seemed very able already exhibited the aforementioned patterns of abilities. We would predict such children could easily handle first grade curricula at four years of age. If we were correct in these judgements, then we ought to look at the first three years of life as our highest priority. This we did.

The psychological literature, in a rare display of power, clearly indicated that children who would underachieve in schools, generally did fine on tests of development (the Gesell, Bayley or even Piagetian tests of

Figure 17.1: Developmental Quotients at Three Months' Intervals of 344 Rural Mississippi Black Children during the Period between Birth and the End of the Third Year of Life

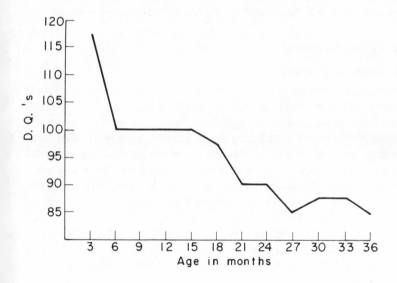

Source: Brown, R.E. and Halpern, F., 'The variable pattern of rural black children', *Clinical Pediatrics*, 1971, vol. 10, no. 7.

sensorimotor intelligence) until the middle of the second year of life.[3]
Figure 17.1 taken from Brown and Halpern's (1971) studies of Mississippi
Delta Region children illustrates the regularly found pattern. See also the
pattern of test scores of Schaefer (1969) and Bayley (1965). It would
appear that part of the reason for the drop in average scores during the
second year is the increasing importance (for testing purposes) of language
and language-related skills from one and a half years on.

I have come to believe that the requirements for adequate human
development are modest during the first seven to nine months of life, so
modest as to be available in even the poorest of homes.[4] The picture
changes, however, when children become able to crawl about and to begin
to process language.

It was our judgement (and so it remains) that the majority of children
who will underachieve in schools will first manifest signs of developmental
delay toward the end of the second year of life and that by three years of
age patterns of future high or low achievement will often be visible. We
therefore decided to concentrate on the second and third years of life.

Quantitative Techniques

The Stream of Experience

We needed a technique to analyze the experiences of one- to three-year-old
children. When we first looked for such techniques, the only available
procedures were those of ecological psychology as espoused by Barker
(1968), Wright (1960), and Schoggen and Schoggen (1968). Their Behavior
Episode Unit (BEU) was an attempt at segmenting and analyzing the
natural ongoing experiences of a child. Unfortunately, the BEU is not a
complete system, but is rather a concept on which to build a system. Using
running records, we induced an inclusive inventory of types of childhood
experiences, developed rules for data collection, created a lengthy manual
and carried out reliability runs. The result is our task instrument, conceptually powerful but with only 67 per cent reliability. More recently
Caldwell (1969) and Clarke-Stewart (1973) have reported on similar
instruments.

The Development of Competence

We developed or borrowed instruments to assess achievement on several
distinguishing dimensions of competence in the one- to three-year-age
range. The following instruments were developed: social competence
behavior checklist; receptive language ability (a performance test); observational capacity (sensing dissonance); and abstract thinking abilities.

Salient Aspects of the Environment

We knew that the primary caretaker was involved in shaping the experiences of children in the age range in question. We were also interested in learning which elements of the physical world the child actually interacted with. A word of warning at this point. The 'environment' is *not* a concept to be bandied about. One well-known creator of diagnostic instruments recently called me to ask for one hour's advice on how to measure the impact of the 'environment' on a child's development. He planned to visit a home for an hour or two to 'measure the environment', much like the way the Federal government 'evaluated' Head Start programs in their early days. Scales for assessing mother-infant interactions are almost as common as rejected research proposals. We were in the awkward position of requiring assessment techniques for measuring factors we had yet to identify specifically. We took some guesses on aspects of caretaker behavior and we time-sampled what children looked at and actually contacted of the physical environment. Four years later, we have finally produced a focused instrument[5] to assess only those aspects of caretaking behavior we believe are really likely to make a difference in a child's development (under ordinary circumstances).

The Longitudinal Natural Experiment

We sought out families who might be doing a great job with their children. We asked nursery- and elementary-school personnel whether they knew of families that were likely to send them beautifully developed children. We also sought out families that sent the low competence child to the first grade. A minority of both groups of families had new babies at home. If the baby was less than one or two years old we asked to be allowed to watch him develop. We have been watching 39 babies develop for over five years. We take a two-hour look every other week for up to two years.

The purpose of the experiment was to see what kinds of experiences, if any, are regularly associated with fine and poor development, and to see if we could identify the environmental inputs to those experiential differences. We were particularly interested in salient environmental factors that are changeable (for the better) as opposed to those we cannot influence (e.g. drug addiction, profound selfishness, serious depression, etc.). In other words, we have been trying to generate hypotheses about effective child-rearing practices.

Subjects

We especially sought out families with modest resources who seem to be very successful at child rearing. We have sought also to study advantaged families with poor track records. With the latter we have been less success-ful. The characteristics of our sample are presented in Table 17.1. We began with 25 children we thought would develop very well and 14 we thought would develop poorly. It is to be noted that our predictions were not perfect. One child we thought would develop rather poorly ranked tenth in overall competence at age three years. This was a remarkable achievement considering the competition. Five children we thought would develop unusually well fell between the twenty-second and thirty-ninth ranks at three years of age.

There was a strong social class effect in our data. Overall competence correlated .40 with social class. Social competence correlated .03 with social class. Nonsocial competence correlated .65 with social class. Note, however, that social class accounts for only 16 per cent of the variance in respect to overall competence.

Table 17.1: Distribution of Subjects with Respect to Age at which Observations were Started, Social Class (SES), Sex and Predicted Competence Ratings

		1-year-olds					2-year-olds				
SES score		I	II	III	IV	V	I	II	III	IV	V
As	Boys	1	1	2	0	0	4	1	3	0	0
	Girls	3	3	2	0	0	2	0	3	0	0
Cs	Boys	0	0	2	1	1	1	0	1	3	0
	Girls	0	0	0	2	1	0	0	2	0	0
Total		4	4	6	3	2	7	1	9	3	0

All subjects = 39

One-year-olds	= 19	Two-year-olds	= 20
Boys	= 21	Girls	= 18
As	= 25	Cs	= 14

Procedures

Figures 17.2 and 17.3 indicate the schedule of data collection of the study.

Results — Experiences Associated with High Levels of Competence

Competence differences began to show up reliably as early as 14½ months of age. Clear differences were more impressive from 24 months of age on. Since our groups tested as similar at 12 months of age, the experiences of the 12 to 15 and 18 to 21 month periods are most interesting (see Figures 17.4 to 17.9). These differences did not often attain statistical significance in our small sample (N = 19, one-year-olds), but we believe they are the most likely to be involved in differential development.

(1) Language Experience

Children are exposed to language in a variety of ways. In our system of analysis we focus on the following types of language experiences: (a) live language directed to the subject — when a person talks to the subject for more than 15 continuous seconds; (b) live language overheard by the subject — when the child listens to live language (not directed toward him) for more than three continuous seconds; (c) TV language — (self-explanatory); (d) other mechanical language — radio and records.

In the above cases children appear to be attending primarily to the language experience *per se*. In other situations, language may be involved, but the child appears to have other purposes in mind. For example, if a mother asks a child to stop doing something, the task is usually coded as *to cooperate* experience. Our language experience analysis therefore does not cover *all* language exposure, but focuses on what might be characterized as *predominantly* linguistic experiences.

Though there are modest differences in total amounts of language experience in the lives of most of our subjects (6.0 per cent of all Ss; top five Ss — 5.8 per cent v. bottom five Ss — 3.3 per cent, at 12-15 months), live language directed to the subject is considerably more prevalent in the experiences of our children developing very well than in the rest of our subjects (5.8 per cent v. 1.9 per cent). (See Tables 17.2 and 17.3.)

(2) Exploration and Mastery of the World of Physical Objects

Consistent with the findings of Piaget (1952) is our repeated finding that most children spend a lot of time interacting with physical objects during the second year of life. Most but not all of the objects are small and portable. Children may stare at these objects, explore their qualities, or practise simple skills (mastery experiences) on them. There seems to be a progression such that exploration is more frequent than mastery at about 12 months of age, but mastery activities gradually become predominant during the second and third years (see Figures 17.4 and 17.7). In our study, this trend is accelerated in children developing well and delayed in those developing poorly (see Figures 17.8 and 17.9).

Figure 17.2: Schedule of Runs — Preschool Project

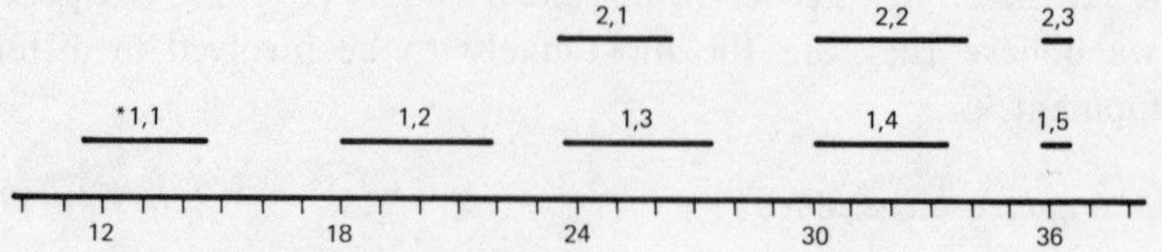

Chronological Age of Child (months)

* first number is the starting age of child, second number is the run number

Figure 17.3: Preschool Project — Details of Observations and Tests within Runs

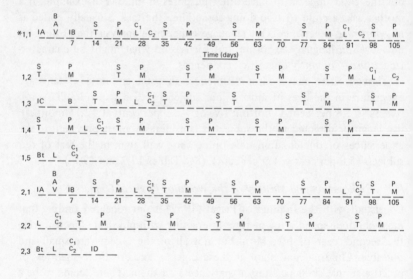

CODE
IA — Interview A
IB — Interview B
IC — Interview C
ID — Interview D
L — Language
A — Auditory Screening
V — Visual Screening
T — Task Observation

S — Social Competence Observation
M — Maternal Behavior Observation
P — Use of the Physical Environment
B — Bayley
Bt — Binet
c_1 — Discrimination Test
c_2 — Abstract Abilities
(Hunt-Uzgiris for 1-yr-old;
Meyer for 2-yr-old)

* first number is the starting age of child, second number is the run number

Figure 17.4: Patterns of Experience, Group — All Subjects, Age 12-15 months (N = 19)

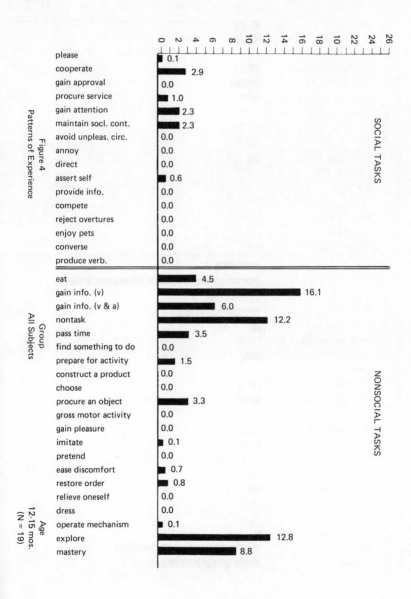

Figure 17.5: Patterns of Experience, Group — Top 5 in Overall Competence, Age 12-15 Months (N = 5)

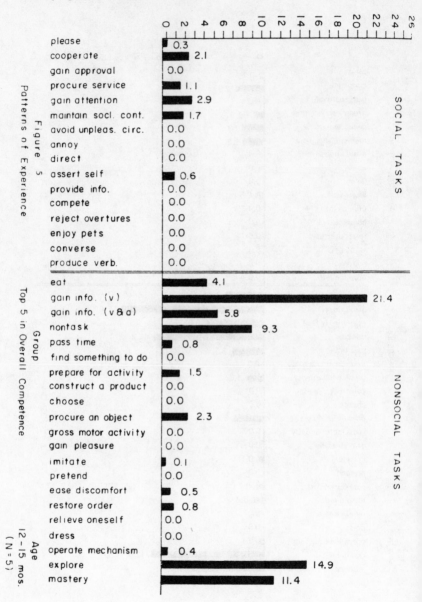

Figure 17.6: Patterns of Experience, Group — Bottom 5 in Overall Competence, Age 12-15 Months (N = 5)

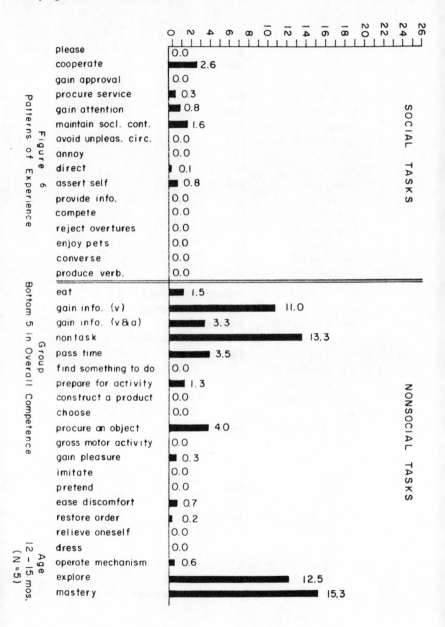

Figure 17.7: Patterns of Experience, Group — All Subjects, Age 18-21 Months (N = 19)

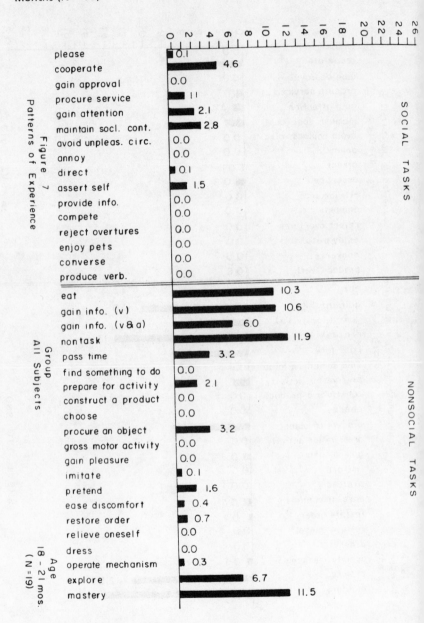

Figure 17.8: Patterns of Experience, Group — Top 5 in Overall Competence, Age 18-21 Months (N = 5)

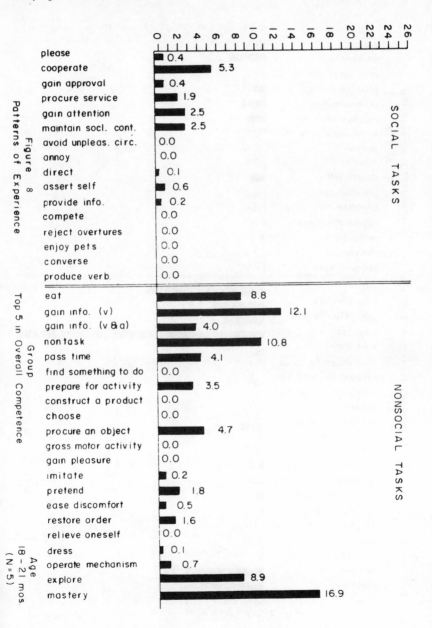

Figure 17.9: Patterns of Experience, Group — Bottom 5 in overall Competence, Age 18-21 Months (N = 5)

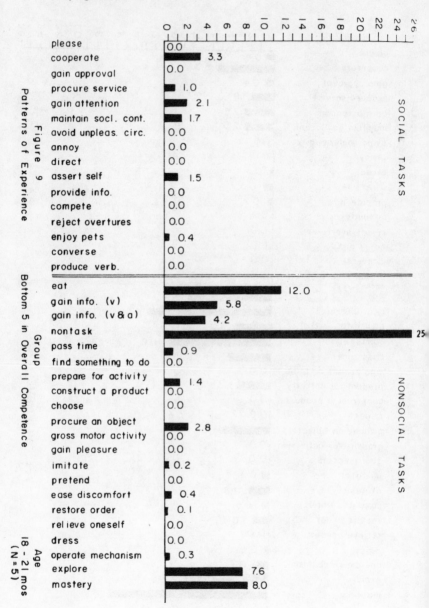

Table 17.2: Types of Language Experiences*, 12-15 Months

Group	Live language directed to S	Live language overheard by S	Mechanical	Sesame St	Total language
All 1-yearolds (N = 19)	4.2	0	0	0	6.0
Overall competence rankings:					
Top 5	5.8	0	0	0	5.8
Bottom 5	1.9	0.2	0.6	0	3.3

* Median per cent duration

Table 17.3: Types of Language Experiences*, 18-21 Months

Group	Live language directed to S	Live language overheard by S	Mechanical	Sesame St	Total language
All 1-year-olds (N = 19)	1.7	1.4	0.4	0	6.0
Overall competence rankings:					
Top 5	1.7	1.5	0	0	4.2
Bottom 5	0.4	0.2	0.4	0	4.0

* Median per cent duration

(3) Pass Time Experience

In our system a child who cannot find anything to keep himself occupied with for more than a few seconds, and cannot leave the field is *passing time*. This experience is a part of everyone's life, especially children in a conventional teacher-centered elementary school (Jackson, 1968). We find more *pass time* experience at 12 to 15 months of age in the lives of poorly developing children (top five Ss — 0.8 per cent v. bottom five Ss — 3.5 per cent; see Figures 17.5 and 17.6) and less at 18 to 21 months of age (top five Ss — 4.1 per cent v. bottom five Ss — 0.9 per cent; see Figures 17.8 and 17.9) as compared with children developing well. We believe it is because of restrictive parental practices in the 12 to 15 month age period and laissez-faire or 'keep away from me' practices in the 18 to 21 month period.

(4)   Nontask

A child who is free to roam and does not engage in any sustained activity for three seconds or longer is said to be in a 'nontask' state in our system. Such behavior is common in childhood (12.2 per cent of all Ss at 12-15 months; 11.9 per cent of all Ss at 18-21 months; see Figures 17.4 and 17.7). It is dramatically high in the lives of children developing poorly (in our sample) during the 18 to 21 months age range (top five Ss – 10.8 per cent v. bottom five Ss – 25.9 per cent; see Figures 17.8 and 17.9). This figure seems to us to be a kind of 'index of emptiness'.

Key Developmental Processes of the First Three Years of Life

We believe a simple and effective way to think about the early development of human competence is to focus on four key processes.

(1)   Language

From seven or eight months on through the next year or two, facility with most receptive language is acquired by most children.

(2)   Social Skills and Attachment

From birth on, but particularly between 7 or 8 and 24 months of age, children are acquiring social skills, establishing some form of primary attachment, acquiring a first view of themselves as social beings and establishing a very complex social contract with their primary caretakers.

(3)   Curiosity

Nearly every 8-month-old is a creature consumed by curiosity. It is the time of life parallel to that in the lives of kittens, puppies, monkeys and even horses when most children are more given to pure exploration than they ever will be again.

(4)   Problem Solving Skills

Piaget's work demonstrates quite impressively how the human mind absorbs many kinds of instrumental learning during the first two years of life. The seemingly simple 'play' of infancy is the basic training for later intelligent activity.

How these four processes fare as a consequence of child-rearing practices seems to us to be fundamental in the development of each child.

Our research has convinced us that it is only a small minority of children who develop as well as they could, in regard to these educational foundations, from eight months on.

Key Stresses of the Period

The 8- or 9-month-old, given the chance to explore, will do so. He will roam the living area for hours seeing exciting, novel and perplexing scenes, where an adult sees only the same old stuff. That fascinating world is not, however, ordinarily a safe world for an infant. It may contain broken objects with sharp edges, material you shouldn't put in the mouth, things that shouldn't be leaned on, etc. It is a world where objects that other people value can sometimes be broken inadvertently. It is an easy place to create disorder, to spill things, to litter. It may even have an older brother that doesn't really like the infant. All these factors *stress* the caretaker. She can solve all these difficulties simultaneously by preventing locomotion with a jump seat or a playpen.

The typical 10-month-old child can crawl, pull-to-stand, and climb units up to eight or so inches in height. Stair climbing seems universally attractive to children of that age. Unfortunately, the ability to climb *down* stairs safely is not acquired for at least another two months. Along with the baby's clumsiness and modest memory, etc., climbing is a common source of stress.

The typical twelve-month-old child can walk unaided and can climb units up to about fourteen inches high. This means he or she can climb a low table, or the average chair or sofa. At this point in development children can climb from chairs onto counters and other high places with skill. I won't belabor the point but considerably more danger is the result.

The 14- to 16-month-old often seems to refuse to cooperate with his mother just for the sake of refusing. He seems to want to contest her will. In our research this is common, therefore normal. In the inexperienced, unprepared mother, the second half of the second year of life can be very trying.

Far and away the source of stress most difficult to deal with is from the behavior of a not-much-older sibling. Repeatedly, we find that when children are spaced less than three years apart families pay a significant price. To the extent that the gap is more than three years the consequences lessen, whereas narrower age differences lead to greater stress.

A first child reared at home lives (usually) in a loving, protective atmosphere for most of his first two years. He rarely comes face to face with aggression or hostility. In contrast, a second child with a sibling a year or a year and a half older inevitably must cope with such forces, day after day, once he begins to crawl about. The young infant finds this task very difficult; mothers often find themselves into at least twelve months of chronically unpleasant policing activities; and worst of all, the older child finds sharing his mother an unfair and unpleasant kind of existence.

This description is not in any sense an exaggeration, although no two family situations are ever exactly alike. More details will be provided in later publications; but suffice it to say, no treatment of child-rearing, in the home, can avoid dealing with this source of stress when siblings are closely spaced and the children are less than four years old.

These stresses, along with the previously mentioned important developments, must be considered when discussing the role of child-rearing practices. To date we perceive three primary functions for caretakers of infants; designer, consultant, and authority. What follows is a description of how the apparently more effective caretakers handled these functions in our group.

(1) Designing the Living Area

They protected the child from the dangers of the home (safety proofing), *and* they protected the home from the child (child proofing), usually ahead of time. They then provided maximum access to the living quarters. They particularly made the kitchen safe and useful. They made kitchen cabinets and safe utensils, etc. available for play.

(2) Consulting

They were available to the child several hours each day to assist, enthuse and soothe when necessary. They used a particular style in responding to overtures. They would usually respond promptly even if only to delay action. They would pause to consider the baby's *purpose of the moment*. They would provide what was needed *with* some language, on target and at or slightly above his level of comprehension. They would add a related idea or two and they would not prolong the exchange longer than the baby wanted.

(3) Authority

Though loving and encouraging and free with praise, these mothers were firm. *No matter how young the infant, they set clear limits.* They spoke a disciplinary language the baby could understand. They did not over-intellectualize or expect the baby to do more than he was capable of, like control strong impulses indefinitely, etc.

The Training Program and the Comparative Experiment

Space limitations preclude an extensive treatment of these topics. Suffice it to say that we have spent the last two years creating and implementing a training program for average families. We begin work with families when their babies are 5 months of age and finish the program when they are 17 months old.

The comparative experiment is our current project. Sixty families of average child-rearing capacities have been assigned to one of four groups on a matched basis. One group is receiving guidance in child-rearing from us. A second group represents an attempt to control for prestige effects. Those families are receiving a comparable amount of guidance from a practised pediatric team. A third group represents an attempt to control for sensitization and test sophistication effects. They receive no guidance, but are visited according to the standard data collection schedule and the infants are tested according to that schedule. In a fourth group, we are only testing the babies before the study begins (for matching purposes) and at two years of age (along with all the others) for evaluation purposes.

Concluding Remarks

What I have described is my idea of a sensible form of educational psychological research. It is far from perfect. It is assailable on many fronts. Nevertheless, it is the only way I know of, at this point in history, to make legitimate use of scientific method in exploring the long-term experiential inputs to the development of babies.

Notes

1.　At various stages, extending over the last nine years, this research has received support from the following: United States Office of Education (OE-5-10-39), under the provisions of the Cooperative Research Program as a project of the Harvard University Center for Research and Development on Educational Differences; the Carnegie Corporation of New York; The Office of Economic Opportunity, Head Start Division (CG-9909 A/2), and the Office of Child Development. Division of HEW (OCD-CB-193). The statements made and views expressed are solely the responsibility of the author.
2.　Our description of a well-developed child is necessarily not free from error. The amount of error is, in part, a function of the accuracy of our work and in part dependent upon the generalizability of these findings to the types of children not in our samples.
3.　This statement covers a lot of territory which I cannot go into although at this point, suffice to say, I exclude children born with serious handicaps, or those badly abused during the first years of life.
4.　This judgement is consistent with the findings of the old Dennis (1935) study of development with minimum environmental stimulation.
5.　The Adult Assessment Scales (1974).

References

Barker, R.G. *Ecological Psychology*. Stanford, Calif.: Stanford University Press, 1968.

Bayley, N. 'Comparisons of mental and motor test scores for ages 1-15 months by sex, birth order, race, geographical location, and education of parents', *Child Development*, 1965, vol. 36, 379-411.

Brown, R.E. and Halpern, F. 'The variable pattern of rural black children', *Clinical Pediatrics*, 1971, vol. 10, no. 7.

Caldwell, B. 'A new approach to behavioral ecology', in J.P. Hill (ed.), *Minnesota Symposia on Child Psychology*, vol. 2. Minneapolis, Minn.: The University of Minnesota Press, 1969, pp. 74-108.

Clarke-Stewart, A.K. 'Interactions between mothers and their young children: characteristics and consequences', *Monographs of the Society for Research in Child Development*, 1973, serial no. 153, vol. 38, nos. 6-7.

Dennis, W. 'The effects of restricted practice upon the reaching, sitting, and standing of two infants', *Genetic Psychology*, vol. 47, 1935.

Jackson, P.W. *Life in Classrooms*. New York: Holt, Rinehart and Winston, 1968.

Lacrosse, E.R., Lee, P.C., Litman, F., Ogilvie, D.M., Stodolsky, S.S. and White, B.L. 'The first six years of life: a report on current research and educational practice', *Genetic Psychology Monographs*, 1970, vol. 82, 161-266.

Murphy, L. *Personality in Young Children*. New York: Basic Books, 1956.

Piaget, J. *The Origins of Intelligence in Children*. New York: W.W. Norton, 1952.

Schaeffer, E. Infant Education Research Project, Washington, DC. A report by the US Department of Health, Education and Welfare, 1969.

Schoggen, P. and Schoggen, M.F. 'Behavior units in observational research'. Presented as part of the APA Symposium, Methodological Issues in Observational Research, San Francisco, Calif., 1968 (mimeo.).

Wenar, C. 'Executive competence and spontaneous social behavior in one-year-olds', *Child Development*, 1972, vol. 43, 256-60.

White, B.L. 'Fundamental early environmental influences on the development of competence', in Merle E. Meyer (ed.), *Third Symposium on Learning: Cognitive Learning*, Western Washington State College, 1972, pp. 79-105.

White, B.L. *Human Infants: Experience and Psychological Development*. Englewood Cliffs, NJ: Prentice-Hall, Inc., 1971.

White, B.L. 'Child development research: An edifice without a foundation', *Merrill-Palmer Quarterly*, 1969, vol. 15, 47-8.

White, B.L., Kaban, B., Shapiro, B. and Constable, E. 'Adult assessment scales', Harvard Preschool Project, 1974.

White, B.L. and Watts, Jean C. *et al. Experience and Environment: Major Influences on the Development of the Young Child*, vol. 1. Englewood Cliffs, NJ: Prentice-Hall, Inc., 1973.

White, R. 'The concept of competence', *Psychological Review*, 1959.

Wright, H.F. 'Observational child study', in P. Mussen (ed.), *Handbook of Research Methods in Child Development*. New York: Wiley, 1960, pp. 71-139.

18 SOCIAL CONDITIONING OF VOCALIZATIONS IN THE INFANT

H.L. Rheingold, J.L. Gewirtz and H.W. Ross

Source: *Journal of Comparative and Physiological Psychology*, 1959, vol. 52, pp. 68-73. Copyright 1959 by the American Psychological Association. Reprinted by permission.

By three months of age the infant gives a well-defined social response to the appearance of adults. He looks at them intently, smiles, becomes active, and vocalizes. This behavior is repeated again and again in sequence. Adults often respond to these acts of the infant; they may only look at the child, but they may also smile to him, touch or caress him, or vocalize in return. Frequently one observes 'answering' social and, in particular, vocal play between mother and child. The adults' responses may therefore play an important part in maintaining and developing social responsiveness in the child (Rheingold, 1956). The principles of operant conditioning (Skinner, 1953) suggest that some of these adult responses, functioning as reinforcers, may affect the development of the child's social behavior (Gewirtz, 1956). Thus, smiling in the infant has been shown to respond to conditioning (Brackbill, 1958).

The present study was an attempt to condition vocalizations in infants. Vocalizations were selected for study because they seem to provide an index of the whole social response (Rheingold, 1956). The reinforcing stimulus was a complex of social acts which resembled those an attentive adult might naturally make when a child vocalizes. If temporal contiguity between the infant's vocalization and the reinforcing stimulus, which follows it, brings about an increase in the vocalizations, conditioning may be said to have occurred. The possibility that the reinforcing stimulus may also have functioned as an arouser of vocalizations will be considered. In any case, the results of the study should provide further understanding about the development of social responsiveness, as well as of speech.

Method

Two parallel experiments were carried out in sequence. In the first, 11 babies (*S*s) were studied, with one experimenter (*E*) and one observer-recorder (*O*), both women. In the second, 10 other *S*s and one *S* from Experiment I were studied with the *E* and *O* of the first experiment changing roles. An experiment was composed of three successive units in each of which three or four *S*s were studied at one time.

261

Subjects

The *S*s were 21 infants, all residents almost from birth in the same institution. (We are grateful to Sister Thecla and the staff of St. Ann's Infant Asylum, Washington, DC, for their generous cooperation.) Their median age was 3.0 months; three-quarters of them were no more than three days older or younger than the median. In each experiment six *S*s were male, five were female. Age was the main criterion for selection. Four possible *S*s were rejected; one seemed immature, two had a very high rate of vocalizing during the first baseline measure, and one was markedly fussy.

The institution offers excellent care and, as is characteristic of institutions, there are multiple caretakers. In general, the *S*s were well developed, healthy, alert, and socially responsive. The *E*s asked for no modifications in the usual caretaking routines. The caretakers knew that the *E*s were observing the development of social behavior, but they did not know the details of the experiment. The caretakers' usual behavior toward the *S*s appeared not to be modified by the conditions of the experiment.

Experimental Conditions

Baseline. In experimental Days 1 and 2 (first and second Baseline days) *E* leaned over the crib with her face about 15 in. above *S*'s and looked at him with an expressionless face, while *O* tallied vocalizations, out of *S*'s sight. Then *E* moved her head as necessary to remain in *S*'s line of vision, a condition which obtained throughout the experiments.

Conditioning. During experimental Days 3 and 4 (first and second Conditioning days), *E* again leaned over the crib with an expressionless face except that when *S* vocalized, *E* made an immediate response and then resumed the expressionless face until the next vocalization. The response, or *reinforcing stimulus*, consisted of three acts executed by *E* simultaneously, quickly, and smoothly. They were a broad smile, three 'tsk' sounds, and a light touch applied to the infant's abdomen with thumb and fingers of the hand opposed. No more than a second of time was required to administer the reinforcer.

At the beginning of the conditioning periods each vocalization was reinforced. Sometimes, as the rate of vocalizing increased, only every second, and later, every third, vocalization was reinforced. In Experiment I, 72 per cent of the reinforcers occurred after *each* vocalization; in Experiment II, 94 per cent. Less frequent reinforcing seemed to depress the rate, at least initially, and, because of the rather severe time restrictions, was abandoned altogether by the end of the study.

Extinction. Experimental Days 5 and 6 (first and second Extinction days) were the same as Days 1 and 2; *E* leaned over the crib with an expressionless face and made no response to *S*'s vocalizations.

The Vocal Response

Every discrete, voiced sound produced by *S* was counted as a *vocalization*. A number of other sounds characteristically made by very young infants, e.g. straining sounds and coughs, and the whistles, squeaks and snorts of noisy breathing, were not counted as vocalizations. Sounds falling under the categories of protests, fusses, and cries (see Emotional Behaviour below) were recorded separately. No attempt was made to record the phonetic characteristics of any of the sounds or their duration.

Observer Agreement. Agreement between two *O*s on the number of vocalizations produced by *S*s in 3-min. periods was high. Counts for 27 periods, using 13 different *S*s, yielded a median percentage agreement of 96 (range, 67 to 100). About half of these reliability measures were obtained at the *S*'s cribs, and the rest from tape recordings made during the experiment. These two techniques yielded similar percentages of observer agreement.

The Unit of Measurement. The unit for statistical analysis was the number of vocalizations an *S* gave in a 3-min. period. The counts were recorded by half-minutes and these were summed to give the score for the 3-min. period. After a rest period of 2 min., in which both *E* and *O* walked away from the baby's crib, another 3-min. count was made. After a second rest period a third count was made.

In each day nine such 3-min. counts were planned, distributed thus: one block of three in the first part of the morning, the second block of three in the late morning, and the third block of three after the midday meal. The minimum amount of time between blocks was 10 min., although usually an hour or more elapsed.

Actually, nine periods of observations were obtained during only 80 per cent of the 132 subject-days (22 *S*s x 6 experimental days). Since three or four *S*s were studied at a time, it was not always possible to find nine periods in a day when each was awake, alert, and content. Further, because the experiments were carried out in the nursery which the *S*s shared with 12 other infants, the presence and activities of these other babies, and of the caretakers in carrying out their routines, sometimes made it impossible to obtain the desired number of periods.

Emotional Behavior

A number of responses which seemed to be 'emotional' were recorded during the observation periods. These were: 'protests', discrete sounds of a whining nature; 'fusses', a series of sounds separated by a catch in the voice, whimpering; 'cries', continuous loud, wailing sounds; 'persistent looking away from E', rolling of the head from side to side or staring to one side or the other of E; and 'marked hand activity', hand play, finger sucking, or face or head rubbing. The last two activities seemed to be attempts to avoid E. Measures of observer-agreement in the recording of these responses were not made.

Each of these responses was given a credit of one for each half-minute in which it occurred. From the sum for each S a mean score was obtained for each experimental day.

Results

Similarity between Experiments

Figure 18.1 presents the means of both experiments for the six experimental days. Each point represents the mean of 11 individual means. It was expected that the effect of the experiment conditions would be similar from experiment to experiment, but the extent to which the

Figure 18.1: Mean Number of Vocalizations on Consecutive Experimental Days

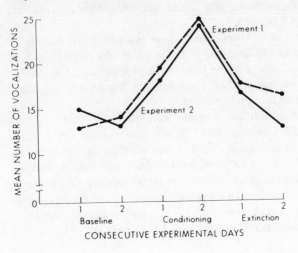

slopes of the curves would be congruent was not predicted.

The amount of similarity between the two experiments was estimated by an analysis of variance (Table 18.1), using Lindquist's Type VI design (1953). The analysis reveals no evidence of a difference between Experiments. Further, no source of variation involving Experiments is significant. (The difference between the two experiments in second Extinction day means is not significant; it suggests, however, that the less frequent reinforcement in Experiment I may have made the behavior more resistant to extinction.)

Three conclusions may be drawn from such close agreement in the results of two parallel experiments, each using different *S*s and different *E*s: first, we are dealing with some relatively stable characteristics of three-month-old infants; second, the results may be accepted with confidence; and third, the results of the separate experiments may be pooled for all remaining analyses . . .

[Details of effect of experimental conditions omitted. See Table 18.1.]

Table 18.1: Analysis of Variance of Effect of Consecutive Experimental Days

Source of variation	df	MS		F
Between subjects	21			
Experiments (1 v. 2)	1	1218		0.03
Error	20	45322		
Within subjects	110			
Conditions (baseline v. conditioning v. extinction)	2	71243	(1)[a]	10.63[b]
Days within conditions (1 v. 2)	1	4205	(2)[a]	1.88
Conditions X Days	2	22917	(3)[a]	9.24[b]
Days X Experiments	1	1738	(2)[a]	0.78
Conditions X Experiments	2	2031	(1)[a]	0.30
Conditions X Days X Experiments	2	866	(3)[a]	0.35
Error 1	40	6703		
Error 2	20	2233		
Error 3	40	2481		

[a] Number in parentheses refers to the error term used. The terms were not pooled because of statistically significant differences among them.

[b] Significant at .001 level.

Amount of Change in Number of Vocalizations

The treatment effects have been found reliable. It seems in order, there-fore, to present the means of vocalizations for each day and to calculate the amount of change produced by the experimental conditions. Under baseline conditions the three-month-old infants gave about 13 to 14 vocalizations in a 3-min. period. Individual differences were wide and ranged from 3 to 37 vocalizations. Using the social reinforcer for one day raised the rate to 18 vocalizations, an increase of 39 per cent. A second day of conditioning elevated the rate to 25, a further increase of 34 per cent. In all, conditioning brought about an increase of 86 per cent. Removing the reinforcer depressed the rate to 17 during the first and to 15 during the second day, the latter approaching very closely the level of baseline performance.

Emotional Behavior

Emotional behavior, while striking when it occurred, was observed in-frequently. The largest mean for any day in both experiments was 3.0, the smallest was 1.9. The order of the means by experimental days was identi-cal in the two experiments. It was: first Extinction day, second Extinction day, second Baseline day, second Conditioning day, first Conditioning day, and first Baseline day. The greater number of emotional responses during Extinction agrees with the findings of others (e.g. Brackbill, 1958; Skinner, 1953; Verplanck, 1955). Because the responses labeled emotional occurred so infrequently and because observer-agreement measures were not made, no further statistical analysis seemed warranted . . .

[Additional findings omitted.]

Discussion

The results of these experiments suggest that:

1. Infants' vocal behavior in a social situation can be brought under experimental control; that is, it appears to be conditionable.
2. A social event composed of an everyday complex of acts, performed by an adult who is not a caretaker, can function as a reinforcing stimulus.
3. The incidence of such behavior can be very quickly modified in as young an organism as the three-month-old infant.

Alternative Explanation

The question raised in the introduction may now be considered. Did the reinforcing stimulus function as an arouser of vocalizations? Would infants have vocalized more often because of the stimulation it provided, even if it had *not* been made contingent upon the infant's behavior? Or, did some part of the reinforcing stimulus (say, the smile) act as a social 'releaser'? The findings appear to be compatible with the conclusion that conditioning occurred: the rate of vocalizing continued to rise on the second day of Conditioning; the rate did not fall to the Baseline level on the first day of Extinction; it continued to fall on the second day of Extinction; and *S*s with low Baseline rates of vocalizing gained under Conditioning, although for them there was often a relatively long time interval (30 sec. or more) between the reinforcing stimulus and the occurrence of the next vocalization. Still, the decisive answer to the question must await an experiment in which the reinforcing stimulus is administered with equal frequency, but never directly after the infant vocalizes.

Nature of the Reinforcer

The results seem to show that some everyday behavior of adults can function as a reinforcing stimulus for an infant. One would like to know from what sources its reinforcing properties arise. In the simplest case, the smiles, sounds, and caresses of adults may be reinforcing only because they provide a change in stimulation. Further information on this matter could be obtained by working with the separate parts of the reinforcing stimulus, one by one; by substituting for them lights or sounds dispensed by a machine; or by using a reinforcer of a less 'affectionate' nature than the one used here appears to be. On the other hand, even for the three-month-old infant the smiles, sounds, and caresses of the adults may function as conditioned reinforcers because of their past association with caretaking acts.

It is possible that the *S*s of this study, living in an institution, may have had a less rich experience with adults. Institutional babies were used as *S*s only because they were more readily available, because more of them could be studied at one time, and because the complicating variable of differences in maternal care could be bypassed. They did not appear however to be 'starved' for attention or affection. Indeed, the attendants were often observed responding to babies when they vocalized. While it is possible that mothers would respond more often, in the absence of a comparative study we believe that infants in general would respond as these infants did.

Relation of Results to Theories of Speech

Since this study was limited to the vocalizing of infants in a social situation, attempts to reconcile the results with theories which account for all classes of prelinguistic utterances (babbling is the class frequently mentioned) cannot be complete. Thus, nothing in the findings of this study is incompatible with, for example, Holt's theory (1931) that the sound which the child hears himself make has reinforcing properties; with Lewis' theory (1951) that the adult's speech calls forth the infant's speech (a kind of imitation); or with Piaget's theory (1952) that vocalizing is perpetuated for its own sake by the processes of assimilation and accommodation. These may be labeled circular theories, for they do not postulate the necessity for any class of events prior to the moment when the infant responds to his own or another's vocalization. The theories of Miller and Dollard (1941) and of Mowrer (1950), on the other hand, are based upon the infant's associating the gratification of his needs and the accompanying vocalizations of the caretaker. Again, the results do not contradict this possibility.

The present study, however, does demonstrate the operation of still another principle: that the speech of the infant, if only in a social situation, can be modified by a response from the environment which is contingent upon his vocalizing. Hence, what happens *after* the infant vocalizes has been shown to be important . . .

References

Brackbill, Y. 'Extinction of the smiling responses in infants as a function of reinforcement schedule', *Child Developm.*, 1958, 29, 115-24.

Gewirtz, J.L. 'A program of research on the dimensions and antecedents of emotional dependence', *Child Developm.*, 1956, 27, 205-21.

Holt, E.B. *Animal Drive*. London: Williams and Norgate, 1931.

Lewis, M.M. *Infant Speech: A Study of the Beginnings of Language* (2nd edn.). New York: Humanities Press, 1951.

Lindquist, E.F. *Design and Analysis of Experiments in Psychology and Education*. Boston: Houghton Mifflin, 1953.

Miller, N.E. and Dollard, J. *Social Learning and Imitation*. New Haven: Yale Univer. Press, 1941.

Mowrer, O.H. *Learning Theory and Personality Dynamics*. New York: Ronald, 1950.

Piaget, J. *The Origins of Intelligence in Children*. New York: Int. Univer. Press, 1952.

Rheingold, H.L. 'The modification of social responsiveness in institutional babies', *Monogr. Soc. Res. Child Developm.*, 1956, 21, no. 63 (no. 2).

Skinner, B.F. *Science and Human Behavior*. New York: Macmillan, 1953.

Verplanck, W.S. 'The control of the content of conversation: Reinforcement of statements of opinion', *J. abnorm. soc. Psychol.*, 1955, 51, 668-76.

SECTION FIVE: SOCIAL COMPETENCE

Introduction

The two papers in this section, by John and Elizabeth Newson and H.R. Schaffer, both focus on the importance for cognitive development of the early social relationship between child and adult. A number of researchers have recently proposed that infants possess a special competence for engaging in dialogue-like interactions with adults: the Newsons' paper briefly describes this research (it is covered in more detail by Schaffer), and suggests that such interactions engender the development of 'intersubjectivity'. This implies that both participants in the interaction come to share topics for 'conversation': these may be behavioral, on the part of either or both partners, or environmental in that objects or events become shared referents. The Newsons argue that this 'marking' or singling out for joint attention plays a central role in aiding the formation of concepts by the child. Further, they see this as forming the foundation of later communication through language, and the whole process of the transmission of culture.

Schaffer's paper elaborates on many of the points raised by the Newsons. After describing some of the relevant research, Schaffer then discusses the necessary cognitive abilities on which dialogue depends, and the role of the mother in at first guiding, and then supporting the interaction. The paper ends with a discussion of the relevance of these early processes for subsequent development.

19 INTERSUBJECTIVITY AND THE TRANSMISSION OF CULTURE

John and Elizabeth Newson

Source: *Bulletin of the British Psychological Society*, 1975, vol. 28, pp. 437-46.

[A shortened form of this paper was given by John Newson at the BPS Annual Conference at Nottingham, April 1975.]

Piaget's Standpoint and the Approach Presented in this Paper

One of the most important debts which developmental psychology owes to Jean Piaget derives from his steadfast insistence that it is *symbolic functioning*, via the establishment of cognitive structures, which provides the key to our understanding of what is important in human psychological development. And Piaget goes on to assert that symbolic activity must clearly be recognized as a function which in some sense emerges, as a result of the child's activities, at a distinctive point in the human infant's natural psychological development: 'At the end of the sensorimotor period, at about one and a half to two years, there appears a function that is fundamental to the development of later behavior patterns. It consists in the ability to represent something (a signified something: object, event, conceptual scheme, etc.) by means of a 'signifier' which is differentiated and which serves only a representative purpose: language, mental image, symbolic gesture and so on' (Piaget and Inhelder, 1969).

Obviously for the purpose of constructing a comprehensive theory concerning the course of subsequent cognitive growth it was necessary to begin somewhere. But instead of beginning, classically, with thought, Piaget takes as his starting-point motor activity, initially of a simple reflex kind, which the child is said to display in the presence of objects. This leads him to emphasize sensorimotor activity, involving the manipulation by the infant of inanimate objects. He goes on to suggest that thought is the 'interiorization' of such actions: 'In order to know objects, the subject must act upon them, and therefore transform them: he must displace, connect, combine, take apart and reassemble them' (Piaget, 1970).

Knowledge, then, originates in activity: originally overt activity of the infant, shown in the physical manipulation of objects. And this leads later to the performance of operations which, as a result of internal processes of organization (equilibration), are not self-evident in the infant's

271

observable behaviour. The primary emphasis is, however, active interaction between the organism and his environment.

It needs to be stated here that the theoretical position which will be outlined in this paper will represent a shift of emphasis rather than an absolute disagreement with Piaget's philosophical standpoint. For instance, we would not quarrel at all with his proposition that 'objective knowledge is not acquired by a mere recording of external information but has its origin in interactions between the subject and objects . . .' (1970, op. cit.). To this statement we merely wish to add that the object with which the human infant interacts most often, and most effectively, particularly in the earliest stages of development, is almost invariably another human being. In this sense the Piagetian standpoint needs to be qualified and elaborated in certain important respects, but in general terms can be accepted as a useful overall conceptual frame of reference. We would also fully agree with Piaget when he asserts, in opposition to empirical behaviourists, that knowledge arises neither from outside the organism, nor from within it. As he puts it: 'The main point of our theory is that knowledge results from *interactions* between the subject and the object, which are *richer* than what the objects can provide by themselves' (1970, op. cit.).

To align Piaget's position with our own it is necessary to enlarge the concept of 'object' to include human beings. Yet human beings are not quite like other objects, in as much as they have the power to communicate with others of their kind and hence to share with them a common culture: an articulated framework or structure of knowledge which is, in a sense, understood only because it is *mutually* understandable. The argument is, then, that knowledge itself originates within an interaction process (highly active on the part of the infant) between the infant himself and other, more mature, human individuals who already possess shared understandings with other communicating beings. Furthermore, these shared understandings are embedded in a uniquely human way of conceptualising the world in spatial and temporal terms. In short, the child only achieves a fully articulated knowledge of his world, in a cognitive sense, as he becomes involved in social transactions with other communicating human beings. Knowing, and being able to communicate what it is that we know, need to be viewed as opposite sides of the same coin.

The Infant's Knowledge of Objects

Piaget's view that the infant's knowledge somehow originates from an internalization of the actions he performs in coordinating hand and eye movements, so as to grapple with inanimate objects, was supported by observations he made upon his own children. He describes their reactions when objects were made to disappear from view by covering them, dropping them silently or hiding them inside containers. One of the infant's most important 'constructions' is said to be that which leads to the discovery of the notion of a permanent object at between nine and twelve months of age. Thus: 'During the first months of existence, there are no permanent objects, but only perceptual pictures which appear, dissolve, and sometimes 'reappear' (1970, op. cit.). At this stage it is suggested that the object is only conceptualised as a result of the actions involved in looking for it.

> One real example is an 11-month-old child who was playing with a ball. He had previously retrieved it from under an armchair when it had rolled there before. A moment later, the ball went under a low sofa. He could not find it under this sofa, so he came back to the other part of the room and looked for it under the armchair, where this course of action had already been successful. [1970, op. cit.]

It should be noticed, in passing, that in this account the infant in question clearly has the capacity both to hold in mind an accurate knowledge of certain relevant spatial locations like 'under the armchair', and to sustain an intention to retrieve an object, such as a ball, when it is no longer in view. However, on the basis of numerous similar observations of strategies used by babies to retrieve hidden or lost objects, Piaget asserts that the achievement of object permanence at around this age represents a major mental achievement: it contributes to a veritable 'Copernican revolution' which babies accomplish in the course of the first 12 to 18 months. It is this evaluation that has stimulated many further studies aimed at verifying that babies do react towards the disappearance or reappearance of objects in the way he describes.

However, our purpose is to do more than study babies' reactions; it is to explain how they themselves become *agents*, directing their own actions. This is a distinction not always made in conventional experimental psychology. Among psychologists working in the experimental tradition, Bower is outstanding. In a recent monograph (Bower, 1974), he has surveyed a wide range of experimental studies which have a bearing upon the way infants behave in the presence of what adults would regard as objects. Bower draws attention to a respectable array of carefully recorded evidence, showing that the human infant is capable of extraordinarily complex feats of behavioural adjustment to external events and circumstances, often from the moment of birth. One surprising finding is that, even within the first two weeks of life, infants are able to reach out and grasp for visually presented objects with a considerable degree of accuracy. 'The hand opens before contact and closes on contact, but too quickly for the contact to have released the hand closure' (Bower, 1974). To demonstrate these responses it is necessary to support the infant in an optimal posture, relieving him of the muscular burden of head control while allowing free movement of the limbs; but when this is done, objects presented at a suitable distance will frequently be attained with delicately appropriate and coordinated hand and arm movements, on a visual cue alone, and without the necessity for practice in hand-eye coordination which Piaget, among others, has assumed to be necessary.

More strikingly still, Bower has fitted certain infants with polarizing spectacles so as to be able to study their reactions to a 'virtual object' (i.e. an object which appears visually to be solid and three-dimensional, but which is in fact produced by stereoscopic techniques). When such a virtual object is substituted for the real object, it is claimed that the infant reaches for it as before, but is then 'upset' to find there is no normal tactual feedback. Bower also asserts that accurate reaching reactions become strangely difficult to elicit from babies after the age of four weeks and only reappear, in the babies he has followed up, around the age of 20 weeks.

Bower's claims, particularly those concerned with the reaction to the virtual object, need to be verified by workers in other laboratories before they can be interpreted unambiguously. There is, as might be expected, much scope for interpreting the behavioural evidence of 'upset' when observing babies of this age, who are only able to sustain their attention for short time spans and are very easily distressed when manipulated for experimental purposes. His work is, however, part of a more pervasive trend among contemporary developmental psychologists to observe and record the behaviour of very young infants and to subject their recordings to detailed and systematic forms of analysis.

Bower's contribution is but one example of a host of recent investigations which have begun to suggest that the human infant is a much more complicated organism than previous generations of developmental psychologists have led us to believe. The well-known experiment by Bruner and Kalnins (Bruner, 1968), showing that infants can adjust their sucking behaviour so as to bring a picture into clear focus, provides a similarly dramatic demonstration of the intrinsic 'cleverness' of the human neonate, and particularly highlights visual sophistication.

Clearly, findings of this kind (and there are similar findings about the accuracy of visual scanning activity in newborn babies) suggest that infants at birth are already possessed of the necessary sensory, motor and neural equipment to make it possible for them to respond appropriately towards real objects in a three-dimensional world. In consequence these results would seem to refute those empiricist theories which have led some psychologists to assume that babies require prolonged experience with objects before they develop such skills. At the same time we need to treat with caution the suggestion, both implicit and explicit in Bower's writing, that the human infant is somehow inherently possessed of the 'knowledge' that seen objects are tangible. Behaviour, however complicated, carries no necessary implication that the organism is capable of appreciating the ends towards which its own behaviour is directed. However accurately a guided missile is able to seek out its target, we do not generally feel it necessary to credit the missile with having *knowledge* about the target as an object, out there, about to be destroyed. Adult human beings do, however, share with one another the capacity to make such conceptualisations, and it seems reasonable to ask how the infant is brought to the point of sharing them.

To do him justice, Bower does devote the final chapter of his monograph to a more considered discussion of cognitive development as such. He also provides an excellent summary of experimental observations upon children's reactions to the disappearance and reappearance of objects or their apparent transformation. At two months an infant can track slowly-moving visual targets, even if they pass behind an obscuring screen and re-emerge at the opposite side. A little later he will be able to back-track visually if the emerging object is radically different from the one which went behind the screen. Between two and four months there seems to be some evidence to suggest that he will respond with a decelerated heart-rate (surprise?) when an object, after being momentarily screened from him, proves to have vanished. Not until about six months will most babies attempt to remove a cloth cover deliberately, i.e. with intent to retrieve a hidden object. Even at a year, infants who observe an object hidden in the experimenter's palm and then placed under a cloth will, after the hand is removed and shown to be empty, still not think to look for the object under the cloth, despite the tell-tale lump to be seen in full view.

One conclusion arising from this review is that the search for definitive evidence that object permanence is suddenly achieved, at one particular instant in the child's mental progress, is unlikely to prove successful. Each method of demonstrating that the child will respond appropriately to a disappearing or reappearing object seems to give rise to a different operational definition of what is meant by the achievement of object permanence. Cumulatively, these demonstrations merely make it increasingly obvious that the human infant is sensitive to a vast number of happenings or events: and that these leave residual memory effects, in the sense that they can be shown to influence his subsequent observable reactions. How early this can be seen will depend to a very great extent upon our social skill in drawing a baby's attention to objects as salient entities within the compass of his attention, and upon our experimental ingenuity in detecting his differential responses in subsequent encounters.

All this does little to provide us with satisfactory evidence for the dramatic arrival within the baby's mental experience of some entirely new level of awareness directed towards objects as such. Perhaps the most secure evidence that the baby can represent objects to himself in the sense that we ourselves do, would be a demonstration that he is able to communicate with some other person about 'objects' in a reliable and consistent way. In short, we need to be very cautious about arguing that objects exist as entities for babies until we have evidence that babies can share with us a certain mutual understanding of event sequences in which we and they are caught up. Human knowledge about the environment — as opposed to mere reactivity towards it — depends upon some measure of agreement between interacting persons about how reality is being construed. It is in this sense that the child's knowledge about objects, and his ability to communicate what he knows, are fundamentally inseparable. At all events, the accounts of both Bower and Piaget seem to place far too little emphasis on the fact that the human infant is also surprisingly *socially* active almost from the moment of birth. Furthermore, he approaches the business of intentional action in a manner which makes sense to himself in the same way as to others, rather than merely reacting to circumstance.

The Primacy of Social Responsiveness in Human Infants

Moving, three-dimensional, self-deforming and noise producing objects have a basic attention-demanding function for the human infant which far exceeds the effect of any static object, however brightly coloured or 'novel' it might otherwise be in terms of such factors as shape or size (Schaffer, 1971). This is a part of the reason why the human face of his mother clearly begins to exert a compelling fascination from the moment when the infant is capable of bringing it into clear focus (i.e. more or less from birth). The patterns of reaction whereby the infant can demonstrate such interest also need to be carefully noted. And when these are examined in slowed down video-recordings of an interacting mother-baby pair, it turns out firstly that the different sensorimotor components of the infant's activity are highly synchronized with each other, and secondly, that his action sequences are temporally organized so that they can mesh — with a high degree of precision — with similar patterns of action produced by his human caretaker. The fact is that, from a very early age indeed, infants appear to be capable of taking part in dialogue-like exchanges with other human beings. Thus, when the adult talks to the infant, the infant displays all the complex gestural accompaniments that one normally expects of attentive listening; and when the adult pauses, the infant can reply with a fully articulated, gesturally animated, conversation-like response. Prolonged social interchanges comprising an alternating succession of passive and active role-taking apparently occur with an effortless spontaneity; and this seems to 'come naturally' not only to the mother, who obviously has a long history of conversation experience, but to her infant who is in most other respects conceptually and socially quite inexperienced. Clearly, observations of this sort add strength to the argument that the infant is somehow *innately primed* to participate in complicated social rituals.

The reciprocal nature of this phenomenon implies, as Colwyn Trevarthen has pointed out (Trevarthen *et al.*, 1976), that the movements of eyes, head, mouth, limbs and voice are based in rhythmic synchronies and patterns which are common to human social interaction regardless of age, race or social custom. Such patterns represent cultural universals which man also shares with many animals lower in the phylogenetic chain, and they thus have very deep biological roots. Indeed, it is probably because these rhythmic coordinations of behaviour are so ubiquitous and pervasive that they have been completely taken for granted, and hence overlooked, in the behaviour of very young infants. Trevarthen's approach might be described as that of a behavioural embryologist: he tends to emphasise the great complexity of genetically based behavioural systems with which the human infant is endowed. He seems inclined to stress the inborn nature of the ability to take part in complex social interaction rituals, and he describes the phenomenon as 'innate intersubjectivity'.

When Trevarthen uses the term 'intersubjectivity', he is referring to a specific kind of sociability which mediates communication between two human subjects. It is his view that infants are inherently responsive to those patterns of temporal movement which typically govern the episodic behaviour cycles characteristic of most living organisms, or at least of those which are phylogenetically advanced enough to engage in social forms of communication. Thus, for instance, the ways in which the eyes of both infant and adult move within the head seem to him to depend upon genetically pre-programmed timing mechanisms which govern the step-like jumps or 'saccades' which are normally made in looking behaviour. The human baby both responds *to*, and responds *with*, actions which are synchronised in accordance with basically shared rhythms.

Beyond this, however, the looking behaviour of neonates — when viewed in slow-motion action replays — is very delicately coordinated with certain hand and arm movements, and even with facial and mouthing movements, all of which are integrated together in such a precisely co-ordinated rhythmic sequence that the total response can be most aptly designated 'pre-speech'. The forms of stimulation which optimally call forth such complex conversation reactions from very young infants are themselves not simple. It may be true, for instance, as other students of neonatal behaviour have pointed out (Condon and Sander, 1974), that human speech conforms to a basic rhythmic pattern of vocalized sound which calls forth precisely synchronized motor movements in newborn babies. But these and other phenomena, such as social smiling, may best be viewed as only part of a more general complex responsiveness to the social approaches we make to babies: reciprocal social responsiveness which is the end product of a biological selection process aimed at the important biological goal of making human communication with babies feasible.

Susan Pawlby, from our own Unit, when interviewing mothers about their early attempts to communicate with their babies, at the preverbal level, found that some of them talked spontaneously about trying to get on the same wavelength. The analogy is an interesting one. As every schoolboy knows, effective communication between a transmitting and a receiving station demands that both stations are at least tuned to the same basic carrier frequency before any transmission of information can take place. The motor action sequences which human beings characteristically employ (intonational pattern, hand gestures, facial movements, etc.) are temporally patterned in ways which are far from random but also in ways to which, as human beings, we are selectively highly responsive. It is obviously dangerous to stretch analogies too far, but it may well be that all information exchange implies a certain basic compatibility in the temporal response characteristics of the communicating individuals.

In two-way communication it may also be essential to arrange that transmission and reception periods alternate according to some rule or device which ensures that one transmitter remains silent while the other is operating, since there would otherwise be gross interference between competing signals on the same wavelength. Trevarthen has not been the only observer to point out that babies seem to be natural conversationalists (Schaffer, 1974), in the sense that they are innately skilled in turn-taking. They look attentive when we speak to them and wait for an appropriate pause or hiatus before they in turn make some gesture, or vocal or pre-vocal response. Opinions differ as to how much the baby's actions are under the puppet-like control of the more experienced partner in such communication sequences. Schaffer (op. cit.) and Shotter (1973) have suggested that it is the skill of the mother which mainly accounts for the alternating form of the dialogue which can be observed: but even so, it may still be the case that infants must be biologically primed in certain very specific respects for it to be possible for mothers to select points for action in the situation so as to give such convincing simulations of the dialogue form which appears to be a feature of all interpersonal communication, regardless of culture.

This brings us to a further reason for wanting to introduce a term such as 'intersubjectivity'. Typically the form of control which a mother exercises in trying to establish communication with her baby is one which makes a great deal of use of his own spontaneous actions. These first appear as coordinated segments of apparently goal-directed activity. As Bower's work shows, the baby's behaviour seems to be 'aimed at' objects and events in the world surrounding him which other human beings would also naturally expect to notice or to find interesting (Bower, 1974). This means that it is possible, almost from birth, for the interacting adult to take his or her cue from the spontaneous actions performed by the baby and to weave these into the form of a dialogue with him. Thus mothers and babies begin to conduct 'conversations' concerning objects and events to which both partners are attentive, even though there is as yet no evidence for verbal understanding on the baby's part. Since, however, the baby plays a very active and self-directed role from the outset, the course of the ensuing dialogue is never strictly under the sole control of either partner. Whatever communication takes place emerges as an intersubjective product of their joint collaboration. The word 'intersubjectivity' therefore usefully draws attention to the general principle that human cognitive understanding arises from a process of *negotiation* between two or more human beings; and it suggests that it may not be sensible to seek the roots of those shared understandings which constitute human knowledge within the action patterns of any one individual viewed in social isolation. (It is in this sense that the word is used by the French philosopher Merleau-Ponty when discussing socialization from the sociological standpoint; see O'Neill, 1973.)

Mother-Baby Interaction Sequences

While paying respect to the inborn predispositions of the human infant, contemporary developmental psychologists are increasingly becoming interested in the functional significance which should be attached to this precocious social activity of normal babies and, more particularly, in how this may be related to the overall course of cognitive and symbolic development. In practice, most mothers are apparently very skilled in sustaining the interest and attention of their babies, both towards themselves and towards significant objects and events which are encountered in the course of everyday life. Mothers also often act as mediators between the baby and outside events. They tend to provide, quite unselfconsciously, forms of feedback which are dramatically attention-compelling because they are contingently geared — in a very delicately timed way — to actions which are spontaneously made by the infant himself. Even in the most straightforward adult-and-baby encounters with objects, the adult's visual monitoring of the baby's activity may be highly critical. Note how, in practice, one is able to elicit simple visual following behaviour in a supine four-week infant using a dangling ring. In this superficially simple task, the test demonstrator will carefully attend, not just to the general state of arousal of the infant, but to his precise focus and line of regard. Having 'hooked' the attention of the infant upon the ring, one then begins gingerly to move it across his field of vision in such a way that the infant's eyes continue to hold the object with successive fixations until eventually the head follows the eyes in that coordinated overall movement pattern which denotes successful tracking. If the test object is moved too suddenly, or is left static too long, the visual attention of the infant will flag and the attempt will have to begin all over again from scratch. In this instance, what is in fact happening is a highly skilled monitoring by the adult and a consequent adjustment of the dangling object, moment by moment, depending on the feedback which is being obtained from the spontaneous actions of the infant. It might even be argued that one is dragging from the infant a complex response which he would be unlikely to give to an object which was moved by mechanical means across his visual field. The resulting action sequence of the infant is therefore a combination of his own activity and *an intelligent manipulation of that activity by the much more sophisticated adult partner.* The adult, by being contingently responsive to the infant in a way which only another human being could be, manages both to hold the infant's attention, and to shape the course of his ongoing activity pattern; and, incidentally, the infant is provided with a sustained looking experience which might not otherwise have occurred.

Confronting a baby with a humanly presented object thus turns out to be complicated even though the baby is required to give his attention only to the movement of a single object. The situation obviously becomes much more difficult to analyse when the baby is called upon to divide his attention between the person presenting the object and the object itself. Yet it is this kind of activity, in which a baby begins to switch his visual attention from his mother to other objects and back again to his mother, which provides her with an extremely rewarding set of social signals and makes her feel that communication between herself and her infant is at last a real possibility. However, visual switching activity also appears to be something more complex than an automatic response to external events. Again it seems to emerge as a product of collaboration, in which the mother as a sophisticated adult capitalises upon the spontaneous actions of her child so as to entrain them into sequences which are potentially useful both as communication gestures and in alerting the baby's attention to events which can become foci of shared reference.

Switching eye direction between contact with another person and contact with shared objects of reference is clearly of enormous significance as a means of sustaining social rapport between any two human beings; and the fact that most babies become proficient in this art at around the age of six months provides us with yet another example of their staggering social precocity. Closely linked with this is the whole question of how babies become able to imitate actions which they see others perform; and here, once more, it can be argued that facility in imitation develops out of a collaboration between two partners in which the adult provides the infant with forms of feedback which are closely linked to the spontaneous actions of the infant himself. Mothers seem to stage-manage the situation in such a way as to draw out of the infant sustained patterns of action which mirror the adult's own actions. A case can be made, then, for saying that the infant's capacity to imitate (and hence to empathize with others) itself develops within the context of spontaneous social exchanges which almost invariably occur between the infant and those who seek to communicate with him in human terms (Newson and Pawlby, 1975).

Problems of Recording and Analysis

Within the two-way interaction games which ordinary mothers spontaneously play with their babies, a very large number of actions which the baby makes are interpreted as communication gestures in the sense that they are incorporated into the dialogue. From the baby's standpoint, these particular actions are apparently rendered significant by the quality and timing of the mother's gestural and vocal reciprocations. The effect is to highlight or 'mark' certain events as having special significance, and hence to *punctuate* the contribution which the baby is making according to a pattern of meaningfulness which is, to some extent, being imposed by the more sophisticated partner. The mother's intonational gestures, often accompanied by dramatic alterations of facial expression, clearly have a powerful effect in alerting the baby's attention to the significance of his own actions.

The attempt to give a detailed sequential description of the alternating flow of communication gestures which typically takes place poses certain methodological problems. One of the most obvious is that the two-way communication process takes place so rapidly, even with very young babies, that it is only possible to look at it in detail by making simultaneous audio-visual recordings which can be slowed down and then replayed as many times as is necessary in order to establish precisely what has taken place during the interchange. Ideally, one needs to encapsulate on the permanent record the signalling actions of both partners, the direction and quality of their changing attentiveness, and the overall setting within which the interaction is taking place. One also needs to be able to relate the activities of each partner to those of the other in an accurate time sequence. And all this is only a minimum technical requirement which must precede the evolution of coding schedules designed to be sensitive to the meaningful content of whatever communication is taking place. Various research workers both in this country and elsewhere are currently preoccupied with such problems, and it is as yet too soon to report any consensus as to the most appropriate strategies for coding and analysis.

Although it is also too early to offer a review of published findings deriving from this particular research approach, some general comments arising from attempts to undertake practical research studies may be of interest. It seems, for instance, that the roles of observer and participant in relation to adult-infant interaction sequences are quite distinct and separate. As a participant, or actor, one inevitably pays maximal attention to the communication gestures of the other partner, i.e. the baby, and one cannot be simultaneously aware of all the subtleties of one's own communication gestures — particularly the nonverbal ones — without putting the smooth functioning of the communication process at risk. This is analogous to thinking too much about the mechanics of the walking process and tripping over one's own feet. This does not imply, however, that a participant may not be able to function as an observer when viewing his own behaviour in retrospect, and indeed there may be considerable advantages in securing this kind of cooperation from mothers. This consideration leads us to yet another reason for invoking the notion of 'intersubjectivity'. In a sense, it is only possible to chart the course of a communication interchange by oneself engaging in such activity as a 'communicant' or practitioner of human communication skills, i.e. as one who has already been initiated into human culture. Thus while the analysis of temporal event sequences lends itself appropriately to computer processing, the identification of the significant events must remain the province of the empathic human observer. Indeed, it may even be the case that, at the preverbal level of communication, the mother herself will sometimes be the only person who can identify certain communication gestures which her baby is currently making, because only she shares a history of common communication experience with that baby (Newson and Shotter, 1974).

Further Theoretical Implications

Evidence is now accumulating which strongly suggests that communication at the preverbal level provides the foundation upon which verbal language can be built. In other words, the representational function which makes language possible seems to develop out of what Werner and Kaplan have called the *primordial sharing situation.*

> In this situation the human infant is 'sharing' rather than 'communicating' an experience (the object of reference) with another person, usually the mother. That is, the primordial sharing situation is a sensorimotor affective 'pre-symbolic situation in which there is little differentiation in the child's experience between himself, the other (typically the mother), and the referential object'. The precursory components for symbolization, however, are present. Together, the mother and child are sharing the same thing. What is still necessary is that the child must differentiate and integrate the primordial sharing situation — himself, from objects of reference, from his means of symbolic communication, from his communicants (others) — so that his symbols represent his objects of reference in a communicative fashion to both others and himself. [Langer, 1970]

In practice, it certainly seems to be necessary to make a fairly fundamental distinction between face-to-face exchanges involving adult and child, and exchanges during which one of the partners (usually the adult) is offering comments upon the elsewhere-directed actions which the other partner (usually the child) is performing. The rules governing social interplay in these two rather obviously different situations do not seem to be the same. It appears to be the case, for instance, that active participation in face-to-face conversational episodes is possible at a much earlier age; and this is in tune with the idea, well supported by observational study, that manual manipulatory competence generally comes surprisingly late in the developmental timetable, as compared with visual exploratory skill. It is, however, the interplay between the child's person-oriented gestures and his object-related actions which is likely to prove a most fruitful area for further research. Very young babies can pay sustained attention to another person and will often respond to people while largely ignoring inanimate objects; it is only during the second half of the first year that they seem to become capable of sustained absorption or play with objects. It may be significant, therefore, that it also takes time for infants to reach the stage where they can alternate their attention appropriately between persons and things. Yet when this does become possible, it opens up a whole new field of collaboration: the child's attention can be drawn not just towards the objects themselves, but towards the fundamental cognitive distinction between objects and the actions which they elicit.

The general proposition that the child's knowledge has its roots in his early social ability receives striking support from yet another source.

Any function in the child's cultural development appears on the stage twice, on two planes, first on the social plane and then on the psychological, first among people as an *intermental category* and then within the child as an *intramental category*. [Vygotsky, 1966]

It is of particular interest that Vygotsky invokes the term 'intermental' which is hardly distinguishable from the term 'intersubjective' as we have used it in this paper.

Summary and Conclusion

Human cognitive competence is predicated upon the fundamental assumption that most of the actions we perform are readily intelligible to other human beings, as are theirs to us. Yet this is obviously not the case with the newborn child, who is quite unable to respond to communications which adults take for granted as 'basic' such as the gesture of pointing towards some object which is clearly visible in his field of view. The child gradually achieves such competence, but only — we now believe — as a result of being positively involved in numerous experiences of reciprocal activity with other human beings. His early experience, being largely socially mediated, very frequently involves being caught up and swept along in exchanges with other communicating persons, who intuitively engage him in alternating-role sequences such that his own natural and spontaneous actions and reactions are assigned a precise function within the context of an apparently meaningful exchange. Through such dialogues-of-action, the infant becomes thoroughly familiar with the role of a skilled communicator, participating in forms of communication long before he is able to understand the full content of what is being communicated.

Involvement in such activity provides what seem to be the optimal conditions for arriving at genuine shared understandings with his partner. The situation is such that the child is under very little constraint, and can freely experiment in his role as actor. At any moment within the dialogue he can ad lib or enlarge upon the part he is being called upon to play, since nearly any variation of his own action or reaction can be compensated for by being incorporated into the ongoing dialogue, which remains understandable in human terms throughout. He is thus massively and repeatedly involved in nonverbal dialogues whose form is governed by some underlying structure of meaning. At the same time, however, the content of any given communication is by no means wholly imposed by the more skilled partner; it arises out of the combined activity of both individuals. Thus the basic human ability to structure knowledge in such a way that it can be shared — the ability to commune with others — derives initially from mothers' 'natural' inclination to treat their babies as if they already had understanding.

The term 'intersubjectivity' has recurred throughout this paper. In using it, attention is being drawn to a fundamental proposition: that the origin of symbolic functioning should be sought, not in the child's activities with inanimate objects, but rather in those idiosyncratic but shared understandings which he first evolves during his earliest social encounters with familiar human beings who are themselves already steeped in human culture.

References

Bower, T.G.R. (1974), *Development in Infancy*. San Francisco: Freeman.

Bruner, J.S. (1968), *Processes of Cognitive Growth in Infancy*, vol. 3. Worcester: Clark Univ. Press.

Condon, W.S. and Sander, L.W. (1974), 'Neonate movement is synchronized with adult speech', *Science*, N.Y. 183, 99-101.

Kalnins, I. and Bruner, J.S. (1973), 'The coordination of visual observation and instrumental behaviour in early infancy', *Perception*, 2, 307-14.

Langer, J. (1970), 'Werner's theory of development', in P.H. Mussen (ed.), *Manual of Child Psychology*, 3rd edn. New York: Wiley.

Newson, J. and Newson, E. (1976), 'On the social origins of symbolic functioning', in V.P. Varma and P. Williams (eds.), *Advances in Educational Psychology*, III. London: Hodder and Stoughton (in press).

Newson, J. and Pawlby, S. (1975), 'On imitation', paper presented to an inter-university colloquium at Nottingham University.

Newson, J. and Shotter, J. (1974), 'How babies communicate', *New Society*, 29, no. 618, 345-7.

O'Neill, J. (1973), 'Embodiment in child development: a phenomenological approach', in H.P. Dreitzel (ed.), *Childhood and Socialization*. New York: Collier-Macmillan.

Piaget, J. (1970), 'Piaget's theory', in P.H. Mussen (ed.), *Manual of Child Psychology*, 3rd edn. New York: Wiley.

Piaget, J. and Inhelder, B. (1969), *The Psychology of the Child*. London: Routledge and Kegan Paul.

Schaffer, H.R. (1971), *The Growth of Sociability*. Harmondsworth: Penguin Books.

Schaffer, H.R. (1974), 'Behavioural synchrony in infancy', *New Scientist*, 62, 16-18.

Schotter, J. (1973), 'Prolegomena to an understanding of play', *J. Theory soc. Behav.*, 3, 47-89.

Trevarthen, C., Hubley, P. and Sheeran, L. (1976), 'Psychological actions in early infancy', *La Recherche* (in press).

Vygotsky, L.S. (1966), 'Development of higher mental functions', in *Psychological Research in the USSR*. Moscow: Progress Publishers.

20 EARLY INTERACTIVE DEVELOPMENT

H.R. Schaffer

Source: H.R. Schaffer (ed.), *Studies in Mother-Infant Interaction* (Academic Press, 1977). Copyright by Academic Press Inc. (London) Ltd.

What are the characteristics of social behaviour in infancy? In the past the motivation for enquiry has come mostly from the intrinsic interest of the problem itself, in that evidence was looked for regarding the capabilities at the beginning of life for what is surely one of the most complex of skills, namely that of forming interpersonal relationships. It is true that some had hoped to find in the first bond formed by the infant with another person the prototype of all subsequent relations: as yet, however, there is no substantiating evidence whatever for such an association. Rather, the primary relationship is an intriguing event in its own right, forming but the first though crucial step in the socialization process.

Increasingly, however, an additional reason for interest in this area has appeared in recent years. It stems from the realization that many functions traditionally treated in psychology as though they 'belonged' to individuals and could thus be studied purely as intrapersonal events generally occur within an *inter*personal context and that is from this context that they derive their functional meaning. Abstraction is, of course, not only permissible but necessary in scientific enquiry; however, the study of early development in particular has furnished us recently with a number of examples showing how vital it is to extend the traditional focus and take note of the *social* dimension of behaviour patterns.

Of these examples that of language is no doubt the best known. Conceived initially as a beneath-the-skin system, as a set of behavioural patterns explicable purely in terms of the psychological organization of the individual, it has increasingly been recognized as in fact deriving its significance primarily from its communicative function and as in need consequently of study in dyadic settings. The change of emphasis from syntactic to semantic features no doubt made this inevitable, but its implications have been explored in particular amongst those attempting to comprehend the very first stages of language acquisition. Instead of seeing language arising *de novo* at the beginning of the second year, it is now being related to the pre-verbal communication patterns that are already established between mother and infant in the early months of life. Language acquisition, in other words, has been firmly placed within a social setting.

287

Amongst other functions in the study of which we see a similar change are concept formation, which Katherine Nelson (1974) in particular has treated in terms of the child's encounters with the people and things that constitute his social environment; the acquisition of skills and of problem solving ability that Kaye (1976) and Wood and Middleton (1975) have described as occurring within a dyadic context; and even attention — surely, according to its traditional treatment, one of the most private of an individual's functions, but now given an interpersonal slant by describing the role of mutuality of attentive focus that develops among mothers and infants. And as a final example let us note that in the considerable body of literature on the sucking response there has until recently been virtually no acknowledgement of the fact that sucking generally implies the presence of another person actively involved in the feeding process — an omission only now beginning to be rectified by work such as that of Kaye (1977).

Changes in Approach

As a result of this trend, an increasing number of investigators are turning to an examination of the earliest social relationship in their search for the developmental antecedents of particular functions. And with this new impetus the study of early social behaviour has begun to take a new direction in terms of both the questions being asked and the techniques being used. A considerable body of data is, of course, already in existence on social development (see the reviews by Maccoby and Masters, 1970, and Ainsworth, 1973) — much of it based on the concept of attachment, to which ethological (Bowlby, 1972), cognitive-developmental (Schaffer, 1971) and social learning (Gewirtz, 1972) interpretations have variously been given. More recent studies, however, are distinguished by the following features:

(1) *Treatment of social behaviour in dyadic terms.* That infants are capable of organized, spontaneous behaviour from the very beginning of life is now richly documented; the implications for the study of early social behaviour are that a dyadic orientation is essential. Thus the mother's task in interacting with her baby is seen to be not one of creating order out of chaos; it is rather a matter of fitting her behaviour in with an already existing organization. Interactions, even the earliest, are thus two-way affairs in which mutual interchange takes place (Bell, 1968).

(2) *The need to postulate some degree of social pre-adaptation.* A neonate may be an essentially a-social creature, in the sense of not being

capable as yet of truly reciprocal social relationships and of not yet having the concept of a person. However, the nature of his early interactive behaviour is such that it is increasingly difficult to avoid the conclusion that in some sense the infant is already prepared for social intercourse. Not that this should surprise us; if an infant arrives in the world with a digestive system to cope with food and a breathing apparatus attuned to the air around him, why should he not also be prepared to deal with that other essential of his environment, people?

(3) *Emphasis on temporal relationships in interactive situations.* As we shall see below, the nature of the infant's pre-adapted organization can, in part, be described in terms of temporal parameters. Behaviour is chunked in time, and dyadic interactions are thus based on an elaborate interweaving of the participants' behavioural flow. Techniques of sequential analysis rather than indices based on total amounts of behaviour collated over time accordingly become the principal means of data reduction.

(4) *The use of microanalytic techniques.* Experience has shown that the temporal relationships just referred to become most evident at microlevels of analysis. This applies, of course, to adult communicative behaviour too, but this level of analysis has been found to be a particularly fruitful one for exploring the manner in which the infant's behaviour meshes with that of his caretakers.

(5) *An interest in processes rather than products.* Whereas the focus of previous work tended to be on the nature of attachment behaviour in its developed form, recent work has concerned itself more with the processes underlying the formation of social relationships, and accordingly questions have been asked as to how these come about rather than when they appear, towards whom they are manifested, or in what way they change across time and situation.

Methodological Issues

New questions often necessitate the use of new methods and techniques. However, in one respect at least the microanalytic examination of mother-infant interaction has been fortunate, namely in the availability of a wide range of technological aids for recording and analysing in great detail behavioural sequences.

One of the disadvantages of microanalytic investigations lies in their labour-intensive nature, for a session lasting just a few minutes can generate a considerable amount of data when analysed in units of a fraction of a second. Under these circumstances it is not surprising to find samples generally to be small (sometimes involving only single cases) and observation sessions to be limited. This makes the problem of generalizing findings thus obtained an acute one — particularly so when the observations are carried out in the laboratory or, for that matter, in a home converted into a laboratory by the presence of obtrusive equipment and even more obtrusive personnel to operate the equipment. The need for replication becomes accordingly an even more urgent one than it normally is.

The problem of replication also looms large with regard to the choice of the units into which behaviour may be analysed. Going to more microscopic levels of analysis inevitably means that conventional response indices and categories are no longer applicable — or at least need to be supplemented by units of a more appropriate scale.

Clearly some agreement has to be reached among investigators for units to assume scientific reality and to be more than something in the beholder's eye.

Interactive studies are, however, throwing up a further class of new variables, namely those that transcend the behaviour of individuals and instead are defined by the responses of both participants in a dyadic situation. Stern (1974), for example, has shown the usefulness of such dyadic states in the study of mutual gazing among mother-infant pairs, employing the four-fold classification given by *both* partners looking at the other, neither looking, or only one or the other doing so. Similarly Duncan (1973) has used the four possible combinations of speaker-auditor behaviour to yield dyadic states, and yet another example is provided by Collis (1977) with the concept of visual co-orientation. Such variables have heuristic value; their particular importance lies, however, in their demonstration that interactive situations need not be reduced to variables pertaining only to individuals but may be treated in terms peculiar to themselves. Not that interactive situations have not given rise to their own sets of terms and concepts: it is indeed difficult to discuss interactions without resorting to words like smooth, synchronized, or successful. Such notions tend to be both complex and value-laden, making agreement as to their usage difficult. Yet, as Hinde (1976) has shown, there is no reason why a relationship cannot be analysed into its constituents and be provided with meaningful indices (see Hinde and Herrmann, 1977), and though some of the more global concepts like communication of reciprocity are still used in an intuitive and sometimes all-embracing fashion, the advent of dyadic state variables points to at least one way of describing interactions in more acceptable objective fashion.

The use of dyadic states does not, however, solve a further problem raised by the study of interactions, namely that of describing and analysing the sequential flow of interactive behaviour. It is only comparatively recently that the nature of this flow has become of interest, particularly in ethological studies (Slater, 1973), and the statistical methods available for sequential analysis are still at a very early stage of development. On the whole these have concerned themselves with intra-individual sequences in order to establish whether an animal's successive responses are independent or whether each is influenced by one or more preceding responses. While in theory the same principles could hold for inter-individual data (Altmann, 1965), in practice such data raise certain extra problems. One of these is that the behaviour of an individual in an interaction sequence is generally dependent not only on the immediately preceding response of his partner but also on his own previous behaviour. Indeed it seems likely that a *cumulative* effect of previous events in a far from simple additive manner ought ideally to be taken into account, thus making simple Markov chain models[†] even less applicable. Taken in conjunction with the likelihood that social behaviour (just like linguistic behaviour) is arranged in complex hierarchical structures about which we know little as yet, it is apparent that there is a considerable need for purely descriptive accounts of interactive structures quite apart from the provision of the necessary statistical tools for their analysis.

Themes in the Study of Early Interactive Development

Some general trends are already beginning to emerge from studies that have undertaken the detailed examination of early interactive behaviour. What follows is an attempt to sketch an outline provided by this work and draw attention to some of the themes highlighted so far.

Social Pre-Adaptation

Given the need for some degree of preparedness for social interaction, how does it manifest itself?

There are two aspects that may be usefully distinguished, namely *structural* and *functional* pre-adaptation. The former refers to the availability of certain structural mechanisms of endogenous[†] origin that serve to bind the young to its caretaker. Thus, just as the infant rhesus monkey is provided with a strong grasping reflex that ensures its hold on the mother's fur, so the human baby comes into the world with an oral apparatus precisely adapted to cope with the nipple and food that the mother will provide, a set of visual structures highly sensitive to those aspects of stimulation that emanate from other people's faces, and auditory equipment selectively attuned to the human voice. A basic compatibility of inherent origins thus exists between the baby and his caretakers that is shown from the first day of life.

Interactions are, however, never static: the baby's mouth is used for sucking, its sensory apparatus for processing information. Functional compatibility is shown in the way these structures are used, and seen in particular in the temporal relationships between the infant's and the adult's responses. There is now an impressive body of evidence to show that from the beginning an infant's behaviour is organized in time and that the periodicity thus found is mostly dependent on centrally regulated microrhythms (as seen in scanning and in sucking) or macrorhythms (as seen, for example, in state changes). These are at first internally regulated but very soon after birth become linked to external events, particularly to caretaker activities (Schaffer, 1977). How this process of entertainment occurs remains one of the main outstanding questions in this field; that it does occur is shown in the finely synchronized inter-personal exchanges described for sucking (Kaye, 1977), vocal behaviour (Schaffer *et al.*, 1977), and visual interaction (Stern, 1974). To some extent, as we shall see below, the resulting 'smoothness' of the relationship is a function of the adult's sensitivity to the on-off flow of the baby's behaviour; to some extent also, however, the entrainment may be based on inherently determined interpersonal synchronies of movement patterns. The complex rules which are subsequently found to regulate the temporal use of communication channels can thus be said to arise from such inherent compatibilities.

The Infant's Interactive Achievements

The realization in the last decade or so that the young infant, far from being a *tabula rasa*,[†] is even at birth already endowed with an impressive set of competencies, should not, of course, blind one to the considerable task ahead of him in reaching full social status. As Ashley Montagu (1950) has put it, 'The wonderful thing about a baby is its promise, not its per-fomance — its promise to perform under certain auspices.' What then does it still have to achieve in the course of the first year or two to fulfil that promise?

The child's major achievement lies in attaining what we may call the *concept of the dialogue*. There are two aspects to this development, expressed respectively by the notions of *reciprocity* and of *intentionality*.

Reciprocity refers to the role which the infant plays in an interaction sequence. There are numerous indications that early dialogues are at first one-sided affairs (*pseudo-dialogues*), that they are sustained only through the mother's initiative in replying to the infant's responses *as if* they had communicative significance. It is not till the end of the first year that the infant will learn that dialogues are two-sided, that they are based on roles which are both reciprocal and interchangeable (actor-spectator, giver-taker, speaker-auditor), and that the playing of these roles and their periodic exchange are managed according to certain rules to which both partners must adhere. Bruner's description (Bruner, 1977) of give-and-take games shows this development clearly: action patterns of a *joint* nature cannot appear until the infant has mastered the idea of reciprocity.

The related notion of intentionality develops once the infant realizes that his behaviour has communicative value and can be used purposively to affect the behaviour of others and to bring about desired results. Intentionality is a slippery concept that cannot easily be defined in operational terms, yet it is useful in expressing the strong impression one gains when observing older infants that they act in full awareness of anticipated goals. The contrast is between the baby who cries because he has a pain and the baby who cries in order to summon his mother to deal with the pain: the one responding reactively, the other with an eye to the future. Through having been involved in dialogues all along and through the consistent responses of others contingent on his behaviour the infant learns that his smiles, vocalizations, gestures and movements are attended to by others and produce particular effects. In time they will therefore be used purposively with the anticipation that others will respond in certain specific ways. Just when the infant becomes capable of such an achievement is still far from certain. However, the argument advanced by Bates *et al.* (1975) is convincing, namely that intentionality does not become evident till the end of the first year, when on attaining sensori-motor stage V the infant becomes capable of differentiating ends from means and thenceforth is able to use objects to interact with adults and adults as a means of obtaining objects. From that stage on he can point for things out of reach, cry for attention, raise his arms to be lifted, repeatedly drop toys out of his pram for the sheer sadistic pleasure of seeing his mother pick them up again, and eventually use words capable of producing a great range of diverse effects.

It becomes apparent that two further developments are closely related to attaining the concept of the dialogue. In the first place, it is necessary for certain *cognitive mechanisms* to develop so that dialogic ability can appear at all. The differentiation of ends from means is only one such mechanism; a more basic one is the differentiation of self from other (without which a dialogue would obviously be an absurdity) and the related growth of object permanence and of representational skills generally. If, moreover, the child is to deal with social events in terms of a remembered past and an anticipated future and not relate them merely to the here-and-now, an expansion in memory capabilities is clearly required. And yet another example is the growth of attention span which will enable the infant to relate to two objects simultaneously and thus, for example, play ball with the mother rather than, as earlier, play with *either* the mother *or* a ball.

The other development refers to the expansion that takes place in the number of *communication channels* available to the child. Some, such as smiling and crying, are present from the early weeks on, but throughout the first year or two an increasing number make their appearance. Gestures such as pointing and demand movements, the ability to follow the other person's gaze, vocalizations of one kind or another and finally the appearance of words all combine to increase vastly the range of subtle meanings which the child can eventually both convey and comprehend.

The Mother's Dyadic Behaviour

What is it that enables an infant eventually to become an accomplished participant in dialogues? Given an inherent basis of pre-adaptation and the necessary cognitive means, the additional factor required seems to be just the sheer opportunity, repeated day after day for month after month, of taking part in dialogue-like exchanges. And it is here that the mother's ability to set up and sustain such exchanges becomes so important.

Mothers need to call upon a variety of dyadic techniques in relating to their infants. For convenience sake these have been classified as phasing, adaptive, facilitative, elaborative, initiating and control techniques and are discussed in these terms in greater detail elsewhere (Schaffer, 1977). For our present purposes it is the first of these, the mother's phasing techniques, that are of relevance. A repeated theme that emerges from the observations reported in the following pages is that early interaction sequences generally begin with the infant's own spontaneous behaviour, that the mother then chimes in to support, repeat, comment upon and elaborate his response, that she holds herself ready to let the infant resume as soon as he wishes, and that in this way she makes it possible for a dialogue-like interaction to be set in motion. Newson (1977) in particular stresses how mothers tend to act as though the infant were already an active communicative partner, endowing his responses with a signal value which, seen from his point of view, they do not in fact possess. The mother thus allows herself to be paced by the infant. She fills in the pauses between his response bursts, and to do so successfully she needs, of course, sensitivity and an exquisite sense of timing.

It is here that we see the importance of the turn-taking pattern found by a number of the contributors in various early interactive situations, for such a pattern is particularly suited to let the infant find out that his behaviour can be used as a means of interacting with another person. It maximizes the opportunity for him to learn that his behaviour is of interest to the mother, that it will be attended to and elicit a response from her, and that it is worth his while to attend to her response in turn. Routine sequences of a predictable nature thus become built up. And it is here that a further phenomenon becomes important, namely that of imitation: as Pawlby (1977) shows, whatever the facts of infants' imitation, imitation *by mothers* is a very common occurrence and accounts for a relatively high proportion of interaction sequences. By repeating the infant's response the mother not only reflects back to him his own behaviour but also produces a stereotyped and therefore predictable form of interaction. And let us also note the extent to which the mother ensures that the infant gets maximum benefit of the information content of her behaviour by exaggerating, repeating, and slowing down her actions and using all the other techniques to which Stern (1977) draws attention.

No wonder that mothers spend so much of any interactive situation in visually attending to the infant, for the appropriateness of their timing and of the nature of their contribution is essential to the continuation of the dialogue. Looking patterns are thus very different from those found in adult dyads, for the mother is holding herself in almost constant readiness to intervene at appropriate moments, without the benefit of the much more varied cues that an adult partner would provide. Far from arbitrarily imposing her behaviour upon the child, she is engaged in continuously monitoring his activities so that she can then time her own interventions in precise synchrony with his. The *when* of her behaviour is thus every bit as important as the *how* if she is to achieve a predictable outcome to the encounter.

Conclusions

How do patterns of communication manifest themselves in the prelinguistic stage? What compatibility is there between the infant and the adult with respect to the mode of communication and its topics? What is the compatibility based on and how is it fostered? These are questions to be answered if we are to explain how the infant becomes capable of participating in interactive situations and growing increasingly skilled at manipulating and recombining social sequences. [. . .]

There are few who would now subscribe to a critical period model of human development according to which early experiences have some decisive long-term effect just because they are early; there are also few, however, who would not agree that in some sense such early patterns do set the scene for what follows by guiding (though by no means irreversibly) the infant in one direction rather than another. Dunn (1977) and Dunn and Richards (1977) examine this very difficult theme in their follow-up study, searching for the consistencies that would enable one to predict across time on the basis of either individual or dyadic measures.

More recently, however, the continuities issue has taken on a new significance with the debate about the precursors of language acquisition. As Bruner (1977) argues, there are strong indications that language skills, far from arising *de novo*, have their roots in earlier interactive events and that the development of verbal communication in the second year must thus be related to the infant's ability to participate in sequences of interpersonal behaviour already evident in the course of the first year. If, as Rommetveit (1968) has put it, one's real concern in learning a language is to communicate messages, and if we follow Halliday (1975) in believing that messages can be meaningfully conveyed long before the child speaks his first word, then the basic problem becomes one of understanding the development of the communicative process in general, with language acquisition being seen as but one offshoot (albeit the most vital one) of this development.

Yet how we can convincingly show that there is indeed a continuity between the pre-verbal and the verbal communicative level, in the sense that the former constitutes a necessary precondition to the latter, remains a problem. One of the customary methods of demonstrating a connection between two developmental events A and B, namely experimentally to deprive the organism of A and see if B still occurs, is obviously not feasible in this instance. The deprivation technique in any case does not provide a pure test, in that it introduces various confounding influences. Similarly another approach, the correlational technique, is not wholly convincing, in that it consists in examining the relationship between parameters of the two functions involved (their age at onset, their amount, and so on) in order to detect similarities, but is then unable to proceed to making statements about the aetiological factors at work.

Under the circumstances it is not surprising to find a tendency to resort to arguments based on the similarity in topography of the functions under discussion, and this may well be as far as we can take it at present. But however persuasive the similarity, one should bear in mind that it provides an argument based on analogy — no more. Developmental continuity therefore remains an assumption. At any rate let us be clear that there are at least three senses in which one may talk of continuity: first with regard to the *functions* of communication (the wish to obtain certain objects, to affect the other person's behaviour, and so on); second with regard to the *constituent skills* required for communication (such as intentionality, role alternation, etc.); and third, with regard to the *situation* in which communication occurs. The last can be particularly misleading: vocal turn-taking, for instance, may be found in quite early interactions, providing them with the 'mature' appearance of later verbal exchanges, and yet this may be brought about entirely by the mother's skill at inserting her vocalizations at appropriate moments into the child's sequence of vocal activity. The continuity, that is, is in this instance inherent in the dyadic situation and does not refer to a constituent skill of the child's.

Any attempt to 'explain' the onset of language in terms of its developmental precursors is thus still fraught with difficulties. But what cannot be doubted is that mother and infant come to share a code of conduct long before they share a linguistic code, that this code has its rules — some universal, some idiosyncratic — which the child acquires in a way that is still far from clear, and that the characteristics of this rule-governed behaviour are now clarifying the processes that underlie the formation of the child's primary social bond.

References

Ainsworth, M.D.S. (1973), 'The development of infant-mother attachment', in B.M. Caldwell and H.N. Ricciuti (eds.), *Review of Child Development Research*, vol. 3, University of Chicago, Chicago.

Altmann, S.A. (1965), 'Sociobiology of rhesus monkeys, II. Stochastics of social communication', *J. theor. Biol.*, 8, 490-522.

Bates, E., Camaioni, L. and Volterra, V. (1975), 'The acquisition of performatives prior to speech', *Merrill-Palmer Q.*, 21, 205-26.

Bell, R.Q. (1968), 'A reinterpretation of the direction of effects in studies of socialization', *Psychol. Rev.*, 75, 81-95.

Bowlby, J. (1972), *Attachment and Loss*, vol. I., *Attachment*, Hogarth, London.

Bruner, J.S. (1977), 'Early social interaction and language acquisition', in H.R. Schaffer (ed.), *Studies in Mother-Infant Interaction*, Academic Press, London.

Collis, G.M. (1977), 'Visual co-ordination and maternal speech', in H.R. Schaffer (ed.), *Mother-Infant Interaction*.

Duncan, S. (1973), 'Toward a grammar for dyadic conversation', *Semiotica*, 9, 29-46.

Dunn, J. (1977), 'Patterns of early interaction: continuities and consequences', in H.R. Schaffer (ed.), *Mother-Infant Interaction*.

Dunn, J. and Richards, M.P.M. (1977), 'Observations on the developing relationship between mother and baby in the neonatal period', in H.R. Schaffer (ed.), *Mother-Infant Interaction*.

Gewirtz, J.L. (1972), 'Attachment, dependence, and a distinction in terms of stimulus control', in J.L. Gewirtz (ed.), *Attachment and Dependency*, Wiley, New York.

Halliday, M.A.K. (1975), *Learning How to Mean*, Arnold, London.

Hinde, R.A. (1976), 'On describing relationships', *J. Child Psychol. Psychiat.*, 17, 1-19.

Hinde, R.A. and Herrmann, J. (1977), 'Frequencies, durations, derived measures and their correlations in studying diadic and triadic relationships', in H.R. Schaffer (ed.), *Mother-Infant Interaction*.

Kaye, K. (1976), 'Infants' effects upon their mothers' teaching strategies', in J.C. Glidewell (ed.), *The Social Context of Learning and Development*, Gardner, New York.

Kaye, K. (1977), 'Toward the origin of dialogue', in H.R. Schaffer (ed.), *Mother-Infant Interaction*.

Maccoby, E. and Masters, J.C. (1970), 'Attachment and dependency', in P.H. Mussen (ed.), *Carmichael's Manual of Child Psychology*, 3rd edn., Wiley, New York and London.

Montagu, A. (1950), *On Being Human*, Abelard-Schuman, New York.

Nelson, K. (1974), 'Concept, word, and sentence: interrelations in acquisition and development', *Psychol. Rev.*, 81, 267-85.

Newson, J. (1977), 'An intersubjective approach to the systematic study of mother-infant interaction', in H.R. Schaffer (ed.), *Mother-Infant Interaction*.

Pawlby, S.J. (1977), 'Imitative interaction', in H.R. Schaffer, (ed.), *Mother-Infant Interaction*.

Rommetveit, R. (1968), *Words, Meanings, and Messages*, Academic Press, New York and London.

Schaffer, H.R. (1971), *The Growth of Sociability*, Penguin, Harmondsworth, Middx.

Schaffer, H.R. (1977), *Mothering*, Open Books, London; Harvard University Press, New York.

Schaffer, H.R., Collis, G.M. and Parsons, G. (1977), 'Vocal interchange and visual regard in verbal and pre-verbal children', in H.R. Schaffer (ed.), *Mother-Infant Interaction*.

Slater, P.J.B. (1973), 'Describing sequences of behavior', in P.P.G. Bateson and P.H. Klopfer (eds.), *Perspectives in Ethology*, Plenum, New York.

Stern, D.N. (1974), 'Mother and infant at play: the dyadic interaction involving facial, vocal, and gaze behaviours', in M. Lewis and L.A. Rosenblum (eds.), *The Effects of the Infant on its Caregiver*, Wiley, New York and London.

Stern, D.N. (1977), 'The infant's stimulus world during social interaction', in H.R. Schaffer (ed.), *Mother-Infant Interaction*.

Wood, D. and Middleton, D. (1975), 'A study of assisted problem-solving', *Br. J. Psychol.*, 66, 181-92.

SECTION SIX: INTELLIGENCE: TESTS AND GENETICS

Introduction

Contemporary understanding of the development of intelligence has progressed a long way from Benjamin Bloom's assertion that 50 per cent of a child's intelligence is formed in the first five years. Intertwined with the issue of development is the problem of the measurement of intelligence in these early years. The concept 'intelligence' poses plenty of problems for those who wish to operationalise it in the form of tests for children over five years, and these problems, and others, are even more acute in the assessment of the pre-school child.

Marjorie Honzik's paper reviews the form and content of the most often-used tests for the age range, and critically analyses their use and the results thereby gathered. After going into the detail of the low correlations found between early test results and those taken later, she questions the current status of this use of tests and suggests that there is much more work needed on the development of more appropriate procedures and instruments.

Robert McCall, in his paper, takes up the discussion from this point, arguing that the tenacious idea of a unitary 'intelligence' factor has misled researchers. His proposal is that it will be more fruitful to look for *changes* as well as continuities in cognitive development, and to consider a wide range of skills as not necessarily developing at the same rate, in the same way, and subject to the same influences. Turning to the controversial issue of the roles of genetic factors, McCall first highlights some of the methodological problems in this research, and then argues that measures of heritability may not be useful in understanding development as these measures are relevant only to differences between individuals, telling us nothing about the general dynamics of development. Neither do heritability estimates indicate to what extent development *might* be susceptible to as yet untried interventions. After returning to the question of test usage, in the light of the heritability discussion, McCall then concludes by proposing a *transitional* model of development.

INTRODUCTION

21 VALUE AND LIMITATIONS OF INFANT TESTS: AN OVERVIEW

Marjorie P. Honzik

Source: M. Lewis (ed.), *Origins of Intelligence* (Plenum Press, 1976), pp. 59-95.

The development of intelligence during infancy is impressive and measurable. The anthropometrist measures growth in head size, which reflects the growth of the brain. The neuropathologist measures cerebral DNA to estimate cell number and possible damage from malnutrition or other causes (Winick, 1970). The psychologist measures behavioral change by means of careful observations of responses to specific tasks. In this chapter we shall review critically infant tests and their contribution to the understanding of mental growth in the first months of life.

The development of mental abilities in infancy is rapid and not easily measured. The adequacy of the tests, the skill of the examiner, and above all, the state of the infant affect mental measurement. Despite these limiting factors, pediatricians, psychologists, neurologists, and parents have found results of testing to be crucial in the diagnosis of specific abilities and deficits; and research workers are turning with increasing frequency to tests to evaluate mental growth and its relevant determinants. We shall discuss sequentially the limitations imposed by the triad of infant, test, and examiner, and then consider the contribution of infant tests to diagnosis and research on infant intelligence.

The Infant

The growth of cognitive functions is intertwined with somatic growth, which makes the testing of the infant a challenge. The baby triples his body weight in the first year but the greatest changes occur in the brain, where there is some increase in cell number but marked increase in cell size, number of dendrites, and in the myelin sheath covering the nerve axons. The weight gain of the brain during early infancy is of greater proportion than the weight gain that takes place in any other somatic area (Dodgson, 1962). Accompanying structural growth are the marked changes in cognitive development that are revealed in the infant's changing perception of and reactions to his world.

The rapidly changing organism requires skillful management by the examiner, who must be continuously sensitive to and vigilant of the marked developmental changes as well as the continuously changing state of each individual child during the testing period.

The requirements of a good test are exacting. Not only does it have to yield reliable and valid scores, but it has to cover the repertoire of cognitive behaviors that are developing and changing from day to day; and clearly it must include materials that will elicit maximum responses at all developmental levels. The perfect assessment, then, takes place when the squalling, sucking, chewing, ever-moving baby is relatively quiescent, attentive, wide-eyed with interest, and above all, responsive to the tester and his toys. The idyllic situation is only achieved with effort on the part of all concerned.

Information processing begins at birth or earlier, but the baby has the greater problem during the paranatal period of accommodating to a life of independent breathing and assimilation of food. Somatic development and change create difficulties in testing at many stages of adjustment during the first years of life. In the immediately postnatal period the infant is often drowsy and unresponsive and the time periods available for testing are very short. Careful observations indicate that infants in the postnatal period are, on the average, alert only 10 per cent of the time. The great ingestion of food relative to body size during the early postnatal months frequently leads to discomfort and colic, which intermittently interfere with the baby's responses. As this stage passes and he is more consistently comfortable, the baby's awareness of strange people and situations becomes apparent. 'Awareness of a strange situation' or 'fear of strangers' may be used as a test item (Bayley, 1969), but this apprehensive stage may make for less than optimal responses on certain test items. The teething child is often more interested in chewing the test equipment than in responding to it. The child who is learning to crawl and walk wants to practise these skills and is proportionately less interested in responding to form boards and problem situations. The skilled tester, using all the patience, perseverence, and charm that he or she can muster, usually can elicit the baby's best responses, but it is not always easy. This descriptive account suggests aspects of the baby's development that may result in errors of measurement in the test results, but it also suggests that we are considering the intellectual development of a living, vibrant, growing organism. The metamorphosis may not be as great as in the butterfly, but the sturdy, almost verbal 2-year-old has come a long way from his immature state at birth. Do the scores on infant tests document these changes? The purpose of this chapter is to answer this question.

Infant Tests

Infant tests reflect the concerns of their authors. Diagnosis was the primary objective of the Gesell (Gesell *et al.*, 1934, 1940, 1941), the Griffiths (1954), and the Brunet-Lézine (1951) tests. Cattell (1940) and Bayley (1933, 1969) were more interested in devising tests that could be used to study the development of mental abilities during the first years of life. However, all five tests have been used in major research projects and all have been and are being used in the diagnosis of individual children. More recently Uzgiris and Hunt (1966) in this country and Audrey Little in Australia have been assembling test items that more specifically test Piaget's stages. Another trend is the use of abbreviated screening tests. The most notable is the Denver Developmental Screening Test (DDST), which is being widely used by pediatricians in the United States and in a number of other countries.

Arnold Gesell of Yale was the pioneer in infant testing. His first degree was in psychology but his approach to infant testing is that of the pediatric neurologist, as indicated by the title of his handbook *Developmental Diagnosis* (with Amatruda, 1941). Griffiths (1954) expresses her indebtedness to Gesell, stating that the justification for a new test is the 'urgency of the need for early diagnosis of mental condition in special cases'. However, she shows greater concern about test standardization and the reliability of the scores than was true of Gesell.

All infant tests include many items first described by Gesell. The Brunet-Lézine test (1951) is a translation into French of the Gesell schedules, but the test items are arranged by age levels. The two tests constructed by American psychologists Bayley (1933, 1969) and Cattell (1940) were developed as research instruments. These investigators were far more attentive than Gesell to the problems of test construction, sampling, and adequate standardization.

These five tests have been widely used. Their distinctive characteristics will be summarized before we discuss the contribution of infant tests to our understanding of intellectual development.

The Gesell Developmental Schedules

Gesell and Amatruda (1941) wrote that 'developmental diagnosis is essentially an appraisal of the maturity of the nervous system with the aid of behavior norms'. Many of the test items in his Developmental Schedules stem from this point of view. For example, he describes the stimulating value of the one-inch cube at successive ages: 'grasps when placed in hand (4 weeks); ocular fixation when cube is placed on table (16 weeks); prehension on sight by palmar grasp (28 weeks); prehension by digital grasp

(40 weeks).' These behaviors are classified as *adaptive behavior*. Other major fields of behavior, according to Gesell, are *motor, language*, and *personal-social*. The motor sequence includes both gross skills, such as sitting and walking, and fine motor skills, such as picking up a small sugar pellet or building with blocks. *Language* behavior is assessed in terms of comprehension as well as vocalizations and use of words. Gesell states that the *personal-social* behavior sequence, consisting of responses to people and self-help items, is 'greatly affected by the kind of home in which the child is reared'. In contrast, he writes of the *motor* scale that it 'is of special interest because it has so many neurological implications', and of *language* behavior that it furnishes clues to the organization of the infant's central nervous system. These distinctions as to the determinants of the subscale scores have never been adequately tested. In fact, cross-cultural research on motor development suggests that child-rearing practices may in part determine gross motor skills. Experiential factors in the home affect not only *personal-social* behaviors but also *language* development and *adaptive* behavior, according to Bernstein (1961), Honzik (1967), and others.

The Gesell schedules yield developmental quotients or DQs obtained by the division of the maturity age by the chronological age of the child. Gesell writes that the 'DQ represents the proportion of normal development that is present at a given age'.

The Gesell schedules are based on extensive observations, but statistical evaluations of the normative findings are not presented, nor is there any attempt to assess the reliability or the validity of the DQs. Gesell's perceptive and almost eloquent descriptions of infant behavior have seldom been equaled:

> . . . the baby can reach with his eyes before he can reach with his hand; at 28 weeks the baby sees a cube; he grasps it, senses surface and edge as he clutches it, brings it to his mouth, where he feels its qualities anew, withdraws it, looks at it on withdrawal, rotates it while he looks, looks while he rotates it, restores it to his mouth, withdraws it again for inspection, restores it again for mouthing, transfers it to the other hand, bangs it, contacts it with the free hand, transfers, mouths it again, drops it, resecures it, mouths it yet again, repeating the cycle with variations — all in the time it takes to read this sentence.

All subsequent authors of infant tests raided the Gesell schedules for test items, with appropriate acknowledgement of indebtedness. The test materials from the Gesell schedules found most frequently in other tests are the red ring and string, the red one-inch cubes, the sugar pellet, and the small dinner bell with handle. These materials are used in the early months to test visual and auditory responses, eye-hand coordinations, and problem solving.

A screening test that not only uses Gesell items but is modeled on it is the Denver Developmental Screening Test (DDST). This test deserves mention because of the care with which it was assembled and because of its wide use in the United States, Canada, and a number of European countries. Frankenburg and Dodds (1967) developed this screening test to 'aid in the early detection of delayed development in young children'. Frankenburg *et al.* (1971) reported on the basis of a few cases that the reliability and validity of this scale is fairly high. They concluded that this screening test used with infants in the first year of life misses approximately 13 per cent of the cases who would obtain an abnormal rating on the Bayley test. Infants and young children earning an abnormal rating on the DDST average psychomotor development indexes (PDIs) of from 50 to 73 on the Bayley.

The Griffiths Scale of Mental Development

The Griffiths scale, published in 1954, resembles the Gesell schedules in some important dimensions. Ruth Griffiths is concerned with diagnosis; she is a perceptive observer of the behaviors of infants, and she wants to avoid any pretense of measuring 'intelligence' in infancy. Her interest was in assembling a good and reliable test that detects deficits in the following areas of functioning: locomotion, personal-social, hearing and speech, eye and hand, and performance. These categories resemble those of Gesell, but Gesell's motor scale is divided into locomotion and performance; his language scale is called more precisely 'Hearing and Speech'; and the adaptive scale is termed simply 'Eye and Hand'. An effort was made to standardize this scale on a representative sample of infants. The distribution of the paternal occupations of the 552 children tested was similar to that of employed males in the United States. A test-retest correlation of 0.87 was reported for 60 infants who were retested after an average interval of 30 weeks. Griffiths wrote that there is nothing necessarily fixed or permanent about an intelligence quotient as such. In addition, she wrote:

> . . . it has often puzzled the writer why psychologists should for so long have expected that the results of a single test, applied in some one particular hour of a child's life, under particular circumstances, should necessarily carry within it any particular implication of finality, or

suggestion that if repeated the ratio of the child's performance to his age should remain unchanged. In no other field of diagnostic work is such a condition expected.

Brunet-Lézine Test

This test follows the Gesell schedules in dividing the test items into the four categories of motor, adaptive, language, and personal-social. However, it differs in that it is a point scale with six test items at each month level, followed by four questions that are asked of the mother or caretaker. The number of test items measuring each of the four behavior categories varies at the different age levels, but for the most part there are two *motor* and four *adaptive* items, and one *motor*, one *language*, and two *personal-social* questions. The test is scored according to the four categories and whether or not the score is based on an observation item or a question. The manual for this test is not available in the United States. The test is used extensively in Europe for diagnosis and was the test of choice of the Stockholm longitudinal study described by Klackenberg-Larsson and Stensson (1968) and Brucefors (1972).

Cattell's Infant Intelligence Scale

This scale was assembled by Psyche Cattell to assess the mental development of a group of normal children in a longitudinal study conducted in the School of Public Health at Harvard. Cases were selected from prenatal clinics. This meant that well-to-do families were excluded from the standardization sample, as were those of the lowest economic levels. Cattell acknowledged 'the vast amount of pioneer work of Gesell' and stated that his battery of tests was used as the foundation for her scale. However, Cattell excluded from her test items of a personal-social nature, since they are influenced to a marked degree by 'home training', and motor items involving the large muscles. Cattell provided objective procedures for administering and scoring the tests. Her test is an age scale with five items listed at each month level in the first year. The standardization was based on a total of 1,346 examinations administered to 274 children, who were tested at ages 3, 6, 9, 12, 18, 24, 30 and 36 months.

The Cattell test has many good points. The items are of interest to the children. The instructions for administering and scoring are clear. Odd-even reliability was 0.56 for the 3-month test, but for the 6-month test it was 0.88, and at subsequent age levels it varied from 0.71 to 0.90.

There are two disadvantages to this test as compared with the Bayley series. Because the standardization testing was done at 3-month intervals the item placements at ages 2, 4, 5, 7, 8, 10 and 11 months are interpolated values. As a result, the transitions from age to age are less smooth than when standardization testing is done at monthly intervals. A second disadvantage is that the total number of test items covering the age period 2-12 months is 55, in contrast to over 100 items in both Bayley's California First Year Mental Scale and in the Brunet-Lézine. Griffiths's scale, which includes both locomotor and performance items, has 155 test items for the age period 1-12 months. Because the Cattell test is shorter than the other tests, it seldom tires the babies. It can usually be completed within a half hour.

The Bayley Scales of Infant Development

These scales, which include both mental and motor tests and a behavior record, are based on more than 40 years of research. Bayley published the California First Year Mental Scale in 1933. Her mental scale includes largely test items that are termed *adaptive* or *language* by Gesell, with a few *personal-social* and *motor* items. The test was assembled to test the children in the Berkeley Growth Study. This cohort was selected from two hospitals; one accepted clinic cases and the other only those who could pay for the delivery. All occupational classes were represented but a disproportionate number of the fathers were students or in the professions. From 47 to 61 babies were tested each month. The preliminary standardization was based on these tests. Split-half reliabilities were only 0.63 and 0.51 for the first two months but at subsequent ages ranged from 0.74 to 0.95.

The 1969 revision of the Bayley Mental and Motor Scales and Behavior Record includes new items and changes in the ordering of the test items. Standardization was done on a stratified United States sample of 1,262 children, with from 83 to 94 tested at each age level. The split-half reliability coefficients for the 1969 scale are higher than those reported for the 1933 version of this test; from 0.81 to 0.93 (Werner and Bayley, 1966). Bayley (1969) wrote that the mental scale was designed to:

> . . . assess sensory-perceptual acuities, discriminations, and the ability to respond to these; the early acquisition of 'object constancy', memory, learning, and problem solving ability; vocalizations and the beginnings of verbal communication; and early evidence of the ability to form generalizations and classifications, which is the basis of abstract thinking.

This test was administered to approximately 50,000 eight-month-old babies born in 12 different hospitals; it was administered as a part of the collaborative study sponsored by the National Institute of Neurological Diseases and Stroke. These test results have been used in many investigations, which will be discussed later in this chapter.

Summary

These are the tests. Test-retest reliability where reported is adequate or good. What of the validity? All five tests have been widely used on research projects. It is only in the findings they have yielded that the value and thus the validity of the tests can be determined.

Prediction from Infant Tests

Gesell and Amatruda (1941) wrote 'diagnosis implies prognosis'. Griffiths did not expect her test score to be predictive. Cattell (1940) noted instances of marked variability in IQs of infants and young children on her test and concluded that 'there is no age from birth to maturity at which it is safe to base an important decision on the results of intelligence tests alone'. The purpose of her test, besides diagnosis, was 'to add to existing knowledge as to the variability in the pattern of mental growth'.

How well do these tests predict? As in most areas of human behavior, it depends! It depends on the integrity of the central nervous system, the genetic blueprint, in subtle and complex ways on experience, and, above all, on the interaction of all these factors. Investigators have begun to sort out the tangled skein and the picture is gradually becoming clearer.

The Gesell, Griffiths, Brunet-Lézine, Cattell, and Bayley tests have all been used extensively in the prediction of later IQs from infant test scores. The method used to portray these results is by interage correlations. Agreement among investigators is high. In Figure 21.1 interage correlations between Bayley's infant test scores and Stanford-Binet Form L IQs at 8 years are shown for the Berkeley Growth Study sample (Bayley, 1949) and the Guidance Study sample (Honzik *et al.*, 1948) born in 1928-9. These interage correlations are remarkably similar to those obtained for a Stockholm sample born between 1955 and 1961 and tested in infancy on the Brunet-Lézine, and tested at 8 years on Form L of the Stanford-Binet (Klackenberg-Larsson and Stensson, 1968; Brucefors, 1972). Neither of these longitudinal studies shows prediction of 8-year IQs from infant mental test scores, but both do show increasing prediction during the age period 1-3 years. This cross-validation of findings is impressive since the studies differ in three major respects: the infant tests used (Bayley versus Brunet-Lézine), cohort difference (Swedish versus United States samples), and a time period difference of 30 years.

These findings are further cross-validated by those of Cattell (1940),

Figure 21.1: Prediction of IQs

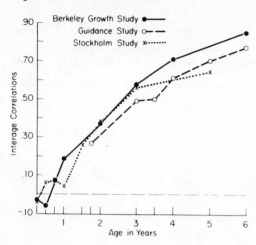

Prediction of IQs on the Stanford-Binet, Form L or L-M, at eight years from earlier scores on the California Infant and Preschool Scales in the Berkeley Growth Study and the Berkeley Guidance Study and from earlier scores on the Brunet-Lézine in the Stockholm Study.

who reported that scores on her test at 3 months correlated 0.10 with 3-year IQs on the Stanford-Binet, and by those of Hindley (1960), who found a correlation of −0.13 between the 3- and 12-month test scores on the Griffiths for a London sample (see Table 21.1). It should be noted here that whereas the babies in the Stockholm and London studies were tested at ages 3, 6, 12, 18 and 24 months, the babies in Bayley's Berkeley Growth Study were tested each month and the scores averaged for 3-month periods for purposes of determining the stability of test scores.

Table 21.1 shows that although the correlations over developmentally long time periods are negligible, adjacent ages yield moderately high *r*s. The findings of this table indicate what has become a truism in longitudinal studies of infants and children: the interage correlations are highly related to the age at testing and inversely related to the interval between tests. The negligible and even negative prediction from test scores obtained during the first months of life does not appear to be a chance phenomenon of one study but rather a developmental fact. What is the explanation? The moderate interage correlations between the 3- and 6-month scores of over 0.50 found in three different countries suggest that the changes in relative position are taking place gradually (Table 21.1).

Table 21.1: Interage Correlations of Infant Mental Test Scores Based on Five Different Tests

| Investigator | Approx. N | Interage correlations (in months) | | | | | |
		3x6 r	3x12 r	2x36 r	6x9 r	6x12 r	6x36[a] r
Bayley (1949) Site: Berkeley Test: Bayley Calif. Infant Test	61	0.57	0.28	−0.09	0.72	0.52	0.10
Klackenberg, Larsson and Stensson (1968) Site: Stockholm Test: Brunet-Lévine	140	0.51	0.36	−0.08	0.70	0.59	−0.05
Hindley (1960, 1965) Site: London Test: Griffiths	29-80	0.53	−0.13	—	—	0.34	0.40
Cattell (1940) Site: Harvard Test: Cattell	35	—	—	0.10	—	—	0.34
Nelson and Richards (1939) Site: Fels Test: Gesell	48-80	—	—	—	—	0.72	0.46

[a]　The 36-month test was the California Preschool Scale in the Bayley study and forms of the Stanford-Binet in the other four investigations.

Brucefors *et al.* (1974), in an analysis of the test results for the Swedish sample, compared two groups of children who showed the greatest gains and losses over the age period 3 months to 8 years. The ascending group at 3 months had an average IQ of 84. The average IQ of this subsample at 8 years was 114 on the Terman-Merrill. The average IQ of the descending group was 111 at 3 months and 84 at 8 years. The rate of change in both of these extreme groups was gradual, with both groups earning the same score at about 18 months. Brucefors's preferred interpretation of the marked changes, which also account in part for the negative correlations between the 3-month and childhood mental test scores, is in terms of *activity level*. Less active infants may be less responsive to test stimuli in the early months and earn lower scores, but they may be acquiring information and developing skills that serve them well at a later age period.

Escalona (1968) wrote that 'inactive babies show more sustained visual attention and do more tactile exploration of the immediate environment . . . up to at least 8 months than do active babies'. In contrast, Escalona reported that 'active babies, between the ages of 4 and 12 weeks, tend to develop responsiveness to relatively distant stimuli earlier, and acquire locomotion and the capacity for purposive manipulation of objects somewhat sooner'. Escalona added that 'the claim that activity level demonstrably affects the course of development does nothing to define the process or mechanisms that account for variations'. She took as a working hypothesis that differences in activity level below the age of 8 months can be attributed to differences in the threshold for the release of movement. This hypothesis suggests a constitutional difference that predisposes the infant to react with activity or inactivity.

Support for the possibility that activity level may play a part in determining the age changes in mental test performance in infancy comes from Bayley and Schaefer (1964). They reported that the boys in the Berkeley Growth Study who had high IQs in later life were as infants calm, happy, and positive in their responses. They found that an abrupt shift in the nature of the correlations with the activity ratings at 18 months coincided with a drop in the boys' *r*s between mental and motor scores. They also found that activity in the child, his mental test scores, and hostility in the mother are correlated in the latter half of the first year but not thereafter. These authors concluded: 'There is here a suggestion that hostile maternal behavior toward sons may goad them to activity and stimulate development until the boys begin to walk.' They added:

> If this is true, then we might postulate that the problems posed by active boys when they start running about and getting into things result in suppressive controls by mothers who are already hostile; at the same time, the accepting permissive mothers are encouraging activity in their relatively passive babies.

A similar trend was reported for the girls, but the impact of the mother's behavior on the girl's test score is much less clear. There is some evidence (Bing, 1963; Honzik, 1967) that the father's role is important in the development of the girls' cognitive skills, and the fathers were not rated in the Berkeley Growth Study. Taken together, these findings suggest that the road to high intellectual performance in later childhood is a complex one. Whether the baby is relatively active or inactive in the first year may itself make a difference, but these individual differences also have an impact on the caretakers, whose responses may further affect cognitive development. In sum, the fact of the low predictions of infants' mental test scores has led to hypotheses and perhaps a model of at least how some of the changes in mental test performance may occur.

Effect of Including Mothers' Reports on Test Scores and Interage Prediction

Correlations between test scores earned at 6 months and 3 years (Table 21.1) indicate that predictions are higher for the Griffiths and Gesell tests than for Bayley's Infant Mental Scale and the Brunet-Lézine. This difference may be due to the fact that the mothers' reports of test behaviors are not included in the scores on the Bayley test but play an important part in the scores on the Gesell and the Griffiths. It is possible that the more intelligent and more educated mother or caretaker gives a clearer picture of the child's behavior than the less able mother, thus adding her capabilities to the individual differences in the babies' test scores. In some instances the mothers' reports would contribute to more accurate scores. For example, Honzik *et al.* (1965) found that infants who were 'suspected' of having neurological impairment from their birth records vocalized with greater frequency during their mental tests at 8 months than was true of the normal control group. The conclusion was reached that the 8-month babies in the control group were more inhibited by the strangeness of the test situation, so vocalized less in the test situation and thus failed the vocalization items on the Bayley. On the Griffiths and the Gesell scales the mothers' reports of vocalizing would have been credited. On future tests it would seem advisable to score a test with and without the caretakers' reports so that the advantages of both scores would be available. This is now possible on the Brunet-Lézine.

Vocalization Factor Score

Many researchers have concluded that early infant test scores are of little value because of the low negative interage correlations obtained when infant scores are compared with IQs obtained during childhood. Bayley's findings are among the most clear-cut in showing little or no prediction, and yet it was from a cluster analysis of the items of her test given each month to the children in the Berkeley Growth Study that a vocalization factor was obtained (Cameron *et al.*, 1967). This factor score is moderately predictive to the age of 36 years, but for girls only (Bayley, 1968). The age of first passing each test item was the score used in the correlation matrix from which the vocalization factor was derived. Vocalization dimension definers include: vocalizes eagerness, vocalizes displeasure, says 'da da' or equivalent, and says two words.

In the same year that Cameron *et al.* published the results of the vocalization factor score, Moore (1968) in England reported for the London sample that a 'speech quotient' derived from the hearing and speech section of the Griffiths scale showed some constancy from 6 to 18 months in girls ($r = 0.51, p < 0.01$) but 'virtually none in boys' ($r = 0.15$).

This sex difference is of borderline statistical significance. Consistent with this finding is the failure of the boys' 6-month speech quotient to predict any later assessment, whereas that of the girls is significantly related to vocabulary at age 3 years. Moore concluded that 'clearly, linguistic development runs a steadier course from an earlier age in female infants'.

The sex difference in stability of vocalizations and a 'speech quotient' was discovered independently from infant tests in London and Berkeley. Further confirmation of this finding was reported by Kagan (1971) in his study of continuity and change in infant behaviors. He found greater continuity and stability in the vocalizations of girls than of boys in a longitudinal study covering the first 3 years of life. He reported that the amount of vocalizing to facial stimuli was relatively stable in girls during the first year and that these vocalization scores predicted verbal behavior, but not overall IQ, at age 2½ years. McCall *et al.* (1972) concluded from these three studies that vocalization in infancy may have a special salience for females that it does not connote for males with respect to predicting later mental test performance.

A Sex Difference in Prediction from Infant Tests

The greater stability of infant vocalizations in girls than in boys suggests that there might be a sex difference in prediction of infant test scores.

McCall *et al.* (1972) reported for the Fels longitudinal data that the 6-month Gesell DQs predicted 3½-year Stanford-Binet IQs for girls ($r = 0.62$, $p < 0.01$), but not for boys ($r = -0.01$). This difference is statistically significant at the 0.02 level. For this same sample the 12-month DQs yielded a fairly high correlation with the 6-year Stanford-Binet IQs for girls ($r = 0.57$, $p < 0.001$), but not for boys ($r = 0.22$, $p < 0.05$). Hindley (1965) also reported a rather marked sex difference in the stability of girls' DQs on the Griffiths as compared with that of boys. Predictions of the 5-year Stanford-Binet IQs from the Griffiths DQs appear in Table 21.2.

In contrast to these results, Klackenberg-Larsson and Stensson (1968) found no sex difference in DQ stability in the Stockholm sample, but they did find significant sex differences in mean DQ scores, favoring the girls at all age levels tested from 3 months to 5 years, and added that 'the differences between the sexes are especially apparent in the language and personal-social scales'.

Goffeney *et al.* (1971) reported the prediction of the Wechsler Intelligence Scale for Children (WISC) scores at age 7 years from the 8-month Bayley test scores for 626 children tested at the University of Oregon Medical School as a part of the Collaborative Project. The mothers in this

Table 21.2: Predictions of 5-Year Stanford-Binet IQs from Griffiths DQs

| Griffiths DQs | 5-year Stanford-Binet IQs | |
	Boys (N = 43) r	Girls (N = 37) r
6 months	0.24	0.41[b]
18 months	0.35[a]	0.48[b]

[a] $p < 0.05$ level
[b] $p < 0.01$ level

Figure 21.2: Mean IQs on the Stanford-Binet, Form L-M, at 4 years according to Scores on the Bayley Mental Scale at 8 months

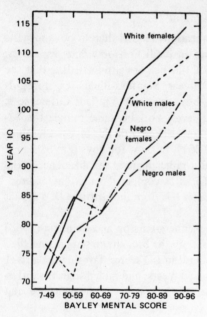

Source: Broman *et al.*, 1975.

sample were below average in socioeconomic status; 63 per cent were black and 37 per cent white. The correlations between the 8-month Bayley test scores and the IQs on the WISC were 0.27 ($p < 0.01$) for the females (0.30, $p < 0.01$ for the black and 0.28, $p < 0.01$ for the white females) and 0.12 ($p < 0.05$) for the males (0.01 ns for the black and 0.16, $p < 0.05$ for the white males). Very similar correlations were obtained when the verbal IQs of the WISC were the predicted scores. The sex difference found in this study was minimally present for the total sample of 19,837 children in the Collaborative Project, which included cohorts born in 12 hospitals (Broman *et al.*, 1975). For this large sample, prediction of 4-year Stanford-Binet IQs from Bayley test scores is shown in Figure 21.2. This figure suggests a much higher relationship between the 8-month and 4-year test scores than is indicated by the correlation coefficients, which are 0.21 for white boys ($N = 4,569$), 0.24 for black boys ($N = 5,507$), 0.23 for white girls ($N = 4,312$), and 0.24 for black girls ($N = 5,507$). These coefficients are all highly significant at better than the 0.01 level because of the large number of cases. These samples included a few children with handicapping conditions that would increase the correlations beyond those found for a normal, neurologically intact sample. In other words, in this large study there is positive but extremely low prediction, which is of negligible practical significance. The sex difference suggests greater mental test stability in girls but is not significant.

Socioeconomic Status and Prediction

The effect of the interaction of socioeconomic status and infant test scores on prediction was described by Willerman *et al.* (1970) for a Collaborative Project subsample of 3,037 babies born at the Boston Lying-In Hospital. This study shows that socioeconomic status has a significant effect on prediction for children earning low mental scores at 8 months. Children with low scores at 8 months living in homes of low socioeconomic status will do poorly on the 4-year Stanford-Binet, while children with low scores at 8 months living in homes of high socioeconomic status will earn above-average IQs at 4 years. Willerman *et al.* concluded that 'poverty amplifies the IQ deficit in poorly developed infants', or stated another way, 'infants retarded at 8 months were seven times more likely to obtain low IQs at age 4 years if they come from the lower socioeconomic status than if they come from a higher socioeconomic level'. This is a provocative paper but there may be alternative interpretations. Some of the children earning low scores at 8 months may be 'slow bloomers' who will eventually develop high verbal or other intellectual skills. The fact that these children live in homes of high socioeconomic status may not be the only determining factor. It may be that they are showing an increasing resemblance to parents who have similar skills. Support for this hypothesis comes from the study of adopted children by Skodak and Skeels (1949), who found that the IQs of adopted children who had never lived with their parents showed an increasing resemblance to the abilities of their own parents but little increase in resemblance to the educational level of the adopting parents during the age period 2-4 years.

Retardation and Minimal Brain Impairment as Factors in Prediction

Relatively high correlations between infant test scores and childhood IQs appear from time to time in the literature. The inclusion of children with very low scores usually accounts for these findings. MacRae (1955) reported a correlation of 0.56 ($p < 0.01$) between ratings based on either the Cattell or the Gesell tests, administered to 40 children under 12 months of age, and WISC IQs obtained at 5 years or older. This coefficient is considerably higher than that usually reported for normal children. We note that some of the children in this sample were living in a home for the mentally deficient. The purpose of the testing was for adoption. MacRae found that the ratings based on the infant test scores were very helpful. More than half the ratings of the babies did not change at all between the first and sixth year, and ratings of only two children changed by more than one rating category. The rating categories were definitely deficient, somewhat below average, average, somewhat above average, and definitely superior.

Knobloch and Pasamanick (1960) also reported significant correlations between infant test scores and later IQs. For 147 prematures considered normal, Gesell DQs at 40 weeks correlated with 3-year Stanford-Binet IQs 0.43; but for 48 children who were 'neurologically or intellectually abnormal', the correlation rose to 0.74. These authors stated that correlations of the same order of magnitude were obtained for both white and black children in this Baltimore sample, suggesting the validity of the findings.

The results indicating greater stability in the test scores of low-scoring babies are of importance to neurologists, pediatricians, psychologists, and others who depend on infant tests in the diagnosis of mental impairment and subnormality.

Diagnostic Value of Infant Tests

A major use of infant tests is in the diagnosis of mental defect. How accurate are these assessments? The fallibility of the tests themselves was suggested earlier in this chapter. On the other hand, the reliability of the tests is reasonably high and all tests are moderately predictive for low-scoring children. Before standardized tests were available, physicians, and especially pediatricians, had to depend entirely on their background of experience in making a diagnosis of mental defect. Their decisions would often have far-reaching effects on the lives of children, especially if institutionalization or adoption were being considered. To what extent does the information from an infant test help in the diagnosis? Illingworth (1960), a pediatrician, described in some detail the need for assistance in assessing the effects of such conditions as neonatal anoxia, head injury, virus encephalitis, or a subdural hematoma. He concluded from a review of the literature that 'there is plenty of evidence that developmental tests, properly used, are of the utmost value'. He went on to say: 'No one, of course, should expect developmental tests when repeated to give a constant value.' He stated that the objective test results should always be supplemented by a history and an evaluation of the quality of performance.

Studies specifically designed to assess the usefulness of infant tests in aiding pediatricians in their diagnosis of handicapping conditions was undertaken by Bierman *et al.* (1964) and Werner *et al.* (1968, 1971), using the data of the Kauai Pregnancy Study. In these extensive investigations of the pre- and postnatal development of all children ($N = 681$) born on the island of Kauai in 1954-5, pediatricians rated the intelligence of the children at about 20 months of age as retarded, low normal, normal, or superior. A total of 93 per cent were rated as normal; 5 per cent as low normal; and 0.6 per cent (1 girl and 3 boys) as retarded. These children were all tested on the Catell at the same age, 20 months. The agreement between the pediatricians' appraisals and the Cattell IQs was not high ($r = 0.32$) but was statistically significant ($p < 0.01$). The 46 per cent (16 out of 35 children) judged below normal by pediatricians at 20 months earned low IQs or were doing poorly in school at ages 5-9 years. The accuracy of these predictions of poor school performance was increased to 75 per cent if the Cattell IQs were taken into account. Bierman *et al.* concluded that the test scores appear to be valuable to the pediatrician who does not want to err in the direction of giving a poor prognosis for a child who may later prove capable of adequate if not superior academic performance. Children who at 20 months had normal Cattell IQs, but were misjudged as below normal in intelligence by the pediatricians, were likely to have poor speech, show abnormal or slow motor development, and be of 'poor physical status'. Children judged *normal* by the pediatricians whose Cattell IQs at 20 months were below 80 were not doing well in school when 6-9 years of age: 'from one half to two-thirds of these children were not capable of average academic work.' In a follow-up at 10 years of all available children in the Kauai study, Werner *et al.* (1968, 1971) reported that the best single predictor of IQ and achievement at age 10 years was the Cattell IQ at age 20 months. For children with IQs below 80 at age 20 months, a combination of Cattell IQ and pediatricians' ratings of intelligence yielded a high positive correlation ($R = 0.80$) with the IQs on the Primary Mental Abilities tests at 10 years. That the results of this study yielded positive results using 20-month Cattell IQs is remarkable. There is probably no age at which testing is more difficult than at the end of the second year, when children want to be autonomous and are therefore negativistic and resistant to adult suggestions, requiring great skill on the part of the examiner.

Infant tests are used to detect the effect of handicapping conditions known to have occurred at an earlier time, such as rubella during the pregnancy or asphyxia during the neonatal period. Honzik *et al.* (1965) compared the 8-month Bayley mental test scores of a group of infants suspected of having neurological handicaps, on the basis of hospital records, with the scores of a matched normal control group from the same hospitals. In this study the birth records of more than 10,000 babies born in seven different hospitals were scrutinized for evidence of complications of pregnancy or delivery and distress during the neonatal period. Of this group approximately 2 per cent were selected as possibly suspected of having brain impairment and were matched with a normal control group using the same records. The testers of the infants (128 males and 69 females) at 8 months were unaware of the neonatal appraisal as suspect or normal and rated most of the children 'normal'. The Bayley mental test scores, however, differentiated the suspect from the control group at between the 0.05 and the 0.01 levels of significance. There were also statistically significant differences in the performance on individual test items. This investigation is noteworthy in showing that infant mental tests at 8 months can be differentiating of deficits that are not obvious even to experienced testers.

Test scores do not always reflect the ill effects of asphyxia during delivery. Ucko (1965) reported no difference in the Griffiths DQs at 6 months of children who were anoxic during the neonatal period when they were compared with a matched normal sample from the London longitudinal study. A difference in the selection procedures in the two studies may account for the findings. Ucko was concerned only with the degree of anoxia or asphyxia. In the Honzik study the pediatrician making the decisions as to whether the infant was suspected of having neurological damage took into account evidences of neurological difficulty, describing the babies as follows: 'Some [babies] were limp, others rigid, some sucked poorly . . . were frequently excessively irritable, and occasional opisthotonus was seen.' Infants are tolerant of some degree of anoxia during the perinatal period, so that probably many of the infants in the Ucko study were not adversely affected by the asphyxia, while in the Honzik study only infants showing some evidence of ill effects were included.

Genetic Studies Using Infant Tests

The only direct evidence of the effect of the genetic structure on intelligence comes from chromosomal studies. The advent of hypotonic treatment of cells led to accurate counts of the number of chromosomes in the cells of normal human beings and the possibility of correlating abnormal counts with tested abilities. One of the dramatic discoveries was that individuals with Down's syndrome, or mongolism, have an extra 21st chromosome. Individuals with this genetic makeup are noticeably slow in their mental and motor development, seldom earning IQs of more than 50. The Bayley scales have been used to compare the abilities of Down's syndrome infants reared at home versus those living in an institution (Bayley *et al.*, 1971). The test scores reflected not only the low scores of these children but also the beneficial effects of a home environment. The mean Bayley IQ of the children reared at home was 50; in the hospital, 35. This difference is statistically significant ($p < 0.005$).

Resemblance in the mental abilities of family members is the most frequently used method of assessing the relevance of heredity. Erlenmeyer-Kimling *et al.* (1963) reported that for most relationship categories the median of the empirical correlations closely approaches the theoretical value predicted on the basis of the genetic relationship alone. The median empirical value of the parent-child correlations is 0.50; the median *r* for fraternal twins, 0.53; and for identical twins reared together, 0.87, and reared apart, 0.75. These coefficients are based on samples of parents and children of school age. Are the findings similar for infant test scores? The answer is interesting. Parent-child resemblance is negligible in the first months of life, and the characteristic statistic of 0.50 is not reached until the end of the preschool period (Bayley, 1954; Hindley, 1962; and Honzik, 1957, 1963). Skodak and Skeels (1949) reported a similar finding for children who were adopted in the first months of life. The correlations between the adopted children's IQs and their natural parents' IQs (or years of schooling) increased from a near-zero at 2 years to statistically significant correlations ($p < 0.05 - 0.01$) at 4 years. The same increase in resemblance was not obtained between the children's IQs and their adoptive parents' years of schooling, although the children's above-average IQs reflected the good environments provided by their adoptive parents. These findings suggest that changes in IQ during the early preschool years are not entirely due to environmental factors. If we can assume that the increasing resemblance between the scores of the natural parents and their children's IQs is due to heredity, the genetic factor still accounts for very little of the total variance in the children's mental test performance.

Twin studies are the ones most frequently cited as showing the effect of genetic similarity on intelligence. Freedman and Keller (1963) tested a group of same-sexed twins every month during the first year on the Bayley scales. These investigators did not know the zygosity of the twins until after the testing period was over. They found that the intrapair difference on the combined mental and motor scales of the monozygotic twins was less in nearly all instances than that of the dizygotic twins ($p < 0.01$). Wilson (1972) and Wilson and Harpring (1972) reported within-pair correlations of monozygotic (MZ) and dizygotic (DZ) twins on the Bayley scales for a group of 261 pairs tested every three months during the first year (see Table 21.3). These coefficients are similar to those found for older children and adults, except that the values for DZ twins are higher. The greater resemblance of fraternal twin babies than that of siblings is in all likelihood the result of the greater similarity in the experience of the twins than in the experiences of single-born children in the same family. There is also the possibility that the experiences of MZ twins are more similar than those of DZ twins. The greater similarity in the genetically similar MZ twins than in the less similar DZ twins suggests hereditary determination, but the crucial study requires that the twins be reared apart so that there is control of experiential factors.

Table 21.3: Within-Pair Correlations of Twins on Bayley Scales (261 Pairs)

Age in months	MZ[a] r	DZ[b] r
3	0.84[c]	0.67
6	0.82	0.74
9	0.81[c]	0.69
12	0.82[c]	0.61

[a] Monozygotic
[b] Dizygotic
[c] $p < 0.05$

A study by Nichols and Broman (1974), based on the 8-month Bayley tests given in the Collaborative Study, reported high intratwin correlations (0.84 for 122 pairs of MZ twins and 0.55 for 227 pairs of DZ twins) but a relatively low correlation of 0.22 for siblings. The low resemblance between the 4,962 siblings tested at 8 months compared with the DZ intrapair *r* of 0.55 suggests that the experience of infants living in the same family can be very different and that the extent of the genetic similarity does not preclude great differences in test scores. There is always the possibility that the siblings were fathered by different men, but this is less likely to have occurred in the Collaborative Study, since the siblings were born and tested within a relatively limited time period. In fact, the authors referred to 'full' siblings, suggesting that blood checks were done on the parents of these siblings. A significant finding in this study was that the high heritability estimate derived from the difference between the MZ and DZ correlations was due to the higher concordance of severe retardation in the MZ pairs. In the MZ sample, removal of all severely retarded children reduced the intrapair correlation of 0.84 to 0.55. Removal of severely retarded children had no effect on the DZ correlation of 0.55 or the sibling *r* of 0.22. These authors added that there was evidence that genetic factors are important in severe retardation on the Bayley scale, since the concordance ratio for retardation was significantly higher in the MZ than the DZ twins. Environmental factors are also implicated in the very low test scores, since the incidence of retardation is significantly higher in the twin samples than among the single siblings.

Experience and Intelligence in Infancy

Interest in the effect of experience on the development of mental abilities has led to an upsurge of investigations of the possible effects of experience on the growth of intelligence in infancy.

The interaction of experience and heredity begins at conception, when the mother's nutrition and health begin to have their effect on the developing embryo. Infant tests are not needed to show the devastating effects of maternal rubella or Western encephalitis on the fetus but are being widely used to assess the effects of maternal and infant malnutrition on the development of the central nervous system (CNS) and intelligence.

Malnutrition

Both the Gesell and the Bayley infant tests have been used extensively in assessments of the effects of malnutrition on intellectual development. Cravioto and Robles (1965) tested the hypothesis that the effect of severe malnutrition on mental development varies as a function of the period of life at which malnutrition is experienced. Twenty infants hospitalized for severe protein-calorie malnutrition were tested on the Gesell scale during hospital treatment and during the rehabilitation period. On the first examination, just after the acute electrolyte disturbance had been corrected, all infants scored considerably below the age norms. During rehabilitation 14 of the children gained in DQs on the Gesell, but the 6 youngest did not, confirming the hypotheses that the younger the infant the greater the adverse effect of poor nutrition. Pollitt and Granoff (1967) cross-validated these findings in Peruvian children with marasmus using the Bayley scales. The scores of this group of previously marasmic infants were compared with those of their siblings who had no unusual medical history and whose measurements were within normal limits. It was found that while the siblings were developing according to age expectation, 17 of the 19 children recovered from marasmus had severe mental and motor retardation. From these studies and those of Mönckeberg (1968) and Chase and Martin (1969), Cravioto and Delicardie (1970) concluded that protein-calorie malnutrition occurring in the first year of life, if severe enough to retard physical growth markedly and to require hospitalization, may have adverse effects on mental development. These authors added that if the duration of the untreated episode is longer than four months, particularly during the first months of life, the effect on mental performance may be so intense as to produce severe mental retardation, which is incompletely corrected by nutritional rehabilitation. With all their limitations, both mental and motor scores of infant tests helped describe the findings objectively and indicate their significance.

Maternal Deprivation

The impetus for studies of the effect of experience on intellectual development has come in part from Bowlby's monograph (1952) describing the ill effects of maternal deprivation. This monograph was the stimulus for research on the ill effects of institutional care, which was reviewed by Ainsworth (1962), Casler (1961), and Yarrow (1961). Casler concluded in his review that in institutional care there is a lack or relative absence of tactile, vestibular, and others forms of stimulation, which accounts for some of the emotional, physical, and intellectual deficits. Casler (1965) later investigated the effects of extra tactile stimulation on infants living in an institution. He found that infants given specific tactile stimulation over a 10-week period performed significantly better on the Gesell Developmental Schedules than did a matched control group. This study, which used a rather small number of cases, should be replicated, but the findings are in line with those of comparative psychologists, such as Harlow (1958), as well as developmental psychologists (Bayley and Schaefer, 1964).

The next question is how long-lasting are the ill effects of institutional care and the good effects of supplemental stimulation. A partial answer is provided by Dennis and Najarian (1957), who tested all the children in a Lebanese crèche where health needs were met but the infants were minimally stimulated. They found that the infants' Cattell IQs were normal at age 2 months but averaged only 63 during the age period 3-12 months. Children tested at ages 4 and 5 years obtained IQs of approximately 90, although they had spent all their lives in the crèche. These results suggest that the period of limited stimulation during infancy had no lasting effect on mental growth. A similar finding was reported by Kagan and Klein (1973) in a cross-cultural study of Guatemalan infants. The rural Guatemalan infant spends most of his life in 'the small dark interior of a windowless hut'. He is usually kept close to his mother but is rarely spoken to or played with. Compared with American infants, he is extremely passive, fearful, unsmiling, and quiet. These Guatemalan infants were retarded with respect to 'activation of hypotheses, alertness, onset of stranger anxiety, and object permanence'. In marked contrast to the infants, the Guatemalan preadolescents were comparable to American middle-class norms on tests of perceptual analysis, inference, recall, and recognition memory. Kagan concluded that 'infant retardation seems to be partially reversible, and cognitive development during the early years more resilient than had been supposed'.

Apparently the effect of added stimulation may last no longer than that of relative deprivation. Rheingold and Bayley (1959) reported transitory gains in social responsiveness in institutionalized infants who were given 'more attentive care' by one person from the sixth to the eighth month. These children performed no better on the Cattell test a year later than did a matched group who received no special attention.

Parent-Child Interaction and Infant Test Scores

Another approach to the problem of evaluating environmental influence is to relate infant test scores to socialization practices in the family. Baldwin *et al.* (1945) were among the first to relate parental behavior to the test scores of infants and young children. He reported that for 94 children in the Fels longitudinal study tested on the Gesell, DQ changes were related to 'freedom to explore', 'emotional warmth', and 'acceleratory methods'. These variables, described in different ways, have been found relevant to gains in IQ in a number of subsequent studies. Bayley and Schaefer (1964) reported for the small but intensively tested Berkeley Growth Study sample that boy babies whose mothers evaluated them positively, granted them some autonomy, and expressed affection for them were 'happy, positive, calm infants'. These boys tended to earn below-average scores on the Bayley tests in the first year but made rapid gains in the next few years, when they were likely to earn high IQs. The authors reported that, conversely, boys who scored high in the first year were active, unhappy, and negative with mothers who were hostile and punitive. These boys tended to have low IQs after 4 years. It is difficult to sort out cause and effect in these relationships. Were the boys' Bayley test scores higher in infancy *because* they were stimulated by the punitive mothers? To what extent did the positive, affectionate mother affect the cognitive development of her son? For girls in this study there was little correlation between the mother's behavior in the first two or three years and their later intelligence. These results were to some extent cross-validated in the much larger Guidance Study sample (Honzik, 1967). Ratings of the *closeness of the mother-son relationship* at 21 months correlated with the mental test scores of the boys at this age ($r = 0.29$, $p < 0.05$). This correlation increased to $0.48 < 0.01$ at 9 years and was still significant at age 40 years (Honzik, 1972). *Closeness of mother to daughter* correlated significantly with the daughter's IQ at 2 years but not thereafter.

In the London longitudinal study Moore (1968) reported a similar increasing correlation between the 'emotional atmosphere of the home', 'toys, books, and experience', and 'example and encouragement' and the children's IQs at 3 and 8 years. The interesting phenomenon here is that although the family variables were rated when the children were aged 2½ years, the correlations, and thus the predictions, of the 8-year IQs were all higher, and significantly so, than the 5-year IQs. Unfortunately Moore did not report the correlation between the family variables and the children's Griffiths DQs at ages 6 months and 12 months, so that age trends cannot be considered from infancy to middle childhood. A major conclusion to be drawn from the four longitudinal studies is that measurable experiences in the home in the first two years may show an increasing correlation with IQs during childhood. It is understandable that evidences of ability of the parents, such as their education or socioeconomic status, would show an increasing correlation with their children's test scores. It is more difficult to comprehend why variables like *mother-son closeness*, which is not related to parental ability, shows an increasing relation to the son's IQ. Actually, later measures of mother-son closeness do not show this correlation, which means that the warmth and concern that the mother has for her son in the early years has a greater effect on his later intellectual functioning than does concurrent favoring and protectiveness in adolescence (Honzik, 1966).

In a study of 41 black babies aged 5 to 6 months, Yarrow *et al.* (1972) differentiated the natural home environment into (1) inanimate stimulation and (2) social stimulation. These two types of environmental variables, obtained from time-sampling observations, were not highly correlated but did correlate significantly with Bayley's mental test scores. It is of interest in this study that the investigators considered the relation of other infant variables to *social* and *inanimate stimulation*. The infant variable *vocalization to bell* correlated significantly with social but not inanimate stimulation. *Goal-directed behaviors* correlated significantly ($p < 0.01$) with both social and inanimate stimulation. Yarrow *et al.* concluded that:

> . . . it is likely that the infant's orientation to objects and to people very early becomes part of a feedback system with the environment. His smiling, vocalizing, and reaching out to people; his visually attending to and manipulating objects tend to be self-reinforcing and thus, to some extent self-perpetuating.

Two investigators have avoided the problem of inherited similarity of parents and children by studying the relation of the family milieu to infant test scores in adopted children. Beckwith (1971) correlated the Cattell IQs of 24 adopted infants with evaluations of their mothers' interactions with them in the home. Cattell IQs (at 8-10 months) were correlated with the infants' 'social experience' ($p < 0.01$) and the extent to which he was 'talked to', 'touched' and 'given an opportunity to explore the house'. In this study no relationship was found between the infants' IQs and the adoptive parents' socioeconomic status, but the IQs did correlate with the natural mothers' socioeconomic class.

Another study of 40 adopted children at age 6 months was reported by Yarrow (1963). The maternal variables for the investigation were carefully chosen and covered three major maternal functions: (1) need gratification and tension reduction, (2) stimulation-learning conditions, and (3) affectional interchange. The maternal variables yielding the highest correlations with the 6-month Cattell IQs were *stimulus adaptation* ($r = 0.85$), *achievement stimulation* ($r = 0.72$), *social stimulation* ($r = 0.65$), and *physical contact* ($r = 0.57$). All these correlations were significant at the 0.01 level or better and were much higher than those reported for the natural mother and children. An important question here is how long-lasting the effects of the early infant experience are. These adopted children were tested again on the WISC at 10 years (Yarrow *et al.*, 1973). Seven of the eight maternal variables assessed when these adopted children were aged 6 months correlated significantly with the WISC IQs at 10 years. However, when the correlations were computed for boys and girls separately, the findings were similar to those reported by Bayley and Schaefer (1964) and others: the relationships were negligible for the girls but highly significant for the boys. The range of rs for the girls was from 0.08 for *achievement stimulation* to 0.24 for *emotional involvement*. The range for the boys was from 0.43 ($p < 0.05$) for *achievement stimulation* to 0.68 ($p < 0.01$) for *physical contact*. These correlations, together with those of other investigators, clearly indicate the importance of early affective relationships and tactual stimulation to mental growth. Fortunately infant mental tests are available and have been used to evaluate the relation of the infant's experience to his test scores concurrently as well as in the prediction of later mental functioning.

Summary

This chapter discusses the available infant tests and the difficulties involved in giving accurate and complete tests in the first year of life. It is noteworthy that the most clear-cut findings are those reported by investigators who are skilled in working with infants, are aware of the pitfalls inherent in assessing infants, and did much of the actual testing themselves. This is true of Bayley, Beckwith, Cattell, Gesell, Hindley, and others.

Reliability and Validity

The Bayley and Cattell infant tests are highly reliable and internally consistent as judged by the correlation of odd with even test items. Test-retest correlations are relatively high over short age periods but decline markedly as the time span between tests lengthens (Bayley, Brunet-Lézine, Cattell, Gesell, and Griffiths). The magnitude of the coefficients and the nature of the interage correlations have been cross-validated by studies in different countries by the use of different tests at different time periods, suggesting that a major determinant of these interrelationships is the rate of development of the human organism. Honzik (1938) noted that the magnitude of the rs varies with the age ratio of the first to the second test. Thus the rs between the 3- and 6-month test scores is roughly 0.50, as is the correlation between the 3- and 6-year scores. This age ratio underestimates the magnitude of the rs as the children grow older but is suggestive of the changing rate of development of mental abilities with age.

Another index of the validity of the tests is the agreement between scores on different tests. Erickson *et al.* (1970) reported a correlation of 0.97 ($p > 0.001$) between the Bayley and the Cattell scores of children who ranged in ability from profoundly retarded to normal, suggesting a high degree of validity of the scores of the children in this ability range.

Prediction from Infant Tests

Predictions based on the test scores of infants depend not only on the growth processes but also on the effects of experience and on the nature of the tests used to measure the developing abilities. The following conclusions are reached from the studies discussed.

1. In neurologically intact infants, scores obtained on currently available tests during the first months of life are not predictive of later intelligence because of immaturity, rapidly changing behaviors, or the overriding significance of other behaviors such as the infant's relative *activity* during this age period (Bayley and Schaefer, 1964; Escalona, 1968).

2. Prediction of later intelligence test scores begins to occur in the second half of the first year in girls only (Hindley, 1960, 1965), and more especially in certain specific abilities, such as vocalizations (Cameron *et al.*, 1967; Kagan, 1971).

3. Prediction of later intelligence does not accelerate until after the second birthday (Bayley, 1949; Brucefors, 1972; Hindley, 1965; Honzik *et al.*, 1948).

4. Prediction is markedly more accurate for low-scoring infants, regardless of whether the low score is due to chromosomal aberrations (e.g. trisomy 21), infection (rubella during the pregnancy), injury, perinatal anoxia, or generalized subnormality of unknown etiology.

5. The effect of experience on test constancy is suggested by a study showing that the interage correlations are noticeably higher for children living in the relatively constant environment of a day-care center (Ramey *et al.*, 1973).

Diagnosis

Evidence from many investigations attests to the value of infant mental tests in the diagnosis of even minimal neurological lags or deficits (Bierman *et al.*, 1964; Honzik *et al.*, 1965). Infant test scores are diagnostic of deprivation experiences as well as of the effects of enriched environments. However, the value of these scores is greater in the assessment of deficits than of superiority, since high scores on infant tests are less stable than average or low scores. Precocity in infancy may reflect early maturing or the effects of a great deal of stimulation rather than higher potential for later above-average cognitive functioning.

What can be done to improve diagnoses? The use of mothers' reports as additional information may add to the value of the examination. It is often possible to determine the mother's estimate of the validity of the test by asking her if the baby responded to the test as she would expect him to or if she was surprised at what he could do.

The infant's reactions to the test and his cognitive style should be recorded and evaluated. These evaluations may prove more useful than the test scores. Freedman and Keller (1963) found that monozygotic twins were significantly more alike than dizygotic twins on Bayley's behavior profile, which is part of the Bayley tests. Actually the behavior profile was more differentiating than the mental and motor scales in this study.

For more adequate diagnoses a greater effort should be made to measure specific abilities and new groups of abilities. Also the findings of investigations of cognitive functioning should be considered as possible additions to the current tests. A premise of Fantz and Nevis's (1967) investigations was that 'the early development of cognitive function is primarily through perception rather than action'. They added that 'later individual differences are more likely to be correlated with the early development of perception and attention than with action'. Although it would not be feasible to duplicate Fantz's experiments in a testing situation, it would be possible to assess infants' attentiveness to schematic drawings as a part of the test. Lewis (1971) wrote that if one views *attention* and its distribution as an information-processing operation, attention can be viewed as a measure of cognitive functioning. Kagan (1971) reported social class differences in attentiveness in the first year, which further suggests its possible relevance to what is termed *intelligence* in the older child. *Attention* is easily assessed in the mental test situation, and if it proves diagnostic or predictive, it should be incorporated into the test score.

Discussion

The value of infant tests is seriously questioned by Lewis (1973) and Lewis and McGurk (1972). This overview suggests why. Infant test scores are not stable over long periods of time, and their relationship to previous and concurrent experience is complex and only beginning to be understood. As Yarrow *et al.* (1973) wrote, 'We are still in a rather primitive state with regard to concepts and methodology for handling the dynamic interplay among these sets of variables'. Perhaps the key word here is *dynamic*. Growth is seldom simple and seldom occurs at a constant rate; instead it is rather highly interactive and occurs at a decelerating rate. A question that has not been raised but may prove highly relevant is whether experiences are more effective during periods of rapid or of relatively slower growth. Our hypotheses from what is known to date about intellectual development over the life span is that the effect of experiences, both those injurious and those beneficial to the organism's cognitive skills, is negatively related to growth and, thus, to age. In other words, the earlier the experience the greater the potential effect. This does not mean that the effects of experience are reflected immediately in the behavior of the infant. Some of the conditions, such as Western encephalitis or maternal care, are known to have more predictable effects on later cognitive development than on current cognitive skills. Another possibly confounding factor, suggested by the higher correlations between maternal care and infant scores in adopted than in own children, is that aspects of optimal maternal care may be negatively relevant to genetic potential. This was actually found in the Guidance Study, where the mother's education, which reflects her ability, was negatively related to the most relevant experiential variable, *closeness of mother and child* (Honzik, 1967).

The critiques of Lewis (1973) and Lewis and McGurk (1972) are valuable in asking some significant and cogent questions about attempts to measure 'intelligence' in infancy. Infant tests obviously do not measure what is measured by the Stanford-Binet, the Wechsler, or primary abilities tests; they measure abilities and skills that, to a large extent, are the bases and precursors of later mental development. It is clear that the tests could be improved by the elimination of items that are more motor than mental and by the addition of new items suggested by recent research. Infant tests, with all their limitations, have served us well. Possibly their main value has been in diagnosis, but they have also contributed substantially to our understanding of the many factors contributing to the development of abilities in the first years of life.

Conclusion

The major question of this review is whether or not test scores accurately describe the growth of mental abilities and reflect the temporary and more permanent effects of experience. This we believe they do, and we believe that with amplification and careful use their value can be enhanced. Standards and reference points are needed and good tests can help serve this need. The purpose of infant testing is to determine the progress of an individual child or the mental development of all children. Prediction of later intellectual functioning is a worthy aim of infant tests but secondary to the more important objective of adding to our understanding and knowledge of the course of development of mental abilities in infancy and early childhood.

References

Ainsworth, M.D., (1962), 'The effects of maternal deprivation: A review of findings and controversy in the context of research strategy', in *Deprivation of Maternal Care: A Reassessment of Its Effects*, World Health Organization, Geneva, Switzerland, p. 97.

Baldwin, A.L., Kalhorn, J. and Breese, F.H., 1945, 'Patterns of parent behavior', *Psychological Monograph, 58* (whole no. 268).

Bayley, N., 1933, *The California First Year Mental Scale*, University of California Press, Berkeley.

Baley, N., 1949, 'Consistency and variability in the growth of intelligence from birth to eighteen years', *Journal of Genetic Psychology, 75*: 165.

Bayley, N., 1954, 'Some increasing parent-child similarities during the growth of children', *Journal of Educational Psychology, 45*: 1.

Bayley, N., 1968, 'Behavioral correlates of mental growth: Birth to 36 years', *American Psychologist, 23*: 1.

Bayley, N., 1969, *Bayley Scales of Infant Development*, Psychological Corp., New York.

Bayley, N., Rhodes, L., Gooch, B. and Marcus, M., 1971, 'Environmental factors in the development of institutionalized children', in J. Hellmuth (ed.), *Exceptional Infant: Studies in Abnormalities*, vol. 2, Brunner/Mazel, New York.

Bayley, N. and Schaefer, E.S., 1964, 'Correlations of maternal and child behaviors with the development of mental abilities: Data from the Berkeley Growth Study', *Monographs for the Society for Research and Child Development, 29* (6, whole no. 97).

Beckwith, L., 1971, 'Relationship between attributes of mothers and their infants' IQ scores', *Child Development, 42*: 1083.

Bernstein, B., 1961, 'Social class and linguistic development: A theory of social learning', in A.H. Halsey, J. Floud and C.A. Anderson (eds.), *Economy, Education and Society*, Free Press, New York.

Bierman, J.M., Connor, A., Vaage, M. and Honzik, M.P., 1964, 'Pediatricians' assessments of the intelligence of two-year-olds and their mental test scores', *Pediatrics, 34*: 680.

Bing, E., 1963, 'Effect of child-rearing practices on development of differential cognitive abilities', *Child Development, 34*: 631.

Bowlby, J., 1952, 'Maternal care and mental health', *Monograph Series*, no. 2 (2nd edn.), World Health Organization, Geneva, Switzerland.

Broman, S.H., Nichols, P.L. and Kennedy, W.A., 1975, *Preschool IQ: Prenatal and Early Developmental Correlates*, Wiley, New York.

Brucefors, A., 1972, 'Trends in development of abilities', paper given at Réunion de coordination des recherches sur la croissance et le développement de l'enfant normal, Institute of Child Health, London.

Brucefors, A., Johannesson, I., Karlberg, P., Klackenberg-Larsson, I., Lichenstein, H. and Svenberg, I., 1974, 'Trends in development of abilities related to somatic growth', *Human Development, 17*: 152.

Brunet, O. and Lézine, P.U.F., 1951, *Le développement psychologique de la première enfance*, Editions Scientifiques et Psychotechniques, Issy-les-Moulineaux.

Cameron, J., Livson, N. and Bayley, N., 1967, 'Infant vocalizations and their relationship to mature intelligence', *Science, 157*: 331.

Casler, L., 1961, 'Maternal deprivation: A critical review of the literature', Monographs of the Society for Research in Child Development, 26 (2: whole no. 80).

Casler, L., 1965, 'The effects of extra tactile stimulation on a group of institutionalized infants', *Genetic Psychology Monographs, 71*: 137.

Cattell, P., 1940, *The Measurement of Intelligence in Infants and Young Children*,

Science Press, New York. Reprinted by Psychological Corp., 1960.

Chase, H.P. and Martin, H.P., 1969, 'Undernutrition and child development', paper read before the Conference on Neuropsychological Methods for the Assessment of Impaired Brain Functioning in the Malnourished Child, Palo Alto, California.

Cravioto, J. and Delicardie, E., 1970, 'Mental performance in school age children', *American Journal of Diseases of Children, 120*: 404.

Cravioto, J. and Robles, B., 1965, 'Evolution of adaptive and motor behavior during rehabilitation from kwashiorkor', *American Journal of Orthopsychiatry, 35*: 449.

Dennis, W. and Najarian, P., 1957, 'Infant development under environmental handicap', *Psychological Monographs, 71* (7, whole no. 436).

Dodgson, M.C.H., 1962, *The Growing Brain: An Essay in Developmental Neurology*, Williams and Wilkins, Baltimore.

Erickson, M.T., Johnson, N.M. and Campbell, F.A., 1970, 'Relationships among scores on infant tests for children with developmental problems', *American Journal of Mental Deficiency, 75*: 102.

Erlenmeyer-Kimling, L. and Jarvik, L.F., 1963, 'Genetics and intelligence: A review', *Science, 142*: 1477.

Escalona, S., 1968, *The Roots of Individuality: Normal Patterns of Individuality*, Aldine Publishing Company, Chicago.

Fantz, R.I. and Nevis, S., 1967, 'The predictive value of changes in visual preferences in early infancy', in J. Hellmuth (ed.), *Exceptional Infant: The Normal Infant*, vol. 1, Brunner/Mazel, New York.

Frankenburg, W.K., Camp, B.W. and Van Natta, P.A., 1971, 'Validity of the Denver Developmental Screening Test', *Child Development, 42*: 475.

Frankenberg, W.K. and Dodds, J.B., 1967, 'The Denver Developmental Screening Test', *Journal of Pediatrics, 71*: 181.

Freedman, D.G. and Keller, B., 1963, 'Inheritance of behavior in infants', *Science, 140*: 196.

Gesell, A. and Amatruda, C., 1941, *Developmental Diagnosis*, Paul B. Hoeber, New York.

Gesell, A., Halverson, H.M., Ilg, F.L., Thompson, H., Castner, B.M., Ames, L.B. and Amatruda, C.S., 1940, *The First Five Years of Life*, Harper, New York.

Gesell, A. and Thompson, H., 1934, *Infant Behavior: Its Genesis and Growth*, McGraw-Hill, New York.

Goffeney, B., Henderson, N.B. and Butler, B.V., 1971, 'Negro-White, Male-female 8-month developmental scores compared with 7-year WISC and Bender Test Scores', *Child Development, 42*: 595.

Griffiths, R., 1954, *The Abilities of Babies*, McGraw-Hill, New York.

Harlow, H.F., 1958, 'The nature of love', *American Psychologist, 13*: 673.

Hindley, C.B., 1960, 'The Griffiths scale of infant development: Scores and predictions from 3 to 18 months', *Journal of Child Psychology and Psychiatry, 1*: 99.

Hindley, C.B., 1962, 'Social class influences on the development of ability in the first five years', *Proceedings of the 14th International Congress of Applied Psychology, Child and Education, 3*: 29.

Hindley, C.B., 1965, 'Stability and change in abilities up to five years: Group trends', *Journal of Child Psychology and Psychiatry, 6*: 85.

Honzik, M.P., 1938, 'The constancy of mental test performance during the preschool period', *Journal of Genetic Psychology, 52*: 285.

Honzik, M.P., 1957, 'Developmental studies of parent-child resemblance in intelligence', *Child Development, 28*: 215.

Honzik, M.P., 1963, 'A sex difference in the age of onset of the parent-child resemblance in intelligence', *Journal of Educational Psychology, 54*: 231.

Honzik, M.P., 1966, 'The environment and mental growth from 21 months to 30 years', *XVIII International Congress of Psychology Proceedings, 11*: 28.

Honzik, M.P., 1967, 'Environmental correlates of mental growth: Prediction from the family setting at 21 months', *Child Development, 38*: 337.

Honzik, M.P., 1972, 'Intellectual abilities at age 40 in relation to the early family environment' in F.J. Monks, W.W. Hartup and J. de Wit (eds.), *Determinants of Behavioral Development*, Academic Press, New York.

Honzik, M.P., Hutchins, J.J. and Burnip, S.R., 1965, 'Birth record assessments and test performance at eight months', *American Journal of Diseases of Children, 109*: 416.

Honzik, M.P., Macfarlane, J.W. and Allen, L., 1948, 'Stability of mental test performance between 2 and 18 years', *Journal of Experimental Education, 17*: 309.

Illingworth, R.S., 1960, *The Development of the Infant and Young Child: Normal and Abnormal*, E. and S. Livingstone Ltd., Edinburgh and London.

Ireton, H., Thwing, E. and Gravem, H., 1970, 'Infant mental development and neurological status, family socioeconomic status, and intelligence at age four', *Child Development, 41*: 937.

Kagan, J., 1971, *Change and Continuity in Infancy*, Wiley, New York.

Kagan, J. and Klein, R.E., 1973, 'Cross-cultural perspectives in early development', *American Psychologist, 28*: 947.

Klackenberg-Larsson, I. and Stensson, J., 1968, 'Data on the mental development during the first five years', in *The Development of Children in a Swedish Urban Community: A Prospective Longitudinal Study, Acta Paediatrica Scandinavica*, Supplement 187, IV, Almqvist and Wiksell, Stockholm.

Knobloch, H. and Pasamanick, B., 1960, 'An evaluation of the consistency and predictive value of the 40-week Gesell Developmental Schedule', paper presented at the Regional Research Meeting of the American Psychiatric Association, Iowa City.

Lewis, M., 1971, 'Individual differences in the measurement of early cognitive growth', in J. Hellmuth (ed.), *Exceptional Infant: Studies in Abnormalities*, vol. 2, Brunner/Mazel, New York.

Lewis, M., 1973, 'Intelligence tests: Their use and misuse', *Human Development, 16*: 1.

Lewis, M. and McGurk, H., 1972, 'Evaluation of infant intelligence', *Science, 178*: 1174.

McCall, R.B., Hogarty, P.S. and Hurlburt, N., 1972, 'Transitions in infant sensorimotor development and the prediction of childhood IQ', *American Psychologist, 27*: 728.

MacRae, J.M., 1955, 'Retests of children given mental tests as infants', *Journal of Genetic Psychology, 87*: 111.

Mönckeberg, F., 1968, 'Effect of early marasmic malnutrition on subsequent physical and psychological development', in N.E. Scrimshaw and J.E. Gordon (eds.), *Malnutrition, Learning and Behavior*, MIT Press, Cambridge, Massachusetts, p. 269.

Moore, T., 1968, 'Language and intelligence: A longitudinal study of the first eight years, Part II: Environmental correlates of mental growth', *Human Development, 11*: 1.

Nelson, V.L. and Richards, T.W., 1939, 'Studies in mental development, III: Performance of twelve-month-old children on the Gesell Schedule and its predictive value for mental status at two and three years', *Journal of Genetic Psychology, 54*: 181.

Nichols, P.L. and Broman, S.H., 1974, 'Familial resemblance in infant mental development', *Developmental Psychology, 10*: 442.

Pollitt, E. and Granoff, D., 1967, 'Mental and motor development of Peruvian children treated for severe malnutrition', *Review of Interamericana Psicologia, 1*: 93.

Ramey, C.T., Campbell, F.A. and Nicholson, J.E., 1973, 'The predictive power of the Bayley Scales of Infant Development and the Stanford-Binet Intelligence Test in a relatively constant environment', *Child Development, 44*: 790.

Rheingold, H.L. and Bayley, N., 1959, 'The later effects of an experimental modification of mothering', *Child Development, 31*: 363.

Skodak, M. and Skeels, H.M., 1949, 'A final follow-up study of 100 adopted children', *Journal of Genetic Psychology, 75*: 85.

Ucko, L.E., 1965, 'A comparative study of asphyxiated and non-asphyxiated boys from birth to five years', *Developmental Medicine and Child Neurology, 7*: 643.

Uzgiris, I.C. and Hunt, J.McV., 1966, 'An instrument for assessing infant psychological development', mimeographed paper, Psychological Development Laboratories, University of Illinois.

Werner, E.E. and Bayley, N., 1966, 'The reliability of Bayley's revised scale of mental and motor development during the first year of life', *Child Development, 37*: 39.

Werner, E.E., Bierman, J.M. and French, F.E., 1971, *The Children of Kauai: A Longitudinal Study from the Prenatal Period to Age 10*, University of Hawaii Press, Honolulu.

Werner, E.E., Honzik, M.P. and Smith, R.S., 1968, 'Prediction of intelligence and achievement at 10 years from 20-month pediatric and psychologic examinations', *Child Development, 39*, 1063.

Willerman, L., Broman, S.H. and Fiedler, M., 1970, 'Infant development, preschool IQ, and social class', *Child Development, 41*: 69.

Wilson, R.S., 1972, 'Twins: Early mental development', *Science, 175*: 914.

Wilson, R.S. and Harpring, E.B., 1972, 'Mental and motor development in infant twins', *Developmental Psychology, 7*: 277.

Winick, M., 1970, 'Fetal malnutrition and growth processes', *Hospital Practice, 5*: 33.

Yarrow, L.J., 1961, 'Maternal deprivation: Toward an empirical and conceptual re-evaluation', *Psychological Bulletin, 58*: 459.

Yarrow, L.J., 1963, 'Research in dimensions of early maternal care', *Merrill-Palmer Quarterly, 9*: 101.

Yarrow, L.J., Goodwin, M.S., Manheimer, H. and Milowe, I.D., 1973, 'Infancy experiences and cognitive and personality development at ten years', in L.J. Stone, H.T. Smith and L.B. Murphy (eds.), *The Competent Infant: Research and Commentary*, Basic Books, New York.

Yarrow, L.J., Rubenstein, J.L., Pedersen, F.A. and Jankowski, J.J., 1972, 'Dimensions of early stimulation and their differential effects on infant development', *Merrill-Palmer Quarterly, 18*: 205.

22 TOWARD AN EPIGENETIC CONCEPTION OF MENTAL DEVELOPMENT IN THE FIRST THREE YEARS OF LIFE

Robert B. McCall

Source: M. Lewis (ed.), *Origins of Intelligence* (Plenum Press, 1976), pp. 97-122.

Despite evidence to the contrary, 'real intelligence' historically has been considered to be a relatively unitary trait, constant over age, and pervasive in its governance of nearly all mental behaviors (Hunt, 1961). Although it is currently fashionable to denigrate such a view, it is still prevalent to some extent. For example, the excitement in certain quarters about brain-wave tests of intelligence because scores reflect a unitary characteristic, are apparently constant over age, and are equally distributed among different cultural groups stands as testimony to the lingering vestiges of a unitary, developmentally constant 'intelligence'.

For decades such a concept has dominated the field of infant testing. Surely, it was reasoned, since a person is born with a certain amount of intelligence that remains with him throughout life, it should be possible to detect some aspects of intelligence even in a young baby. After all, intelligence simply grows in quantity with development (like height) but undergoes no qualitative changes, and one's relative standing remains the same over the years.

When infant tests could not predict from the first year of life to childhood IQ, the concept of a unitary, constant intelligence did not wither. Instead people blamed the infant tests for being unreliable (which they are not), or they claimed that the infant tests measured the wrong thing. Intelligence was really there in the miniaturized adult form — if we only knew how to measure it.

After several infant tests had been developed, none of which predicted later IQ from first-year scores, it began to appear that psychologists might never behaviorally ferret out the intelligence that hid within a human infant. This led to the ultimate retreat: the infant possesses intelligence, but he simply does not have the behavioral repertoire to display it. This argument wraps the unitary, constant notion of intelligence in a security blanket that can never be penetrated by the chilling winds of scientific inquiry.

There have always been dissenting voices. Gesell said he never intended his tests to measure 'intelligence', and therefore he did not expect that they would predict later IQ. Stott and Ball (1965) and Bayley (1970) argued that mental performance underwent qualitative transformations and was not one thing that simply became more visible with development. And Piaget's (1952) comprehensive epigenetic view of development was in direct contradiction to the traditional conception of intelligence. As Piaget's influence gained in America, several investigators created assessments of infancy based upon Piagetian sensorimotor milestones (e.g. Uzgiris and Hunt and Corman and Escalona). While these Piaget-based assessments seem to have a certain face validity, there are far less actual psychometric data for these new forms of infant assessment than for the traditional methods. The upshot is a general dissatisfaction or disinterest in attempting to assess general mental development in human infants.

I believe we really have not taken Piagetian notions of development very seriously, and we have used infant tests to search for the wrong phenomena. It is ironic that the field of developmental psychology — presumably a study of *changes* over age — has spent much of its time looking for developmental continuities (Wohlwill, 1973). Finding little developmental stability, why haven't we inferred that changes are predominant and tried to describe such qualitative transitions in infant behavior?

In this paper I review selected portions of the data on stability and change in general infant test performance and then describe a slightly different strategy for viewing these data. I wish to persuade the reader that there are orderly and reasonable transitions that take the human infant successively through periods dominated by stimulus detection, exploration, imitation, vocal-verbal behavior, and symbolic language functioning. I will speculatively propose that despite these several qualitative transitions, there are one or two guiding themes that are not single abilities, skills, or g,[†] but common functions served in turn by different sets of behaviors and skills.

Stability and Change in Infant Test Performance

Cross-Age Correlations

If infant tests reflect something of a unitary, developmentally constant 'intelligence', then we should expect fairly strong age-to-age correlations among test scores within the infancy period and some prediction to childhood IQ.

Within Infancy. The issue of whether there are age-to-age correlations for infant tests was recently polarized by Lewis and McGurk (1972, 1973), Matheny (1973), and Wilson (1973). Lewis and McGurk argued for 'no reliable relationship between successive measures of infant intelligence during the first 24 months of life' (1972, p. 1,176), whereas Wilson presented moderate age-to-age correlations for a large sample of twins. Table 22.1 presents a few of the age-to-age correlations within the first three years of life for the precursor of the Bayley Infant Scale used in

Table 22.1: Age-to-Age Correlations for Infant Tests and Childhood IQ from the Fels and Berkeley Longitudinal Studies

Fels, Gesell[a]

Months	6	12	18
12	0.59		
18	0.52	0.57	
24	0.40	0.57	0.71

Berkeley, California (Bayley)[b]

Months	(4, 5, 6)	(10, 11, 12)	(18, 21, 24)
(10, 11, 12)	0.52		
(18, 21, 24)	0.23	0.60	
(27, 30, 36)	0.10	0.45	0.80

Fels (above) and Berkeley (below), Stanford-Binet[c]

Years	9	10	11	12
9		0.90	0.82	0.81
10	0.88		0.90	0.88
11	0.90	0.92		0.90
12	0.82	0.90	0.93	

[a]   Correlations between raw Gesell total scores for samples of 184-224 subjects from the Fels study (McCall *et al.*, 1972).
[b]   Correlations between standardized scores averaged over available tests at the three ages in months (from Bayley, 1949, p. 181).
[c]   Stanford-Binet age-to-age correlations for the Fels study above the diagonal (from Sontag *et al.*, 1958, p. 28) and for the Berkeley Growth Study below the diagonal (Bayley, 1949, p. 183).

the Berkeley Growth Study as reported by Bayley (1949) and for the Gesell Developmental Schedule employed in the Fels Longitudinal Study. As might be expected, the correlations are higher the shorter the interval between assessments, and they tend to increase as the infant gets older. These values are more similar to those of Wilson's twins than those of Lewis and McGurk's singleton sample.

While the age-to-age correlations for infant test scores are not zero, neither are they impressively high. This is especially true when one considers the proportion of shared variance (obtained by the squaring of these test-retest rs) and when these correlations are compared with analogous figures for childhood IQ assessments. For example, a typical correlation for a one-year test-retest interval for IQ between 9 and 12 years of life exceeds 0.90, but such values are in the 0.50s for infant tests in the first two years.

These results are typical and lead to the conclusion that while there is some degree of correspondence in relative infant test performance across 6- and 12-month intervals, the degree of association is not strong, especially when compared with analogous data from childhood IQ test-retest performance of the same children. The changes in relative position from one age to the next are more impressive than the similarities.

Infancy to Childhood. Given the modest age-to-age correlations within the infancy period, what is the level of prediction to childhood IQ scores for normal children? A summary of such data is presented in Table 22.2. These values represent correlations of test scores given to infants between 1 and 30 months of life with their childhood IQ scores obtained between 3 and 18 years. The correlation at any one test-retest interval represents the median over several different correlations reported by a variety of studies. These data follow the general trends observed for test-retest correlations within the infancy period (i.e. Table 22.1) in which the correlations are highest over the shorter retest intervals and highest for older children. Generally speaking, there is essentially no correlation between performance during the first six months of life with IQ score after age 5; the correlations are predominantly in the 0.20s for assessments made between 7 and 18 months of life when one is predicting IQ at 5-18 years; and it is not until 19-30 months that the infant test predicts later IQ in the range of 0.40-0.55.

Perhaps other variables have diluted these predictions — such as the reliability of the tests and sex differences. First, the low correlations are not totally a function of the reliability of the infant test, which is approximately as reliable after the third month of life as the Stanford-

Binet during childhood (McCall *et al.*, 1972). Second, these predictive correlations have rarely been calculated separately for the sexes, and some studies report that predictability occurs at a younger age (e.g. 12 months versus 18-24 months) and attains higher levels for girls than for boys (McCall *et al.*, 1972). Nevertheless, the basic trend observed in Table 22.2 holds true for both sexes. Third, there have been some attempts to supplement the infant test with measures of the socioeconomic status of the parents to make multivariate predictions of childhood IQ. At the young ages the socioeconomic status of the parents predicts childhood IQ better than the infant test, and it is not until 12 months for girls and 18 months for boys that the infant test increases the predictability. Finally, some have tried to look at specific behaviors within the infant test battery for their potential to predict later IQ. There has been one, but only one, notable discovery: the propensity of infant girls to vocalize in the testing context during the first year of life has shown correlations as high as 0.74 with verbal IQ at 26 years (Cameron *et al.*, 1967). This finding gains some support from other longitudinal studies (Kagan, 1969; McCall *et al.*, 1972; Moore, 1967). However, apart from vocalization by female infants, the predictions of specific item clusters to childhood IQ are generally not higher than for the total infant test score (McCall *et al.*, 1972).

Table 22.2: Median Correlations between Infant Tests and Childhood IQ for Normal Children

Childhood age (years)	Age in infancy (months)[a]			
	1–6	7–12	13–18	19–30
8–18	0.01	0.20	0.21	0.49
	(12/4)[b]	(8/2)	(6/2)	(9/2)
5–7	0.01	0.06	0.30	0.41
	(7/5)	(5/4)	(5/4)	(16/4)
3–4	0.23	0.33	0.47	0.54
	(7/4)	(5/3)	(6/4)	(16/3)

Alternative Approaches. Whenever an expected relationship is not observed, it is possible that the 'right' sample, age period, or combination of measures has not been tried. First, the above discussion concerns the relative lack of prediction from infancy to later IQ for essentially 'normal' samples. Of course, what constitutes normality is a matter of definition, but an exceptionally low score on an infant test, even in the first few months of life and even if a pediatrician has not diagnosed the infant as high risk, has some contemporary and predictive significance regarding developmental progress (Honzik *et al.*, 1965; McCall *et al.*, 1972; Werner *et al.*, 1968). But extremely high scores on an infant test in the first year are not predictive, and conversely, children who have IQs of 140 or higher at 4 years are essentially indistinct from the total population on the Bayley infant test at 8 months (Willerman and Fiedler, 1974). Thus, while the infant tests have diagnostic and predictive value when extremely low scores are involved, there is only modest cross-age consistency for 'normal' samples, including those with very high scores (McCall *et al.*, 1972).

Perhaps it is too much to ask that single infant scores should predict later IQ. For example, Gesell and others (Anastasi, 1968) have suggested that prediction to childhood IQ might be improved if the pattern of developmental change in infant test scores were considered. This approach has not been attempted in any serious way, though some preliminary analyses of the Berkeley Growth Study data have failed to reveal a relationship between pattern of infant test performance during the first two years of life and later IQ or change in IQ. Moreover, different patterns of IQ change between 2½ and 17 years are not associated with infant test scores or changes in infant test performance during the first two years. Of course, infant test performance over the first two years of life and childhood IQ between 2½ and 17 years may represent such gross developmental periods that important, but developmentally specific, relationships are obscured. These analyses are being continued.

Second, infant test scores might be supplemented with assessments of the child's personality or more specific parental behaviors. Child behaviors during the test session and in the home as well as specific parental-infant interaction variables have been shown to be modestly related to traditional and Piagetian test scores during the first two years of life (e.g. Bayley and Schaefer, 1964; Décarie, 1965; Matheny *et al.*, 1974; Wachs *et al.*, 1971). Whether prediction to childhood IQ would be enhanced significantly by the use of a combination of test scores (the total or specific item subsets) and such personality-social behaviors is still an open question.

Heredity-Environment and Infant Test Performance

The heredity-environment issue that has raged over childhood IQ performance has not been lost on infant testers. Before we take up this issue itself, it will be helpful to distinguish the general level of a child's performance from his developmental pattern or profile. *General level* denotes the average of a child's scores over some developmental period. In contrast, *developmental pattern* refers to the rises and falls in relative score over a given age span — whether the child increases, decreases, rises and then falls, etc. It is conceivable for general level and pattern to be independent of one another. That is, children could show rises in score value whether they averaged a developmental quotient (DQ) of 85 or 135. Further, two groups of children could have the same general level (e.g. DQ = 100) but some might show steep rises, others gradual declines, and still others U or inverted-U patterns. In actual fact, however, level and pattern are not independent, since infants having different age trends are also likely to have different general levels. The analysis of genetic correlates of differences in infant test performance has been done for the case in which general level and developmental profile are both permitted to determine the comparison groups as well as for the case in which only change in test score over age is involved. However, since general level and developmental profile are not independent in nature, this distinction is somewhat artificial.

Heritability

General Level Plus Developmental Pattern. Freedman and Keller (1963) reported that Bayley infant test performance between 2 and 12 months of age was more similar within monozygotic (MZ) than dizygotic (DZ) twins (20 pairs). Using the data from the Louisville Twin Study, Wilson (1972a, 1974; Wilson and Harpring, 1972) has also presented within-pair correlations for MZ and DZ twins. McCall (1972a; McCall *et al.*, 1973) compared siblings with unrelated children from the Fels sample, and Nichols and Broman (1974) presented correlations for monozygotic and dizygotic twins as well as for siblings from the Collaborative Perinatal Project. What can be concluded from these studies with respect to the heritability of the general level of infant test performance?

These data suggest extraordinarily consistent and high correlations within pairs of MZ twins — rs between 0.81 and 0.85, values that approach (and sometimes exceed) the reliability of the test based upon singleton infants. The correlations for DZ twins are less consistent but always lower than for MZs, rs ranging between 0.55 and 0.74 for samples containing different ages, races, and sexes. So far there appears to be some heritability for the general level of infant test performance since the within-pair correlations for MZ twins are higher than for DZ twins by approximately 0.07 to 0.30.

This conclusion is made suspect by a variety of methodological problems (McCall, 1972a,b; McCall *et al.*, 1973; Wachs, 1972; Wilson, 1972b) and the disturbing fact that the correlations for singleton siblings are fairly consistent across studies and very modest in size — 0.15-0.37. If DZ twins and siblings both share 50 per cent of their genes on the average, why is the correlation among DZ twins from two to five times larger than for siblings?

Nichols and Broman (1974) have provided a possible answer. In the Collaborative Perinatal Project there was a tendency for serious retardation to be six to nine times more frequent among twins than among single births. Obviously this figure depends on how one defines retardation, but Nichols and Broman used a very conservative definition in which less than 1 in 10,000 children should be retarded if the distribution of scores were normal. Moreover, the incidence of severe retardation is almost twice as great among MZ as among DZ twins, and both MZ twin members are twice as likely to be retarded as are both members of DZ pairs. Therefore, there is heritability for severe retardation on the Bayley at 8 months of age. But what happens to the MZ versus DZ correlations when such retarded children are eliminated from the sample and only 'normals' remain? When this was done, Nichols and Broman reported that the correlations for MZ and DZ twins are virtually identical — $r = 0.55$! Therefore *among normal twins* there is no evidence for heritability of general level at 8 months of age.

But even after severe retardates are eliminated from the twin sample, the within-pair correlation for DZs is two to three times the correlation for siblings. McCall (1972a; McCall *et al.*, 1973) and Nichols and Broman (1974) have suggested that twins may have much more similar prenatal environments than do siblings, as suggested by the fact that concordance for retardation was 3.6 times more likely among DZ twins than among siblings (Nichols and Broman, 1974). Since DZ twins and singleton siblings are genetically comparable, some nongenetic factor (e.g. prenatal environment) must be involved. Moreover, twins tend to be tested at the same age on the same day, whereas a test at the same chronological age may be administered to siblings in different calendar years. Finally, no one really knows how much of the sibling correlation is due to common environmental factors, since no one has tested unrelated infants reared in the same home as an environmental control for the sibling relationship. In any case, the sibling correlations of 0.15-0.37 for infant test scores are substantially below the median sibling correlation of 0.55 (Jensen, 1969) for child and adult IQ.

The conclusion seems to be that there is heritability for serious mental retardation detectable by infant tests, but when such severe cases are eliminated there is no evidence for heritability of infant test score among twins in the first year of life. Further, samples of twins are not typical representatives of samples of singletons for nongenetic reasons — concordance for retardation is substantially more frequent among DZ twins than among siblings, despite their genetic comparability. Presumably, prenatal and perinatal environments are more similar and more risky for DZ twins than for siblings. Moreover testing procedures favor higher correlations for twins than for siblings. Finally, although siblings do correlate above zero, it is not yet possible to separate environmental from genetic contributors to this correlation, which is substantially lower than for childhood IQ. The evidence for a strong heritable component to infant test performance in the first year of life among normal infants is weak at best and more probably negligible (Scarr-Salapatek, 1974).

It is clear from the literature on the heritability of childhood IQ (Jensen, 1969), from the increasing correlations with development between the IQs of biological parents and their adopted children (Honzik, 1957), and from the emerging correlations with age between infant scores obtained from a parent (as an infant) and his child as an infant (Eichorn, 1969; McCall *et al.*, 1973) that there is a gradual increase in heritability for general mental test performance after the first year, which reaches adult levels between 4 and 6 years of age. These observations suggest that individual differences in mental test performance become progressively more closely associated with differences in the genetic composition of those individuals.

It is interesting to note that increasing heritability roughly coincides with the introduction of verbal items on the infant tests and the increased emphasis on verbal and abstract-symbolic reasoning on the IQ tests. Moreover, as heritability rises, so do the cross-age correlations between IQ retests. These observations are consistent with the proposition that the development of mental performance undergoes major qualitative shifts during the first few years of life, but that once verbal skills and abstract reasoning are available the general nature of behaviors called *intellectual* by our society is established and cross-age IQ correlations approach their highest levels.

Pattern Over Age. When it comes to the heritability of the pattern of infant test performance over age, the issues are the same but the data on both sides of the argument are less decisive. Wilson (1972a,b; 1974) and Wilson and Harpring (1972) have argued that MZ twins are more similar in their developmental profile for several developmental periods (e.g. 3-12 months, 12-24 months, 18-36 months, and 3-5 years) but not between 5 and 6 years. McCall (1972a,b; McCall *et al.*, 1973) has criticized the results for the first two years of life and many of his comments also apply to Wilson's later publication (1974). In contrast to Wilson's twin data, McCall's analysis of the infant test scores from the Fels study indicated no greater pattern similarity for singleton siblings than for unrelated children during the first year, during the second year, and during the first two years, or for IQ test performance between 3 and 12 years, between 3 and 6 years, or between 6 and 12 years of age (McCall *et al.*, 1973). Moreover, the issue is further complicated to the extent that the findings and implications of the Nichols and Broman (1974) data on the heritability of mental retardation among twins versus singleton siblings are also applicable to the pattern of test scores over age. Objectively one would conclude that the waters are too muddy and that there is no unambiguous evidence either way on the heritability of profile contour. In a less charitable moment, however, I am yet to be convinced of any genetic correlates of developmental profile in infant test or childhood IQ performance.

Environmental Influences

Regardless of the questions concerning the heritability data, it seems unequivocal that there is a major genetic component to individual differences in infant test performance that is larger than for childhood IQ. Nevertheless, it is quite another issue to specify what those environmental circumstances might be. Most attempts to relate traditional indices of between-family environmental differences to Gesell and Bayley test performance in the first year have been unsuccessful. For example, parental education and other presumed measures of socioeconomic status do not relate to mental test performance until 2-5 years of age (McCall *et al.*, 1972). In contrast, socioeconomic status shows correlations between 0.25 and 0.50 for childhood IQ.

Of course, general SES may be too abstract and far removed from the actual functional parent-child interactions. These may nevertheless influence certain infant skills that in turn are masked when the total score is used. An indication that some of the environmental factors in infant and childhood test performance may be rather complicated and specific is implied in the sibling comparisons for developmental profile. If siblings are not more similar in their pattern of test scores over age, then changes within the infancy and childhood periods are apparently not related to those general intellectual characteristics of the home that are likely to be shared by siblings of that family. Such attributes as parental value for intellectual behaviors, reward for intellectual and academic performance, parental modeling of such behaviors, and the opportunity for educational and enriching experiences — factors that are frequently proposed as environmental determinants for IQ — are apparently not correlates of developmental change in infant and childhood mental test performance (though they may influence general level). One possible implication is that particular environmental events do not have the same influence on all children or even the same child at different ages (McCall *et al.*, 1973).

One conclusion seems to be that there are major nongenetic factors affecting the general level and developmental pattern of infant test performance, and that these factors are probably not global in character or easily summarized under 'general social status' or 'intellectual climate of the home'. In view of Nichols and Broman's (1974) data suggesting prenatal nongenetic influences on retardation rates among twins, perhaps one could search for early biological rather than social environmental influences on first-year infant test performance.

Interpretation. A summary of the above data represents a curious anomaly: both the heritability and the correlations between mental test performance and general indices of socioeconomic status increase with age. How can ostensible environmental and genetic contributions to mental test performance *both* increase? There are many possible explanations, but I favor one that emphasizes the proposition that the qualitative nature of mental performance − and thus its environmental and genetic determinants − changes over the infancy period. Thus nongenetic biological circumstances (e.g. prenatal environment, nutrition, state, and cooperativeness) may be related to infant test performance in the first few months because the test emphasizes basic perceptual alertness, neuromotor functions, and sensorimotor and social responsiveness − factors that may be relatively inconsistent within an infant from one testing to another. But such factors become less important with development, because the skills being tested emphasize vocabulary, verbal fluency, reasoning, and memory − abilities that are influenced by social-educational experiences and that are more stable across time for an individual. Thus the larger nongenetic variance in first-year infant test performance may be a function of temporary biological and social factors that we have largely failed to specify and measure, whereas the environmental factors that influence later test performance are of a different genre, more social-educational than earlier, more stable across time, and more commonly measured.

Actually the heritability values reported above, which inspired this speculation, have very little implication for the nature of the development of mental performance. First, very low heritabilities (e.g. for first-year test performance) do not necessarily imply that genes have no role in infant mental development. Heritability values only reveal the extent to which *differences between infants* are associated with differences in their geno-types. Who would deny that the infant's neuromotor development and general ontogeny of behavioral propensities and skills are not heavily dependent upon genetic codes and programs? To interpret a low or zero heritability as indicating that development of these characteristics is totally environmental is to postulate a new kind of creation. Rather, *differences* between infants in their general level or developmental pattern of test performance are not predominantly reflections of their differences in genetic composition. Indeed, as proposed above, it is possible that early in infancy such development is so characteristic of the species that differences between individuals simply constitute variations in measurement error, contemporary emotional or attention states, co-operativeness, time since the last nap or feeding, and other uninteresting, transient, but nevertheless nongenetic variables.

But the converse of this argument is also true. Even though herita-bilities for childhood IQ are high, this fact alone does not imply that environment plays no role or that it makes a vastly subordinate con-tribution to the development of childhood mental skills. Again, herita-bilities refer to the possible genetic correlates of differences between individuals, not necessarily to the basic development of such character-istics in the species. Moreover, high heritabilities themselves do not provide an indication of how easily a phenotype trait can be altered by appropriate and timely intervention — hair color can be changed easily but one's sex cannot. Phenylketonuria and TB once had high heritabilities, but these diseases are largely under medical control now. With respect to IQ, a high heritability does not necessarily imply that it cannot be changed, and Heber's Milwaukee project (Heber *et al.*, 1972) demonstrated that IQs can be raised as much as two standard deviations (e.g. 30 points) by early intervention and education.

In short, high or low heritabilities for general level or developmental profile do not tell us much about the dynamics of mental development in infants and children.

Infant Tests as a Psychometric Tool

Given the above discussion, what is the status of infant tests as a psycho-metric assessment technique?

A Question of Validity

First, the tests are clearly valuable in detecting abnormality and retarda-tion. After reviewing the literature on the use of infant tests in detecting abnormality, McCall *et al.* (1972) concluded that:

> . . . infant tests may have contemporary as well as predictive utility in identifying pathological and 'suspect' conditions in infancy, and a very low score on an infant test, even though a pediatrician does not classify the child as abnormal (and vice versa), may have diagnostic value. [p. 730]

However, with regard to essentially normal samples, test scores from the first year of life have essentially no practical utility in predicting later performance. In view of this fact, some have gone so far as to suggest that infant tests be abandoned as assessments of individual differences among essentially normal children (Lewis and McGurk, 1972, 1973). A frequent response to the empirical failure of infant tests to predict later IQ is that they were never intended to do so, and while they do not have predictive validity they have contemporary validity as an assessment of a child's current developmental status (e.g. Bayley, 1970). But somehow this claim is meaningless to many psychologists. Apparently, the faith in a constant, unitary intelligence is so strong that many feel that if the infant test has no predictive validity it has no validity whatsoever. What purpose is served to know a child's current developmental status if it tells nothing about that child's future performance?

Consider an analogous situation in pediatrics. A physician finds a newborn's birth weight an important piece of information, especially in conjunction with an estimate of the child's gestational age, despite the fact that among normal children birth weight does not predict stature in childhood. The 'small-for-dates' newborn may have a variety of special problems that can be monitored or treated but that are unique to the newborn period. Birth weight is a valid sign of current status without much predictive utility. Analogously, infant tests are sensitive to behavioral and neurological abnormalities, and the infant test coupled with a skilled pediatrician can be quite valuable in diagnosing abnormality (McCall *et al.*, 1972).

But does the infant test have contemporary validity for normal infants? Unfortunately there is precious little traditional psychometric validity data for normal samples, largely because there is no obvious criterion against which the infant test can be evaluated. Pediatric judgment of developmental progress is a possibility, but the tests represent an attempt to make just such clinical impressions more objective and accurate. Indeed the tests have become the criterion of infant developmental status. The face validity of infant assessments is so great that there is relatively little 'mental' behavior that characterizes an infant that is not represented on these tests. It is small wonder that each new infant test differs only slightly from its predecessors and correlates rather highly with them (McCall *et al.*, 1972). This 'criterion problem' may force us into accepting or rejecting infant tests largely on the basis of their face validity and contemporary utility.

White Elephant

Perhaps infant researchers have been chasing a white elephant. The assumption underlying the research reviewed above is that there is continuity in infant test performance during the first year or two of life, but the results are not profoundly supportive of that view, especially for the first year of life. Indeed a theme that recurs in the interpretation of these results suggests marked developmental transitions in the fundamental character of infant mental performance.

Ironically, developmental psychologists are not prone to investigate changes. The history of developmental psychology, especially within the context of longitudinal studies, represents the quest for continuity and stability and not the attempt to describe ontogenetic change. We have correlated scores and behaviors at one age with the same or different scores and behaviors at a very distant age. Having limited ourselves to this strategy, what else could we find? We either obtain significant correlations and pronounce the existence of stability, or we do not obtain such correlations and are left with the ambiguities of accepting the null hypothesis. Since the only acceptable scientific product of such a strategy is the 'discovery' of continuity, our theoretical conceptions and statistical methods have denied us the privilege of observing development, a term that implies change and transformation with age (McCall, 1974; Wohlwill, 1973). In this sense, we have rarely studied infant mental development.

Assuming the infant tests are reliable samples of a significant portion of the infant's behavioral repertoire, it might be profitable to explore the test protocols for the purpose of describing such qualitative transitions in the development of mental behavior. If these transitions are marked, the determinants of one type of behavior at one age may be quite different from the determinants of another type of behavior at a developmentally distant age, and there may not be a sizable correlation between precocity at one age and precocity at quite another age. However, since it is reasonable to expect that a child who finishes a given stage early relative to other children should embark on the next stage (but not necessarily quite distant stages) relatively early, there may be correlational relationships among rather specific types of behaviors at adjacent developmental periods that might reveal the nature of these transitions. In short, perhaps we should shift our attention from an attempt to find stability and continuity to an attempt to describe and hypothesize about the nature of developmental change in infant mental behavior.

Developmental Transitions in Mental Behavior

Analysis of the Fels Data

McCall *et al.* (1972) recently attempted to pursue this course by examining responses to the items on the Gesell at 6, 12, 18 and 24 months for subjects in the Fels Longitudinal Study. The purpose was to look at more specific item clusters rather than total test scores and to determine paths of correlational association between item sets at one age and item sets at adjacent ages. Principal components analyses were performed on the item responses separately at each age, and then the component scores from these analyses were correlated across age.

The first principal components at each age correlated among themselves for both males and females. No other set of components showed such a strong correlational pattern across all the ages. Statistically these results are not surprising, but their advantage lies in the fact that the first principal components at each age contain fewer items than the total test, and one can be more specific about which behaviors are involved in these major developmental transitions.

At 6 months the items loading on the first principal component were interpreted to reflect visually guided exploration of perceptual contingencies. For example, the items 'reaches for dangling ring', 'lifts inverted cup', 'bangs spoon on table', 'splashes in tub', 'conscious of fallen objects', and 'pats table' all describe manipulation that produces some clear, contingent perceptual consequence. The fact that Piaget (1952) emphasized such behavior in his concept of circular response and that infants (e.g. in Rovee and Rovee, 1969; Siqueland, 1969; Watson, 1972) as well as animals (e.g. in McCall, 1965, 1966) will perform simple responses in order to produce a contingent perceptual event makes this interpretation appealing.

The exploration of perceptual contingencies at 6 months correlated with a mixture of sensorimotor and social imitation plus rudimentary vocal-verbal behavior at 12 months. While many items at 12 months have previously been interpreted to reflect fine motor skill, most of these items request the infant to imitate the examiner in performing a rather simple motor behavior, one that is well within the physical competence of the child. Consequently the items 'rings bell in imitation', 'imitates rattle of spoon in cup', 'builds tower of two to three cubes', 'puts cube in cup', 'performance box', and 'scribbles in imitation' all require the child to imitate the examiner's simple motor action. Also loaded on this component were several diverse behaviors that seemed to reflect the learning of social interactions and simple verbal skills (e.g. 'waves bye-bye', 'says three to five words', 'says bye-bye or hello' and 'plays peek or pat-a-cake'). This implies that social-verbal behavior and imitation of fine motor behaviors are related activities, and it seems reasonable that the child who develops the tendency to imitate does so in a social context, playing reciprocal sensorimotor and vocal-verbal imitation games with his parents. The similarity to Piaget's (1951) theorizing as well as to Hunt's (1961) interpretation of it is striking.

These behaviours at 6 and 12 months were correlated with verbal and motor imitation items (e.g. 'scribbles in imitation', 'repeats things said' and 'throws ball in box') and especially verbal production ('names pictures', 'repeats things said', 'says five or more words', 'requests things at table', 'names watch', 'uses two or more words together') and verbal comprehension ('points to several pictures', 'points to parts of body') at 18 months.

By 24 months the main developmental trend was even more strongly verbal in character. While imitation was still present (e.g. 'imitates simple drawn patterns', 'puts cube in cup, plate, box'), the predominant theme featured the verbal skills of production and labeling ('names five pictures', 'names watch', 'asks for things at table by name', 'names five familiar objects', 'uses color names'), verbal comprehension ('points at several pictures', 'listens to stories with pictures'), and fluent verbal production and grammatical maturity ('speaks in sentences', 'tells name', 'tells experiences', 'uses pronouns', 'asks for things at table by name', 'knows prepositions').

These data provide a more specific description of the possible nature of transitions in mental behaviour than might be obtained from a simple look at total scores. Although the analyses were not done with an *a priori* theory in mind, the results are remarkable consistent with Piaget's description of mental development in the first two years of life. That is, at 6 months the child is predominantly an explorer of perceptual consequences: he studies the perceptual-cognitive information or uncertainty in his environment. An important aspect of this exploration is the contingent consequences to his physical interaction with the environment. By 12 months his 'environment' is more likely to include social beings with whom he engages in reciprocal imitation of sensorimotor and rudimentary verbal behaviors. As his ability increases to symbolize mentally, his language improves and he continues to imitate the verbal-vocal social behavior of adults as well as to demonstrate skills in vocabulary comprehension and production. By 24 months the dominant theme has evolved into grammatical fluency and production.

Very preliminary analyses are under way of the Berkeley Growth Study infant test data in collaboration with Dorothy Eichorn, Study Director, and Paul Mussen, Director of the Institute of Human Development, University of California at Berkeley. The early results of analyses similar to those reported above for the Fels data are quite concordant with these interpretations.

Speculations on a Theory of Epigenetic Developmental Transitions

Sensorimotor Behavior and Language. At a general level these observations are consistent with a Piagetian concept of epigenetic development in which qualitatively different behaviors build upon their predecessors, unfolding in a logical sequence. An important point is that there are relationships between diverse behavioral emphases (e.g. sensorimotor exploration, imitation and language) within and across ages that suggest it would be profitable to consider early language, for example, as somehow emerging from, or at least related to, antecedent sensorimotor behaviors.

Formerly, many language scholars believed in innate language acquisition (e.g. McNeill, 1970). The infant was so dominated by inherited structures which predisposed him to language that almost no experience, save the presence of a language environment, was necessary for language to unfold according to a maturational schedule. Simplified, language began when the child uttered his first word. On the other side, researchers of sensorimotor and perceptual-cognitive behavior in early infancy rarely concerned themselves with language. They acknowledged that language was an important development, but no concerted attempt was made to view the phenomena of exploration, conjugate reinforcement, or sensorimotor imitation in early infancy as being related to the subsequent emergence of language. In contrast, Piaget described epigenetic transitions in which sensorimotor behavior became intimately meshed with the development of language, but American scientists studied only one behavioural aspect of Piaget's theory at a time and even then it was often not researched developmentally. In American research Piaget is popular in pieces, not for his developmental purview.

More recently there have been major shifts within the language community that are more friendly to the notion that early language might represent a logical outgrowth of sensorimotor behavior. No longer is early language thought to be simply the unfolding of an innate language, complete with its own grammar, that is manifested regardless of the adult language environment. Rather, it is now recognized that language develops because the child needs to communicate something (Brown, 1973). Brown and others see early one- and two-word sentences not as exemplars of a pivot-open grammar but rather as servants to semantic goals. The child's early utterances are attempts to communicate or declare something meaningful, and the semantic categories that early language fulfills are remarkable similar to sensorimotor learning and behavior.

For example, prominent semantic functions of early language are *nomination, recurrence, nonexistence, location,* and *agent-action-object* declarations (Brown, 1973). The child's incessant naming of objects (e.g. 'that ball') and requests for recurrence (e.g. 'more ball') presupposes that the child recognizes objects and actions. Nomination is not unlike the Piagetian sensorimotor recognitory assimilation in which the child reels off a set of motor actions that have been habitually associated with a given object or event. The infant is likely to wander past a mechanical toy and give it a shove to produce a varied set of sights and sounds; in the same way, when he passes the stove he says 'stove' and perhaps attributes a quality of heat to it by simply stating 'hot'. His requests for recurrence of objects or events are very similar to the circular responses in which the child repeats an action to reproduce an interesting sight or sound. His propensity to declare the nonexistence of an object (e.g. 'all-gone-ball') presupposes the capacity of object permanence as well as an expectation that an object or an event should exist or occur in a given situation but that such an expectation has not been confirmed. Similarly he frequently utters pronouncements on the location of objects (e.g. 'book table') that require a concept of object permanence and a memory in which he knows the object does not disappear but changes location (e.g. 'where X?'). Such prerequisites are developed in early sensorimotor experience. Finally, when two- and three-word sentences arrive, they often fall into the agent-action-object category. Piaget believes that very early in infancy the child does not perceive agent, action and object as independent from one another but comes to this perception through sensorimotor interaction with his environment. The child's experience with manipulating objects and observing the consequences of his manipulation represents a direct sensory analogue for agent-action-object verbal utterances (Brown, 1973).

The Fels data reveal correlations between early sensorimotor behavior and elementary language. These results may challenge the simplistic notion that language begins with the first word. While one must be careful not to infer that events that come developmentally early necessarily cause those that follow, a correlation at least suggests that maturational precocity at one stage relates to maturational precocity at a later stage. Further, there is the possibility that the correlation implies more than just stability in general development and maturation — perhaps such particular sensori-motor behaviors indeed represent necessary antecedent schema for language to build upon. At the very least such hypotheses cannot be so glibly dismissed as was once fashionable.

Developmental Themes. Although the behaviors at various points during the first three years of life differ in their qualitative details, they never-theless seem to serve common purposes or themes. These purposes fall roughly into two classes. The first is the *reduction of perceptual-cognitive uncertainty*. The child takes in information about the world and frequently checks on the validity of that information. During the first year he explores the attributes of objects — their size, color, texture, weight, plasticity, and function. Later he discovers there is something else to be learned about objects and events: they have names ('that ball'), locations ('book table'), and attributes ('big ball'), and are possessed by certain people ('Johnny ball'), etc.

A second pervasive function is a corollary of the first. The child has an influence on his environment — behaviors that we might call *affectance* (White, 1959). At first the child manipulates objects as if he were asking, 'What can this object do?' Later, after he is more familiar with the nature of the object, the emphasis shifts from what the *object* can do to what *he* can do with the object (Hutt, 1970). When language is available, he may simply describe his affectance behaviors in the manner of a verbal circular response. For example, after throwing a ball down the stairs and out of sight, the child may describe the event (e.g. 'ball go'), declare its dis-appearance or nonexistence (e.g. 'all-gone ball'), or state a wish for its recurrence (e.g. 'more ball'). Even one-word utterances often represent attempts to affect the environment, not just describe it, such as a request for milk expressed when the child says 'milk' while pointing to the milk carton or holding an empty glass. And how effective is the defiant 'No!' in producing responses from a parent? Later, agent-action-object utter-ances are employed to affect environmental consequences (e.g. 'I wanna cookie'). How analogous are the child's early manipulation of objects, circular responses, and gesturing to these simple verbal attempts to pro-duce environmental (inanimate and social) consequences?

The proposal is that the reduction of perceptual-cognitive uncertainty — discovering the attributes and functions of objects and events in one's world — and the propensity of infants toward affecting their environment are themes or functions that underlie many of the diverse behaviors that evolve sequentially during the first three years.

Transitions. The data presented above suggest an orderly set of transitions guided by these themes. During the first few months the infant is simply a stimulus-detection device. He attends to objects as a function of their perceptual information, which may be embodied in their physical structure (e.g. contour density, brightness and movement) or their discrepancy from familiar experiences. As the child's motor abilities develop, he uses them to serve exploration by moving himself near objects of interest and manipulating them to expose their various features. The process of acquiring perceptual information about an object is tantamount to attributing rudimentary meaning to it, since we call an object or an event 'meaningful' partially as a function of the number of remembered associations called forth by its character and function. With the child's propensity to explore he discovers that objects roll, bounce, make noise, change shape, etc., when manipulated. Such contingent and/or conjugate reinforcement enhances the manipulatory behavior, and the child not only learns the static physical properties of an object but also what it can do. As the child becomes able to distinguish between himself as the agent and the action he performs and both of these from the object and its consequence, he explores different means to the same or different ends and what *he* can do with the object rather than what the object can do. Again the themes are perceptual-cognitive uncertainty and its corollary affectance.

It is at this point that sensorimotor imitation begins to play a more prominent role. At first, imitation tends to be adults imitating baby, who then repeats his own action. This is pseudoimitation because the child does not imitate a new behavior but merely repeats one that is already in his repertoire. Nevertheless such imitation games represent a social extrapolation of the exploration of perceptual-cognitive uncertainty and contingent consequences of the child's action. Perhaps the infant accidentally sighs and blows a bubble through his drool, the parent imitates him forthwith, the child repeats the action, and he is immediately rewarded by the parent who imitates him again. He is not only exploring the nature of this social object but also his social affectance.

Vocal behavior is a favorite activity for these pseudoimitation games. Moreover vocal behavior seems to serve the same functions as sensorimotor exploration: the reduction of perceptual-cognitive uncertainty through nomination (i.e. labeling or requests for labels, 'dat?' or 'what dat?'), attribution, location, etc., and social affectance (requests for recurrence or the 2-year-old's defiant 'No!'). Objects have size, shape, color, and now verbal labels, 'I can make an object rock, fall, wiggle, and with language I can make other people vocalize, smile, talk to me, fetch me a cookie, and even get angry.' If the functions that early language serves are well practised in the sensorimotor period and transferred from the inanimate world to the social world by imitation, it is reasonable to expect that language comprehension precedes production at this stage (Blank, 1974).

The discussion above suggests that elementary vocalization and labeling, requests for recurrence, attribution, location, and agent-action-object utterances are simple verbal analogues to well-exercised sensorimotor behaviors. But why does more advanced language behavior develop? Blank (1974) has suggested that sensorimotor behavior, such as gestures and their verbal analogues, are inefficient next to more advanced verbal behavior and are nearly useless when it comes to expressing cognitions and affectance with respect to objects that are not present in the immediate environment. If a youngster wants to play with the big-wheeler that is on a shelf in the garage, it is about as efficient to point at it as it is to ask for it verbally. But how does a child at home obtain by gestures alone a big-wheeler that he saw yesterday on TV? Language is needed. And how does a young child respond nonverbally to a parent's demand, '*How* did this mess get here?' or '*Why* did you pour the ink in the bathtub?' No amount of gesturing can deal with 'how' and 'why' questions. Gesturing and sensorimotor actions simply become inefficient next to the potentiality of language for serving the goals of acquiring information and meaning about objects and affecting one's environment. Moreover, the social environment makes demands on the child that simply cannot be handled by gestural responses. Parents model the appropriate verbal behaviors and reward the child for imitating them. In the simplest terms the themes of reducing uncertainty and affectance are the same; only the behavioral method has shifted from gestures to words.

Notice that beyond the level of elementary vocalization and verbal labeling and comprehension, more advanced language depends heavily on the symbolic function and memory. The most basic of these appears to be object permanence: the child must remember that an object exists after it has disappeared in order to declare its disappearance or nonexistence verbally and request its recurrence. Moreover there is no way for the child to handle the 'not here' and 'not now' situations that reward the development of advanced language concepts and communication skills without having representational thought and perceptual/verbal memory.

The sequence and nature of the behaviors that form the main set of developmental transitions in the Fels data are consistent with this developmental scenario.

Acknowledgment

Portions of the research reported in this paper were sponsored by Public Health Service grants NIE 6-00-3-0008 and HD-04160 to Robert B. McCall, by FR-15537, HD-00868, and FR-00222 to the Fels Research Institute, and by the Samuel S. Fels Fund of Philadelphia. The Fels data are the result of 45 years of effort by numerous staff individuals under the direction of Lester W. Sontag and now Frank Falkner and by the enduring faith of Samuel Fels and later the foundation that he endowed. I thank Carol Dodds, Dorothy Eichorn, Robert Kavanaugh, Rosemary Raterman, and Joanne Steinhiber for their several contributions to this paper.

References

Anastasi, A., 1968, *Psychological Testing*, Macmillan, New York.
Bayley, N., 1949, 'Consistency and variability in the growth of intelligence from birth to eighteen years', *Journal of Genetic Psychology, 75*: 165.
Bayley, N., 1970, 'Development of mental abilities', in P.H. Mussen (ed.), *Carmichael's Manual of Child Psychology* (3rd edn), vol. 1, Wiley, New York, p. 1163.
Bayley, N. and Schaeffer, E.S., 1964, 'Correlations of maternal and child behaviors with development of mental ability: Data from the Berkeley Growth Study', *Monographs of the Society for Research in Child Development, 29* (97).
Blank, M., 1974, 'Cognitive functions of language in the preschool years', *Developmental Psychology, 10*: 229.
Brown, R., 1973, *A First Language*, Harvard University Press, Cambridge, Massachusetts.
Cameron, J., Livson, N. and Bayley, N., 1967, 'Infant vocalizations and their relationship to mature intelligence', *Science, 157*: 331.
Décarie, T., 1965, *Intelligence and Affectivity in Early Childhood*, International Universities Press, New York.
Eichorn, D.H., September 1969, 'Developmental parallels in the growth of parents and their children', Presidential Address, Division 7, APA.
Freedman, D.G. and Keller, B., 1963, 'Inheritance of behavior in infants', *Science, 140*: 196.
Heber, R., Garber, H., Harrington, S., Hoffman, C. and Falender, C., December 1972, 'Rehabilitation of families at risk for mental retardation', progress report, Rehabilitation Research and Training Center in Mental Retardation, University of Wisconsin, Madison.
Honzik, M.P., 1957, 'Developmental studies of parent-child resemblance in intelligence', *Child Development, 28*: 215.
Honzik, M.P., Hutchings, J.J. and Burnip, S.R., 1965, 'Birth record assessments and test performance at eight months', *American Journal of Diseases in Children, 109*: 416.
Hunt, J.McV., 1961, *Intelligence and Experience*, Ronald Press, New York.
Hutt, C., 1970, 'Specific and diversive exploration', in H.W. Reese and L.P. Lipsitt (eds.), *Advances in Child Development and Behavior*, vol. 5, Academic Press, New York, p. 119.
Jensen, A.R., 1969, 'How much can we boost IQ and scholastic achievement?',

Harvard Educational Review, 39: 1.

Kagan, J., 1969, 'On the meaning of behavior: Illustrations from the infant', *Child Development, 40*: 1121.

Lewis, M. and McGurk, H., 1972, 'Evaluation of infant intelligence', *Science, 178*: 1,174.

Lewis, M. and McGurk, H., 1973, 'Testing infant intelligence', *Science, 182*: 737.

Matheny, A.P., Jr., 1973, 'Testing infant intelligence', *Science, 182*: 734.

Matheny, A.P., Jr., Dolan, A.B. and Wilson, R.S., 1974, 'Bayley's infant behavior record: Relations between behaviors and mental test scores', *Developmental Psychology, 10*: 696.

McCall, R.B., 1965, 'Stimulus-change in light-contingent bar pressing', *Journal of Comparative and Physiological Psychology, 59*: 258.

McCall, R.B., 1966, 'The initial-consequent-change surface in light-contingent bar pressing', *Journal of Comparative and Physiological Psychology, 62*: 35.

McCall, R.B., 1972a, 'Similarity in developmental profile among related pairs of human infants', *Science, 178*: 1004.

McCall, R.B., 1972b, 'Similarity in IQ profile among related pairs: Infancy and childhood', Proceedings of the American Psychological Association meeting, Honolulu, p. 79.

McCall, R.B., 1974, 'Critique of a field, review of *The Study of Behavioral Development* by J.E. Wohlwill', *Science, 184*: 673.

McCall, R.B., Hogarty, P.S. and Hurlburt, N., 1972, 'Transitions in infant sensorimotor development and the prediction of childhood IQ', *American Psychologist, 27*: 728.

McCall, R.B., Appelbaum, M.I. and Hogarty, P.S., 1973, 'Developmental changes in mental performance', *Monographs of the Society for Research in Child Development, 38* (3, serial no. 150).

McNeill, D., 1970, 'The development of language' in P.H. Mussen (ed.), *Carmichael's Manual of Child Psychology* (3rd edn.), vol. 1, Wiley, New York, p. 1061.

Moore, T., 1967, 'Language and intelligence: A longitudinal study of the first eight years, Part I: Patterns of development in boys and girls', *Human Development, 10*: 88.

Nichols, P.L. and Broman, S.H., 1974, 'Familial resemblances in infant mental development', *Developmental Psychology, 10*: 442.

Piaget, J., 1951, *Play, Dreams, and Imitation in Childhood*, translation of *La formation du symbole chez l'enfant*, by C. Gattegno and F.N. Hodgson, Norton, New York.

Piaget, J., 1952, *The Origins of Intelligence in Children*, International Universities Press, New York.

Rovee, C.K. and Rovee, D.T., 1969, 'Conjugate reinforcement of infant exploratory behavior', *Journal of Experimental Child Psychology, 8*: 33.

Scarr-Salapatek, S., February 1974, 'Genetic determinants of infant development: An overstated case', paper presented at the American Association for the Advancement of Science, San Francisco.

Siqueland, E.R., April 1969, 'The development of instrumental exploratory behavior during the first year of human life', paper presented at SRCD, Santa Monica.

Sontag, L.W., Baker, C.T. and Nelson, V.L., 1958, 'Mental growth and personality development: A longitudinal study', *Monographs of the Society for Research in Child Development, 23* (68).

Stott, L.H. and Ball, R.S., 1965, 'Infant and preschool mental tests: Review and evaluation', *Monographs of the Society for Research in Child Development, 30* (101).

Wachs, T.D., 1972, 'Technical comment', *Science, 178*: 1005.

Wachs, T.D., Uzgiris, I.C. and Hunt, J.McV., 1971, 'Cognitive development in infants of different age levels and from different environmental backgrounds: An explanatory investigation', *Merrill-Palmer Quarterly, 17*: 283.

Watson, J.S., 1972, 'Smiling, cooing, and "the game" ', *Merrill-Palmer Quarterly, 18*: 323.

Werner, E.E., Honzik, M.P. and Smith, R.S., 1968, 'Prediction of intelligence and achievement at 10 years from 20 months pediatric and psychologic examinations', *Child Development, 39*: 1063.

White, R.W., 1959, 'Motivation reconsidered: The concept of competence', *Psychological Review, 66*: 297.

Willerman, L. and Fiedler, M.F., 1974, 'Infant performance and intellectual precocity', *Developmental Psychology, 45*: 483.

Wilson, R.S., 1972a, 'Twins: Early mental development', *Science, 175*: 914.

Wilson, R.S., 1972b, 'Technical comment', *Science, 178*: 1006.

Wilson, R.S., 1973, 'Testing infant intelligence', *Science, 182*: 734.

Wilson, R.S., 1974, 'Twins: Mental development in the preschool years', *Developmental Psychology, 10*: 580.

Wilson, R.S. and Harpring, E.B., 1972, 'Mental and motor development in infant twins', *Developmental Psychology, 7*: 277.

Wohlwill, J.F., 1973, *The Study of Behavioral Development*, Academic Press, New York.

SECTION SEVEN: LONGITUDINAL STUDIES

Introduction

This final section follows on logically from the previous section, which was beginning to develop some ideas on how to represent adequately the complexity of early cognitive development. In the first paper, Jerome Kagan discusses the conflict between desires for simple, all encompassing models and theories, and the possibility (that McCall raised in the previous section) that there may be many relatively independent processes operating. He focuses particularly on the use of the concept of stage, arguing that although the term may have a *descriptive* use, it is not helpful as an *explanatory* concept. The final part of this paper discusses the importance of context variables on infant behaviour, which Kagan believes have been inadequately considered as yet.

In the second paper, Thomas Bower follows a similar line to Kagan: he draws on recent research to suggest that there are indeed, a number of different competences that show individual courses of development, such as conservation and object permanence. What is shared by these, Bower suggests, is a cyclical growth process in which skills appear in embryonic form, disappear, and then reappear at new levels of organization.

The final report, by Judith Dunn, is of a study of mother-infant interaction, and its continuities and discontinuities, that is an example of the sort of research that might begin to take account of the various theoretical issues raised in this and the previous sections.

23 THREE THEMES IN DEVELOPMENTAL PSYCHOLOGY

Jerome Kagan

Source: L.P. Lipsitt (ed.), *Developmental Psychobiology: The Significance of Infancy* (Lawrence Erlbaum, 1976), pp. 129-37.

The eras of an intellectual discipline are delineated by sets of central questions, each yoked to preferred methods of inquiry. Some questions are answered, if only temporarily; many are discarded because they were improperly framed; most are reworded to accommodate to new information. Physicists know why eclipses occur, do not worry about the 'aether', and attempt to determine the number of basic particles rather than define an atom.

Psychologists too, have answered, discarded, or rephrased questions during the short history of the discipline. We now have some insight into the nature of color vision, do not ask about the essence of will, and probe the conditions that monitor the performance of a coherent set of actions rather than seek the intrinsic meaning of reinforcement. Developmental psychologists, in a field with an even shorter history, have clarified some puzzles that provoked brooding among sixteenth century scholars. Infants apparently see hues as adults (Bornstein, 1975) and are afraid of events they do not understand (Kagan, 1976). We have stopped looking for the spirits that bewitch infants, and have begun to substitute statements about the developmental course of specific competences in task contexts for principles about intelligence.

One of the most vital changes in perspective regards the role of experience. We used to ask, 'How does experience alter the child's behavior?' because we assumed that all experience had some effect on the young child. We now entertain the possibility that maturational constraints render some experiences irrelevant, for the effect of experience is dependent in part on its timing. Hence, we wish to know how the developing brain uses varied experience to permit change. Developmental psychologists generally wish to understand four quite different classes of phenomena:

1. We want to explain normative ontogenetic changes in those behaviors and competences that appear to be universal and appreciate that the interaction of maturational and environmental events is necessary to

361

account for the fundamental phenomena.

2. We wish to explain interindividual variation in behavior in specific contexts during a particular developmental stage. Some children do not show object permanence until 1 year; others display this ability at 7 months.

3. We wish to explain intraindividual variation in different contexts during the same era; a child is likely to smile at a mask of a human face at 5 months of age, but not to a car rolling down a ramp. At 30 months the probability of smiling to these two events is completely reversed.

4. Finally, we wish to explain extreme deviance, phenomena like schizophrenia, suicide and autism, which, like freak waves on an ocean's surface, are unusually difficult to predict.

The Relation between Biological Maturation and Psychological Experience

The lawful changes that occur over the human lifespan are obviously under the guidance of the rather strict script contained in the genome, which guarantees that we will crawl before we run and mimic before we speak. All 2-year-olds carry a small number of potentialities, which attract them to contour and curvilinearity and dispose them to stop playing when a stranger enters the room. Ernst Mayr (1974) has called these *closed systems*. The *open systems* are created by the experiential events that control the variability and the time of appearance of inherited competences, as well as the intensity, frequency and asymptotic level of functioning of these dispositions. These open systems define the profile of psychological characteristics that allow us to detect class, regional, ethnic and national differences with greater ease than is good for us or for society. The complementary action of closed and open systems is a new way of phrasing the sentence, which appears in a similar form in almost every textbook on human behavior. The interactions between biological and environmental forces determine the psychological growth of the organism. What does that 14-word sentence mean?

Our inability to answer that question and invent a crisp metaphor for the textbook phrase is multidetermined. One reason derives from the historical debate between science and the church that began almost five centuries ago. The accommodation of each institution to the other led to a treaty that 'awarded' material events to science and psychic ones to the church. Each institution was supposed to honor the intellectual sovereignty of the other. The major philosophical statements written in the seventeenth and eighteenth centuries were attempts to keep this truce sturdy as the assumptions of science became more appealing than those of the church. There is a second reason — less profound but of course of consequence. Analysis, which is the preferred strategy of science, assumes a special form in psychology. Since psychological phenomena are so variable, social scientists were drawn to statistical techniques that were based on the presupposition that one could analyze a unitary phenomenon – say a child's height, achievement score in reading, or hallucinations – into separate biological and experimental causes and assign a weight to each. We resist Whitehead's metaphysics, which assumes that the raw materials of science are occasions of experience, each with a duration and an essential unity:

> Any attempt to analyze it into component parts injures it in some way. But we cannot do anything with it unless we do analyze it. A first step toward analysis is to dissect the unity into an experiencing subject and an experienced object. The dividing line between these two is both arbitrary and artificial. It can be drawn through various positions and wherever it is drawn it is never anything more than a convenience. [Waddington, 1975, p. 4]

A favorite model of analysis is the multiple-regression equation, whose partial coefficients imply that some factors are more important than others. This conceptualization of nature often prevents us from viewing an event as the product of a coherence of forces. Consider a Christmas snowfall created by the complementary interaction of humidity and temperature. It seems inappropriate to ask which factor is more critical, or to assign different beta weights to temperature and humidity. We seem to have less trouble acknowledging such complementary interactions when both forces are in a material mode than when the names for the forces originate in different metalinguistic domains, such as biology and psychology.

The power of analysis in biological research has persuaded many of the utility of treating discrete, material neurological elements as primary and the less discrete psychological events as part of the former. But consider the case of a Taiwanese merchant who visits a shaman because of a chronic pain in his chest. The local shaman tells the merchant that he has angered an ancestor and, if he makes restitution, he will be relieved. He leaves the shaman with less distress than when he arrived (Kleinman, 1975).

Many Western physicians and psychologists are likely to spend hours arguing whether the symptom resulted primarily from psychological or physiological factors. But suppose there is a synergy between the merchant's physiology and his psychology. Many Taiwanese with a similar physiology but fewer worries might not develop the same somatic symptoms; many with a similar collection of uncertainties but not the same physiology would not have the distress. An infant with brain stem damage resulting from perinatal anoxia who is raised in a familial environment in which little psychological acceleration occurs will display cognitive deficits at age 6. A child with the same set of birth conditions growing up in an environment that provides many opportunities for cognitive development will not display the intellectual deficit (Broman, Nichols and Kennedy, 1975). A black child in an all white classrooom produces a certain quality of psychological tension; the same child in a black classroom does not. Each of these examples, and we could offer many more, illustrates a more general principle, namely, mutual interaction between an element and the larger field in which it exists creates a new entity. The new entity is not a part of either the element or the field, and the sentences that describe the transcendental entity cannot be completely replaced with sentences that describe the original element and field without losing some meaning. A hallucination is a part of neither the brain nor the structures created by past history. The field of physics provides the best metaphor. An electric charge in an electromagnetic field mutually influence each other. The charge is described in terms of velocity and energy, the field is described in terms of strength, and their interaction produces a third, quite different phenomenon — radiation — which is described in terms of frequency. The radiation is neither part of the field nor part of the charge; it is a product of the interaction of charge and field.

Mental phenomena (for example, the perception of red, the ability to recall five numbers, or smiling to a face) are analogous to radiation, for they result from the mutual interaction of neural structures and psychological processes in the larger field we call the central nervous system. The perception of red is no more a part of the cells of the central nervous system than radiation is part of the field or the electric charge that generated it. Biological forces contribute to and are necessary for psychological phenomena, but the characteristics of the latter are, like radiation, a product of the interaction. The most detailed knowledge of neural organization, including all the significant synapses in a chicken embryo at a given stage of embryogenesis, would not permit prediction of the actual movements of the embryo at that stage. All we can say is that the state of differentiation of the nervous system at a given stage limits the range of behavioral potentialities. The maturation of the nervous system sets both constraints and permissiveness on the range of behaviors possible, but cannot explain them.

Consider the universal developmental phenomenon of 'separation anxiety'. The infant must be at a particular stage of cognitive maturation in order to protest his caretaker's departure (Kagan, 1976) for such distress rarely occurs before 8 months of age. During the period from 8 to 24 months, when protest is most likely to occur, the enormous variation in the frequency and intensity of the protest that follows maternal departure is likely to be a function of the interaction of experience and the child's temperament. Firstborn 1-year-olds living in an infant house on an Israeli kibbutz protest separation with greater intensity than laterborns; Bushmen children living on the Kalahari Desert are more likely to display separation distress than American children during the normal period of its display.

A second illustration of this idea comes from our recent longitudinal study of Chinese and Caucasian children, some of whom were being reared totally at home, some of whom were attending a day care center. The children were observed in a pair of play sessions at 13, 20 and 29 months. Initially they played with an interesting set of toys while their mother read a magazine. After almost half an hour of play, an unfamiliar child of the same sex and ethnicity and that child's mother were introduced into the room. Changes in duration of playing, vocalization and proximity to the mother were coded as indexes of the child's degree of apprehension to the unfamiliar peer. Chinese and Caucasian home-reared children showed an inverted U-shaped function for inhibition of play with a peak inhibition at 20 months (Kagan, 1976). That is, there was a greater decrease in time playing, comparing solo with peer session, at 20 months than at 13 or 29 months for both ethnic groups. However, the degree of apprehension, as indexed by proximity to mother, inhibition of vocalization and inhibition of play, was significantly greater for the Chinese than for the Caucasian children.

Biological changes in the central nervous system, interacting with the experiences that characterize the larger field, lead most children to display maximal apprehension to an unfamiliar peer somewhere in the middle of the second year. Processes probably related to the temperament of the Chinese child and special experiences in the home contribute to a greater level of apprehension. This finding suggests that one must distinguish between growth functions for phenomena dictated by a maturational script and individual variation, within a particular developmental era, in the level or quality of the behavioral phenomenon. We suggest that it is not always useful to assign different beta weights to the genetic forces that direct the maturational events or temperamental dispositions and to the experiential field in which these forces operate. We can and must discover the functional relations among these forces, as physicists have discovered the functional relationships among charge, field and radiation.

The Meaning of Stage

Although psychological change seems at the surface to be continuous, some psychologists believe that it is theoretically useful to organize these changes into stages. The word stage has two meanings — one descriptive and the other theoretical. The former, which is relatively easy to understand, refers to a correlation among clusters of psychological characteristics during particular periods in development. Embryologists distinguish between the stage of the embryo and that of the fetus, the latter being characterized by growth and enlargement of organs rather than differentiation. At a descriptive level that distinction seems reasonable and even helpful, but it does not explain anything about growth. It is a little like saying that an automobile journey from Boston to New York consists of two stages — one prior to the Merritt Parkway where traffic is light, and one from the Merritt Parkway to Manhattan where traffic is heavy.

Most psychologists are dissatisfied with a descriptive concept of stage and want a theoretical construct that states something about the necessary relations between the structures and processes of successive eras.

Campos' important contribution (Campos, 1976) implies the emergence of a stage toward the end of the first year. Campos reports cardiac acceleration to the visual cliff among 9-month-olds, but deceleration at 5 months of age. This difference in the direction of heart rate to the deep side of the cliff before and after 9 months of age is one example from a very large set of behavioral changes that appear between 7 and 13 months. For example, there is a dramatic increase in attention to transformations of familiarized auditory and visual events between 7 and 9 months of age in both American and Guatemalan children. There is also an increase in inhibition in the reaching for novel objects, and the emergence of stranger and separation anxiety. Should these changes be viewed as the product of a new common structure or a new process? A clue to the answer comes from the fact that there is a major increase in the ability to retrieve information from memory somewhere around 8 to 10 months of age. For example, 5-8-month-old children in the '*A* not *B*' object permanence paradigm will not perform correctly when the delay between hiding the object in the new place and allowing the child to reach is long, say 7 seconds, but will perform correctly if the delay is short, for example, 1-3 seconds. Delayed-response performance tests on monkeys also point to the growth of memory processes in the middle of the first year (see Rosenblum and Alpert, 1974).

It is likely that the changes that occur between 8 and 13 months result in large measure from an increase in the ability to retrieve structures from memory that represent events and objects that are not in the immediate field. The 9-month-old, but not the 6-month-old, is able to retrieve (not just recognize) schemata for events not in his or her present field that happened more than a few seconds earlier. Schaffer has also suggested that the ability to activate from memory schemata for absent objects and to use them to evaluate a situation are critical for the changes that occur at this time (Schaffer, 1974). We are suggesting that the stage we call 'short-term memory' collapses soon after every experience in the child under 8 months. But after that time changes in the central nervous system allow the infant to retrieve information transduced earlier. The data imply that the essence of the performance we call the 'object concept' is not the acquisition of a new structure (the belief that objects are permanent) but rather the emergence of a new cognitive competence.

The movement called 'developmental psychobiology' recognizes the temporary usefulness of psychological stages that are monitored by a child's changing biology, for the psychological functioning of a 4-year-old is obviously different from that of a 1-year-old. But it is less obvious that the additional assumption of a thick cord of connection between stages, a contingent relation between earlier and later structures, is as useful. This idea is attractive to the Western mind because of a predilection toward the notion of unitary deep structures that explain phenotypically diverse performances. It is less pleasing to consider successive classes of behavior, each resting on its own base. Modern stage theories satisfy a deep longing for a hidden unity that weaves experience into a seamless fabric. We do not like to see anything wasted or thrown away; perhaps that is why the principle of conservation of energy is so aesthetic. The possibility that the intensity, variety and excitement of the first years of life, together with the extreme parental effort those years require, could be discarded like wrapping paper that is no longer needed is a little too threatening to our Puritan spirit. But given the available evidence, we should at least remain open to that idea.

The Power Concept

The major disquiet I feel is that the power of situational context in infant behavior is often ignored. Intelligence, smiling, attention, or fear, tend to be treated as if they were attributes of the child rather than the product of interactions between the child and the task context. I noted in a recent paper (Kagan, 1976) that Western psychologists prefer to posit abstract attributes that are minimally constrained by context. One speaks of hostile or depressed people and rarely feels it necessary to specify target and occasion. Mischel's (1968) cogent criticism of this affinity for traits reflects a growing corpus of empirical data which implies that we must specify the target and occasion of motivational and attitudinal dimensions. A similar criticism applies to cognitive competences. Generalizations about memory, reasoning, planfulness, or perceptual analysis rarely specify the problem context in detail or restrict developmental principles to classes of problem situations. There is minimal generality to the concrete operational groupings across different tasks during the transitional period from 5 to 7 years of age. Similarly, quality of recognition memory is dependent on the information to be remembered, as planfulness is dependent on the nature of the task. But we have not applied this new appreciation to the work on infants.

The unpublished results of an analysis of a large body of longitudinal data gathered on over 75 Chinese and Caucasian children who have been observed eight times from 3.5 through 29 months makes this point in bold relief. Several different auditory and visual episodes were administered to the children at each age, and the child's attention, vocalization, fretting, smiling, and motor activity were coded. For example, on one episode the child interacted with an adult female. On another the child heard taped speech; on another the child was shown a visual event in which a 2-inch block was taken from a box and moved in front of the infant for a series of trials; on another the child saw a small wooden car roll down a wooden ramp and strike a Styrofoam object at the bottom of the ramp. The behavioral variables did not display impressive generality across all of the episodes. A child who was highly attentive or irritable on one episode was not necessarily attentive or fretful on another. There was also a remarkable lack of stability in reactivity across age. Although lower-class children were less attentive than middle-class children to some of the episodes at 3.5 months, there were no class differences in level of attention to the same episodes from 5 through 29 months. Although the Caucasian children smiled more in response to some of the episodes (especially the female examiner and the block episode), they did not smile more than the Chinese in response to the episode in which the car rolled down the ramp. Moreover, behavioral differences between social classes or ethnic groups on a particular test at a particular age often did not occur at another age. Freedman's suggestion that Chinese newborns are less labile than Caucasians on the Cambridge Infant Scale is an interesting and important result. But it does not necessarily mean that lability is a generalized attribute of Caucasian children that will appear in all contexts and at all ages. We must begin to replace statements about abstracted traits with statements about dispositions in classes of contexts.

References

Bornstein, M.H. (1975), 'Qualities of color vision in infancy', *Journal of Experimental Child Psychology, 19*, 401-19.

Broman, S.H., Nichols, P.L. and Kennedy, W.A. (1975), *Preschool IQ: Prenatal and Early Development Correlates.* Hillsdale: Lawrence Erlbaum Assoc.

Compos, J.J. (1976), 'Comments on "Infancy, Biology and Culture" ', in L.P. Lipsitt (ed.), *Developmental Psychobiology.* Lawrence Erlbaum.

Kagan, J. (1976), 'Emergent themes in human development', *American Scientist, 64*, 186-96.

Kleinman, A. (1975), *The Cultural Construction of Clinical Reality Comparisons of Practitioner-Patient Interaction in Taiwan.* Unpublished manuscript.

Mayr, E. (1974), 'Behavior programs and evolutionary strategies', *American Scientist, 62*, 650-9.

Mischel, W. (1968), *Personality and Assessment.* New York: Wiley.

Rosenblum, L.A. and Alpert, S. (1974), 'Fear of strangers and specificity of attachment in monkeys', in M. Lewis and L.A. Rosenblum (eds.), *The Origins of Fear.* New York: Wiley, pp. 165-94.

Schaffer, H.R. (1974), 'Cognitive components of the infant's response to strangeness', in M. Lewis and L.A. Rosenblum (eds.), *The Origins of Fear.* New York: Wiley, pp. 11-24.

Waddington, C.H. (1975), *The Evolution of an Evolutionist.* Ithaca, New York: Cornell University Press.

24 REPETITION IN HUMAN BEHAVIOR

Thomas G.R. Bower

Source: *Merrill-Palmer Quarterly*, 1974, vol. 20 (4), pp. 303-18.

A foundation that underpins a great deal of theoretical and experimental effort in developmental psychology is the belief that behavioral growth is a continuous, incremental process with the child necessarily getting better and better at any task as he grows. The whole concept of an IQ depends on this assumption. It is this assumption that underpins the prototypical experiment in child psychology, the experiment in which children of one age are shown to be incapable of some task while children of an older age are shown to be capable of the task. In such experiments, and I have published a number of them myself, the conclusion is often that a segment of development takes place between age 1 and 2, and is then over. In this paper I would like to challenge the idea that development is a continuous, incremental process, with developed accomplishments becoming part of the permanent range of competences of the growing child. Rather, I will argue, development is a cyclic process with competences developing and then disappearing, to reappear anew at a later age; development is not a continuous linear process but rather a series of waves, with whole segments of development reoccurring repetitively.

There are many phenomena that could be used to illustrate this argument. One of the simplest and best known occurs in the course of the development of walking. As everyone knows, newborn infants can walk soon after birth, provided they are not required to maintain their posture by themselves. The behaviour is obviously very different from mature walking, although they show the same sequential organization in time. This organized patterning of movements disappears in the months after birth, and does not reappear until the onset of walking proper, usually some 8-10 months later. There is no obvious explanation of why an organized pattern of movements should fade out in this way. The most obvious explanation would seem to be in terms of disuse; the pattern of movements is not normally exercised and so simply dies away. This kind of explanation would seem to be ruled out by the numerous studies which have exercised the behavior frequently and vigorously, without however arresting its decline. The fact that use cannot prevent the disappearance of primary walking would seem to support a maturational theory of the sort put forward by Humphrey (1969); according to her theory the disappearance

370

of any primary behavior results from normal growth processes in which higher cortical centers take the function of lower centers, with inhibitory connections growing in first, and thereby suppressing behavior. However, it would seem to me that such an explanation, if taken as much more than a metaphorical description, runs into the problem of explaining why it is that practice of early walking, while it does not prevent the disappearance of the primary behavior, undoubtedly facilitates the appearance of secondary or mature walking, producing highly significant accelerations of this phase of the behavior. How is it that practice of a behavior that disappears can facilitate the appearance of a later behavior, no matter how structurally similar the two are? That seems even more mysterious than the disappearance of an organized, adapted pattern of behavior that is used.

There are similar puzzles to be found in the analysis of auditory manual coordination, as shown in the development of aurally guided reaching. Until recently the only studies of the development of aurally guided reaching were the superb clinical observations of blind infants that were made by Fraiberg and her associates (Fraiberg, 1968; Fraiberg and Freedman, 1964; Fraiberg, Siegel and Gibson, 1966). Fraiberg found that in blind infants reaching towards a sound source develops slowly, if at all, in the second half of the first year of life. Fraiberg assumed that similar auditory guided reaching would develop much faster in sighted infants, who could use vision as a mediator to help establish the coordination between ear and hand. For a variety of theoretical reasons I was interested in checking this assumption. Accordingly a large number of sighted infants were run in test conditions designed to simulate the test conditions used by Fraiberg with her blind patients. The infants were placed in a light-tight room and the lights switched off, so that the infants were in total darkness. A noise-making toy was then introduced within reach of the infants. In one condition the toy was a soft fur-covered duck containing a small loudspeaker emitting 1 squeak per second; in the other condition the toy was a bell which was rung by hand. The room was illuminated with an 875 μm light source. The infants' behavior was recorded via an infra red sensitive TV system. The infants were given three minutes in which to reach for the toy. After this the lights were switched on and the infants allowed to reach for the toy in the light. The results indicated that infants up to about six months were as likely to reach for the auditorily defined toy as for the visually defined toy. Their accuracy was as high in the auditory as in the visual condition, when the noise-making toy was in the middle, though lower when the toy was off the midline. This is just what one would expect given the psychophysics of auditory localization and the growth problems of the auditory system. Location of a sound source is specified by the difference between the time of arrival of a sound stimulus at one ear and its time of arrival at the other ear. Since the distance between the two ears changes continuously during growth there can be no invariant stimulus specifying the radial direction of any sound source, save for the midline direction, which is specified by a zero difference in arrival time at all times during growth. The psychophysical coordination specifying that a sound source is in the midline plane could thus be built in, or could be easily acquired. (For an extended discussion of this problem see Bower, 1974).

Table 24.1: A Comparison of Auditory-Motor Localization and Visual-Motor Localization in Infants under Six Months

	Success rate %	
Object position	Auditory-motor	Visual-motor
30° left	48	100
Middle	92	96
30° right	33.5	100

For infants older than six months the results were quite different. These infants would not reach for the auditorily defined target at all, regardless. They tended to sit with arms limp, making no attempt to get their hands to the auditorily defined object. In the visual situation by contrast these infants took the object rapidly and without difficulty. Only in some of the very oldest infants (12 months) was there any renewed effort to get at the audible but invisible object.

Here then is an example of a sensory-motor coordination that fades away and then recovers. There are many possible explanations of this cycle of development. One obvious explanation is that vision simply becomes the predominant modality in sighted infants so that the use of audition simply atrophies. This is a possible explanation but an unlikely one given that the pattern of development is the same in blind infants. Fraiberg's studies of blind infants from six months up have already been described. Their performance at comparable ages was about the same as that of sighted infants. In addition it would seem that blind infants initially have auditory-manual coordination and then lose it at about the same time as sighted infants. Urwin (1973) has studied the development of this coordination in one infant, blind as a result of agenesis of the eyes;

the coordination was there at sixteen weeks but disappeared around 24 weeks, about the time it seems to disappear in sighted infants. The infant was given a great deal of practice in using the coordination. This practice was of no avail in arresting the decline of the coordination. It thus seems that we can invoke neither lack of use nor the increasing importance of other modalities to explain the disappearance of this useful coordination.

One could also attempt to explain the change of behavior in terms of the requirements of the motor component of the coordination. It would seem from a number of studies that as infants grow older the role of vision in the guidance of reaching becomes more and more important and may become critical enough that reaching will not take place in the absence of vision. If this were the case it could be that the auditory-manual coordination is still there but cannot be expressed as a result of the new requirements of the motor system. We have attempted to test this hypothesis with the following experiment. Infants were shown a toy in the light. Before they could reach for it, the lights were extinguished leaving the infants in darkness. The toy in this experiment was soundless. Its position during the phase in which reaching could occur was specified only in visual memory. The infants could see neither the toy nor themselves. We know from a previous experiment (Bower and Wishart, 1972) that 4-5 month old infants have no problems in such a situation. They reach out and take the object without difficulty. If the visual requirements of reaching itself are responsible for the apparent decline in auditory-manual coordination, there should be a similar decline in this situation, a decline which could hardly be attributed to a decline in visual trace memory itself (Bower, 1967). The results of the experiment were not straightforward. There was a decline with age in the frequency of capture of the toy in darkness. However this decline was entirely due to a loss of accuracy in reaching in darkness. The number of attempts to reach did not decline at all. The detailed results thus are quite different from those obtained with the audible object, where there were no attempts to reach at all.

It thus seems that the decline in behavior in the auditory test situation results from a loss of the 'knowledge' that a sound can specify a tangible object. This instance of repetition differs somewhat from the first example given, walking. Here the primary and secondary behaviors are identical rather than merely similar. What is lost seems to be an item of knowledge rather than anything as specific as a pattern of movements. On the other hand the decline in both cases seems to be inevitable and cannot be arrested by use. We do not at this time know whether practice of the early phase of auditory-manual coordination will accelerate the appearance of

Figure 24.1: Percentage of Blind and Sighted Babies Attaining Success in Reaching for an Auditorily Defined Object

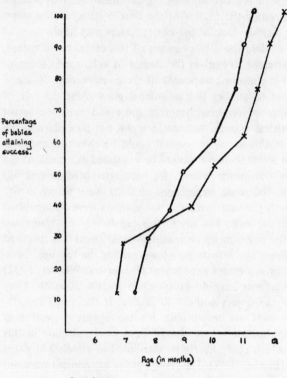

x   Blind babies
o   Sighted babies

the later phase. In one sighted subject who was given extended practice during the first phase the second phase did emerge very precociously. However, Urwin's blind subject, who was given extensive practice during the first phase, has shown no such gain. Obviously a great deal of further research will be required before we can conclude anything about acceleration here.

The instances of repetition presented thus far could be described as instances of literal repetition: the behaviors in the first and second phases are identical or at least very similar. I should like now to turn to two instances of what would seem to be formal rather than literal repetition, instances in which the behaviors involved are quite different, although the problems to be solved seem to be formally the same. The first comes from the development of the object concept. Infants between the ages of 12 and 20 weeks show a peculiar pattern of erroneous responding in tracking tests (Bower, Broughton and Moore, 1971; Bower and Paterson, 1973). For example, if one presents such an infant with a stationary object in the center of a track that then moves to the right of the track where it stops, before returning to the center, where it pauses before repeating the cycle, one can readily — within a few cycles of movement — establish smooth, competent-looking tracking behavior. If, however, after several cycles, one moves the object from the center to the left, rather than the right, these competent-looking infants will look, not to the left, but to the right. In other words, these infants will ignore the visible displacement of the object and look for it where they have previously seen it.

Infants stop making such errors around the age of 20 weeks. At this time infants, as gauged by their eye movements, know a great deal about the properties of objects. They know that objects still exist when they have gone behind screens (Charlesworth, 1966; Bower, 1971), they can infer where objects are going when they see them move behind screens (Bower, Broughton and Moore, 1971; Mundy-Castle and Anglin, 1969) and they seem able to infer what has happened when one object goes behind a screen and a different one emerges (Bower, Broughton and Moore, 1971, op. cit.). These capacities seem to disappear completely when the infant is confronted with the standard Piagetian object permanence test (Piaget, 1937) in which an object is made to vanish by having a cloth or cup dropped over it. Infants in such a situation act as if they thought the vanished object no longer existed, in total contrast to their sophisticated, developmentally prior eye tracking behavior. Furthermore, recall the description given of the typical eye tracking error of infants of less than 20 weeks. These infants look for an object where they have previously seen it, ignoring its perfectly visible movements. The words are almost precisely those used by Piaget (1937) and others (Gratch, 1971) to describe errors made by considerably older infants in a quite different task. I am referring to the error characteristic of infants in stage IV of the development of the object concept. If one shows such infants a toy and then hides the toy under one of two simultaneously visible cloths, the infants will be able to retrieve the toy without difficulty. On a second trial if the toy is hidden under the same cloth, the infants will retrieve it without difficulty. If, however, on the third trial, one hides the toy under the other, allowing the infant to watch the whole hiding sequence, the infant will search for the toy, not where it is, but rather under the cloth where he has previously found it. The formal similarity between these two errors is quite striking. The same words could be used to describe both without doing violence to either. The differences are nonetheless considerable. The response systems involved are totally different. The specific stimulus situations are quite different. Yet at a more formal level of description the two errors seem to be the same, involving a repetition of some developmental process. In a case like this it is hard to know whether the repetition is coincidental, or whether it reflects a genuine repetition. A strict S-R viewpoint, as advocated by Bruner (1966a), would insist that the seeming repetition is coincidental and cannot be real since the stimulus situations and behaviors are so different. Theorists with a more abstract idea of the processes controlling behavior, such as Piaget (1967) and Bruner himself wearing a different hat, would probably argue that the seeming repetition is a genuine repetition. The first interest this phenomenon had for me was the indication it gave that cognitive development was not the smooth continuous, unitary, process it had always seemed to be. Either the knowledge that the 'eye' had at 5 months was lost by the age of 8 months or the information available to control the eye was in a compartment of the mind, separate from that available to control the hand. The former alternative would align the phenomenon with the two previous instances of repetition discussed here; the latter would imply the sort of schizoid mentality attributed to the infant by Schaffer (1971) among others. A direct experiment to decide between these two hypotheses would seem easy enough but unfortunately has not been carried out, so far as I know. However, a theoretically much more sophsticated set of experiments has been carried out by Brown (1973). Brown argued that the stimulus situations were so different that we need not invoke either the idea of repetition or that of compartment-alization. In particular she has argued that the infants' sophisticated eye tracking behavior depends on comprehension of the spatial relationship 'behind' whereas success in the Piagetian tasks depends on comprehension of the spatial relationship 'inside'. The evidence substantiating this hypo-thesis is set out elsewhere (Bower, 1974). More relevant to our present purposes is the deduction that infants who are capable of the eye tracking tasks that rely on comprehension of the relationship 'behind' should be capable of the same tasks if they are required to solve them by using their hands. This deduction was tested and it was found that infants of 20-24 weeks could indeed retrieve objects that had been hidden behind screens, while refusing — or seeming unable — to retrieve objects that had been hidden inside cups. This ability, however, disappeared with increasing age, until ability to cope with 'behind' relations was no better than ability to cope with 'inside' relations. The ability to cope with behind relations of course came back, in time, roughly contemporaneously with the ability to cope with inside relations. Inasmuch as ability to cope with behind

Figure 24.2: Eye Tracking Behavior

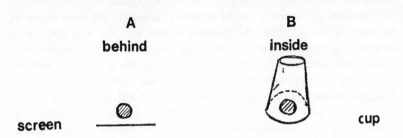

When an object goes *behind* another, the object and the occluder are in different spatial locations. By contrast, when an object goes *inside* another, object and occluder have the same place in space.

relations can be taken as prototypical of the abilities that appear by the age of 20 weeks, then these abilities do disappear to reappear at a later age. The seeming formal repetition thus involves a literal repetition. Further, the repetition has similar properties to the simpler repetitions discussed earlier, in that infants practised on the first phase of the sequence, either the eye tracking or retrieving objects from behind screens were considerably accelerated in their success with the later tasks (Bower and Paterson, 1972; Brown, 1973). However, early practice, at least in retrieving objects from behind screens, did not prevent the decline of the early ability (Brown, 1973). It thus seems that even the repetition within the object concept although not tied to specific behaviors as are the other repetitions discussed here, shows enough of the same properties to be listed with them.

The last instance of repetition that I wish to discuss is repetition within the development of the ability to conserve. Conservation is the ability to detect that a value on some quantitative dimension such as volume or weight is invariant under shape transformation. We usually think of conservation developing between 5 years and 9 years. However, as Piaget (1941) has always emphasized, some forms of conservation develop during infancy. The one I wish to discuss is conservation of weight (Mounoud and Bower, 1974). The development of anticipatory responses to weight is fascinating. At about the age of 6 months infants seem to anticipate that objects will weigh something but that is about the limit of their capacities. If one hands an object to an infant of this age, his arm will typically drop under the weight and then recover, the recovery being followed, usually, by transport of the object to the mouth. If one gives the same object to the baby a second time, the response occurs with the arm drop being virtually the same. In fact the arm drop does not vary no matter how many times one presents the object. If one presents an infant with an object twice as large and twice as heavy one will obtain an arm drop that is approximately twice as great as that obtained with the original object. It thus seems that infants of this age apply the same response to all objects regardless of their past experience with either the specific object or similar objects. They do not seem to 'know' that the same object always weighs the same or that weight is related to size. One comes to the same conclusion if one looks at force of grasp rather than arm movement. Infants of 6-7 months apply the same force of grasp to objects regardless of their weight, showing no correction even when the object is in the hand and its weight can be sensed directly. Practice does not change the force of grasp until fatigue sets in.

By the age of about 9 months some development has taken place. The infant of this age will make an initial error when presented with an object. On the second presentation, however, the error is greatly reduced, while by the third it is so small as to be unmeasurable. This is true of both arm movement and force of grasp. It thus seems that by 9 months of age infants know that the same object will weigh the same on each presentation. However, these infants do not yet relate weight to size. Practice with one object does not reduce the error on presentation of another object twice — or half — the size. Infants who have taken a brass rod 2.5 cm in diameter and of length 2.5 cm do no better on presentation of another brass rod of the same diameter and length 5.0 cm than infants who have had no experience of the first rod. The infants are thus incapable of serial prediction of weight from visual characteristics. At 12 months this ability has developed. Infants of this age, run with the pair of brass rods described above, do as well on their first trial with the second rod as infants with two prior trials with that rod. Infants of this age know that the same object weighs the same on each presentation and that the longer an object is, the heavier it will be. It is at this point that one can meaningfully begin to test for weight conservation in infants. We used a variety of procedures to test for this ability. One of the simplest utilized a ball of plasticine. The infants were given the ball three times. As expected their error on taking it declined to virtually zero on the third trial. Then with the infants watching, the ball was rolled out into a sausage shape which was then given to the infant. If the infant realized that weight is invariant under shape transformation, he would have done as well on this fourth trial as on the third trial. This did not happen. All of the infants tested seemed to think that since the sausage was longer, it must therefore be heavier, with the result that their arm flew up on presentation of the elongated object. The converse happened if one began with the sausage and transformed it into a ball. We got the same results using a hinged rod that could be extended or doubled up. Force of grasp showed exactly the same pattern of responding, with weight being predicted from length and no realization that weight is independent of shape. By the age of 18 months this pattern of errors had disappeared. The infants showed behavioral conservation of weight. This behavioral conservation is formally the same as the verbal conservation that comes in much later. The errors are the same and the formal requirements for success are the same, but the two sequences of development are about 5 years apart in time.

The development of conservation as described above would seem to exemplify purely formal repetition. However, there is evidence that the formal repetition involves a literal repetition as well. Sheeran (1973) has studied the maintenance of behavioral conservation in nursery school children. She found that 3½-year-olds showed perfect behavioral conservation. These children were incapable of comprehending the verbal formulation of the conservation problem. 4½-year-olds by contrast, who could comprehend but not solve the verbal formulation of the problem, showed the same errors as 12-month-olds when presented with the behavioral version of the task. Their behavioral conservation had disappeared. Older children who could show verbal conservation also showed behavioral conservation once again. It seems as if formal repetition involves literal repetition as well.

Table 24.2: Mean Change in Arm Position after Third Presentation before Transformation and on First Presentation after Transformation in the Two Age Groups Studied[a]

Age (years)	Before transformation	After transformation
3, 2	0.3	0.9[b]
4, 10	2.4	7.8[c]

[a] Change is measured in mm from a photograph superimposing the arm position on taking the object and 250 msec later

[b] N.S.

[c] p .03.

The few examples of repetition in development that I have given here do not by any means constitute an exhaustive list. Repetition has been demonstrated in pattern presentation (Carpenter, personal communication, 1973), the development of reaching (Bower, Broughton and Moore, 1970), development of imitation (Dunkeld, 1973), the development of spatial concepts (Piaget, 1948; Bruner, 1968), concepts of number (Bever, Mehler and Epstein, 1968), and of course linguistic development (Bever, Foder and Weksel, 1965). I could reasonably argue that there are more repetitive phenomena in development than there are continuous incremental processes. Given that repetition is a widespread phenomenon, what is its theoretical significance? Are repetitive phemomena mere curiosities or do they indicate something truly central to the process of development? The first question that should be asked of each instance of repetition, is whether the two phases of the development are actually connected with one another. This is a very difficult question to ask in the context of behavioral development, since the relevant experiments are so hard to do (Bower, 1974). The only paradigm we can legitimately use in all cases is the acceleration paradigm. If practice of the first phase of a repetitive sequence accelerates the appearance of the second phase, with all other variables held constant, then, I think, we can reasonably conclude that the two phases of development stand in some kind of causal relationship to one another. As was indicated above, there is this kind of relationship in the development of walking and within the development of the object concept. There is also some evidence of such acceleration in the development of visually guided reaching (White and Held, 1966; Bower, 1973a) as well as the tentative evidence on acceleration in auditorily guided reaching that was mentioned above. As for the long-term repetition in such areas as weight conservation, I know of no systematic studies attempting to show acceleration. However, I have been told that the children of potters in a primitive society, who play with clay from an early age, show considerably accelerated development of verbally indexed conservation of matter (Mundy-Castle, personal communication, 1973). This may indicate a long-term effect of practice in the behavioral skill. Unfortunately despite the interest in this problem that was shown some years ago (Bruner, 1966b), I know of no systematic studies of this kind of problem. Such studies are required and will be well worth the labor they will necessarily involve.

In addition to these acceleration studies there is some evidence that the first phase of a skill or concept may be a *necessary* acquisition if the second phase is to appear at all. This seems to be the case for the development of the concept of space. Some blind children do not develop an adequate concept of space; those who do seem to have had vision for that period of infancy that is necessary to develop a behavioral expression of the concept (Drever, 1955). Subsequent lack of vision does not seem to be critical, provided the first phase of the concept has been acquired.

It seems to me that these studies, few as they are, indicate that we should take repetition seriously. If it turns out that the first phase of a concept or skill is necessary for the mature expression of that concept or skill, then the practical consequences are enormous. As Piaget and others have shown, there are almost no mature concepts that do not have a behavioral expression in infancy. The theoretical consequences of taking repetitive phenomena seriously are equally great. For example, it seems profitless to study the development of conservation as something occurring between 5 years and 9 years of age, if this phase of the development is entirely specified by development occurring in infancy. At this point we cannot say that the first phase of any sequence specifies the later phase. However, it seems to me that there is enough evidence tentatively to support Piaget's arguments that this is the case, enough evidence at least to justify a full-scale attack on the problem of repetition.

References

Bever, T.G., Foder, J.A. and Weksel, W. (1965), 'Is linguistics empirical?', *Psychological Review*, vol. 72.

Bever, T.G., Mehler, J. and Epstein, J. (1968), 'What children do in spite of what they know', *Science*, vol. 162.

Bower, T.G.R. (1974), *Aspects of Development in Infancy*. San Francisco: W.H. Freeman and Co.

Bower, T.G.R., Broughton, J.M. and Moore, M.K. (1970), 'Demonstration of intention in the reaching behavior of neonate humans', *Nature*, vol. 228.

Bower, T.G.R. (1967), 'The development of object permanence: Some studies of existence constancy', *Perception and Psychophysics*, vol. 2.

Bower, T.G.R. (1971), 'The object in the world of the infant', *Scientific American*, vol. 225.

Bower, T.G.R., Broughton, J.M. and Moore, M.K. (1971), 'The development of the object concept as manifested by changes in the tracking behavior of infants between 7 and 20 weeks of age', *Journal of Experimental Child Psychology*, vol. 11.

Bower, T.G.R. and Paterson, J.G. (1972), 'Stages in the development of the object concept', *Cognition*, vol. 1, no. 1.

Bower, T.G.R. and Wishart, J.G. (1972), 'The effects of motor skill on object permanence', *Cognition*, vol. 1, no. 2, 1972.

Bower, T.G.R. (1973a), 'Space perception and the object concept', in L.B. Cohen and P. Salapatek (eds.), *Infant Perception*. New York: Academic Press, in press.

Bower, T.G.R., unpublished manuscript. (1973b)

Bower, T.G.R. and Paterson, J.G. (1973), 'The separation of place, movement and object in the world of the infant', *Journal of Experimental Child Psychology*, vol. 15.

Brown, I.E. (1973), *A Study on the Development of the Object Concept: Inside is not Behind*, unpublished MA thesis, Department of Psychology, Edinburgh University.

Bruner, J.S., Olver, R.R. and Greenfield, P.M. (1966a), *Studies in Cognitive Growth*. New York: John Wiley and Sons.

Bruner, J.S. (1966b), *The Process of Education*. Cambridge, Mass.: Harvard University Press.

Bruner, J.S. (1968), *Processes of Cognitive Growth: Infancy*. Clark University Press.

Charlesworth, W.R. (1966), 'Persistence of orienting and attending behavior in infants as a function of stimulus-locus uncertainty', *Child Development*, vol. 37.

Drever, J. (1955), 'Early learning and the perception of space', *American Journal of Psychology*, vol. 68.

Dunkeld, J. (1973), unpublished manuscript. Department of Psychology, Edinburgh University.

Fraiberg, S. (1968), 'Parallel and divergent pattern in blind and sighted infants', *Psychoanalytic Study of the Child*, vol. 23.

Fraiberg, S. and Freedman, D.A. (1964), 'Studies in the ego development of the congenitally blind infant', *Psychoanalytic Study of the Child*, vol. 19.

Fraiberg, S., Siegel, B.L. and Gibson, R. (1966), 'The role of sound in the search behavior of a blind infant', *Psychoanalytic Study of the Child*, vol. 21.

Gibson, E.J. (1969), *Principles of Perceptual Learning and Development*. New York: Appleton-Century-Crofts.

Gratch, G. and Landers, W.F. (1971), 'Stage IV of Piaget's theory of infants' object concept: A longitudinal study', *Child Development*, vol. 42.

Humphrey, T. (1969), 'Postnatal repetition of human pre-natal activity sequences with some suggestions of their neuroanatomical basis', in R.J. Robinson (ed.), *Brain and Early Behaviour*. London: Academic Press.

Mounoud, P. and Bower, T.G.R. (1974), 'Conservation of weight in infants', *Cognition*, in press.

Mundy-Castle, A.C. and Anglin, J. (1969), 'The development of looking in infancy'. Paper presented at SRCD Conference, Santa Monica, April.

Piaget, J. (1955), *The Construction of Reality in the Child*. London: Routledge and Kegan Paul. (Original French edn., 1937.)

Piaget, J. (1956), *The Child's Conception of Space*. London: Routledge and Kegan Paul. (Original French edn., 1948.)

Piaget, J. (1967), *Biologie et Connaissance*. Editions Gallimard.

Piaget, J. (1941), 'Le mecanisme du développement mental', *Arch. de Psychologie*, vol. 28.

Schaffer, H.R. (1971), *The Growth of Sociability*. London: Penguin Books.

Sheeran, L. (1973), *Vertical decalage in weight conservation between sensorimotor and Conceptual Levels*. Unpublished MA thesis, Department of Psychology, Edinburgh University.

Urwin, C. (1973), *The Development of a Blind Baby*. Unpublished manuscript, read at Edinburgh University, January.

Wertheimer, M. (1961), 'Psychomotor coordination of auditory-visual space at birth', *Science*, vol. 134.

White, B. and Held, R. (1966), 'Plasticity of sensori-motor development in the human infant', in J.F. Rosenblith and W. Allinsmith (eds.), *The Cause of Behavior*. Boston: Allyn and Bacon.

25 MOTHER-INFANT RELATIONS: CONTINUITIES AND DISCONTINUITIES OVER THE FIRST 14 MONTHS

Judy F. Dunn

Source: *Journal of Psychosomatic Research*, 1976, vol. 20, pp. 273-7.

The early relationship between mother and baby has in recent years received much attention from developmental psychologists.[1] Interest has largely been focused on early communication between mother and baby, and the link between this exchange and the later development of language. But in addition the question of how far difficulties of adjustment between mother and baby in the early weeks might show continuity with later difficulties in the relationship has been much discussed. Mother-child pairs vary widely in the quality and frequency of their interaction in the first months: how are these differences related to the quality of the child's subsequent relationship with the mother? Could they for example be used to pick out the mother-child pairs at risk of later difficulties of adjustment? Can we find any links between these differences and the later development of the child?

To begin to answer these questions we need longitudinal data, and in this paper I want to discuss some findings from a study of 77 mother-child pairs followed from prenatal interview until the children were 5. The study was initiated by M.P.M. Richards, and was carried out in Cambridge. Detailed description of the study, and reports and discussion of the results are available in other publications.[2,3,4,5] Here I shall briefly summarise some general implications of the study's findings for our ideas on continuities in development.

The study was based primarily on direct observations of mother and baby at home. The schedule of visits is shown in Table 25.1. The sample was selected as a low-risk group on medical and social grounds, and the babies were delivered at home. We were particularly interested in the contribution of individual differences between newborn babies to the patterns of interaction, and with this in mind we made a number of different assessments of the baby's behaviour other than those derived from the observations of mother and baby together. Two of these measures that will be discussed here were made in the sucking test developed by Waldrop and Bell;[6] this test gives us measures of the baby's rate of sucking, and of the baby's reaction to the removal of a pacifier. Babies show marked individual differences in these responses, differences which are stable from day to day over the newborn period.

Table 25.1: Outline of Procedures used in the First 14 Months

2-5 weeks before delivery	Interview of mother.
Delivery	Precoded medical information collected by midwife. Observation of first mother-infant interaction (when observer present).
Days 2, 3, 8, 9, 10	Observation of a feeding session. Collection of attitude and interview information.
Days 0-10	Continuous diary kept by mother of baby's time spent in cot, feeding, crying, bathing, out of cot.
Day 8 or 9	Neurological examination, sucking test (Waldrop and Bell, 1966).
8 weeks. 2 visits	Observation of a feeding session and 2 non-feeding baby awake periods. 48-hour diary kept by mother.
14, 20 and 30 weeks	Two observations and 48-hour diary at each age.
14 months	Two observations (tape-recorded) and 48-hour diary.

The First Ten Days Post-Partum

During the first ten days we found that there was no evidence for a simple unitary dimension of maternal warmth. The smoothness and coordination of the feed, which is often assumed to reflect underlying sensitivity on the mother's part, was related to the course of labour and delivery, and to the differences between babies reflected in the sucking test measure of latency to cry when the pacifier was removed. Coordination of the feed was not related to a group of measures of mother's behaviour reflecting affectionate interest in the baby: looking at the baby, smiling at the baby, and talking affectionately to the baby. However it was interesting that this cluster of maternal measures *was* positively correlated with the measure of individual differences between babies in rate of sucking. A multiple regression analysis for each observation variable with the 'background' variables (parity, sex, feed type (breast or bottle), labour and delivery factors, neurological examination and sucking test measurements) showed that, for the mother's 'affectionate talk' variable, the suck rate measure was of prime importance. This indicates that differences between babies in sucking behaviour are related to the affectionate behaviour shown by the mother during feeds.

These findings underline the importance of the baby as contributor to early differences between mother-baby pairs in interaction patterns. We cannot, however, assume that the baby's behaviour in the sucking test, done on the eighth day, is independent of the care he has received since birth. Even though the sucking test measures are made so early in life, and are stable from day to day, it is quite possible that the differences in sucking behaviour are related to the differences in mothering experienced by the babies. This association between the mother's affectionate behaviour and the suck rate measure raises a problem of great importance in studies of maternal or infant behaviour: that no measures of the behaviour of either mother or baby can be assumed to be independent of the course of previous interaction between them. The findings also raise the question of which aspect of the individual differences in patterns of inter-action between mother and child will show continuity to later days, and which reflect special features of the earliest exchange and adjustment in the post-partum period.

Observations between 2 and 7 Months

Over the first seven months we found marked individual differences between mothers on measures of how much they talked to, and touched the babies, and measures of how responsive they were to the babies' noises. These measures were highly correlated both within and between feeds: that is, a mother who at 8 weeks talked a lot to her baby, also touched him a lot and was very responsive to his noises, when compared with the other mothers in the sample, and she continued to be among the most responsive and vocal mothers over the first 7 months. These differences in mothering style were not related to the differences in measures of coordination shown in the early feeds. Relative difficulty in the early feeds does not, in this sample at least, predict any of the later differences of affectionate interest or interaction between mother and baby. Two further points must be made about this consistency in differences in maternal style. First, it is quite possible that individual differences between babies contributed to the consistent pattern, since we found correlations between the babies' behaviour in the sucking test, and the measures of maternal touching and talking at 14 and 20 weeks. There was a negative correlation between the measures of latency to react to the removal of the teat, in the sucking test, and the later scores of maternal touching and talking.

Second, when we examined the maternal response to infant crying we did not find the same consistent pattern of individual differences over time. Rather, the way in which a mother responded to her baby's crying was importantly influenced by the level of irritability of the baby at previous visits. This suggests that a mother's response to her baby's crying is not a useful index of maternal 'sensitivity' or interest in the baby, unless the level of irritability of the baby is taken into account.

Observations at 14 Months

The observations when the child was 14 months showed that there was a large range of individual differences in measures of the 'conversational' exchange of looks, smiles, noises and objects between mother and baby. We found that there were high correlations between the amount the mother talked to the baby and the measure of a baby looking at, vocalising to, and giving, showing or pointing out objects to his mother. Tape-recordings of the verbal exchange, made during the observations, showed us that the mother's responsiveness to the baby's utterances was also correlated with the measure of the amount of maternal talking. However, we must not take this simply as a measure of the mother's responsiveness to the child, without taking account of the child's behaviour, since we found that the percentage of the child's utterances that the mother responded to depended on the number of child utterances that were demands for help, or particular objects. Again we come back to the point that measures of maternal responsiveness are confounded with individual differences in child behaviour.

At this point in the study, one of the questions that we were interested in concerned the relation between observational measures of a mother's interest in and response to her baby, and the features of maternal speech which those studying language acquisition have found to be important in promoting language growth in children at this very early stage of language development.

As a first step in making a comparison between these two facets of mothering style, we looked at the relation between Nelson's[7] categories of 'acceptance', 'rejection' and 'direction' in the mother's verbal replies to her child and the observational measures. In her study of language acquisition, Nelson found that maternal speech characterised by a high degree of 'acceptance' facilitated language growth in the child.

Our analysis showed that *how* the mother replied to her baby's utterances was not related to *whether* she replied. The verbal feedback measures of acceptance, direction and rejection showed no significant correlations with the observational measures of responsiveness. Are we then, with these verbal measures, picking up on differences in maternal style which only become apparent when the children are beginning to use language? How do the earlier differences between mother-child pairs

Table 25.2: Spearman Rank Correlations between 1st-10-day Measures and Measures from 60 Weeks (N = 30)

1st 10 Days	60-weeks measure			
	Mother vocalise	% Baby utterances responded to	% Baby utterances as demands	Acceptance
Factor 2	0.31[a]	0.55[b]	0.39[a]	0.30
Suck rate	—	0.46[b]	0.45[b]	—

[a] $p < .05$
[b] $p < .01$

relate to these differences at 14 months? And what might the consequences of these differences be for the child's later development?

Table 25.2 shows that there are indeed correlations between some measures from the post-partum period and from 14 months. The factor (Factor 2) from the observations made in the first ten days on which maternal affectionate talking, looking, smiling at the baby, and the measure of the baby's suck rate were loaded, is positively correlated with the 14 month measures of maternal vocalising to the baby, and with the percentage of baby utterances responded to. These correlations again raise the problem of using measures as if they reflected exclusively 'maternal' or 'infant' behaviour. Table 25.2 shows that the baby suck rate measure from day 8 is correlated with the measures of mother behaviour at 14 months, and with the percentage of demands in the baby utterances. We must not, then, assume that any connection between the early days and the second year reflects continuity in either mother behaviour or baby behaviour alone; rather, the pattern of associations found here underlines the point that it is more meaningful to describe the connection across time as being between individual differences in mother-child pairs, rather than between measures of mother's or baby's behaviour.

We have found, then, differences in patterns of interaction that show continuity between the first ten days and 14 months. How far do these differences matter in terms of the child's later development? Our study follows the children until they reach school, and a variety of tests and interviews are carried out when the children are 3, 4½ and 5 years. Now it has been suggested that the experience of a sensitive and responsive mother during the first year of life has a powerful effect on the development of infant 'competence' and communication skills. It is, however, very difficult to relate measures of competence in the first 18 months to later measures of intelligence. It is interesting to note, then, that in our study we did not find any association between measures of maternal responsiveness in the first year, and the child's IQ measured at 4 years with the Stanford-Binet test. However a correlation *was* found between the measure of maternal verbal 'acceptance' from the transcripts of maternal speech to the child at 14 months, and the child's IQ at 4½ years.

For those aspects of intellectual development assessed in the IQ test, then, the feature of the environment that has been shown to be important was a style of maternal talking when the child was 14 months, rather than a simple measure of responsiveness from the first year. Obviously the range of variation within the sample is of great importance here, and generalisations should not be made from this study without taking this into account. It is also clear that it is a wide open possibility that there might be connections between maternal responsiveness and later differences in the child's social behaviour, and indeed in the child's approach to intellectual problems. However, the connections found here should alert us to the possible discontinuities in developmental patterns, and to the dangers of too-simple notions about the over-riding importance of early experience.

Acknowledgements

The research described here was supported by a grant from the Nuffield Foundation; it was initiated by M.P.M. Richards with whom the author collaborated in carrying out the study. We would like to thank the Midwives of the City of Cambridge, and the mothers for their generous help.

References

1.   Schaffer, H.R. (ed.), *Studies in Mother-Infant Interaction. The Loch Lomond Symposium.* Academic Press, London (1976).
2.   Richards, M.P.M. and Bernal, J.F., 'An observational study of mother-infant interaction', in N. Blurton-Jones (ed.), *Ethological Studies of Child Behaviour.* Cambridge University Press, Cambridge (1972).
3.   Dunn, J.F., 'Consistency and change in styles of mothering', in *Parent-Infant Interaction. Ciba Foundation Symposium 33.* Elsevier, Amsterdam (1975).
4.   Dunn, J.F. and Richards, M.P.M., 'Observations on the developing relationship between mother and baby in the new-born period', in H.R. Schaffer (ed.), *Studies in Mother-Infant Interaction.* Academic Press, London (1976).
5.   Dunn, J.F., 'Patterns of early interaction: continuities and consequences',

in H.R. Schaffer (ed.), *Studies in Mother-Infant Interaction*. Academic Press, London (1976).
6.   Waldrop, M.F. and Bell, R.Q., 'Effects of family size and density on newborn characteristics', *Amer. J. of Orthopsychiatry, 36*, 544 (1966).
7.   Nelson, K., 'Structure and strategy in learning to talk', *Monogr. Soc. Res. Child Devel.*, 149 (1973).

GLOSSARY OF TECHNICAL TERMS

Ankle clonus: most body muscles are normally in a slight state of tension. This is often called muscle 'tone' or 'tonus'. 'Clonus' is the opposite of tonus. Ankle clonus is the extent to which the ankle joint is not held in position by muscle tone, i.e. the looseness or floppiness of the ankle.

Apgar (rating): assessment of a neonate's physiological functioning immediately after birth in five areas: respiratory effort, heart rate, skin colour, muscle tone and reflex irritability. Each of these has three possible scores: 0, 1 and 2. An infant fully functioning in all areas would thus score 10.

Cinching: restraining an infant's movements, swaddling, for example, by wrapping with a shawl.

CNS: central nervous system.

Cross-sectional sample: sample of individuals from whom data are collected on one occasion (e.g. at a given age), usually with a view to comparisons with similar samples at different age levels. So, a *cross section* of 3, 4 and 5 year-olds might be given a test and the results analysed for developmental trends. By contrast a *longitudinal sample* involves the following up of the *same* individuals over a period of time, e.g. testing at 3, 4 and 5 years.

DQ: developmental quotient. Calculated in the same way as intelligence quotient: DQ = developmental age/chronological age x 100, i.e. a DQ of 100 indicates development at the normal rate.

EEG (electroencephalogram): recording of the fluctuations of electrical potentials across different parts of the brain, collected by the use of electrodes attached to various parts of the scalp.

Electroretinogram: record of fluctuations of electrical potentials of the retina, collected by the use of electrodes attached either to the skin around the eye, or surgically inserted into the retinal region.

Endogenous: arising from within the individual.

Genotype: genetically encoded traits and characters. Normally used in biology in connection with physical traits, but in psychology used for behavioural traits.

IQ: intelligence quotient. Calculated by assessing an individual's mental age, normally by use of a standardised intelligence test of tests. IQ = mental age/chronological age x 100, i.e. a person whose mental age is the same as their chronological age has an IQ of 100.

Lability: an individual's state is said to be labile when it is especially sensitive, and changes markedly as a result of environmental stimulation.

Markov chain: mathematical model that assigns probabilities to transitions from one state to succeeding states; essentially a step-by-step model. Felt by many theoreticians to be of very limited use in explaining behaviour.

Moro reflex: if support is suddenly removed from an infant's head (particularly) or another part of the body, a stereotyped reaction occurs in which the head is flung back, the eyes close, and the arms and legs are suddenly extended, the arms then often being brought together in front of the body. This is the Moro reflex. It can also be elicited by sudden noise.

Ontogenetic: pertaining to the development of the individual as opposed to phylogeny (q.v.).

Pacifier: American term for dummy.

Phylogenetic: pertaining to the development of the species.

Rooting: Semi-automatic searching for the nipple by the infant; can be elicited by a light touch on the side of the mouth or cheek.

Second formant transition: three basic frequency bands occur in speech. These are known as formants. Changes or transitions in these (particularly the second) play an important role in forming particular speech sounds.

Tabula rasa: literally, 'blank slate'. View of the infant as relying entirely on learning and environmental stimulation for its mental development.

Time-sampling: a means of collecting data on behaviour by observing what is occurring at particular points in time, with regular intervals between observations.

Tonic neck response: a stereotyped position of the head and arms in neonates, also known as 'fencing posture' because of its similarity to a fencer's posture. The arm on the side to which the head is turned is fully extended, and the other arm held high. Occurs when child is prone on its back.

Tonus: state of tension in muscle (see ankle clonus).

Trimester: three month period.

Umwelt: literally 'experience-world'. The world as perceived by an individual.

Vestibular stimulation: stimulation of the organs of balance in the middle ear, e.g. by a child being picked up, or laid down.

Voicing: speech sounds are either voiced or unvoiced. In voiced sounds, the vocal chords produce a sound; in unvoiced, they are silent.

VTR: video-tape recording.

INDEX

activity level, and mental development
310-11
affectance *see* intentionality
affectionate behaviour from adults:
    and conditioning 262, 264, 266-7
    and mental development 323-6
    and suck rate 384
    theories about 72-7
Ahrens, R. 115-16
Appel, K.J. 192-3
appetitional behaviour, and conditioning
208-28
Arapesh society, infants in 18, 20-1
Atayal society, children in 100
attention:
    and mental development 328
    to auditory stimuli 129
    to visual stimuli 123-5
auditory discrimination 131-40, 220-2

Bayley Scales of Infant Development
    see tests on infants
Berkeley Growth Study 308, 311, 323-4,
    337, 339
Berlin, B. *et al.* 85
Berlyne, D.E. 236
birth experiences of infants 18-20
Blank, M. 354
Boas, F. 90
Bower, T.G.R. *et al.* 151-77, 163-4,
    165, 182, 273-4, 275, 279, 370-81
Bowlby, John 76
breast feeding:
    and Arapesh infants 21
    and Guatemalan infants 59
    and Zinacanteco infants 46
Brown, I.E. 376
Brucefors, A. *et al.* 310
Bruner, J.S. *et al.* 91, 93, 94, 95, 376
Brunet-Lezine Tests *see* tests on
    infants

Cattell's Infant Intelligence Scale
    see tests on infants
child-rearing:
    'hygienist' principles of 70-4
    in Arapesh society 20-1
    in Western society 64-79

child-rearing – *cont.*
    'individualism' principles of 77-9
    'natural development' principles of
    74-7
    'religious' principles of 67-70
Chinese and Western infants 364-6,
    368-9
Chomsky, N. 88
Cole, M. *et al.* 96, 97
commonality, in infant development
85-9
competence, development of:
    and language experience 247, 255
    and mother-child interaction 258
    and 'nontask time' 256
    and 'pass time' 255-6
    and sensorimotor experience 247
    environmental factors in 238-59
    in first three years 243-59
competence, in six-year-old child:
    attentional abilities 242
    intellectual abilities 241-2
    linguistic abilities 241
    social abilities 240-1
conditioned responses:
    and auditory discrimination 220-2
    and voluntary responses 255-7
    appetitional 207-28
    head-turning 209-10, 213-14, 225-6
    individual differences in 222-4
    non-nutritive sucking 232-6
    stages in 216-19
    vocalisation 261-8
conformity, and Zinacanteco infants
52-3
conservation, development of 88-9, 92
    repetition in 377-9
crawling, in Ganda infants 28-9
culture:
    and mental development 92-103
    differences in 84-5

Dasen, P.P. 86-7
Denver Development Screening Test
    see tests on infants

elicited responses, in newborn infants
44-5

392